Comprehensive Model of the

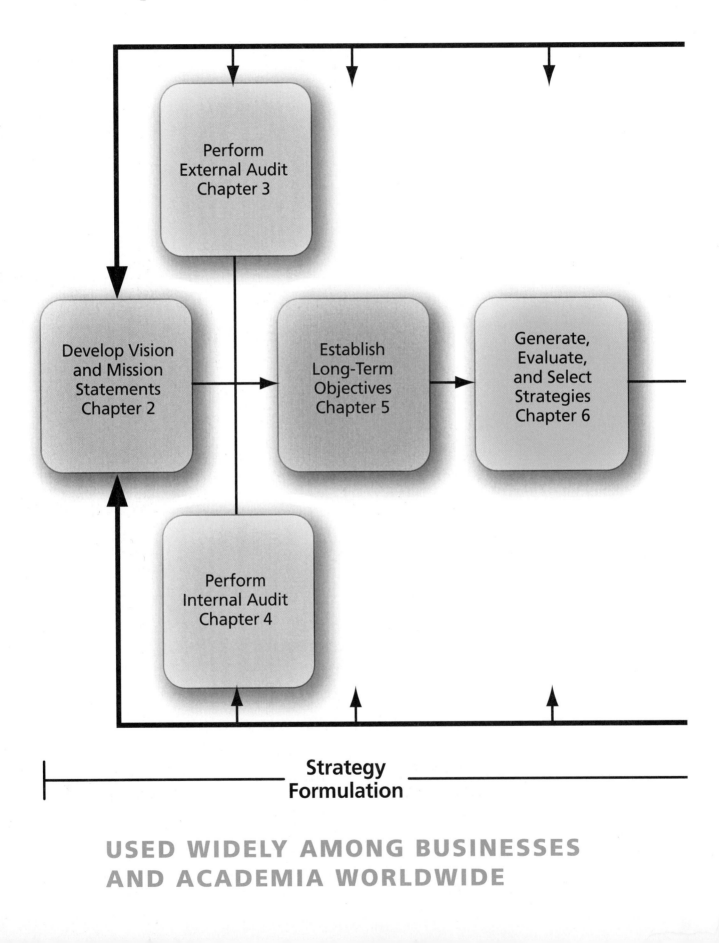

Perform
External Audit
Chapter 3

Develop Vision
and Mission
Statements
Chapter 2

Establish
Long-Term
Objectives
Chapter 5

Generate,
Evaluate,
and Select
Strategies
Chapter 6

Perform
Internal Audit
Chapter 4

Strategy
Formulation

USED WIDELY AMONG BUSINESSES
AND ACADEMIA WORLDWIDE

Strategic Management Process

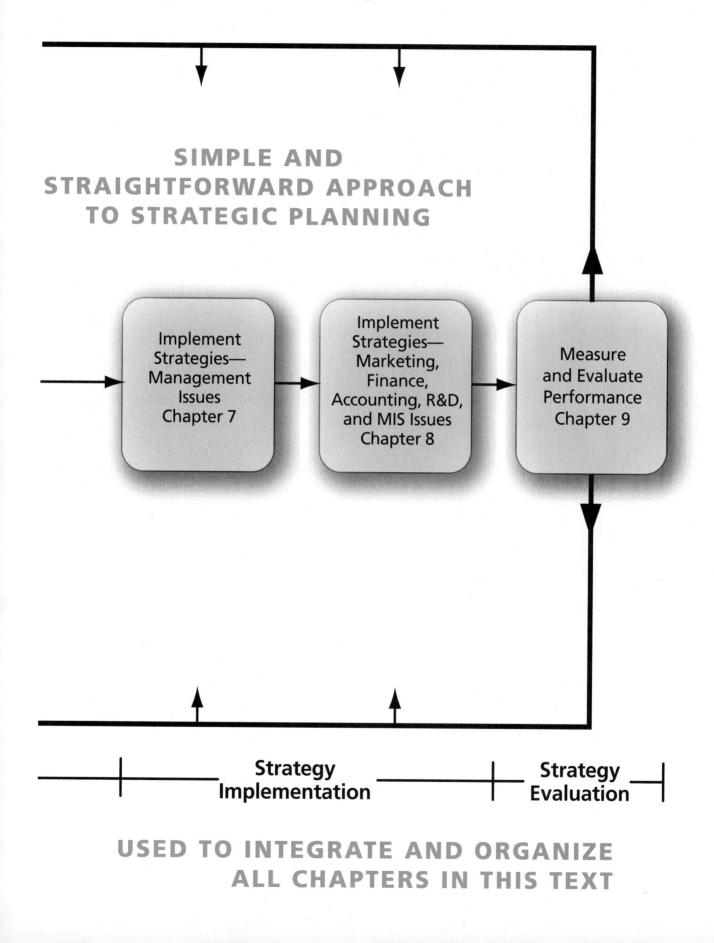

SIMPLE AND
STRAIGHTFORWARD APPROACH
TO STRATEGIC PLANNING

Implement
Strategies—
Management
Issues
Chapter 7

Implement
Strategies—
Marketing,
Finance,
Accounting, R&D,
and MIS Issues
Chapter 8

Measure
and Evaluate
Performance
Chapter 9

Strategy
Implementation

Strategy
Evaluation

USED TO INTEGRATE AND ORGANIZE
ALL CHAPTERS IN THIS TEXT

twelfth edition

Strategic Management

• CONCEPTS

Fred R. David

FRANCIS MARION UNIVERSITY

FLORENCE, SOUTH CAROLINA

PEARSON EDUCATION

To Joy, Forest, Byron, and Meredith—
my wife and children—
for their encouragement and love.

Library of Congress Cataloging-in-Publication Data

David, Fred R.
  Strategic management : concepts / Fred R. David. — Twelfth ed.
    p. cm.
  ISBN-13: 978-0-13-601569-7
  ISBN-10: 0-13-601569-7
  1. Strategic planning. I. Title.

HD30.28.D3785 2009
658.4'012—dc22

2007051138

Editor-in-Chief: David Parker
Product Development Manager: Ashley Santora
Assistant Editor: Kristen Varina
Editorial Assistant: Elizabeth Davis
Marketing Manager: Nikki Jones
Marketing Assistant: Ian Gold
Associate Managing Editor: Suzanne DeWorken
Project Manager, Production: Ann Pulido
Permissions Project Manager: Charles Morris
Senior Operations Supervisor: Arnold Vila
Senior Art Director: Janet Slowik
Interior Design: Liz Harasymczuk
Cover Design: Liz Harasymczuk
Cover Photo: Adam Gault/Digital Vision/Getty Images, Inc.
Director, Image Resource Center: Melinda Patelli
Manager, Rights and Permissions: Zina Arabia
Manager, Visual Research: Beth Brenzel
Manager, Cover Visual Research & Permissions: Karen Sanatar
Image Permission Coordinator: Ang'John Ferreri
Composition: Laserwords
Full-Service Project Management: Thistle Hill Publishing Services, LLC
Printer/Binder: Quebecor World Color/Dubuque
Typeface: 10/12 Times

Credits and acknowledgments borrowed from other sources and reproduced, with permission, in this textbook
appear on the appropriate page within text.

Pearson Education LTD.
Pearson Education Singapore, Pte. Ltd
Pearson Education, Canada, Ltd
Pearson Education–Japan

Pearson Education Australia PTY, Limited
Pearson Education North Asia Ltd
Pearson Educación de Mexico, S.A. de C.V.
Pearson Education Malaysia, Pte. Ltd.

10 9 8 7 6 5 4 3 2 1
ISBN-13: 978-0-13-601569-7
ISBN-10: 0-13-601569-7

Brief Contents

Contents

Part 5
Strategic Management Case Analysis 320

Preface

The business world today is considerably different and more complex than it was just two years ago when the previous edition of this text was published. Today, we experience private-equity firms acquiring hundreds of companies, rising consumer and business concern about global warming and pollution, high oil and gasoline prices, extensive outsourcing, a migration of work to China and India, more attention on business ethics, ballooning federal budget deficits, continued globalization, consolidation within industries, a European Union in dispute over its constitution, and intense rivalry in almost all industries. E-commerce continues to alter the nature of business to its core.

Thousands of strategic alliances and partnerships, even among competitors, formed in recent years. Hundreds of companies have declared bankruptcy and corporate scandals have highlighted the need for improved business ethics and corporate disclosure of financial transactions. Downsizing, rightsizing, reengineering, and countless divestitures, acquisitions, and liquidations have permanently altered the corporate landscape in the last two years. Thousands of firms have begun global operations and thousands more have merged. Thousands have prospered and yet thousands more have failed in the last two years. Many manufacturers have become e-commerce suppliers and long-held competitive advantages have eroded as new ones have formed.

Both the challenges and opportunities facing organizations of all sizes today are greater than ever. Illegal immigration across the U.S.–Mexico border has reached emergency levels. There is less room than ever for error today in the formulation and implementation of a strategic plan. This textbook provides a systematic effective approach for developing a clear strategic plan.

Changes made in this twelfth edition are aimed squarely at illustrating the effect of this new world order on strategic-management theory and practice. Due to the magnitude of the changes affecting companies, cultures, and countries, every page of this edition has been updated. The first edition of this text was published in 1986 and since that time it has grown to be one of, if not the most widely read strategic management books in the world. This text now is published in nine languages other than English.

This twelfth edition provides updated coverage of strategic-management concepts, theory, research, and techniques in the chapters. Every sentence and paragraph has been scrutinized, modified, clarified, deleted, streamlined, updated, and improved to enhance the content and caliber of presentation. The structure of this edition parallels the last, with nine chapters and a Cohesion Case, but the improvements in readability and coverage are dramatic. Every chapter features strategic-management concepts and practices presented in a clear, focused, and relevant manner with hundreds of new examples integrated throughout.

The skills-oriented, practitioner perspective that historically has been the foundation of this text is enhanced and strengthened in this edition. New and expanded coverage of strategic-management theories and research herein reflect companies' use of concepts such as value chain analysis (VCA), Balanced Scorecard, resource-based view (RBV), benchmarking, restructuring, and outsourcing. To survive and prosper in the new millennium, organizations must build and sustain competitive advantage. This text is now trusted around the world to provide future and present managers the latest skills and concepts needed to effectively formulate and efficiently implement a strategic plan—a game plan if you will—that can lead to sustainable competitive advantage for any type of business.

Our mission in preparing the twelfth edition of *Strategic Management: Concepts* was "to create the most current, well-written strategic management textbook on the market—a book that is exciting and valuable to both students and professors." Based on comments from 49 reviewers of the prior edition, new strategic-management research and practice, such as the Industrial Organizational (I/O) Model, Market Commonality, Value Chain Analysis, Balanced Scorecard, and First Mover Advantages, are incorporated and supported by hundreds of new practical examples. There is a brand-new Cohesion Case on Walt Disney—2008 which replaces the prior Google case. Nearly all of the twelfth edition Experiential Exercises have been revamped, replaced, or improved.

The 49 reviewers (listed below) and I believe you will find this edition to be the best strategic management textbook available for communicating both the excitement and value of strategic management. Concise and exceptionally well organized, this text is now published in English, Chinese, Spanish, Thai, German, Japanese, Farsi, Indonesian, Indian, and Arabic. A version in Russian is being negotiated. On five continents, this text is widely used in colleges and universities at both the graduate and undergraduate levels. In addition, thousands of companies, organizations, and governmental bodies use this text as a management guide, making it perhaps the most widely used strategic planning book in the world.

This textbook meets all AACSB-International guidelines for the business policy and strategic-management course at both the graduate and undergraduate levels, and previous editions have been used at more than 500 colleges and universities. Prentice Hall maintains a separate Web site for this text at www.prenhall.com/david. The author maintains the Strategic Management Club Online at www.strategyclub.com, which offers many benefits for strategic-management and business policy students.

Chapter Themes

As listed below, two themes permeate all chapters in this edition and contribute significantly to making it timely, informative, exciting, and valuable. Boxed insert "Perspectives" in each chapter link concepts being presented to each theme. Nearly all of the boxed inserts are new to this edition.

1. **Global Factors Affect Virtually All Strategic Decisions** The global theme is enhanced in this edition because doing business globally has become a necessity, rather than a luxury in most industries. Nearly all strategic decisions today are affected by global issues and concerns. There is new global coverage in each chapter consistent with the growing interdependence among countries and companies worldwide. The dynamics of political, economic, and cultural differences across countries directly affect strategic-management decisions. Doing business globally is more risky and complex than ever. The global theme illustrates how organizations today can effectively do business in an interlocked and interdependent world community.

2. **Preserving the Natural Environment Is a Vital Strategic Issue** Unique to strategic-management texts, the natural environment theme is strengthened in this edition in order to promote and encourage firms to conduct operations in an environmentally sound manner. This theme now includes social responsibility, sustainability, and business ethics issues. Countries worldwide have enacted laws to curtail the pollution of streams, rivers, the air, land, and sea.

Global warming is now undeniable and even oil companies are supporting emission restrictions as consumers are demanding responsible action from companies and politicians. Thousands of companies are "going green." The strategic efforts of both companies and countries to preserve the natural environment are described herein. More and more businesses are issuing Sustainability Reports to detail their efforts to curb global warming and operate in an environmentally-friendly manner. Respect for the natural environment has become an important concern for consumers, companies, society, and AACSB-International.

Twelfth Edition Design Features

There are some nice design features in this edition. For the first time ever, four photos in vivid color are present in each chapter and are tied directly to (1) chapter opening, (2) global perspective, (3) natural environment perspective, and (4) Walt Disney end-of-chapter experiential exercises. These four small photos per chapter make the twelfth edition much more visually appealing. In the prior edition, only chapter opening photos were present.

The comprehensive strategic-management model is displayed at the front cover of the text. At the start of each chapter, the section of the comprehensive strategy model covered in that chapter is highlighted and enlarged so students can see the focus of each chapter in the basic unifying comprehensive model.

Time-Tested Features

This edition continues to offer many special time-tested features and content that have made this text so successful for nearly twenty years. Historical trademarks of this text that are strengthened in this edition include:

Chapters: Time-Tested Features

- This text meets AACSB-International guidelines which support a practitioner orientation rather than a theory/research approach. It offers a skills-oriented approach to developing a vision and mission statement; performing an external audit; conducting an internal assessment; and formulating, implementing, and evaluating strategies.
- The global and natural environment themes permeate all chapters and examine strategic-management concepts in these important perspectives.
- The author's writing style is concise, conversational, interesting, logical, lively, and supported by numerous current examples throughout.
- A simple, integrative strategic-management model appears in all chapters and on the inside front cover of the text. This model is widely utilized for strategic planning among consultants and companies worldwide. One reviewer said: "One thing I have admired about David's text is that he follows the fundamental sequence of strategy formulation, implementation, and evaluation. There is a basic flow from mission/purposes to internal/external environmental scanning to strategy development, selection, implementation, and evaluation. This has been, and continues to be, a hallmark of the David text. Many other strategy texts are more disjointed in their presentation, and thus confusing to the student, especially at the undergraduate level."

- A Cohesion Case follows Chapter 1 and is revisited at the end of each chapter. This Cohesion Case allows students to apply strategic-management concepts and techniques to a real organization as chapter material is covered, which readies students for case analysis in the course.
- End-of-chapter Experiential Exercises effectively apply concepts and techniques in a challenging, meaningful, and enjoyable manner. Eighteen exercises apply text material to the Cohesion Case; ten apply textual material to a college or university; another ten exercises send students into the business world to explore important strategy topics. The exercises are relevant, interesting, and contemporary.
- There is excellent pedagogy in this text, including Notable Quotes and Objectives to open each chapter, and Key Terms, Current Readings, Discussion Questions, and Experiential Exercises to close each chapter.
- There is excellent coverage of strategy formulation issues such as business ethics, global versus domestic operations, vision/mission, matrix analysis, partnering, joint venturing, competitive analysis, governance, and guidelines for conducting an internal/external strategy assessment.
- There is excellent coverage of strategy implementation issues such as corporate culture, organizational structure, outsourcing, marketing concepts, financial analysis, and business ethics.
- A systematic, analytical approach is presented in Chapter 6, including matrices such as the SWOT, BCG, IE, GRAND, SPACE, and QSPM.
- The chapter material is again published in four-color.
- "Visit the Net" Internet exercises are available online at www.prenhall.com/david or at the www.strategyclub.com Web site and in the page margins of the text. This feature reveals the author's recommended Web sites for locating additional information on the concepts being presented, and greatly enhances classroom presentation in an Internet environment since the recommended sites have been screened closely to assure that each is well worth visiting in class. This feature also provides students with substantial additional material on chapter concepts.
- The Web site www.prenhall.com/david, provides chapter updates and support materials.
- The nine chapters are organized in the same manner as the previous edition.
- For the chapter material, the outstanding ancillary package includes a comprehensive *Instructor's Manual,* computerized test bank, and PowerPoints.

What's New to This Edition in the Chapters

In addition to the special time-tested trademarks described above, this edition includes some exciting new features, changes, and content designed to position this text as the clear leader and best choice for teaching business policy and strategic management.

First of all, the new Cohesion Case on the Walt Disney Company features one of the most successful, well-known, best managed, and largest family entertainment companies in the world. In addition to its theme parks worldwide, Disney owns Touchstone Pictures, Miramax Films, Pixar, ESPN Zone, 17 hotels at the Walt Disney World Resort, ABC News, Disney Channel, and more. It is a fun company and real challenge for students to address strategic issues facing Disney.

Experiential Exercises at the end of each chapter apply concepts to the Disney Cohesion Case and ready students for case analysis when they complete the chapter material. Over the past twenty years, the Cohesion Case for this text has changed from Ponderosa Steakhouse in the first and second editions, to Hershey Foods in the third through seventh editions, to AOL in the eighth edition, to American Airlines in the ninth edition, Krispy Kreme in the tenth, Google in the eleventh, and now Walt Disney, which is a great company for students to focus upon throughout the semester.

In this edition, new features, changes, and content common to all nine chapters include:

- New Global and Natural Environment boxed inserts.
- New examples throughout.
- New Visit the Net (VTN) Web sites provided in the page margins. Many universities now teach in Internet-ready classrooms and utilize Web sites during lectures. These sites are hot-linked at the www.prenhall.com/david and www.strategyclub.com Web sites.
- Improved coverage of global issues and concerns.
- Expanded coverage of business ethics.
- All new current readings at the end of each chapter reveal new, relevant strategic-management research.
- More international flavor than ever. There is excellent new coverage of cultural and conceptual strategic-management differences across countries.
- New research and theories of seminal thinkers in strategy development such as Ansoff, Chandler, Porter, Hamel, Prahalad, Mintzberg, and Barney are included. Scholars such as these have brought strategic management to its present place in modern business. Practical aspects of strategic management are still center-stage and the trademark of this text.
- Substantial new material on business ethics throughout. Corporate fraud, scandals, and illegalities are numerous, so we in academia must be certain to emphasize that "good ethics is good business." This notion is tied to the natural environment theme in this edition.

In addition to the above changes listed above, some specific chapter by chapter changes in this twelvth edition are:

Chapter 1

- There is a new Global Perspective boxed insert regarding the extent that U.S. firms dominate industries.
- There is a new Strategies in Action Table featuring McDonalds and American General.
- Experiential Exercises 1A and 1B have been overhauled.
- There are new examples throughout.

Chapter 2

- Eight new vision statements are provided along with new "Author's Comments" about each one.
- Six new mission statements are provided along with new "Author's Comments" about each one.
- Updated Global Perspective is provided.
- Updated Natural Environment Perspective is provided.
- Experiential Exercises 2A and 2B have been overhauled.
- New examples throughout.

Chapter 3

- New Natural Environment Perspective on climate change
- New Global Perspective on auto producers in China
- Deleted section on "The U.S.–Mexico Border"
- Deleted section on "Russia's Economy"
- Deleted section on "China: Opportunities and Threats"
- New EFE Matrix on ten-theatre cinema complex.
- New examples throughout.
- Experiential Exercises 3A, 3D, and 3E have been overhauled.

Chapter 4

- New Natural Environment Perspective on EU use of chemicals.
- New Global Perspective on work week variation across countries.
- New IFE Matrix on a retail computer store.
- New examples throughout.
- Experiential Exercise 4A has been overhauled.

Chapter 5

- New heading and material on private-equity firm acquisitions.
- New Global Perspective on joint venturing in India.
- Over 80 new examples.
- New material on joint ventures.
- New material on cooperating with rival firms.
- Deleted section on "Joint Ventures in Russia."
- Experiential Exercises 5A and 5C overhauled.

Chapter 6

- New Natural Environment Perspective on developing a SustainabilityReport.
- New SWOT Matrix for a retail computer store.
- New Global Perspective on comparing corporate tax rates worldwide.
- New strategy detail provided to support SPACE Matrix and BCG Matrix.
- New BCG, IE, and QSPM Matrices.
- New examples thoughout.
- All Experiential Exercises updated.

Chapter 7

- New coverage of Six Sigma, the quality-boosting process improvement technique.
- New coverage of ESOPs, including a new table listing the eight largest in the United States.
- New coverage on women's issues, including a new table listing the ten best firms for women to work for.
- Deleted the section "The Russian Culture."
- Revised Natural Environment Perspective on environmental training of students in colleges and universities.

- New examples throughout.
- Experiential Exercise 7A has been overhauled.

Chapter 8

- Substantially more information is provided on "How to Develop Projected Financial Statements," including a full new example of this concept worked out in detail for Mattel, Inc. Many students have trouble with these financial concepts, yet they need to show what impact their recommended strategies would have on this firm's financial future.
- New coverage and examples on calculating a company's worth, including use for the first time of Yahoo's Enterprise Value technique.
- New Natural Environment Perspective on "Strategic Management of Your Health." This is the author's favorite new Boxed Insert in this edition and it focuses on "wellness campaigns" at companies.
- All Experiential Exercises fully updated.
- New examples throughout.

Chapter 9

- New Natural Environment Perspectve on the pollution situation in China.
- Revised/updated Global Perspective on use of atomic energy.
- Fully updated Experiential Exercises.
- New examples throughout.

Instructor's Resource Center

At **www.prenhall.com/irc**, instructors can access a variety of print, digital, and presentation resources available with this text in downloadable format. Registration is simple and gives you immediate access to new titles and new editions. As a registered faculty member, you can download resource files and receive immediate access and instructions for installing course management content on your campus server.

If you ever need assistance, our dedicated technical support team is ready to help with the media supplements that accompany this text. Visit **www.247. prenhall.com** for answers to frequently asked questions and toll-free user support phone numbers.

The following supplements are available to adopting instructors (for detailed descriptions, please visit **www.prenhall.com/irc**):

- **Instructor's Resource Center (IRC) on CD-ROM**—ISBN: 0-13-813210-0
- **Printed Instructor's Manual with Test Item File**—ISBN: 0-13-813217-8
- **PowerPoints** – available on the IRC (both online and on CD-Rom)
- **TestGen Test Generating Software**—Available at the IRC Online.
- **Custom Videos on DVD**—ISBN: 0-13-813212-7

Companion Website

This text's Companion Website at **www.prenhall.com/david** contains valuable resources for both students and professors, including an interactive student study guide.

CourseSmart Textbooks Online

CourseSmart Textbooks Online is an exciting new choice for students looking to save money. As an alternative to purchasing the print textbook, students can subscribe to the same content online and save up to 50% off the suggested list price of the print text. With a CourseSmart etextbook, students can search the text, make notes online, print out reading assignments that incorporate lecture notes, and bookmark important passages for later review. For more information, or to subscribe to the CourseSmart eTextbook, visit www.coursesmart.com.

Special Note to Students

Welcome to business policy or strategic management, whichever title this course has at your university. This is a challenging and exciting course that will allow you to function as the owner or chief executive officer of different organizations. Your major task in this course will be to make strategic decisions and to justify those decisions through oral and written communication. Strategic decisions determine the future direction and competitive position of an enterprise for a long time. Decisions to expand geographically or to diversify are examples of strategic decisions.

Strategic decision making occurs in all types and sizes of organizations, from Exxon and IBM to a small hardware store or small college. Many people's lives and jobs are affected by strategic decisions, so the stakes are very high. An organization's very survival is often at stake. The overall importance of strategic decisions makes this course especially exciting and challenging. You will be called upon in this course to demonstrate how your strategic decisions could be successfully implemented.

In this course, you can look forward to making strategic decisions both as an individual and as a member of a team. No matter how hard employees work, an organization is in real trouble if strategic decisions are not made effectively. Doing the right things (effectiveness) is more important than doing things right (efficiency). For example, ineffective strategies led to revenue declines of 71 percent and 10 percent in 2006 for Avis Budget Group and American Express, respectively. Boston Scientific and the *New York Times* had profit declines of 670 percent and 309 percent, respectively that year. Even well known firms such as Nortel, Circuit City, Eastman Kodak, La-Z-Boy, Citigroup, New Century Financial, Cadbury Schweppes, and Motorola are struggling with ineffective strategies. Many American newspapers are faltering as consumers increasingly switch to interactive media for news.

You will have the opportunity in this course to make actual strategic decisions, perhaps for the first time in your academic career. Do not hesitate to take a stand and defend specific strategies that you determine to be the best based on tools and concepts in this textbook. The rationale for your strategic decisions will be more important than the actual decision, because no one knows for sure what the best strategy is for a particular organization at a given point in time. This fact accents the subjective, contingency nature of the strategic-management process.

Use the concepts and tools presented in this text, coupled with your own intuition, to recommend strategies that you can defend as being most appropriate for the organizations that you study. You will also need to integrate knowledge acquired in previous business courses. For this reason, strategic management is often called a capstone course; you may want to keep this book for your personal library.

This text is practitioner-oriented and applications-oriented. It presents techniques and content that will enable you to formulate, implement, and evaluate strategies in all kinds of profit and nonprofit organizations. The end-of-chapter Experiential Exercises allow you to apply what you've read in each chapter to the new Walt Disney Cohesion Case and to your own university.

Definitely visit the Strategic Management Club Online at www.strategyclub.com. The templates and links there will save you time in performing analyses and will make your work look professional. Work hard in policy this term and have fun. Good luck!

Acknowledgments

Many persons have contributed time, energy, ideas, and suggestions for improving this text over twelve editions. The strength of this text is largely attributed to the collective wisdom, work, and experiences of business policy professors, strategic-management researchers, students, and practitioners. Names of particular individuals whose published research is referenced in this edition of this text are listed alphabetically in the Name Index. To all individuals involved in making this text so popular and successful, I am indebted and thankful.

Many special persons and reviewers contributed valuable material and suggestions for this edition. I would like to thank my colleagues and friends at Auburn University, Mississippi State University, East Carolina University, and Francis Marion University. These are universities where I have served on the management faculty. Scores of students and professors at these schools helped shape the development of this text. Many thanks go to the following 49 reviewers of the prior edition whose comments shaped this twelfth edition:

Joseph Adamo, Cazenovia College

Asad Aziz, University of Colorado

John Bade, Washington University

Henry Beam, Western Michigan University

James Beierlein, Penn State University

Carl Broadhurst, Campbell University

Doug Cannon, Lindenwood University

Val Calvert, San Antonio College

Debi Cartwright, Truman State University

Ronald Decker, University of Wisconsin at Eau Claire

Jonathan Elimimian, Albany State University

Monique Forte, Stetson University

Charles Forrest, Lindenwood University

Mike Frandsen, Albion College

John Frankenstein, Brooklyn College/City University of New York

Steven Frankforter, Winthrop University

Jeff Furman, Boston University

Debbie Gilliard, Metropolitan State College of Denver

George Gresham, Texas A&M University at Kingsville

Robert Gulbro, Athens State University

Carol Himelhoch, Siena Heights University

Gordon Holbein, University of Kentucky

Phillip Jutras, Regis College

David Kimball, Elms College

Robert Ledman, Georgia Southwestern State University

Ugbo Mallam, Paul Quinn College

William Martello, St. Edward's University

Brenda McAleer, University of Maine at Augusta

Norman McElvany, Johnson State College

Joe Mosca, Monmouth University

Richard Mpoyi, Middle Tennessee State University

Carolyn Mueller, Stetson University

Carl Nelson, Polytechnic University

James O'Connor, University of Texas at El Paso

Don Okhomina, Fayetteville State University

David Olson, California State University at Bakersfield

Jeffrey Parker, Jacksonville State University

James Schiro, Central Michigan University College of Professional Studies

Mike Schraeder, Troy University

Karen Silva, Johnson & Wales

James Smith, Dana College

William Tita, Northeastern University

David Vequist, University of the Incarnate World

Richard Weaver, National University

Morrison Webb, Manhattanville College

Michael Welch, Loyola University Chicago

Kenneth Wendeln, Kelley School of Business, Indiana University at Indianapolis

Floyd Willoughby, Oakland University

Nancy Wyant, International College

I especially appreciate the wonderful work completed by the twelfth edition ancillary authors as follows:

Case Instructor's Manual—Forest David, Francis Marion University

Instructor's Manual—Tracy Ryan, Virginia Commonwealth University

Test Item File and PowerPoints—Charles Seifert, Siena Collega

Internet Study Guide—Amit J. Shah, Frostburg State University

Scores of Prentice Hall employees and salespersons have worked diligently behind the scenes to make this text a leader in the business policy market. I appreciate the continued hard work of all those persons.

I also want to thank you, the reader, for investing the time and effort to read and study this text. It will help you formulate, implement, and evaluate strategies for any organization with which you become associated. I hope you come to share my enthusiasm for the rich subject area of strategic management and for the systematic learning approach taken in this text.

Finally, I want to welcome and invite your suggestions, ideas, thoughts, comments, and questions regarding any part of this text or the ancillary materials. Please call me at 843–661–1431, fax me at 843–661–1432, e-mail me at strategy29@aol.com, or write me at the School of Business, Francis Marion University, Florence, South Carolina 29501. I sincerely appreciate and need your input to continually improve this text in future editions. Your willingness to draw my attention to specific errors or deficiencies in coverage or exposition will especially be appreciated.

Thank you for using this text.

Fred R. David

Users of the Eleventh Edition

Following is a small sampling of schools that have used the eleventh edition of this textbook.

Alabama University–Birmingham
Albany State University
American University
Arizona State University
Auburn University at Montgomery
Bob Jones University
California State–Long Beach
Carnegie Mellon University
Central Michigan University
College of Charleston
Colorado State University–Pueblo
Delaware State University
Eastern Michigan University
Eastern Oregon University
Fordham University–Rose Hill
Hofstra University
Humboldt State University
Indiana State University
Indianan University–Kokomo
Iona College
Jackson State University
Johns Hopkins University
Johnson & Wales University
Kentucky State University
La Salle University
Loyola–Chicago
Loyola College
Marshall University
Maryland College Park University
Millsaps College
Mississippi State University
Murray State University
New Mexico State University
New York University
Niagara University
Nicholls State University
North Carolina Wesleyan College

Norfolk State University
Oakland University
Oral Roberts University
Pennsylvania State University–University Park
Philadelphia University
Rider University
Rochester College
Saint Xavier University
Saint Bonaventure University
Saint Leo University
Saint Louis University
Saint Mary's University
Saint Thomas University
Sam Houston State University
Seton Hall University
Southern Wesleyan University
Stetson University
Tennessee State University–Main Campus
Texas Tech University
Texas Wesleyan University
Trinity University
Troy University–Main Campus
University Missouri–Kansas City
University of Alabama–Huntsville
University of California–Riverside
University of Colorado–Boulder
University of Hawaii–Manoa Campus
University of Maine at Augusta
University of Memphis
University of Miami
University of Minnesota–Minneapolis
University of Minnesota–Saint Paul
University of Mobile

University of Nebraska–Lincoln

University of Nevada–Las Vegas

University of Nevada–Reno

University of New Mexico

University of New Orleans

University of North Dakota

University of San Francisco

University of Tennessee–Chattanooga

University of Texas–El Paso

University of Texas–Pan American

University of Texas–San Antonio

University of Toledo

University of Wisconsin–Green Bay

Virginia Commonwealth University

Virginia State University

Virginia Union University

Voorhees College

Washington University

Western Kentucky University

Winona State University

Wright State University

West Virginia University at Parkersburg

About the Author

Dr. Fred R. David is the sole author of three mainstream strategic-management textbooks: (1) *Strategic Management: Concepts and Cases*, (2) *Strategic Management Concepts*, and (3) *Strategic Management Cases*. These texts have been on a two-year revision cycle since 1986, when the first edition was published. They are among the best if not the best-selling strategic-management textbooks in the world and are used at more than 500 colleges and universities. Prestigious universities that have used these textbooks include Harvard University, Duke University, Carnegie-Mellon University, John Hopkins University, the University of Maryland, University of North Carolina, University of Georgia, Florida State University, San Francisco State University, and Wake Forest University.

This strategic-management textbook has been translated and published in Chinese, Japanese, Farsi, Spanish, Indonesian, Indian, Thai, and Arabic, and is widely used across Asia and South America. It is the best-selling strategic-management textbook in Mexico, China, Peru, Chile, Japan, and number two in the United States. Approximately 90,000 students read Dr. David's textbook annually as well as thousands of businesspersons. The book has led the field of strategic management for more than a decade in providing an applications/practitioner approach to the discipline.

A native of Whiteville, North Carolina, Fred R. David received a B.S. degree in Mathematics and an MBA from Wake Forest University before being employed as a bank manager with United Carolina Bank. He received a Ph.D. in Business Administration from the University of South Carolina where he majored in Management. Currently the TranSouth Professor of Strategic Management at Francis Marion University (FMU) in Florence, South Carolina, Dr. David has also taught at Auburn University, Mississippi State University, East Carolina University, the University of South Carolina, and the University of North Carolina at Pembroke. He is the author of 150 referred publications, including 39 journal articles, 53 proceedings publications, and 58 business policy cases. David has articles published in such journals as *Academy of Management Review*, *Academy of Management Executive*, *Journal of Applied Psychology*, *Long Range Planning*, and *Advanced Management Journal*. He serves on the Editorial Review Board of the *Advanced Management Journal*.

Dr. David has received a Lifetime Honorary Professorship Award from the Universidad Ricardo Palma in Lima, Peru. He delivered the keynote speech at the twenty-first Annual Latin American Congress on Strategy hosted by the Centrum School of Business in Peru. Dr. David recently delivered an eight-hour Strategic Planning Workshop to the faculty at Pontificia Universidad Catolica Del in Lima, Peru, and an eight-hour Case Writing/Analyzing Workshop to the faculty at Utah Valley State College in Orem, Utah. He has received numerous awards, including FMU's Board of Trustees Research Scholar Award, and the university's Award for Excellence in Research given annually to the best faculty researcher on campus, and the Phil Carroll Advancement of Management Award, given annually by the Society for the Advancement of Management (SAM) to a management scholar for outstanding contributions in management research. He has given the graduation commencement speech at Troy University for the last two years.

David served for three years on the Southern Management Association's Board of Directors. Through his Web site, www.checkmateplan.com, Dr. David actively assists businesses across the country and around the world in doing strategic planning. He has developed and markets the CheckMATE Strategic Planning Software, which is an industry-leading business planning software package (www.checkmateplan.com).

Strategic Management

• CONCEPTS

Part 1 • Overview of Strategic Management

1 The Nature of Strategic Management

Graduation Day. *Source:* Bryan David.

chapter objectives

After studying this chapter, you should be able to do the following:

1. Describe the strategic-management process.

2. Explain the need for integrating analysis and intuition in strategic management.

3. Define and give examples of key terms in strategic management.

4. Discuss the nature of strategy formulation, implementation, and evaluation activities.

5. Describe the benefits of good strategic management.

6. Explain why good ethics is good business in strategic management.

7. Explain the advantages and disadvantages of entering global markets.

8. Discuss the relevance of Sun Tzu's *The Art of War* to strategic management.

9. Discuss how a firm may achieve sustained competitive advantage.

10. Explain ISO 14000 and 14001.

This chapter provides an overview of strategic management. It introduces a practical, integrative model of the strategic-management process; it defines basic activities and terms in strategic management; and it discusses the importance of business ethics.

This chapter initiates two themes that permeate all the chapters of this text. First, *global considerations impact virtually all strategic decisions*! The boundaries of countries no longer can define the limits of our imaginations. To see and appreciate the world from the perspective of others has become a matter of survival for businesses. The underpinnings of strategic management hinge upon managers' gaining an understanding of competitors, markets, prices, suppliers, distributors, governments, creditors, shareholders, and customers worldwide. The price and quality of a firm's products and services must be competitive on a worldwide basis, not just on a local basis. A "Global Perspective" box is provided in each chapter of this text to emphasize the importance of global factors in strategic management.

A second theme is that *the natural environment has become an important strategic issue.* Global warming, bioterrorism, and increased pollution suggest that perhaps there is now no greater threat to business and society than the continuous exploitation and decimation of our natural environment. Mark Starik at George Washington University says, "Halting and reversing worldwide ecological destruction and deterioration . . . is a strategic issue that needs immediate and substantive attention by all businesses and managers." According to the International Standards Organization (ISO), and in this textbook, the word *environment* refers to the natural environment and is defined as "surroundings in which an organization operates, including air, water, land, natural resources, flora, fauna, humans, and their interrelation." A "Natural Environment Perspective" box is provided in each chapter to illustrate how firms are addressing natural environment concerns.

What Is Strategic Management?

Once there were two company presidents who competed in the same industry. These two presidents decided to go on a camping trip to discuss a possible merger. They hiked deep into the woods. Suddenly, they came upon a grizzly bear that rose up on its hind legs and snarled. Instantly, the first president took off his knapsack and got out a pair of jogging shoes. The second president said, "Hey, you can't outrun that bear." The first president responded, "Maybe I can't outrun that bear, but I surely can outrun you!" This story captures the notion of strategic management, which is to achieve and maintain competitive advantage.

Defining Strategic Management

Strategic management can be defined as the art and science of formulating, implementing, and evaluating cross-functional decisions that enable an organization to achieve its objectives. As this definition implies, strategic management focuses on integrating management, marketing, finance/accounting, production/operations, research and development, and computer information systems to achieve organizational success. The term *strategic management* in this text is used synonymously with the term *strategic planning*. The latter term is more often used in the business world, whereas the former is often used in academia. Sometimes the term *strategic management* is used to refer to strategy formulation, implementation, and evaluation, with *strategic planning* referring only to strategy formulation. The purpose of strategic management is to exploit and create new and different opportunities for tomorrow; *long-range planning,* in contrast, tries to optimize for tomorrow the trends of today.

The term *strategic planning* originated in the 1950s and was very popular between the mid-1960s and the mid-1970s. During these years, strategic planning was widely believed to be the answer for all problems. At the time, much of corporate America was "obsessed" with strategic planning. Following that "boom," however, strategic planning was cast aside during the 1980s as various planning models did not yield higher returns. The 1990s, however, brought the revival of strategic planning, and the process is widely practiced today in the business world.

A strategic plan is, in essence, a company's game plan. Just as a football team needs a good game plan to have a chance for success, a company must have a good strategic plan to compete successfully. Profit margins among firms in most industries have been so reduced that there is little room for error in the overall strategic plan. A strategic plan results from tough managerial choices among numerous good alternatives, and it signals commitment to specific markets, policies, procedures, and operations in lieu of other, "less desirable" courses of action.

The term *strategic management* is used at many colleges and universities as the subtitle for the capstone course in business administration—Business Policy—which integrates material from all business courses. The Strategic Management Club Online at www.strategyclub.com offers many benefits for business policy and strategic management students.

Stages of Strategic Management

The *strategic-management process* consists of three stages: strategy formulation, strategy implementation, and strategy evaluation. *Strategy formulation* includes developing a vision and mission, identifying an organization's external opportunities and threats, determining internal strengths and weaknesses, establishing long-term objectives, generating alternative strategies, and choosing particular strategies to pursue. Strategy-formulation issues include deciding what new businesses to enter, what businesses to abandon, how to allocate resources, whether to expand operations or diversify, whether to enter international markets, whether to merge or form a joint venture, and how to avoid a hostile takeover.

Because no organization has unlimited resources, strategists must decide which alternative strategies will benefit the firm most. Strategy-formulation decisions commit an organization to specific products, markets, resources, and technologies over an extended period of time. Strategies determine long-term competitive advantages. For better or worse, strategic decisions have major multifunctional consequences and enduring effects on an organization. Top managers have the best perspective to understand fully the ramifications of strategy-formulation decisions; they have the authority to commit the resources necessary for implementation.

Strategy implementation requires a firm to establish annual objectives, devise policies, motivate employees, and allocate resources so that formulated strategies can be executed. Strategy implementation includes developing a strategy-supportive culture, creating an effective organizational structure, redirecting marketing efforts, preparing budgets, developing and utilizing information systems, and linking employee compensation to organizational performance.

Strategy implementation often is called the "action stage" of strategic management. Implementing strategy means mobilizing employees and managers to put formulated strategies into action. Often considered to be the most difficult stage in strategic management, strategy implementation requires personal discipline, commitment, and sacrifice. Successful strategy implementation hinges upon managers' ability to motivate employees, which is more an art than a science. Strategies formulated but not implemented serve no useful purpose.

Interpersonal skills are especially critical for successful strategy implementation. Strategy-implementation activities affect all employees and managers in an organization. Every division and department must decide on answers to questions, such as "What must we do to implement our part of the organization's strategy?" and "How best can we get the job done?" The challenge of implementation is to stimulate managers and employees throughout an organization to work with pride and enthusiasm toward achieving stated objectives.

Strategy evaluation is the final stage in strategic management. Managers desperately need to know when particular strategies are not working well; strategy evaluation is the primary means for obtaining this information. All strategies are subject to future modification because external and internal factors are constantly changing. Three fundamental strategy-evaluation activities are (1) reviewing external and internal factors that are the bases for current strategies, (2) measuring performance, and (3) taking corrective actions.

VISIT THE NET

Provides nice narrative regarding strategy formulation and implementation at Southern Polytechnic State University. (www.spsu.edu/planassess/strategic.htm)

Strategy evaluation is needed because success today is no guarantee of success tomorrow! Success always creates new and different problems; complacent organizations experience demise.

Strategy formulation, implementation, and evaluation activities occur at three hierarchical levels in a large organization: corporate, divisional or strategic business unit, and functional. By fostering communication and interaction among managers and employees across hierarchical levels, strategic management helps a firm function as a competitive team. Most small businesses and some large businesses do not have divisions or strategic business units; they have only the corporate and functional levels. Nevertheless, managers and employees at these two levels should be actively involved in strategic-management activities.

Peter Drucker says the prime task of strategic management is thinking through the overall mission of a business:

> . . . that is, of asking the question, "What is our Business?" This leads to the setting of objectives, the development of strategies, and the making of today's decisions for tomorrow's results. This clearly must be done by a part of the organization that can see the entire business; that can balance objectives and the needs of today against the needs of tomorrow; and that can allocate resources of men and money to key results.[1]

Integrating Intuition and Analysis

The strategic-management process can be described as an objective, logical, systematic approach for making major decisions in an organization. It attempts to organize qualitative and quantitative information in a way that allows effective decisions to be made under conditions of uncertainty. Yet strategic management is not a pure science that lends itself to a nice, neat, one-two-three approach.

Based on past experiences, judgment, and feelings, most people recognize that *intuition* is essential to making good strategic decisions. Intuition is particularly useful for making decisions in situations of great uncertainty or little precedent. It is also helpful when highly interrelated variables exist or when it is necessary to choose from several plausible alternatives. Some managers and owners of businesses profess to have extraordinary abilities for using intuition alone in devising brilliant strategies. For example, Will Durant, who organized General Motors Corporation, was described by Alfred Sloan as "a man who would proceed on a course of action guided solely, as far as I could tell, by some intuitive flash of brilliance. He never felt obliged to make an engineering hunt for the facts. Yet at times, he was astoundingly correct in his judgment."[2] Albert Einstein acknowledged the importance of intuition when he said, "I believe in intuition and inspiration. At times I feel certain that I am right while not knowing the reason. Imagination is more important than knowledge, because knowledge is limited, whereas imagination embraces the entire world."[3]

Although some organizations today may survive and prosper because they have intuitive geniuses managing them, most are not so fortunate. Most organizations can benefit from strategic management, which is based upon integrating intuition and analysis in decision making. Choosing an intuitive or analytic approach to decision making is not an either–or proposition. Managers at all levels in an organization inject their intuition and judgment into strategic-management analyses. Analytical thinking and intuitive thinking complement each other.

Operating from the I've-already-made-up-my-mind-don't-bother-me-with-the-facts mode is not management by intuition; it is management by ignorance.[4] Drucker says, "I believe in intuition only if you discipline it. 'Hunch' artists, who make a diagnosis but don't check it out with the facts, are the ones in medicine who kill people, and in management kill businesses."[5] As Henderson notes:

> The accelerating rate of change today is producing a business world in which customary managerial habits in organizations are increasingly inadequate. Experience alone was an adequate guide when changes could be made in small increments. But intuitive and experience-based management philosophies are grossly inadequate when decisions are strategic and have major, irreversible consequences.[6]

VISIT THE NET

Reveals that strategies may need to be constantly changed. (www. csuchico.edu/mgmt/strategy/ module1/sld041.htm)

In a sense, the strategic-management process is an attempt both to duplicate what goes on in the mind of a brilliant, intuitive person who knows the business and to couple it with analysis.

Adapting to Change

The strategic-management process is based on the belief that organizations should continually monitor internal and external events and trends so that timely changes can be made as needed. The rate and magnitude of changes that affect organizations are increasing dramatically. Consider, for example, e-commerce, laser surgery, the war on terrorism, the aging population, the Enron scandal, and merger mania. To survive, all organizations must be capable of astutely identifying and adapting to change. The strategic-management process is aimed at allowing organizations to adapt effectively to change over the long run. As Waterman has noted:

> In today's business environment, more than in any preceding era, the only constant is change. Successful organizations effectively manage change, continuously adapting their bureaucracies, strategies, systems, products, and cultures to survive the shocks and prosper from the forces that decimate the competition.[7]

E-commerce and globalization are external changes that are transforming business and society today. On a political map, the boundaries between countries may be clear, but on a competitive map showing the real flow of financial and industrial activity, the boundaries have largely disappeared. The speedy flow of information has eaten away at national boundaries so that people worldwide readily see for themselves how other people live. People are traveling abroad more: 10 million Japanese annually travel abroad. People are emigrating more: Germans to England and Mexicans to the United States are examples. We have become a borderless world with global citizens, global competitors, global customers, global suppliers, and global distributors!

As the Global Perspective indicates, U.S. firms are challenged by large rival companies in many industries. General Motors' sales decreased 16.6 percent in early 2007 while Ford Motor's sales decreased 19 percent during the same time that Toyota Motor's sales rose 9.5 percent and Honda Motor's sales rose 2.4 percent. To say U.S. firms are being challenged in the automobile industry is an understatement. But this situation is true in many industries. Citigroup cut nearly 17,000 jobs in 2007 in a major restructuring, striving to compete. Westinghouse Electric is one of many landmark American firms that have recently been acquired by companies located outside the United States. Now owned by Japan's Toshiba, Westinghouse in 2007 won a $5.3 billion contract to build four nuclear power plants in China. This was the largest nuclear reactor contract ever for any firm. Based in Nagoya, Japan, that country's largest car maker, Toyota, surpassed General Motors in 2007 as the world's top producer of cars. GM is in the midst of a painful restructuring and has recently incurred billion-dollar annual losses.

The need to adapt to change leads organizations to key strategic-management questions, such as "What kind of business should we become?" "Are we in the right field(s)?" "Should we reshape our business?" "What new competitors are entering our industry?" "What strategies should we pursue?" "How are our customers changing?" "Are new technologies being developed that could put us out of business?"

VISIT THE NET

Reveals that actual strategy results from planned strategy coupled with reactive changes. (www. csuchico.edu/mgmt/strategy/ module1/sld032.htm)

Key Terms in Strategic Management

Before we further discuss strategic management, we should define nine key terms: competitive advantage, strategists, vision and mission statements, external opportunities and threats, internal strengths and weaknesses, long-term objectives, strategies, annual objectives, and policies.

Competitive Advantage

Strategic management is all about gaining and maintaining *competitive advantage.* This term can be defined as "anything that a firm does especially well compared to rival firms."

GLOBAL PERSPECTIVE
The Largest Companies in the World

*F*orbes magazine's annual ranking of the world's largest companies reveals that U.S. firms are being challenged in many industries. The world's largest thirty companies are listed here. Note that only twelve U.S. companies are in the top 30 in sales worldwide.

Rank	Company	2006 Sales ($mil.)	Country
1	Wal-Mart Stores	348,650	USA
2	ExxonMobil	335,086	USA
3	Royal Dutch Shell	318,845	Netherlands
4	BP	265,906	United Kingdom
5	General Motors	207,349	USA
6	DaimlerChrysler	199,985	Germany
7	Chevron	195,341	USA
8	Toyota Motor	179,024	Japan
9	Total	175,051	France
10	ConocoPhillips	167,578	USA
11	General Electric	163,391	USA
12	Ford Motor	160,123	USA
13	ING Group	153,439	Netherlands
14	Citigroup	146,558	USA
15	Allianz	125,329	Germany
16	HSBC Holdings	121,508	United Kingdom
17	Fortis	121,186	Netherlands
18	Bank of America	116,574	USA
19	ENI	113,595	Italy
20	American Intl Group	113,194	USA
21	Volkswagen Group	112,610	Germany
22	Siemens Group	110,819	Germany
23	UBS	105,587	Switzerland
24	JP Morgan Chase	99,302	USA
25	Sinopec-China Petrol	99,026	China
26	AXA Group	98,845	France
27	Berkshire Hathaway	98,539	USA
28	Carrefour	97,726	France
29	Dexia	95,785	Belgium
30	Deutsche Bank	95,496	Germany

Source: Adapted from Scott DeCarlo, "2000 World Leaders: The World's Biggest Public Companies," *Forbes* (April 16, 2007): 143.

When a firm can do something that rival firms cannot do, or owns something that rival firms desire, that can represent a competitive advantage. Getting and keeping competitive advantage is essential for long-term success in an organization. The Industrial/Organizational (I/O) and the Resource-Based View (RBV) theories of organization (as discussed in Chapters 3 and 4, respectively) present different perspectives on how best to capture and keep competitive advantage—that is, how best to manage strategically. Pursuit of competitive advantage leads to organizational success or failure. Strategic management researchers and practitioners alike desire to better understand the nature and role of competitive advantage in various industries.

Normally, a firm can sustain a competitive advantage for only a certain period due to rival firms imitating and undermining that advantage. Thus it is not adequate to simply obtain competitive advantage. A firm must strive to achieve *sustained competitive advantage* by (1) continually adapting to changes in external trends and events and internal capabilities, competencies, and resources; and by (2) effectively formulating, implementing, and evaluating strategies that capitalize upon those factors. For example, newspaper circulation in the United States is steadily declining. Most national newspapers are rapidly losing market share to the Internet, cable, radio, television, magazines, and other media that consumers use to stay informed. Daily newspaper circulation in the United States totals about 55 million copies annually, which is about the same as it was in 1954. Strategists ponder whether the newspaper circulation slide can be halted in the digital age. The six broadcast networks—ABC, CBS, Fox, NBC, UPN, and WB—are being assaulted by cable channels, video games, broadband, wireless technologies, satellite radio, high-definition TV, and TiVo. The three original broadcast networks captured about 90 percent of the prime-time audience in 1978, but today their combined market share is less than 50 percent.[8]

An increasing number of companies are gaining a competitive advantage by using the Internet for direct selling and for communication with suppliers, customers, creditors, partners, shareholders, clients, and competitors who may be dispersed globally. E-commerce allows firms to sell products, advertise, purchase supplies, bypass intermediaries, track inventory, eliminate paperwork, and share information. In total, e-commerce is minimizing the expense and cumbersomeness of time, distance, and space in doing business, thus yielding better customer service, greater efficiency, improved products, and higher profitability.

The Internet and personal computers are changing the way we organize our lives; inhabit our homes; and relate to and interact with family, friends, neighbors, and even ourselves. The Internet promotes endless comparison shopping, which thus enables consumers worldwide to band together to demand discounts. The Internet has transferred power from businesses to individuals. Buyers used to face big obstacles when attempting to get the best price and service, such as limited time and data to compare, but now consumers can quickly scan hundreds of vendor offerings. December 2006 online sales in the United States rose 25 percent to $24.6 billion, while traditional sales increased only 5 percent to $457.4 billion.[9] Both the number of people shopping online and the average amount they spend is increasing dramatically. Online shopping is expected to increase from 7 percent of all shopping today to an eventual peak of 15 percent in ten years, because shoppers still enjoy touching and viewing merchandise. Apparel is expected to become the largest product category of online sales by 2009. Most traditional retailers have learned that their online sales can boost in-store sales as they utilize their Web sites to promote in-store promotions.

Consumers spent more money online for clothes than computers in 2006 for the first time ever. Apparel sales should hit $22.1 billion in 2007 with computer hardware/software at $20.1 billion, followed by autos and auto parts ($19.6 billion), and home furnishings ($12.3 billion).[10] Ten percent of all clothing sales in 2007 were purchased online, a dramatic shift in how people shop. The top three online apparel retailers are Victoria's Secret, L.L. Bean, and Gap.

The Internet has changed the very nature and core of buying and selling in nearly all industries. It has fundamentally changed the economics of business in every single industry worldwide. Broadband, e-trade, e-commerce, e-business, and e-mail have become an integral part of everyday life worldwide. Business-to-business e-commerce is five times greater than consumer e-commerce.

Strategists

Strategists are the individuals who are most responsible for the success or failure of an organization. Strategists have various job titles, such as chief executive officer, president, owner, chair of the board, executive director, chancellor, dean, or entrepreneur. Jay Conger, professor of organizational behavior at the London Business School and author of *Building Leaders,* says, "All strategists have to be chief learning officers. We are in an extended period of change. If our leaders aren't highly adaptive and great models during this period, then our companies won't adapt either, because ultimately leadership is about being a role model."

Strategists help an organization gather, analyze, and organize information. They track industry and competitive trends, develop forecasting models and scenario analyses, evaluate corporate and divisional performance, spot emerging market opportunities, identify business threats, and develop creative action plans. Strategic planners usually serve in a support or staff role. Usually found in higher levels of management, they typically have considerable authority for decision making in the firm. The CEO is the most visible and critical strategic manager. Any manager who has responsibility for a unit or division, responsibility for profit and loss outcomes, or direct authority over a major piece of the business is a strategic manager (strategist). In the last five years, the position of chief strategy officer (CSO) has emerged as a new addition to the top management ranks of many organizations, including Sun Microsystems, Network Associates, Clarus, Lante, Marimba, Sapient, Commerce One, BBDO, Cadbury Schweppes, General Motors, Ellie Mae, Cendant, Charles Schwab, Tyco, Campbell Soup, Morgan Stanley, and Reed-Elsevier. This new corporate officer title represents recognition of the growing importance of strategic planning in the business world.[11]

Strategists differ as much as organizations themselves, and these differences must be considered in the formulation, implementation, and evaluation of strategies. Some strategists will not consider some types of strategies because of their personal philosophies.

Strategists differ in their attitudes, values, ethics, willingness to take risks, concern for social responsibility, concern for profitability, concern for short-run versus long-run aims, and management style. The founder of Hershey Foods, Milton Hershey, built the company to manage an orphanage. From corporate profits, Hershey Foods today cares for over one thousand boys and girls in its School for Orphans.

Vision and Mission Statements

Many organizations today develop a *vision statement* that answers the question "What do we want to become?" Developing a vision statement is often considered the first step in strategic planning, preceding even development of a mission statement. Many vision statements are a single sentence. For example, the vision statement of Stokes Eye Clinic in Florence, South Carolina, is "Our vision is to take care of your vision." The vision of the Institute of Management Accountants is "Global leadership in education, certification, and practice of management accounting and financial management."

Mission statements are "enduring statements of purpose that distinguish one business from other similar firms. A mission statement identifies the scope of a firm's operations in product and market terms."[12] It addresses the basic question that faces all strategists: "What is our business?" A clear mission statement describes the values and priorities of an organization. Developing a mission statement compels strategists to think about the nature and scope of present operations and to assess the potential attractiveness of future markets and activities. A mission statement broadly charts the future direction of an organization. An example of a mission statement is Microsoft's:

> Microsoft's mission is to create software for the personal computer that empowers and enriches people in the workplace, at school and at home. Microsoft's early vision of a computer on every desk and in every home is coupled today with a strong commitment to Internet-related technologies that expand the power and reach of the PC and its users. As the world's leading software provider, Microsoft strives to produce innovative products that meet our customers' evolving needs. At the same time, we understand that long-term success is about more than just making great products. Find out what we mean when we talk about Living Our Values (www.microsoft. com/mscorp).

External Opportunities and Threats

External opportunities and *external threats* refer to economic, social, cultural, demographic, environmental, political, legal, governmental, technological, and competitive trends and events that could significantly benefit or harm an organization in the future. Opportunities and threats are largely beyond the control of a single organization—thus the word *external*. The wireless revolution, biotechnology, population shifts, high gas prices, changing work values and attitudes, illegal immigration issues, and increased competition from foreign companies are examples of opportunities or threats for companies. These types of changes are creating a different type of consumer and consequently a need for different types of products, services, and strategies. Many companies in many industries face the severe external threat of online sales capturing increasing market share in their industry.

Other opportunities and threats may include the passage of a law, the introduction of a new product by a competitor, a national catastrophe, or the declining value of the dollar. A competitor's strength could be a threat. Unrest in the Middle East, rising energy costs, or the war against terrorism could represent an opportunity or a threat.

A basic tenet of strategic management is that firms need to formulate strategies to take advantage of external opportunities and to avoid or reduce the impact of external threats. For this reason, identifying, monitoring, and evaluating external opportunities and threats are essential for success. This process of conducting research and gathering and assimilating external information is sometimes called *environmental scanning* or industry analysis. Lobbying is one activity that some organizations utilize to influence external opportunities and threats.

Internal Strengths and Weaknesses

Internal strengths and *internal weaknesses* are an organization's controllable activities that are performed especially well or poorly. They arise in the management, marketing, finance/accounting, production/operations, research and development, and management information systems activities of a business. Identifying and evaluating organizational strengths and weaknesses in the functional areas of a business is an essential strategic-management activity. Organizations strive to pursue strategies that capitalize on internal strengths and eliminate internal weaknesses.

Strengths and weaknesses are determined relative to competitors. *Relative* deficiency or superiority is important information. Also, strengths and weaknesses can be determined by elements of being rather than performance. For example, a strength may involve ownership of natural resources or a historic reputation for quality. Strengths and weaknesses may be determined relative to a firm's own objectives. For example, high levels of inventory turnover may not be a strength to a firm that seeks never to stock-out.

Internal factors can be determined in a number of ways, including computing ratios, measuring performance, and comparing to past periods and industry averages. Various types of surveys also can be developed and administered to examine internal factors such as employee morale, production efficiency, advertising effectiveness, and customer loyalty.

Long-Term Objectives

Objectives can be defined as specific results that an organization seeks to achieve in pursuing its basic mission. *Long-term* means more than one year. Objectives are essential for organizational success because they state direction; aid in evaluation; create synergy; reveal priorities; focus coordination; and provide a basis for effective planning, organizing, motivating, and controlling activities. Objectives should be challenging, measurable, consistent, reasonable, and clear. In a multidimensional firm, objectives should be established for the overall company and for each division.

Strategies

Strategies are the means by which long-term objectives will be achieved. Business strategies may include geographic expansion, diversification, acquisition, product development, market penetration, retrenchment, divestiture, liquidation, and joint ventures. Strategies currently being pursued by some companies are described in Table 1-1.

Strategies are potential actions that require top management decisions and large amounts of the firm's resources. In addition, strategies affect an organization's long-term

TABLE 1-1 Example Strategies in Action in 2007

McDonald's Corp.

The world's largest restaurant chain by number of outlets, Big Mac is doing fantastic both in the United States and abroad. In recent months, McDonald's began opening drive-through restaurants in China, closed twenty-five sites in the United Kingdom, and disposed of a supply-chain operation in Russia. Big Mac in 2007 is opening 800 new restaurants in China, Japan, and Russia. Shares of McDonald's stock increased 42 percent in 2006 as sales for the year eclipsed $41 billion. Big Mac is working to eliminate trans fats from its food (New York City is requiring this of all restaurants in 2007). McDonald's plans in 2008 to turn ownership of about 2,300 restaurants in Canada and the United Kingdom over to licensees.

American General

A Fortune 500 company based in Piscataway, New Jersey, American General split into three businesses in 2007: air-conditioning systems, bath-and-kitchen business, and vehicle-control systems. The firm also is renaming itself Trane, after its flagship air-conditioning brand name. The company plans to divest the bath-and-kitchen division and to spin off its vehicle-control division into a publicly traded company named Wabco. Led by CEO Fred Poses, American General employs about 62,000 persons and has manufacturing operations in twenty-eight countries.

prosperity, typically for at least five years, and thus are future-oriented. Strategies have multifunctional or multidivisional consequences and require consideration of both the external and internal factors facing the firm.

Annual Objectives

Annual objectives are short-term milestones that organizations must achieve to reach long-term objectives. Like long-term objectives, annual objectives should be measurable, quantitative, challenging, realistic, consistent, and prioritized. They should be established at the corporate, divisional, and functional levels in a large organization. Annual objectives should be stated in terms of management, marketing, finance/accounting, production/operations, research and development, and management information systems (MIS) accomplishments. A set of annual objectives is needed for each long-term objective. Annual objectives are especially important in strategy implementation, whereas long-term objectives are particularly important in strategy formulation. Annual objectives represent the basis for allocating resources.

Policies

Policies are the means by which annual objectives will be achieved. Policies include guidelines, rules, and procedures established to support efforts to achieve stated objectives. Policies are guides to decision making and address repetitive or recurring situations.

Policies are most often stated in terms of management, marketing, finance/accounting, production/operations, research and development, and computer information systems activities. Policies can be established at the corporate level and apply to an entire organization at the divisional level and apply to a single division, or at the functional level and apply to particular operational activities or departments. Policies, like annual objectives, are especially important in strategy implementation because they outline an organization's expectations of its employees and managers. Policies allow consistency and coordination within and between organizational departments.

Substantial research suggests that a healthier workforce can more effectively and efficiently implement strategies. The national center for health promotion estimates that more than 80 percent of all U.S. corporations have no-smoking policies. no-smoking policies are usually derived from annual objectives that seek to reduce corporate medical costs associated with absenteeism and to provide a healthy workplace. Ireland recently banned smoking in all pubs and restaurants. A no-smoking ban went into effect on January 1, 2007 in all restaurants in Belgium, Hong Kong, Alberta (Canada), Thailand, and Louisiana. Also on that date, Washington, DC's smoking ban extended to bars, and many other cities banned smoking in public places, including Columbia, Missouri; Garden City, Kansas; Greenville, South Carolina; Scranton, Pennsylvania; Hattiesburg, Mississippi; Evansville, Indiana; Bloomington, Illinois; and Oxford, Alabama.

The Strategic-Management Model

The strategic-management process can best be studied and applied using a model. Every model represents some kind of process. The framework illustrated in Figure 1-1 is a widely accepted, comprehensive model of the strategic-management process.[13] This model does not guarantee success, but it does represent a clear and practical approach for formulating, implementing, and evaluating strategies. Relationships among major components of the strategic-management process are shown in the model, which appears in all subsequent chapters with appropriate areas shaped to show the particular focus of each chapter.

Identifying an organization's existing vision, mission, objectives, and strategies is the logical starting point for strategic management because a firm's present situation and condition may preclude certain strategies and may even dictate a particular course of action. Every organization has a vision, mission, objectives, and strategy, even if these elements are not consciously designed, written, or communicated. The answer to where an organization is going can be determined largely by where the organization has been!

FIGURE 1-1

A Comprehensive Strategic-Management Model

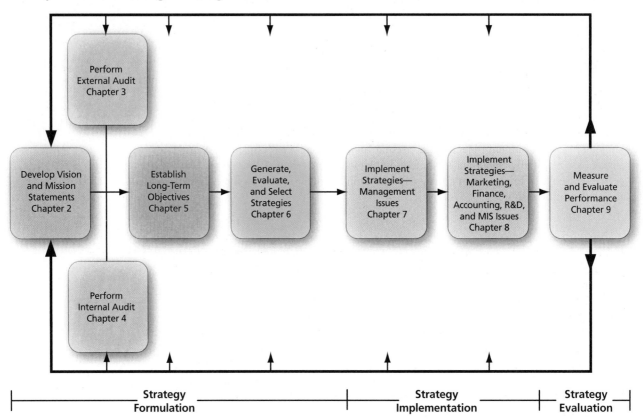

Source: Fred R. David, "How Companies Define Their Mission," *Long Range Planning* 22, no. 3 (June 1988): 40.

The strategic-management process is dynamic and continuous. A change in any one of the major components in the model can necessitate a change in any or all of the other components. For instance, a shift in the economy could represent a major opportunity and require a change in long-term objectives and strategies; a failure to accomplish annual objectives could require a change in policy; or a major competitor's change in strategy could require a change in the firm's mission. Therefore, strategy formulation, implementation, and evaluation activities should be performed on a continual basis, not just at the end of the year or semiannually. The strategic-management process never really ends.

The strategic-management process is not as cleanly divided and neatly performed in practice as the strategic-management model suggests. Strategists do not go through the process in lockstep fashion. Generally, there is give-and-take among hierarchical levels of an organization. Many organizations semiannually conduct formal meetings to discuss and update the firm's vision/mission, opportunities/threats, strengths/weaknesses, strategies, objectives, policies, and performance. These meetings are commonly held off-premises and are called *retreats*. The rationale for periodically conducting strategic-management meetings away from the work site is to encourage more creativity and candor from participants. Good communication and feedback are needed throughout the strategic-management process.

Application of the strategic-management process is typically more formal in larger and well-established organizations. Formality refers to the extent that participants, responsibilities, authority, duties, and approach are specified. Smaller businesses tend to be less formal. Firms that compete in complex, rapidly changing environments, such as technology companies, tend to be more formal in strategic planning. Firms that have many divisions, products, markets, and technologies also tend to be more formal in applying strategic-management concepts. Greater formality in applying the strategic-management process is usually positively associated with the cost, comprehensiveness, accuracy, and success of planning across all types and sizes of organizations.[14]

Benefits of Strategic Management

Strategic management allows an organization to be more proactive than reactive in shaping its own future; it allows an organization to initiate and influence (rather than just respond to) activities—and thus to exert control over its own destiny. Small business owners, chief executive officers, presidents, and managers of many for-profit and nonprofit organizations have recognized and realized the benefits of strategic management.

Historically, the principal benefit of strategic management has been to help organizations formulate better strategies through the use of a more systematic, logical, and rational approach to strategic choice. This certainly continues to be a major benefit of strategic management, but research studies now indicate that the process, rather than the decision or document, is the more important contribution of strategic management.[15] *Communication is a key to successful strategic management.* Through involvement in the process, managers and employees become committed to supporting the organization. Dialogue and participation are essential ingredients.

The manner in which strategic management is carried out is thus exceptionally important. A major aim of the process is to achieve the understanding of and commitment from all managers and employees. Understanding may be the most important benefit of strategic management, followed by commitment. When managers and employees understand what the organization is doing and why, they often feel that they are a part of the firm and become committed to assisting it. This is especially true when employees also understand linkages between their own compensation and organizational performance. Managers and employees become surprisingly creative and innovative when they understand and support the firm's mission, objectives, and strategies. A great benefit of strategic management, then, is the opportunity that the process provides to empower individuals. *Empowerment* is the act of strengthening employees' sense of effectiveness by encouraging them to participate in decision making and to exercise initiative and imagination, and rewarding them for doing so.

More and more organizations are decentralizing the strategic-management process, recognizing that planning must involve lower-level managers and employees. The notion of centralized staff planning is being replaced in organizations by decentralized line-manager planning. For example, Walt Disney Co. recently dismantled its strategic-planning department and gave those responsibilities back to the Disney business divisions. Former CEO Michael Eisner had favored the centralized strategic-planning approach, but new CEO Robert Iger dissolved Disney's strategic-planning department within weeks of his taking over the top office at Disney. The process is a learning, helping, educating, and supporting activity, not merely a paper-shuffling activity among top executives. Strategic-management dialogue is more important than a nicely bound strategic-management document.[16] The worst thing strategists can do is develop strategic plans themselves and then present them to operating managers to execute. Through involvement in the process, line managers become "owners" of the strategy. Ownership of strategies by the people who have to execute them is a key to success!

Although making good strategic decisions is the major responsibility of an organization's owner or chief executive officer, both managers and employees must also be involved in strategy formulation, implementation, and evaluation activities. Participation is a key to gaining commitment for needed changes.

An increasing number of corporations and institutions are using strategic management to make effective decisions. But strategic management is not a guarantee for success; it can be dysfunctional if conducted haphazardly.

VISIT THE NET

Explains in detail how to develop a strategic plan and compares this document to a business plan. (www.planware.org/strategy. htm#1)

VISIT THE NET

Provides excellent narrative on the "Benefits of Strategic Planning," "Pitfalls of Strategic Planning," and the "Steps in Doing Strategic Planning." (www.entarga.com/stratplan/index.htm)

Financial Benefits

Research indicates that organizations using strategic-management concepts are more profitable and successful than those that do not.[17] Businesses using strategic-management concepts show significant improvement in sales, profitability, and productivity compared to firms without systematic planning activities. High-performing firms tend to do systematic planning to prepare for future fluctuations in their external and internal environments. Firms with planning systems more closely resembling strategic-management theory generally exhibit superior long-term financial performance relative to their industry.

High-performing firms seem to make more informed decisions with good anticipation of both short- and long-term consequences. On the other hand, firms that perform poorly often engage in activities that are shortsighted and do not reflect good forecasting of future conditions. Strategists of low-performing organizations are often preoccupied with solving internal problems and meeting paperwork deadlines. They typically underestimate their competitors' strengths and overestimate their own firm's strengths. They often attribute weak performance to uncontrollable factors such as a poor economy, technological change, or foreign competition.

Dun & Bradstreet reports that more than 100,000 businesses in the United States fail annually. Business failures include bankruptcies, foreclosures, liquidations, and court-mandated receiverships. Although many factors besides a lack of effective strategic management can lead to business failure, the planning concepts and tools described in this text can yield substantial financial benefits for any organization. An excellent Web site for businesses engaged in strategic planning is www.checkmateplan.com.

Nonfinancial Benefits

Besides helping firms avoid financial demise, strategic management offers other tangible benefits, such as an enhanced awareness of external threats, an improved understanding of competitors' strategies, increased employee productivity, reduced resistance to change, and a clearer understanding of performance–reward relationships. Strategic management enhances the problem-prevention capabilities of organizations because it promotes interaction among managers at all divisional and functional levels. Firms that have nurtured their managers and employees, shared organizational objectives with them, empowered them to help improve the product or service, and recognized their contributions can turn to them for help in a pinch because of this interaction.

In addition to empowering managers and employees, strategic management often brings order and discipline to an otherwise floundering firm. It can be the beginning of an efficient and effective managerial system. Strategic management may renew confidence in the current business strategy or point to the need for corrective actions. The strategic-management process provides a basis for identifying and rationalizing the need for change to all managers and employees of a firm; it helps them view change as an opportunity rather than as a threat.

Greenley stated that strategic management offers the following benefits:

1. It allows for identification, prioritization, and exploitation of opportunities.
2. It provides an objective view of management problems.
3. It represents a framework for improved coordination and control of activities.
4. It minimizes the effects of adverse conditions and changes.
5. It allows major decisions to better support established objectives.
6. It allows more effective allocation of time and resources to identified opportunities.
7. It allows fewer resources and less time to be devoted to correcting erroneous or ad hoc decisions.
8. It creates a framework for internal communication among personnel.
9. It helps integrate the behavior of individuals into a total effort.
10. It provides a basis for clarifying individual responsibilities.
11. It encourages forward thinking.
12. It provides a cooperative, integrated, and enthusiastic approach to tackling problems and opportunities.
13. It encourages a favorable attitude toward change.
14. It gives a degree of discipline and formality to the management of a business.[18]

Why Some Firms Do No Strategic Planning

Some firms do not engage in strategic planning, and some firms do strategic planning but receive no support from managers and employees. Some reasons for poor or no strategic planning are as follows:

VISIT THE NET

Gives reasons why some organizations avoid strategic planning. (www.mindtools.com/plfailpl.html)

- *Poor reward structures*—When an organization assumes success, it often fails to reward success. When failure occurs, then the firm may punish. In this situation, it is better for an individual to do nothing (and not draw attention) than to risk trying to achieve something, fail, and be punished.
- *Firefighting*—An organization can be so deeply embroiled in crisis management and firefighting that it does not have time to plan.
- *Waste of time*—Some firms see planning as a waste of time because no marketable product is produced. Time spent on planning is an investment.
- *Too expensive*—Some organizations are culturally opposed to spending resources.
- *Laziness*—People may not want to put forth the effort needed to formulate a plan.
- *Content with success*—Particularly if a firm is successful, individuals may feel there is no need to plan because things are fine as they stand. But success today does not guarantee success tomorrow.
- *Fear of failure*—By not taking action, there is little risk of failure unless a problem is urgent and pressing. Whenever something worthwhile is attempted, there is some risk of failure.
- *Overconfidence*—As individuals amass experience, they may rely less on formalized planning. Rarely, however, is this appropriate. Being overconfident or overestimating experience can bring demise. Forethought is rarely wasted and is often the mark of professionalism.
- *Prior bad experience*—People may have had a previous bad experience with planning, that is, cases in which plans have been long, cumbersome, impractical, or inflexible. Planning, like anything else, can be done badly.
- *Self-interest*—When someone has achieved status, privilege, or self-esteem through effectively using an old system, he or she often sees a new plan as a threat.
- *Fear of the unknown*—People may be uncertain of their abilities to learn new skills, of their aptitude with new systems, or of their ability to take on new roles.
- *Honest difference of opinion*—People may sincerely believe the plan is wrong. They may view the situation from a different viewpoint, or they may have aspirations for themselves or the organization that are different from the plan. Different people in different jobs have different perceptions of a situation.
- *Suspicion*—Employees may not trust management.[19]

Pitfalls in Strategic Planning

Strategic planning is an involved, intricate, and complex process that takes an organization into uncharted territory. It does not provide a ready-to-use prescription for success; instead, it takes the organization through a journey and offers a framework for addressing questions and solving problems. Being aware of potential pitfalls and being prepared to address them is essential to success.

Some pitfalls to watch for and avoid in strategic planning are these:

- Using strategic planning to gain control over decisions and resources
- Doing strategic planning only to satisfy accreditation or regulatory requirements
- Too hastily moving from mission development to strategy formulation
- Failing to communicate the plan to employees, who continue working in the dark
- Top managers making many intuitive decisions that conflict with the formal plan
- Top managers not actively supporting the strategic-planning process
- Failing to use plans as a standard for measuring performance
- Delegating planning to a "planner" rather than involving all managers
- Failing to involve key employees in all phases of planning

VISIT THE NET

Provides nice discussion of the limitations of strategic planning process within an organization. (www.des.calstate.edu/limitations.html)

- Failing to create a collaborative climate supportive of change
- Viewing planning as unnecessary or unimportant
- Becoming so engrossed in current problems that insufficient or no planning is done
- Being so formal in planning that flexibility and creativity are stifled.[20]

Guidelines for Effective Strategic Management

Failing to follow certain guidelines in conducting strategic management can foster criticisms of the process and create problems for the organization. An integral part of strategy evaluation must be to evaluate the quality of the strategic-management process. Issues such as "Is strategic management in our firm a people process or a paper process?" should be addressed.

Even the most technically perfect strategic plan will serve little purpose if it is not implemented. Many organizations tend to spend an inordinate amount of time, money, and effort on developing the strategic plan, treating the means and circumstances under which it will be implemented as afterthoughts! Change comes through implementation and evaluation, not through the plan. A technically imperfect plan that is implemented well will achieve more than the perfect plan that never gets off the paper on which it is typed.[21]

Strategic management must not become a self-perpetuating bureaucratic mechanism. Rather, it must be a self-reflective learning process that familiarizes managers and employees in the organization with key strategic issues and feasible alternatives for resolving those issues. Strategic management must not become ritualistic, stilted, orchestrated, or too formal, predictable, and rigid. Words supported by numbers, rather than numbers supported by words, should represent the medium for explaining strategic issues and organizational responses. A key role of strategists is to facilitate continuous organizational learning and change.

R. T. Lenz offered some important guidelines for effective strategic management:

Keep the strategic-management process as simple and nonroutine as possible. Eliminate jargon and arcane planning language. Remember, strategic management is a process for fostering learning and action, not merely a formal system for control. To avoid routinized behavior, vary assignments, team membership, meeting formats, and the planning calendar. The process should not be totally predictable, and settings must be changed to stimulate creativity. Emphasize word-oriented plans with numbers as back-up material. If managers cannot express their strategy in a paragraph or so, they either do not have one or do not understand it. Stimulate thinking and action that challenge the assumptions underlying current corporate strategy. Welcome bad news. If strategy is not working, managers desperately need to know it. Further, no pertinent information should be classified as inadmissible merely because it cannot be quantified. Build a corporate culture in which the role of strategic management and its essential purposes are understood. Do not permit "technicians" to co-opt the process. It is ultimately a process for learning and action. Speak of it in these terms. Attend to psychological, social, and political dimensions, as well as the information infrastructure and administrative procedures supporting it.[22]

An important guideline for effective strategic management is open-mindedness. A willingness and eagerness to consider new information, new viewpoints, new ideas, and new possibilities is essential; all organizational members must share a spirit of inquiry and learning. Strategists such as chief executive officers, presidents, owners of small businesses, and heads of government agencies must commit themselves to listen to and understand managers' positions well enough to be able to restate those positions to the managers' satisfaction. In addition, managers and employees throughout the firm should be able to describe the strategists' positions to the satisfaction of the strategists. This degree of discipline will promote understanding and learning.

No organization has unlimited resources. No firm can take on an unlimited amount of debt or issue an unlimited amount of stock to raise capital. Therefore, no organization can pursue all the strategies that potentially could benefit the firm. Strategic decisions thus always have to be made to eliminate some courses of action and to allocate organizational resources among others. Most organizations can afford to pursue only a few corporate-level strategies at any given time. It is a critical mistake for managers to pursue too many strategies at the same time, thereby spreading the firm's resources so thin that all strategies are jeopardized. Joseph Charyk, CEO of the Communication Satellite Corporation (Comsat), said, "We have to face the cold fact that Comsat may not be able to do all it wants. We must make hard choices on which ventures to keep and which to fold."

Strategic decisions require trade-offs such as long-range versus short-range considerations or maximizing profits versus increasing shareholders' wealth. There are ethics issues too. Strategy trade-offs require subjective judgments and preferences. In many cases, a lack of objectivity in formulating strategy results in a loss of competitive posture and profitability. Most organizations today recognize that strategic-management concepts and techniques can enhance the effectiveness of decisions. Subjective factors such as attitudes toward risk, concern for social responsibility, and organizational culture will always affect strategy-formulation decisions, but organizations need to be as objective as possible in considering qualitative factors.

Business Ethics and Strategic Management

Business ethics can be defined as principles of conduct within organizations that guide decision making and behavior. Good business ethics is a prerequisite for good strategic management; good ethics is just good business!

VISIT THE NET

Describes "Why Have a Code of Ethics" and gives "Guidelines on Writing a Code of Ethics." (www.ethicsweb.ca/codes)

A rising tide of consciousness about the importance of business ethics is sweeping the United States and the rest of the world. Strategists are the individuals primarily responsible for ensuring that high ethical principles are espoused and practiced in an organization. All strategy formulation, implementation, and evaluation decisions have ethical ramifications.

Newspapers and business magazines daily report legal and moral breaches of ethical conduct by both public and private organizations. The biggest payouts for class-action legal fraud suits ever were against Enron ($7.16 billion), WorldCom ($6.16 billion), Cendant ($3.53 billion), Tyco ($2.98 billion), AOL Time Warner ($2.5 billion), Nortel Networks ($2.47 billion), and Royal Ahold ($1.09 billion).

Managers and employees of firms must be careful not to become scapegoats blamed for company environmental wrongdoings. Harming the natural environment is unethical, illegal, and costly. When organizations today face criminal charges for polluting the environment, firms increasingly are turning on their managers and employees to win leniency for themselves. Employee firings and demotions are becoming common in pollution-related legal suits. Managers being fired at Darling International, Inc., and Niagara Mohawk Power Corporation for being indirectly responsible for their firms polluting water exemplifies this corporate trend. Therefore, managers and employees today must be careful not to ignore, conceal, or disregard a pollution problem, or they may find themselves personally liable. In this regard, more and more companies are becoming ISO 14001 certified, as indicated in the "Natural Environment Perspective" on pages 20–21.

A new wave of ethics issues related to product safety, employee health, sexual harassment, AIDS in the workplace, smoking, acid rain, affirmative action, waste disposal, foreign business practices, cover-ups, takeover tactics, conflicts of interest, employee privacy, inappropriate gifts, security of company records, and layoffs has accentuated the need for strategists to develop a clear code of business ethics. United Technologies Corporation has issued a twenty-one-page code of ethics and named a new vice president of business ethics. Baxter Travenol Laboratories, IBM, Caterpillar Tractor, Chemical Bank, ExxonMobil, Dow Corning, and Celanese are firms that have formal codes of business ethics. A *code of business ethics* can provide a basis on which policies can be devised to guide daily behavior and decisions at the work site.

VISIT THE NET

An excellent Web site to obtain additional information regarding business ethics is (www.ethicsweb. ca/codes); it describes "Why Have a Code of Ethics" and gives "Guidelines on Writing a Code of Ethics."

VISIT THE NET

Professor Hansen at Stetson University provides a strategic management slide show for this entire text. (www.stetson.edu/ ~rhansen/strategy)

Merely having a code of ethics, however, is not sufficient to ensure ethical business behavior. A code of ethics can be viewed as a public relations gimmick, a set of platitudes, or window dressing. To ensure that the code is read, understood, believed, and remembered, organizations need to conduct periodic ethics workshops to sensitize people to workplace circumstances in which ethics issues may arise.[23] If employees see examples of punishment for violating the code and rewards for upholding the code, this helps reinforce the importance of a firm's code of ethics.

An ethics "culture" needs to permeate organizations! To help create an ethics culture, Citicorp developed a business ethics board game that is played by forty thousand employees in forty-five countries. Called "The Word Ethic," this game asks players business ethics questions, such as how do you deal with a customer who offers you football tickets in exchange for a new, backdated IRA? Diana Robertson at the Wharton School of Business believes the game is effective because it is interactive. Many organizations, such as Prime Computer and Kmart, have developed a code-of-conduct manual outlining ethical expectations and giving examples of situations that commonly arise in their businesses. Harris Corporation's managers and employees are warned that failing to report an ethical violation by others could bring discharge.

One reason strategists' salaries are high compared to those of other individuals in an organization is that strategists must take the moral risks of the firm. Strategists are responsible for developing, communicating, and enforcing the code of business ethics for their organizations. Although primary responsibility for ensuring ethical behavior rests with a firm's strategists, an integral part of the responsibility of all managers is to provide ethics leadership by constant example and demonstration. Managers hold positions that enable them to influence and educate many people. This makes managers responsible for developing and implementing ethical decision making. Gellerman and Drucker, respectively, offer some good advice for managers:

> All managers risk giving too much because of what their companies demand from them. But the same superiors, who keep pressing you to do more, or to do it better, or faster, or less expensively, will turn on you should you cross that fuzzy line between right and wrong. They will blame you for exceeding instructions or for ignoring their warnings. The smartest managers already know that the best answer to the question "How far is too far?" is don't try to find out.[24]

NATURAL ENVIRONMENT PERSPECTIVE
Using ISO 14000 Certification to Gain Strategic Advantage

Based in Geneva, Switzerland, the ISO (International Organization for Standardization) is a network of the national standards institutes of 147 countries, one member per country. ISO is the world's largest developer of standards. Widely accepted all over the world, ISO standards are voluntary because the organization has no legal authority to enforce their implementation. ISO itself does not regulate or legislate. Governmental agencies in various countries, such as the Environmental Protection Agency in the United States, have adopted ISO standards as part of their regulatory framework, and the standards are the basis of much legislation. Adoptions are sovereign decisions by the regulatory authorities, governments, and/or companies concerned.

What Are ISO 14000 and ISO 14001?

ISO 14000 refers to a series of voluntary standards in the environmental field. The ISO 14000 family of standards concerns the extent to which a firm minimizes harmful effects on the environment caused by its activities and continually monitors and improves its own environmental performance. Included in the ISO 14000 series are the ISO 14001 standards in fields such as environmental auditing, environmental performance evaluation, environmental labeling, and life-cycle assessment. ISO 14001 is a set of standards adopted by thousands of firms worldwide to certify to their constituencies that they are conducting business in an environmentally friendly manner. ISO 14001 standards offer a universal technical standard for environmental compliance that more and more firms are requiring not only of themselves but also of their suppliers and distributors.

Requirements for ISO 14001 Certification

The ISO 14001 standard requires that a community or organization put in place and implement a series of practices and procedures that, when taken together, result in an environmental management system. ISO 14001 is not a technical standard and as such does not in any way replace technical requirements embodied in statutes or regulations. It also does not set prescribed standards of performance for organizations. The major requirements of an EMS under ISO 14001 include the following:

- Establish an EMS that includes commitments to prevention of pollution, continual improvement in overall environmental performance, and compliance with all applicable statutory and regulatory requirements.
- Identify all aspects of the organization's activities, products, and services that could have a significant impact on the environment, including those that are not regulated.
- Set performance objectives and targets for the management system that link back to three policies: (1) prevention of pollution, (2) continual improvement, and (3) compliance.
- Implement an EMS to meet environmental objectives that include training employees, establishing work instructions and practices, and establishing the actual metrics by which the objectives and targets will be measured.
- Audit the operation of the EMS.
- Take corrective actions when deviations from the EMS occur.

Conclusion

ISO 14001 standards on air, water, and soil quality, and on emissions of gases and radiation, contribute to preserving the environment in which we all live and work. The U.S.

Wyoming, Yellowstone National Park, Mammoth Hot Springs. *Source:* Andy Holligan (c) Dorling Kindersley

Environmental Protection Agency (EPA) now offers a guide entitled "Environmental Management Systems (EMS): An Implementation Guide for Small and Medium Sized Organizations." The publication offers a plain-English, commonsense guide to becoming ISO 14001 certified. Not being ISO 14001 certified can be a strategic disadvantage for towns, counties, and companies as people today expect organizations to minimize or, even better, to eliminate environmental harm they cause.

Source: Adapted from the www.iso14000.com Web site and the www.epa.gov Web site.

A man (or woman) might know too little, perform poorly, lack judgment and ability, and yet not do too much damage as a manager. But if that person lacks character and integrity—no matter how knowledgeable, how brilliant, how successful—he destroys. He destroys people, the most valuable resource of the enterprise. He destroys spirit. And he destroys performance. This is particularly true of the people at the head of an enterprise. For the spirit of an organization is created from the top. If an organization is great in spirit, it is because the spirit of its top people is great. If it decays, it does so because the top rots. As the proverb has it, "Trees die from the top." No one should ever become a strategist unless he or she is willing to have his or her character serve as the model for subordinates.[25]

No society anywhere in the world can compete very long or successfully with people stealing from one another or not trusting one another, with every bit of information requiring notarized confirmation, with every disagreement ending up in litigation, or with government having to regulate businesses to keep them honest. Being unethical is a recipe for headaches, inefficiency, and waste. History has proven that the greater the trust and confidence of people in the ethics of an institution or society, the greater its economic strength. Business relationships are built mostly on mutual trust and reputation. Short-term decisions based on greed and questionable ethics will preclude the necessary self-respect to gain the trust of others. More and more firms believe that ethics training and an ethics culture create strategic advantage.

Some business actions considered to be unethical include misleading advertising or labeling, causing environmental harm, poor product or service safety, padding expense accounts, insider trading, dumping banned or flawed products in foreign markets, lack of equal opportunities for women and minorities, overpricing, hostile takeovers, moving jobs overseas, and using nonunion labor in a union shop.[26]

Internet fraud, including hacking into company computers and spreading viruses, has become a major unethical activity that plagues every sector of online commerce from banking to shopping sites. More than three hundred Web sites now show individuals how to hack into computers; this problem has become endemic nationwide and around the world.

Ethics training programs should include messages from the CEO emphasizing ethical business practices, the development and discussion of codes of ethics, and procedures for discussing and reporting unethical behavior. Firms can align ethical and strategic decision making by incorporating ethical considerations into long-term planning, by integrating ethical decision making into the performance appraisal process, by encouraging whistle-blowing or the reporting of unethical practices, and by monitoring departmental and corporate performance regarding ethical issues.

In a final analysis, ethical standards come out of history and heritage. Our predecessors have left us with an ethical foundation to build upon. Even the legendary football coach Vince Lombardi knew that some things were worth more than winning, and he required his players to have three kinds of loyalty: to God, to their families, and to the Green Bay Packers, "in that order."

Comparing Business and Military Strategy

A strong military heritage underlies the study of strategic management. Terms such as *objectives, mission, strengths*, and *weaknesses* first were formulated to address problems on the battlefield. According to *Webster's New World Dictionary,* strategy is "the science of planning and directing large-scale military operations, of maneuvering forces into the most advantageous position prior to actual engagement with the enemy." The word *strategy* comes from the Greek *strategos,* which refers to a military general and combines *stratos* (the army) and *ago* (to lead). The history of strategic planning began in the military. A key aim of both business and military strategy is "to gain competitive advantage." In many respects, business strategy is like military strategy, and military strategists have learned much over the centuries that can benefit business strategists today. Both business and military organizations try to use their own strengths to exploit competitors' weaknesses. If an organization's overall strategy is wrong (ineffective), then all the efficiency in the world may not be enough to allow success. Business or military success is generally not the happy result of accidental strategies. Rather, success is the product of both continuous attention to changing external and internal conditions and the formulation and implementation of insightful adaptations to those conditions. The element of surprise provides great competitive advantages in both military and business strategy; information systems that provide data on opponents' or competitors' strategies and resources are also vitally important.

Of course, a fundamental difference between military and business strategy is that business strategy is formulated, implemented, and evaluated with an assumption of *competition,* whereas military strategy is based on an assumption of *conflict.* Nonetheless, military conflict and business competition are so similar that many strategic-management techniques apply equally to both. Business strategists have access to valuable insights that military thinkers have refined over time. Superior strategy formulation and implementation can overcome an opponent's superiority in numbers and resources.

Both business and military organizations must adapt to change and constantly improve to be successful. Too often, firms do not change their strategies when their environment and competitive conditions dictate the need to change. Gluck offered a classic military example of this:

> When Napoleon won, it was because his opponents were committed to the strategy, tactics, and organization of earlier wars. When he lost—against Wellington, the Russians, and the Spaniards—it was because he, in turn, used tried-and-true strategies against enemies who thought afresh, who were developing the strategies not of the last war but of the next.[27]

Similarities can be construed from Sun Tzu's writings to the practice of formulating and implementing strategies among businesses today. Table 1-2 provides narrative excerpts from *The Art of War.* As you read through Table 1-2, consider which of the principles of war apply to business strategy as companies today compete aggressively to survive and grow.

The Nature of Global Competition

For centuries before Columbus discovered America and surely for centuries to come, businesses have searched and will continue to search for new opportunities beyond their national boundaries. There has never been a more internationalized and economically competitive society than today's. Some U.S. industries, such as textiles, steel, and consumer electronics, are in complete disarray as a result of the international challenge.

Organizations that conduct business operations across national borders are called *international firms* or *multinational corporations.* The term *parent company* refers to a firm investing in international operations, while *host country* is the country where that business is conducted. The strategic-management process is conceptually the same for multinational firms as for purely domestic firms; however, the process is more complex for international firms because of the presence of more variables and relationships. The social, cultural, demographic, environmental, political, governmental, legal, technological, and competitive opportunities and threats that face a multinational corporation are almost limitless, and the number and complexity of these factors increase dramatically with the number of products produced and the number of geographic areas served.

More time and effort are required to identify and evaluate external trends and events in multinational corporations than in domestic corporations. Geographical distance, cultural and national differences, and variations in business practices often make communication between domestic headquarters and overseas operations difficult. Strategy implementation can be more difficult because different cultures have different norms, values, and work ethics.

Advancements in telecommunications are drawing countries, cultures, and organizations worldwide closer together. Foreign revenue as a percent of total company revenues already exceeds 50 percent in hundreds of U.S. firms, including ExxonMobil, Gillette, Dow Chemical, Citicorp, Colgate-Palmolive, and Texaco. Unilever had $10 billion and $21.3 billion in domestic and foreign revenues, respectively, in 2006. A primary reason why most domestic firms are engaging in global operations is that growth in demand for goods and services outside the United States is considerably higher than inside. For example, the domestic food industry is growing just 3 percent per year, so Kraft Foods, the second largest food company in the world behind Nestle, is focusing on foreign acquisitions. Shareholders and investors expect sustained growth in revenues from firms; satisfactory

TABLE 1-2 Excerpts from Sun Tzu's *The Art of War* Writings

- War is a matter of vital importance to the state: a matter of life or death, the road either to survival or ruin. Hence, it is imperative that it be studied thoroughly.
- Warfare is based on deception. When near the enemy, make it seem that you are far away; when far away, make it seem that you are near. Hold out baits to lure the enemy. Strike the enemy when he is in disorder. Avoid the enemy when he is stronger. If your opponent is of choleric temper, try to irritate him. If he is arrogant, try to encourage his egotism. If enemy troops are well prepared after reorganization, try to wear them down. If they are united, try to sow dissension among them. Attack the enemy where he is unprepared, and appear where you are not expected. These are the keys to victory for a strategist. It is not possible to formulate them in detail beforehand.
- A speedy victory is the main object in war. If this is long in coming, weapons are blunted and morale depressed. When the army engages in protracted campaigns, the resources of the state will fall short. Thus, while we have heard of stupid haste in war, we have not yet seen a clever operation that was prolonged.
- Generally, in war the best policy is to take a state intact; to ruin it is inferior to this. To capture the enemy's entire army is better than to destroy it; to take intact a regiment, a company, or a squad is better than to destroy it. For to win one hundred victories in one hundred battles is not the acme of skill. To subdue the enemy without fighting is the supreme excellence. Those skilled in war subdue the enemy's army without battle.
- The art of using troops is this: When ten to the enemy's one, surround him. When five times his strength, attack him. If double his strength, divide him. If equally matched, you may engage him with some good plan. If weaker, be capable of withdrawing. And if in all respects unequal, be capable of eluding him.
- Know your enemy and know yourself, and in a hundred battles you will never be defeated. When you are ignorant of the enemy but know yourself, your chances of winning or losing are equal. If ignorant both of your enemy and of yourself, you are sure to be defeated in every battle.
- He who occupies the field of battle first and awaits his enemy is at ease, and he who comes later to the scene and rushes into the fight is weary. And therefore, those skilled in war bring the enemy to the field of battle and are not brought there by him. Thus, when the enemy is at ease, be able to tire him; when well fed, be able to starve him; when at rest, be able to make him move.
- Analyze the enemy's plans so that you will know his shortcomings as well as his strong points. Agitate him to ascertain the pattern of his movement. Lure him out to reveal his dispositions and to ascertain his position. Launch a probing attack to learn where his strength is abundant and where deficient. It is according to the situation that plans are laid for victory, but the multitude does not comprehend this.
- An army may be likened to water, for just as flowing water avoids the heights and hastens to the lowlands, so an army should avoid strength and strike weakness. And as water shapes its flow in accordance with the ground, so an army manages its victory in accordance with the situation of the enemy. And as water has no constant form, there are in warfare no constant conditions. Thus, one able to win the victory by modifying his tactics in accordance with the enemy situation may be said to be divine.
- If you decide to go into battle, do not anounce your intentions or plans. Project "business as usual."
- Unskilled leaders work out their conflicts in courtrooms and battlefields. Brilliant strategists rarely go to battle or to court; they generally achieve their objectives through tactical positioning well in advance of any confrontation.
- When you do decide to challenge another company (or army), much calculating, estimating, analyzing, and positioning bring triumph. Little computation brings defeat.
- Skillful leaders do not let a strategy inhibit creative counter-movement. Nor should commands from those at a distance interfere with spontaneous maneuvering in the immediate situation.
- When a decisive advantage is gained over a rival, skillful leaders do not press on. They hold their position and give their rivals the opportunity to surrender or merge. They do not allow their forces to be damaged by those who have nothing to lose.
- Brillant strategists forge ahead with illusion, obscuring the area(s) of major confrontation, so that opponents divide their forces in an attempt to defend many areas. Create the appearance of confusion, fear, or vulnerability so the opponent is helplessly drawn toward this illusion of advantage.

(Note: Substitute the words *strategy* or *strategic planning* for *war* or *warfare*)

Source: Adapted from *The Art of War* and from the Web site www.ccs.neu.edu/home/thigpen/html/art_of_war.html.

growth for many firms can only be achieved by capitalizing on demand outside the United States. Computer shipments grew 21 percent in China in 2006, so Dell has greatly expanded its operations in China. Joint ventures and partnerships between domestic and foreign firms are becoming the rule rather than the exception!

Fully 95 percent of the world's population lives outside the United States, and this group is growing 70 percent faster than the U.S. population! The lineup of competitors in virtually all industries today is global. Global competition is more than a management fad. General Motors, Ford, and Chrysler compete with Toyota and Hyundai. General Electric and Westinghouse battle Siemens and Mitsubishi. Caterpillar and John Deere compete with Komatsu. Goodyear battles Michelin, Bridgestone/Firestone, and Pirelli. Boeing competes with Airbus. Only a few U.S. industries—such as furniture, printing, retailing, consumer packaged goods, and retail banking—are not yet greatly challenged by foreign competitors. But many products and components in these industries too are now manufactured in foreign countries.

International operations can be as simple as exporting a product to a single foreign country or as complex as operating manufacturing, distribution, and marketing facilities in many countries. U.S. firms are acquiring foreign companies and forming joint ventures with foreign firms, and foreign firms are acquiring U.S. companies and forming joint ventures with U.S. firms. This trend is accelerating dramatically. International expansion is no guarantee of success, however.

Advantages and Disadvantages of International Operations

Firms have numerous reasons for formulating and implementing strategies that initiate, continue, or expand involvement in business operations across national borders. Perhaps the greatest advantage is that firms can gain new customers for their products and services, thus increasing revenues. Growth in revenues and profits is a common organizational objective and often an expectation of shareholders because it is a measure of organizational success.

In addition to seeking growth, firms have the following potentially advantageous reasons to initiate, continue, and expand international operations:

1. Foreign operations can absorb excess capacity, reduce unit costs, and spread economic risks over a wider number of markets.
2. Foreign operations can allow firms to establish low-cost production facilities in locations close to raw materials and/or cheap labor.
3. Competitors in foreign markets may not exist, or competition may be less intense than in domestic markets.
4. Foreign operations may result in reduced tariffs, lower taxes, and favorable political treatment in other countries.
5. Joint ventures can enable firms to learn the technology, culture, and business practices of other people and to make contacts with potential customers, suppliers, creditors, and distributors in foreign countries.
6. Many foreign governments and countries offer varied incentives to encourage foreign investment in specific locations.
7. Economies of scale can be achieved from operation in global rather than solely domestic markets. Larger-scale production and better efficiencies allow higher sales volumes and lower-price offerings.

A firm's power and prestige in domestic markets may be significantly enhanced with various stakeholder groups if the firm competes globally. Enhanced prestige can translate into improved negotiating power among creditors, suppliers, distributors, and other important groups.

There are also numerous potential disadvantages of initiating, continuing, or expanding business across national borders. One risk is that foreign operations could be seized by nationalistic factions. Other disadvantages include the following:

1. Firms confront different and often little-understood social, cultural, demographic, environmental, political, governmental, legal, technological, economic, and competitive forces when internationally doing business. These forces can make communication difficult between the parent firm and subsidiaries.
2. Weaknesses of competitors in foreign lands are often overestimated, and strengths are often underestimated. Keeping informed about the number and nature of competitors is more difficult when internationally doing business.
3. Language, culture, and value systems differ among countries, and this can create barriers to communication and problems managing people.
4. Gaining an understanding of regional organizations such as the European Economic Community, the Latin American Free Trade Area, the International Bank for Reconstruction and Development, and the International Finance Corporation is difficult but is often required in internationally doing business.

5. Dealing with two or more monetary systems can complicate international business operations.

6. The availability, depth, and reliability of economic and marketing information in different countries vary extensively, as do industrial structures, business practices, and the number and nature of regional organizations.

Conclusion

All firms have a strategy, even if it is informal, unstructured, and sporadic. All organizations are heading somewhere, but unfortunately some organizations do not know where they are going. The old saying "If you do not know where you are going, then any road will lead you there!" accents the need for organizations to use strategic-management concepts and techniques. The strategic-management process is becoming more widely used by small firms, large companies, nonprofit institutions, governmental organizations, and multinational conglomerates alike. The process of empowering managers and employees has almost limitless benefits.

Organizations should take a proactive rather than a reactive approach in their industry, and they should strive to influence, anticipate, and initiate rather than just respond to events. The strategic-management process embodies this approach to decision making. It represents a logical, systematic, and objective approach for determining an enterprise's future direction. The stakes are generally too high for strategists to use intuition alone in choosing among alternative courses of action. Successful strategists take the time to think about their businesses, where they are with their businesses, and what they want to be as organizations—and then they implement programs and policies to get from where they are to where they want to be in a reasonable period of time.

It is a known and accepted fact that people and organizations that plan ahead are much more likely to become what they want to become than those that do not plan at all. A good strategist plans and controls his or her plans, while a bad strategist never plans and then tries to control people! This textbook is devoted to providing you with the tools necessary to be a good strategist.

Success in business increasingly depends upon offering products and services that are competitive on a world basis, not just on a local basis. If the price and quality of a firm's products and services are not competitive with those available elsewhere in the world, the firm may soon face extinction. Global markets have become a reality in all but the most remote areas of the world. Certainly throughout the United States, even in small towns, firms feel the pressure of world competitors. Nearly half of all the automobiles sold in the United States, for example, are made in Japan and Germany.

We invite you to visit the David page on the Prentice Hall Companion Web site at www.prenhall.com/david for this chapter's review quiz.

Key Terms and Concepts

Annual Objectives (p. 13)
Business Ethics (p. 19)
Code of Business Ethics (p. 19)
Competitive Advantage (p. 7)
Empowerment (p. 15)
Environmental Scanning (p. 11)
External Opportunities (p. 11)
External Threats (p. 11)
Host Country (p. 23)
Internal Strengths (p. 12)
Internal Weaknesses (p. 12)
International Firms (p. 23)
Intuition (p. 6)
ISO 14000 (p. 20)

ISO 14001 (p. 20)
Long-Range Planning (p. 4)
Long-Term Objectives (p. 12)
Mission Statements (p. 11)
Multinational Corporations (p. 23)
Parent Company (p. 23)
Policies (p. 13)
Strategic Management (p. 4)
Strategic-Management Model (p. 14)
Strategic-Management Process (p. 5)
Strategic Planning (p. 4)
Strategies (p. 12)
Strategists (p. 10)
Strategy Evaluation (p. 5)
Strategy Formulation (p. 5)
Strategy Implementation (p. 5)
Sustained Competitive Advantage (p. 9)
Vision Statement (p. 11)

Issues for Review and Discussion

1. Explain why the strategic management class is often called a "capstone course."
2. What aspect of strategy formulation do you think requires the most time? Why?
3. Why is strategy implementation often considered the most difficult stage in the strategic-management process?
4. Why is it so important to integrate intuition and analysis in strategic management?
5. Explain the importance of a vision and a mission statement.
6. Discuss relationships among objectives, strategies, and policies.
7. Why do you think some chief executive officers fail to use a strategic-management approach to decision making?
8. Discuss the importance of feedback in the strategic-management model.
9. How can strategists best ensure that strategies will be effectively implemented?
10. Give an example of a recent political development that changed the overall strategy of an organization.
11. Who are the major competitors of your college or university? What are their strengths and weaknesses? What are their strategies? How sucessful are these institutions compared to your college?
12. If you owned a small business, would you develop a code of business conduct? If yes, what variables would you include? If no, how would you ensure that ethical business standards were being followed by your employees?
13. Would strategic-management concepts and techniques benefit foreign businesses as much as domestic firms? Justify your answer.
14. What do you believe are some potential pitfalls or risks in using a strategic-management approach to decision making?
15. In your opinion, what is the single major benefit of using a strategic-management approach to decision making? Justify your answer.
16. Compare business strategy and military strategy.
17. What do you feel is the relationship between personal ethics and business ethics? Are they— or should they be—the same?
18. Why is it important for all business majors to study strategic management since most students will never become a chief executive officer nor even a top manager in a large company?
19. Explain why consumption patterns are becoming similar worldwide. What are the strategic implications of this trend?
20. What are the advantages and disadvantages of beginning export operations in a foreign country?
21. Describe the content available on the SMCO Web site at www.strategyclub.com.
22. List four financial and four nonfinancial benefits of a firm engaging in strategic planning.
23. Why is it that a firm can normally sustain a competitive advantage for only a limited period of time?
24. Why it is not adequate to simply obtain competitive advantage?
25. How can a firm best achieve sustained competitive advantage?
26. Compare and contrast ISO 14000 and 14001.

Notes

1. Peter Drucker, *Management: Tasks, Responsibilities, and Practices* (New York: Harper & Row, 1974): 611.

2. Alfred Sloan, Jr., *Adventures of the White Collar Man* (New York: Doubleday, 1941): 104.

3. Quoted in Eugene Raudsepp, "Can You Trust Your Hunches?" *Management Review* 49, no. 4 (April 1960): 7.

4. Stephen Harper, "Intuition: What Separates Executives from Managers," *Business Horizons* 31, no. 5 (September–October 1988): 16.

5. Ron Nelson, "How to Be a Manager," *Success* (July–August 1985): 69.

6. Bruce Henderson, *Henderson on Corporate Strategy* (Boston: Abt Books, 1979): 6.

7. Robert Waterman, Jr., *The Renewal Factor: How the Best Get and Keep the Competitive Edge* (New York: Bantam, 1987). See also *BusinessWeek* (September 14, 1987): 100. Also, see *Academy of Management Executive* 3, no. 2 (May 1989): 115.

8. Ethan Smith, "How Old Media Can Survive in a New World," *Wall Street Journal* (May 23, 2005): R4.

9. Gian Fulgoni, "Web Can Pay Off for Traditional Retailers," *Wall Street Journal* (December 23, 2006): A7.

10. Jayne O'Donnell, "Computers Bumped from Top of Online Sales," *USA Today* (May 14, 2007): 1B.

11. Daniel Delmar, "The Rise of the CSO," *Organization Design* (March–April 2003): 8–10.

12. John Pearce II and Fred David, "The Bottom Line on Corporate Mission Statements," *Academy of Management Executive* 1, no. 2 (May 1987): 109.

13. Fred R. David, "How Companies Define Their Mission," *Long Range Planning* 22, no. 1 (February 1989): 91.

14. Jack Pearce and Richard Robinson, *Strategic Management,* 7th ed. (New York: McGraw-Hill, 2000): 8.

15. Ann Langley, "The Roles of Formal Strategic Planning," *Long Range Planning* 21, no. 3 (June 1988): 40.

16. Bernard Reimann, "Getting Value from Strategic Planning," *Planning Review* 16, no. 3 (May–June 1988): 42.

17. G. L. Schwenk and K. Schrader, "Effects of Formal Strategic Planning in Financial Performance in Small Firms: A Meta-Analysis," *Entrepreneurship and Practice* 3, no. 17 (1993): 53–64. Also, C. C. Miller and L. B. Cardinal, "Strategic Planning and Firm Performance: A Synthesis of More Than Two Decades of Research," *Academy of Management Journal* 6, no. 27 (1994): 1649–1665; Michael Peel and John Bridge, "How Planning and Capital Budgeting Improve SME Performance," *Long Range Planning* 31, no. 6 (October 1998): 848–856; Julia Smith, "Strategies for Start-Ups," *Long Range Planning* 31, no. 6 (October 1998): 857–872.

18. Gordon Greenley, "Does Strategic Planning Improve Company Performance?" *Long Range Planning* 19, no. 2 (April 1986): 106.

19. Adapted from: www.mindtools.com/plreschn.html.

20. Adapted from the Web sites: www.des.calstate.edu/limitations.html and www.entarga.com/stratplan/purposes.html.

21. Dale McConkey, "Planning in a Changing Environment," *Business Horizons* (September–October 1988): 66.

22. R. T. Lenz, "Managing the Evolution of the Strategic Planning Process," *Business Horizons* 30, no. 1 (January–February 1987): 39.

23. Joann Greco, "Privacy—Whose Right Is It Anyhow?" *Journal of Business Strategy* (January–February 2001): 32.

24. Saul Gellerman, "Why 'Good' Managers Make Bad Ethical Choices," *Harvard Business Review* 64, no. 4 (July–August 1986): 88.

25. Drucker, 462, 463.

26. Gene Laczniak, Marvin Berkowitz, Russell Brooker, and James Hale, "The Ethics of Business: Improving or Deteriorating?" *Business Horizons* 38, no. 1 (January–February 1995): 43.

27. Frederick Gluck, "Taking the Mystique out of Planning," *Across the Board* (July–August 1985): 59.

Current Readings

Adner, R., and P. Zemsky. "A Demand-Based Perspective on Sustainable Competitive Advantage." *Strategic Management Journal* 27, no. 3 (March 2006): 215.

Bigley, Gregory A., Will Felps, and Thomas M. Jones. "Ethical Theory and Stakeholder-Related Decisions: The Role of Stakeholder Culture." *The Academy of Management Review* 32, no. 1 (January 2007): 137.

Boiral, Olivier. "Global Warming: Should Companies Adopt a Proactive Strategy?" *Long Range Planning* 39, no. 3 (June 2006): 315.

Bower, Joseph L., and Clark G. Gilbert. "How Managers' Everyday Decisions Create—or Destroy—Your Company's Strategy." *Harvard Business Review* (February 2007): 72.

Cardy, Robert L., and T. T. Selvarajan. "Competencies: Alternative Frameworks for Competitive Advantage." *Business Horizons* 49, no. 3 (May–June 2006): 235.

Certo, S. Trevis, and Matthen Semadeni. "Strategy Research and Panel Data: Evidence and Implication." *Journal of Management* 32, no. 3 (June 2006): 449.

Certo, Samuel C., S. Trevis Certo, and Christopher R. Reutzel. "Spotlight on Entrepreneurship." *Business Horizons* 49, no. 4 (July-August 2006): 265.

Clement, Ronald W. "Just How Unethical Is American Business?" *Business Horizons* 49, no. 4 (July–August 2006): 313.

Dane, Erik, and Michael G. Pratt. "Exploring Intuition and Its Role in Managerial Decision Making." *The Academy of Management Review* 32, no. 1 (January 2007): 33.

Dew, N., S. Read, S. D. Saravathy, and R. Wiltbank. "What to Do Next? The Case for Non-Predictive Strategy." *Strategic Management Journal* 27, no. 10 (October 2006): 981.

Etzion, Dror. "Research on Organizations and the Natural Environment, 1922-Present: A Review." *Journal of Management* 33, no. 4 (August 2007): 637.

Harrison, Ann E., and Margaret S. McMillan. "Dispelling Some Myths About Offshoring." *The Academy of Management Perspectives* 20, no. 4 (November 2006): 6.

Heine, K., and N. Stieglitz. "Innovations and the Role of Complementarities in a Strategic Theory of the Firm." *Strategic Management Journal* 28, no. 1 (January 2007): 1.

Hill, Linda A. "The Tests of a Leader: Becoming the Boss." *Harvard Business Review* (January 2007): 48.

Hill, Linda A. "The Tests of a Leader: Perspectives Moments of Truth." *Harvard Business Review* (January 2007): 15.

Hitt, Michael A. "Spotlight on Strategic Management." *Business Horizons* 49, no. 5 (September–October 2006): 349.

Hutzchenreuter, Thomas, and Ingo Kleindienst. "Strategy Process Research: What Have We Learned and What Is Still to Be Explored." *Journal of Management* 32, no. 5 (October 2006): 673.

Pangarkar, Nitin, and Jie Wu. "Rising to the Global Challenge: Strategies for Firms in Emerging Markets." *Long Range Planning* 39, no. 3 (June 2006): 295.

Pudelko, Markus. "Some Good Recipes for Globalization—But Quite a Few Ingredients Are Missing." *The Academy of Management Perspectives* 20, no. 2 (May 2006): 78.

Sonenshein, Scott. "The Role of Construction, Institution, and Justification, in Responding to Ethical Issues at Work: The Sensemaking-Institution Model." *The Academy of Management Review* 32, no. 4 (October 2007): 1022.

Walfisz, Martin, Timothy L. Wilson, and Peter Zackariasson. "Real-Time Strategy: Evolutionary Game Development." *Business Horizons* 49, no. 6 (November–December 2006): 487.

COHESION CASE 2008   **DISNEY**

Walt Disney Company—2007

Dr. Mernoush Banton

Florida International University

www.disney.com

NYSE: DIS

Headquartered in Burbank, California, Walt Disney Company for eighty years has captured the attention of millions of people around the world, offering family entertainment at theme parks, resorts, recreations, movies, TV shows, radio programming, and memorabilia. Under new CEO Bob Iger who replaced Michael Eisner in 2005, Disney's net income soared 38 percent in 2007 to $4.68 billion, while revenues climbed 5.2 percent to $35.5 billion. Disney had two box-office smash hits in 2006: (1) *Cars* and (2) *Pirates of the Caribbean: Dead Man's Chest.* Then in 2007, Disney's *Pirates of the Caribbean Two* movie as well as *Meet the Robinsons* and also *Ratatouille,* a movie from Disney's Pixar division, were hits. CEO Iger is trying, however, to resuscitate the Disneyland theme parks in Paris and Hong Kong. He has put Disney movies and ABC shows on Apple's iPod, which too has greatly benefited Disney. He plans to spend $1.1 billion in 2008–2011 to revitalize the Disney California Adventure in Anaheim, California, which has not been doing well.

History

Mr. Walt Disney and his brother Roy arrived in California in the summer of 1923 to sell his cartoon called *Alice's Wonderland.* A distributor named M. J. Winkler contracted to distribute the *Alice Comedies* on October 16, 1923, and the Disney Brothers Cartoon Studio was founded. Over the years, the company produced many cartoons, from *Oswald the Lucky Rabbit* (1927) to *Silly Symphonies* (1932), *Snow White and the Seven Dwarfs* (1937), and *Pinocchio* and *Fantasia* (1940). The name of the company was changed to Walt Disney Studio in 1925.

Mickey Mouse balloons.
Source: Lourens Smak/Alamy Images

Mickey Mouse emerged in 1928 with the first cartoon in sound. In 1950, Disney completed its first live-action film, *Treasure Island,* and in 1954, the company began television with Disneyland anthology series. In 1955, Disney's most successful series, *The Mickey Mouse Club*, began. Also in 1955, the new Disneyland Park in California was opened.

Disney created a series of releases from the 1950s through the 1970s, including *The Shaggy Dog, Zorro, Mary Poppins,* and *The Love Bug*. Mr. Walt Disney died in 1966. In 1969, the Disney studio started its educational films and materials. Another important time of Disney's history was opening the Walt Disney World project in Orlando, Florida in 1971. In 1982, the Epcot Center opened as part of Walt Disney World. In 1983, Tokyo Disneyland opened.

After leaving the network television in 1983, the company created a popular cable network, The Disney Channel. In 1985, Disney's Touchstone division began the successful *Golden Girls* and *Disney Sunday Movie*. In 1988, Disney opened Grand Floridian Beach and Caribbean Beach Resorts at Walt Disney World along with three new gated attractions: the Disney/MGM Studios Theme Park, Pleasure Island, and Typhoon Lagoon. At the same time, filmmaking hit new heights as Disney for the first time led Hollywood studios in box-office gross. Some of the successful films were: *Who Framed Roger Rabbit, Good Morning Vietnam, Three Men and a Baby*, and later, *Honey, I Shrunk the Kids; Dick Tracy; Pretty Woman;* and *Sister Act*. Disney moved into new areas by starting Hollywood Pictures and acquiring the Wrather Corp. (owner of the Disneyland Hotel) and television station KHJ (Los Angeles), which was renamed KCAL. In merchandising, Disney purchased Childcraft and opened numerous highly successful and profitable Disney Stores.

By 1992, Disney's animation began reaching even greater audiences with *The Little Mermaid, The Beauty and the Beast,* and *Aladdin*. Hollywood Records was formed to offer a wide selection of recordings ranging from rap to movie soundtracks. New television shows, such as *Live with Regis and Kathy Lee, Empty Nest, Dinosaurs,* and *Home Improvement*, expanded Disney's television base. For the first time, Disney moved into publishing, forming Hyperion Books, Hyperion Books for Children, and Disney Press, which released books on Disney and non-Disney subjects. In 1991, Disney purchased *Discover* magazine, the leading consumer science monthly. As a totally new venture, Disney was awarded, in 1993, the franchise for a National Hockey League team, the Mighty Ducks of Anaheim.

In 1992, Disneyland Paris opened in France. Disney successfully completed many projects throughout the 1990s by venturing into Broadway shows, opening up 725 Disney Stores, acquiring the California Angels baseball team, opening Disney's Wide World of Sports in Walt Disney World, and acquiring Capital Cities/ABC.

From 2000 to 2007, Disney created new attractions in its theme parks, produced many successful films, opened new hotels, and built Hong Kong Disneyland. For eight decades, Walt Disney Company has successfully established itself as a pioneer in the field of family entertainment.

Internal Issues

Corporate Structure and Mission

As indicated in Exhibit 1-1, Walt Disney Company operates using a strategic business unit (SBU) type organizational structure consisting of four SBUs (1) Disney Consumer Products, (2) Studio Entertainment, (3) Parks and Resorts, and (4) Media Networks and Broadcasting. Note all the well-known large divisions that are part of the Disney umbrella of companies, ranging from ESPN Inc. to Buena Vista Records to ABC Television and more. This is a huge, well-known and well-managed, diversified corporation. Disney is financially strong as indicated in Exhibits 1-2 and 1-3.

Disney does not have a stated vision statement.

The company's mission statement is as follows:

> The mission of Walt Disney Company is to be one of the world's leading producers and providers of entertainment and information. Using our portfolio of brands to differentiate our content, services and consumer products, we seek to develop the most creative, innovative and profitable entertainment experiences and related products in the world.

Financials By Segment

Exhibit 1-4 reveals Disney's revenue and operating income by each business segment. Note that the Disney Media Networks segment brings in the most revenues and operating income. This segment, as well as the Parks & Resorts segment, is growing. However, the company's Studio Entertainment segment and their Consumer Products segment have experienced declining revenues in the last three years. These are problem areas for the company.

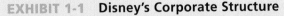

EXHIBIT 1-1 **Disney's Corporate Structure**

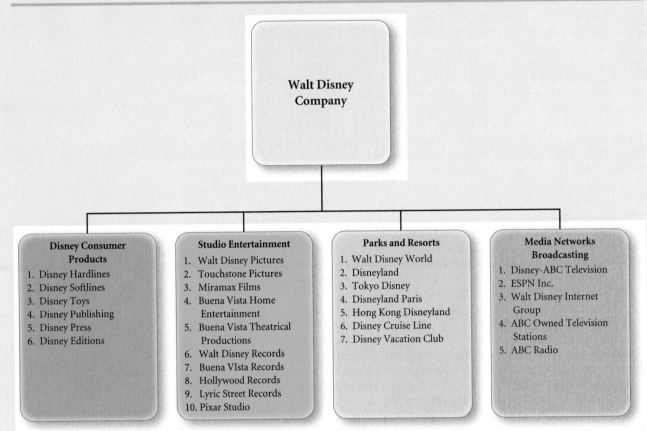

EXHIBIT 1-2 **Consolidated Income Statement**

(In Millions, Except Per Share Data)	2007	2006	2005	2004
Revenues	$ 35,510	$ 34,285	$ 31,944	$ 30,752
Costs and expenses	(28,729)	(28,807)	(27,837)	(26,704)
Gains on sale of equity investment and businesses	1,052	70	26	—
Restructuring and impairment (charges) and other credits, net	—	18	(32)	(64)
Net interest expense	(593)	(592)	(597)	(617)
Equity in the income of investees	485	473	483	372
Income before income taxes, minority interests and the cumulative effect of accounting change	7,725	5,447	3,987	3,739
Income taxes	(2,874)	(1,890)	(1,241)	(1,197)
Minority interests	(177)	(183)	(177)	(197)
Income before the cumulative effect of accounting change	4,674	3,374	2,569	2,345
Cumulative effect of accounting change	13	—	(36)	—
Net income	$ 4,687	$ 3,374	$ 2,533	$ 2,345
Earnings per share before the cumulative effect of accounting change:				
Diluted	$ 2.25	$ 1.64	$ 1.24	$ 1.12
Basic	$ 2.34	$ 1.68	$ 1.27	$ 1.14

(continued)

EXHIBIT 1-2   Consolidated Income Statement—continued

Cumulative effect of accounting change per share	$	—	$	—	$	(0.02)	$	—
Earnings per share:								
Diluted	$	2.25	$	1.64	$	1.22	$	1.12
Basic	$	2.34	$	1.68	$	1.25	$	1.14
Average number of common and common equivalent shares outstanding:								
Diluted		2,092		2,076		2,089		2,106
Basic		2,004		2,005		2,028		2,049

Source: Walt Disney Company—*Form 10K* 2006 and 2007.

EXHIBIT 1-3   Consolidated Balance Sheet

(In Millions, Except Per Share Data)	2007	2006	2005
Assets			
Current assets			
Cash and cash equivalents	$ 3,670	$ 2,411	$ 1,723
Receivables	5,032	4,707	4,585
Inventories	641	694	626
Television costs	559	415	510
Deferred income taxes	862	592	749
Other current assets	550	743	652
Total current assets	11,314	9,562	8,845
Film and television costs	5,123	5,235	5,427
Investments	995	1,315	1,226
Parks, resorts and other property, at cost			
Attractions buildings and equipment	30,260	28,843	27,570
Accumulated depreciation	(15,145)	(13,781)	(12,605)
	15,115	15,062	14,965
Projects in progress	1,147	913	874
Land	1,171	1,192	1,129
Total Fixed Assets	17,433	17,167	16,968
Intangible assets, net	2,494	2,907	2,731
Goodwill	22,085	22,505	16,974
Other assets	1,484	1,307	987
Total Assets	$60,928	$59,998	$53,158
Liabilities and Shareholders' Equity			
Current liabilities			
Accounts payable and other accrued liabilities	$ 5,949	$ 5,917	$ 5,339
Current portion of borrowings	3,280	2,682	2,310
Unearned royalties and other advances	2,162	1,611	1,519
Total current liabilities	11,391	10,210	9,168
Borrowings	11,892	10,843	10,157
Deferred income taxes	2,573	2,651	2,430
Other long-term liabilities	3,024	3,131	3,945
Minority interests	1,295	1,343	1,248
Total Liabilites	30,175	28,178	26,948

(continued)

EXHIBIT 1-3   Consolidated Balance Sheet—continued

Shareholders' equity
Preferred stock $.01 per value
Authorized—100 million shares, Issued—none
Common stock, $.01 per value
Authorized—3.6 billion shares.
Issued—2.6 billion shares at September 29, 2007

and 2.5 billion at October 1, 2006	24,207	22,377	13,288
Retained earnings	24,805	20,630	17,775
Accumulated other comprehensive loss	(157)	(8)	(572)
	48,855	42,999	30,491
Treasury stock, at cost 436.0 million shares at September 30, 2006 and 192.8 million shares at October 1, 2005	(18,102)	(11,179)	(4,281)
Total Shareholders' Equity	30,753	31,820	26,210
Total Liabilities and Shareholders' Equity	$60,928	$59,998	$53,158

Source: Walt Disney Company—*Annual Report* 2006 and 2007.

Exhibit 1-5 provides Disney's revenue and operating income by geographic region. Note that Disney derives 77 percent of its revenue and 76 percent of its operating income from operations in the United States and Canada. The company's revenues and income are both growing in all regions of the world, with Europe being second behind the United States/Canada in both revenues and income.

EXHIBIT 1-4   Revenue and Operating Income by Segment

(In Millions)	2007	2006	2005	2004
Revenue				
Media Networks	$15,046	$14,638	$13,207	$11,778
Parks & Resorts	10,626	9,925	9,023	7,750
Studio Entertainment				
Third parties		7,410	7,499	8,637
Intersegment		119	88	76
	7,491	7,529	7,587	8,713
Consumer Products				
Third parties		2,312	2,215	2,587
Intersegment		(119)	(88)	(76)
	2,347	2,193	2,127	2,511
Total Consolidated Revenues	$35,510	$34,285	$31,944	$30,752
Segment operating income				
Media Networks	$ 4,285	$ 3,610	$ 3,209	$ 2,574
Parks & Resorts	1,710	1,534	1,178	1,077
Studio Entertainment	1,210	729	207	662
Consumer Products	631	618	543	547
Total segment operating income	$ 7,827	$ 6,491	$ 5,137	$ 4,860

Source: Walt Disney Company—*Annual Report* 2006 and 2007.

EXHIBIT 1-5   Revenue and Operating Income by Region

(In Millions)	2007	2006	2005	2004
Revenue				
United States and Canada	$27,286	$26,565	$24,806	$24,012
Europe	5,898	5,266	5,207	4,721
Asia/Pacific	1,732	1,917	1,451	1,547
Latin America and Other	594	537	480	472
	$35,510	$34,285	$31,944	$30,752
Segment operating income				
United States and Canada	$ 6,042	$ 4,938	$ 3,963	$ 3,307
Europe	1,192	918	738	868
Asia/Pacific	437	542	386	582
Latin America and Other	156	93	50	103
	$ 7,827	$ 6,491	$ 5,137	$ 4,860

Source: Walt Disney Company—*Annual Report* 2006 and 2007.

Business Segments

In percentage terms, Disney revenues by segment in 2006 were derived from Media Networks (43 percent), Parks & Resorts (29 percent), Studio Entertainment (22 percent), and Consumer Products (6 percent). Operating income was derived from Media Networks (55 percent), Parks & Resorts (24 percent), Studio Entertainment (11 percent), and Consumer Products (10 percent). The Studio Entertainment segment thus created 22 percent of revenues but only 11 percent of operating income in 2006, somewhat of a problem.

Media Networks/Broadcasting

Disney owns ABC Television Network, which includes ABC Entertainment, ABC Daytime, ABC News, ABC Sports, ABC Kids, Touchstone Television, and ABC Radio. Also included in this segment, Disney owns ESPN, Disney Channel, ABC Family, Toon Disney, SOAPnet, and Buena Vista Television. Disney has equity interest in Lifetime Entertainment Services, A&E Television Networks, E! Entertainment, ESPN, History Channel, The Biography Channel, Hyperion Books, and Disney Mobile.

The increase in revenue in this segment was primarily due to growth from cable and satellite operators, which are generally derived from fees charged on a per-subscriber basis, contractual rate increases, and higher adverting rates at ESPN. The increase in broadcasting revenue was due to growth at the ABC Television Network and increased sales of Touchstone Television series. The growth at the ABC Television Network was primarily due to an increase in primetime advertising revenues resulting from higher rates and advertising revenues from the Super Bowl. Increase in sales from Touchstone Television series was as a result of higher international syndication and DVD sales of hit dramas such as *Lost, Grey's Anatomy,* and *Desperate Housewives,* as well as higher third-party license fees led by *Scrubs,* which completed its fifth season of network television.

In February 2006, Disney and Citadel Broadcasting Corporation (Citadel) announced an agreement to merge the ABC Radio business, which consists of 22 of Disney's company-owned radio stations and the ABC Radio Network, with Citadel. The ESPN Radio and Radio Disney networks and station businesses are not included in the transaction.

Two major TV networks of Walt Disney Company (ABC and ESPN) recently struck a deal with cable operator Cox Communication whereby these companies now offer hit shows and football games on demand. While advertising in the network is a source of additional revenue for the broadcasters, it requires selectivity for charging for each episode. Video-on-demand is a major industry and growing rapidly, expected to be a 3.9 billion-dollar industry by 2010.

Recently, Disney unveiled Disney Xtreme Digital, a networking site aimed at children less than 14 years of age. This service competes against MySpace (owned by News Corporation). Walt Disney just reported an increase in fiscal 2007 second-quarter net income mostly as a result of strong gains at cable network ESPN and surprise movie hits such as *Wild Hogs*. Major

EXHIBIT 1-6   Media Network Segment: Revenue and Operating Income

(In Millions)	2007	2006	2005	2004	2007 vs. 2006	2006 vs. 2005	2005 vs. 2004
					CHANGE		
Revenue							
Cable Networks	$ 9,167	$ 8,001	$ 7,262	$ 8,001	12%	10%	13%
Broadcasting	5,879	6,637	5,945	6,637	(1)%	12%	11%
Total	$15,046	$14,638	$13,207	$14,638	7%	11%	12%
Segment operating income							
Cable Networks	$ 3,582	$ 3,004	$ 2,745	$ 2,329	19%	9%	18%
Broadcasting	703	606	464	245	48%	31%	89%
Total	$ 4.285	$ 3,610	$ 3,209	$ 2,574	23%	12%	25%

Source: Walt Disney Company, *Annual Report* 2006 and 2007.

investments have been placed in new releases and sequences to be released in the second and third quarter of 2007. The Media Networks division generated the highest profit of any Disney segment during the second quarter of 2007.

In November 2006, Disney sold its 39.5 percent interest in E! Entertainment Television (E!) to Comcast (which owned the remainder of the interests in E!) for $1.2 billion. This resulted in an after-tax income of $0.5 billion, which was recorded in the first quarter of fiscal year 2007. Specific financial information for the Media Networks segment is provided in Exhibit 1-6. Disney's domestic broadcast television stations are listed in Exhibit 1-7 while its international media network operations are listed in Exhibit 1-8. Analysts expect Disney's revenues derived from Internet operations to rise 40 percent in 2007 and another 30 percent in 2008 (*Standard & Poor's Stock Report*—April 28, 2007).

Parks and Resorts

Disney owns and operates Walt Disney World Resort and Cruise Lines in Florida, Disneyland Resort in California, ESPN Zone facilities in many states, 17 hotels at the Walt Disney World Resort, Disney's Fort Wilderness Camping and Recreation, Downtown Disney, Disney's Wide World of Sports, Disney Cruise Line, 7 Disney Vacation Club Resorts, Adventures by Disney, and 5 resort locations with 11 theme parks on 3 continents. With theme parks, Disney has 51 percent ownership in Disneyland Resort Paris, 43 percent ownership in Hong Kong Disneyland,

EXHIBIT 1-7   Disney's Domestic Broadcast Television Stations (2007)

MARKET	TV STATION	ANALOG CHANNEL	TELEVISION MARKET RANKING
New York, NY	WABC-TV	7	1
Los Angeles, CA	KABC-TV	7	2
Chicago, IL	WLS-TV	7	3
Philadelphia, PA	WPVI-TV	6	4
San Francisco, CA	KGO-TV	7	5
Houston, TX	KTRK-TV	13	10
Raleigh-Durham, NC	WTVD-TV	11	29
Fresno, CA	KFSN-TV	30	55
Flint, MI	WJRT-TV	12	66
Toledo, OH	WTVG-TV	13	71

Source: Walt Disney Company, *Form 10K* (2007).

EXHIBIT 1-8 **Disney's International Cable Satellite Networks and Broadcast Operations**

PROPERTY	ESTIMATED SUBSCRIBERS (In Millions)	OWNERSHIP %
ESPN(1)	92	80.0
ESPN2(1)	91	80.0
ESPN Classic(1)	62	80.0
ESPNEWS(1)	51	80.0
Disney Channel(1)	89	100.0
International Disney Channels(2)	54	100.0
Toon Disney(1)	57	100.0
Lifetime Television(1)	92	50.0
A&E(1)	92	37.5
ABC Family(1)	91	100.0
The History Channel(1)	91	37.5
E! Entertainment Television(1)	89	39.6
A&E International(2)	75	37.5
Lifetime Movie Network(1)	51	50.0
Lifetime Real Women(2)	16	50.0
Jetix Europe(2)	46	73.7
Jetix Latin America(2)	15	100.0
SOAPnet(1)	53	100.0
Style(1)	44	39.6
The Biography Channel(1)	39	37.5
History International(1)	39	37.5

(1) Estimated U.S. subscriber counts according to Nielsen Media Research as of September 30, 2006.

(2) Not rated by Nielsen. Subscriber count represents number of subscribers receiving the service based on internal management reports.

Source: Walt Disney Company, *Form 10K* (2006).

100 percent ownership in Tokyo Disney Resort as well as Disneyland in both California and Florida. Exhibit 1-9 summarizes Disney's parks and resort holdings.

Disney revenues at its Parks and Resorts division increased 10 percent in 2006 to $9.9 billion due to increases of $647 million and $255 million at its domestic and international resorts, respectively. Higher guest spending was due to a higher average daily hotel room rate, higher average ticket prices, and greater merchandise spending at both resorts.

Disney's 50th anniversary celebration at its parks and resorts increased attendance and hotel occupancy. International revenue growth reflected the first full year of theme park operations at Hong Kong Disneyland Resort as compared to the prior year when the park opened in mid-September 2005. Disneyland Resort Paris also experienced increased revenues. Some of the increase in revenue was offset by the unfavorable impact of foreign currency translation as a result of the strengthening of the U.S. dollar against the Euro. Operating income from the Parks and Resorts segment increased 30 percent, or $356 million, to $1.5 billion. Exhibit 1-10 presents Disney's attendance, per capita theme park guest spending, and hotel statistics for its domestic

EXHIBIT 1-9   Disney's Offerings under Parks and Resorts

WALT DISNEY WORLD RESORTS	DISNEYLAND RESORT	DISNEYLAND RESORT PARIS	HONG KONG DISNEYLAND RESORT	TOKYO DISNEY RESORT	DISNEY CRUISE LINE	ESPN ZONE	WALT DISNEY IMAGINEERING
Epcot	Disneyland	Disneyland Park	Hong Kong Disneyland	Tokyo Disneyland			
Disney-MGM Studios	Disneyland's California Adventure	Walt Disney Studios Park	Resort Facilities	Tokyo DisneySea			
Magic Kingdom	Resort Facilities						
Disney's Animal Kingdom							
Resort Facilities							

Source: Walt Disney Company, *Form 10K* (2006).

EXHIBIT 1-10   Disney Parks and Resorts Data (2006 versus 2005)

	EAST COAST RESORTS		WEST COST RESORTS		TOTAL DOMESTIC RESORTS	
	FY 2006	FY 2005	FY 2006	FY 2005	FY 2006	FY 2005
Increase in attendance	5%	5%	6%	4%	5%	5%
Increase in per capital guest spending	1%	2%	8%	14%	3%	5%
Occupancy	86%	83%	93%	90%	87%	83%
Available room nights (in thousands)	8,834	8,777	810	810	9,644	9,587
Per room guest spending	$211	$199	$287	$272	$218	$206

Source: Walt Disney Company—*Annual Report* (2006).

properties. Exhibit 1-11 provides 2006 attendance figures for Disney theme parks. These parks accounted for almost 30 percent of Disney's 2006 revenues, and reported a 30 percent increase in operating income.

The company also has been hosting VIP tours (additional fees apply), offering added-value services such as number of attractions being covered along with personal guided tours, preferred seating, and front-of-line access to rides. The company also offers package deals for major corporations and schools.

Disney has plans to change its concept of the theme parks from the masses to a more concentrated perspective. This strategy would allow Disney to offer more stand-alone theme parks and resorts in cities and beaches, as well as Disney-branded retail and dining districts, and smaller and more sophisticated parks. Disney is also planning to build time-share vacation homes in places like the Caribbean. Two of the challenges with this strategy would be (1) tailoring the niche attractions to the local markets while keeping the Disney brand reputation, and (2) avoiding cannibalization of existing parks and attractions.

Studio Entertainment

Disney produces live-action and animated motion pictures, direct-to-video programming, musical recordings, and live-stage plays. Disney motion pictures are distributed under the names Walt Disney Pictures and Television, Touchstone Pictures, Hollywood Pictures, Miramax Films, and Buena Vista Home Entertainment International that includes Walt Disney Records, Buena Vista Records, Hollywood Records, Lyric Street Records, and Disney Music Publishing. In May 2006, Disney acquired Pixar, a computer animation leader. As of September 2006,

EXHIBIT 1-11 Disney Theme Park Attendance in 2006 (In Millions)

PARK	ATTENDANCE (IN MILLIONS)
Magic Kingdom (Florida)	16.64
Disneyland (California)	14.73
Tokyo Disneyland	12.90
Tokyo Disney Sea	12.10
Disneyland Paris	10.60
Epcot (Florida)	10.46
Disney-MGM Studios (Florida)	9.10
Animal Kingdom (Florida)	8.91
California Adventure	5.95
Hong Kong Disneyland	5.20
Walt Disney Studios Paris	2.20

Source: Adapted from Merissa Marr, "Disney's $1 Billion Adventure," *Wall Street Journal* (October 17, 2007): p. B1 and B4.

Disney had released 894 full-length movies, 77 full-length animated features, and 542 cartoon shorts. Product offerings include Pay-per-View, Pay Television, Free Television, Pay Television 2, and International Television.

Disney revenues from its Studio Entertainment segment decreased 1 percent, or $58 million, to $7.5 billion primarily due to lower worldwide home entertainment. The increase in worldwide theatrical motion picture distribution revenues was primarily due to the strong box-office performance of selected movies. Operating income from this segment increased $522 million to $729 million.

In August 2005, Disney entered into a film financing arrangement with a group of investors who funded $500 million or about 40 percent of the production and marketing costs of a slate of up to thirty-two live-action films, excluding certain titles such as *The Chronicles of Narnia: The Lion, The Witch and The Wardrobe* and, in general, sequels to previous films, in return for approximately 40 percent of the future net cash flows generated by these films. By entering into minority-owned business transactions, Disney is reducing the risks as well as rewards from the performance of live-action firm production and distribution.

Consumer Products

Disney's Consumer Products segment includes partners with licenses, manufacturers, publishers, and retailers worldwide who design, promote, and sell a wide variety of products based on new and existing Disney characters. The product offerings are: Character Merchandise and Publications Licensing, Books and Magazines, Buena Vista Games, DisneyShopping.com, and The Disney Store. Products include books, interactive games, food and beverages, fine art, apparel, toys, and even home décor.

Disney's 2006 revenues from this segment increased 3 percent to $2.2 billion. Sales growth at Buena Vista Games was due to the release of self-published titles based on *The Chronicles of Narnia: The Lion, The Witch and The Wardrobe, Chicken Little,* and *Pirates of the Caribbean.* Sales growth at Merchandise Licensing was driven by higher earned royalties across multiple product categories, led by the strong performance of *Cars, Disney Princess,* and *Pirates of the Caribbean* merchandise.

Operating income of this segment increased 14 percent to $618 million, mostly due to growth at Merchandise Licensing. The decrease at Buena Vista Games was driven by increased product development spending on future self-published titles. In 2006, Disney sold 365 of its stores to the Children's Place under a franchising agreement.

Competition

For an organization as large and diversified as Walt Disney Company, competitors differ in each segment of business. Time Warner is a major competitor to Disney and is composed of five divisions: AOL, Cable, Filmed Entertainment, Networks, and Publishing. Time Warner

Disney versus the Industry — Comparative Data

DIRECT COMPETITOR COMPARISON

	DIS	TWX	INDUSTRY
Market Cap	$ 71.40B	81.43B	2.24B
Employees	133,000	92,700	1.69K
Quarterly Rev Growth	0.60%	9.20%	7.30%
Revenue	$ 35.20B	45.17B	946.15M
Gross Margin	19.33%	42.45%	34.61%
EBITDA	$ 8.74B	12.08B	135.44M
Operating Margins	18.12%	17.95%	16.55%
Net Income	$ 4.54B	5.12B	9.58M
EPS	$ 2.123	1.549	0.08
P/E	$ 16.97	13.89	19.35
PEG (5 yr expected)	1.37	1.54	1.54
P/S	2.02	1.79	2.37

DIS = Walt Disney Company

TWX = Time Warner Inc.

Industry = Entertainment - Diversified

Source: Adapted from finance.yahoo.com (May, 2007).

owns Time Inc., AOL, Warner Brothers, and TBS Networks. Walt Disney generally is classified as Entertainment-Diversified, which directly competes with Time Warner, Inc. (as shown in Exhibit 1-12). Note that Disney's EPS and P/E ratios are below the industry average but above Time Warner Inc.

CBS Corporation and News Corporation directly compete with the Walt Disney Company in the Media Network segment, but are not rivals in the Consumer Products and Parks and Resorts segments. CBS Corporation was a part of Viacom, Inc. but now operates independently under CBS Corp. News Corporation is a diversified international media and entertainment company that operates in eight segments: Filmed Entertainment, Television, Cable Network Programming, Direct Broadcast Satellite Television, Magazines and Inserts, Newspapers, Book Publishing, and Other. Due to recent corporate restructuring for both CBS Corporation and News Corp., there are no industry data available for comparison purposes. Competition for each segment of Walt Disney is discussed below.

Competition — Media Networks/Broadcasting

Global media is a $1 trillion industry that includes advertising, cable firms, newspapers, radio, and television. This industry is dominated by conglomerates Walt Disney, Time Warner Inc., New York Times, News Corp., and CBS Corporation. Typically, these companies prosper during election years due to heavy advertising revenue invested by the politicians. Special events such as the Olympics also generates additional advertising revenue for such companies.

Walt Disney competes for viewers primarily with other television networks, independent television stations, and other video media such as cable and satellite television programming services, DVD, video games, and the Internet. Radio networks compete with other radio network stations and programming services. Advertising dollars, a major source of income for Walt Disney, also competes with other advertising media such as newspapers, magazines, billboards, and the Internet. According to Research Alert (25 [7]: 3, April 06, 2007), an overwhelming majority of consumers (92.5 percent) regularly or occasionally research products online before buying them in person. Men (43.7 percent) are significantly more likely than women (26.7 percent) to regularly research products online before buying. As a trend, younger consumers are more likely than older consumers to research products online; 25–34-year-olds (95 percent) are more likely than all other age groups to do so.

EXHIBIT 1-13 **Disney Rival Firms in Media
Networks/Broadcasting — Percent**

INDICATES ATTRACTIVENESS OF THAT OUTLET TO
CONSUMERS AGE 18–24

Discovery Networks	72%
Disney/ESPN Media Networks	68%
MTV Networks	52%
Turner Entertainment Networks	48%
Scripps Networks	43%
NBC Universal Cable	39%
Comcast Cable Networks	34%
Fox Cable Networks	31%

Source: Adapted from *Multichannel News*, 28 (10): 30, March 05, 2007.

Consumers 18–24 are more likely than other age groups to share information about products they've searched for online using a variety of media, such as text messaging and instant messaging. Men, more likely than women, use new technologies such as blogs and online communities to share their opinions. Exhibits 1-12 and 1-13 reveal some major competitors to Disney in this segment of business, as well as percentages that indicate attractiveness of that venue to consumers age 18–24.

CBS Corporation is comprised of the following segments: Television, Radio, Outdoor, and Publishing. CBS Television is comprised of CBS Network and its own television stations, television production and syndication, Showtime, and CSTV Networks. In 2006, the CBS Television segment of this corporation contributed 66 percent of total revenue (approximately $9.4 billion). The Radio segment of CBS Corp. owns radio stations in most of the large U.S. markets and the revenue primarily is generated from advertising sales. In 2006, the Radio segment of CBS Corp. generated 14 percent of the company's total revenue (approximately $2.0 billion).

News Corp., with $25.3 billion in revenue, operates in eight industry segments: Filmed Entertainment, Television, Cable Network Programming, Direct Broadcast Satellite Television, Magazines and Inserts, Newspapers, Book Publishing, and Other. For the fiscal year of 2006, the Filmed Entertainment, Television, Cable Network Programming, and Direct Broadcast Satellite Television contributed 68.8 percent or $17.4 billion to the company's total revenue. The company has been moving aggressively toward digital technologies such as broadband, mobility, storage, and wireless. In 2005, News Corp. acquired MySpace.com, the Internet's most popular social networking site, and IGN.com (a gaming and entertainment site). The company has reported an increase in traffic at most of their preexisting sites such as newspaper, cable networks, and local TV stations.

In June 2007, Fox TV, owned by News Corp., had the most popular shows on television with an average audience of 6.7 million every night, followed by CBS with 7.6 million viewers during each prime time, Walt Disney Company's ABC with 5.4 million viewers per night, and finally NBC (owned by General Electric Company) with 4.8 million viewers during each prime-time period.

Disney also has to compete with satellite providers such as DirecTV in the media network and broadcasting segment. It has been reported that DirecTV has had steady sales growth for the past four quarters from 8 percent to 16 percent with earnings growth jumping from 222 percent to 667 percent over the same period.

Time Warner's media and entertainment segments own AOL, Cable, Filmed Entertainment, Networks, and Publishing. The Cable segment services primarily analog and digital video services, and advanced services such as VOD and HDTV with set-top boxed equipped with digital video recorders. To improve this segment of their business, Time Warner just acquired Adelphia for $8.9 billion in cash. Its Film Entertainment segment produces and distributes theatrical motion pictures and television shows. The Network segment consists of HBO and Cinemax pay television programming services. The Publishing segment publishes magazines and Web sites in a variety of areas and has a strategic alliance with Google, Inc. Exhibit 1-14 provides Time Warner's revenue by segment.

EXHIBIT 1-14   Time Warner Inc. Revenue (In Millions) by Segment (2006)

SEGMENT	REVENUE
Cable	11,767
AOL	7,866
Filmed Entertainment	10,625
Networks	10,273
Publishing	5,278

Source: Time Warner Inc., *Form 10K* (2006).

Competition — Parks and Resorts

Disney's theme parks and resorts compete with all other forms of entertainment, lodging, tourism, and recreational activities. Many uncontrollable factors impact this Disney segment, including business cycle and exchange rate fluctuations, travel industry trends, amount of available leisure time, oil and transportation prices, and weather patterns. Seasonality is another concern for this segment as all of the theme parks and the associated resort facilities are operated on a year-round basis. Historically, the theme parks and resort business experiences fluctuations in theme park attendance and resort occupancy resulting from the seasonal nature of vacation travel and local entertainment excursions. Peak attendance and resort occupancy generally occur during the summer months when school vacations take place and during early-winter and spring-holiday periods. Disney's three largest theme parks, Magic Kingdom in Orlando, Tokyo Disneyland, and Disneyland Paris, had in 2005 16.2, 13.0, and 10.2 million visitors.

According to a survey conducted by the International Association of Amusement Parks and Attractions, in 2005, 335 million people visited over 600 amusement parks in the United States, generating $11.2 billion in revenue. The attendance in amusement parks has continued to increase and is projected to continue in a steady growth. In 2004, 28 percent of Americans claimed they had visited an amusement park and one half had plans to do so in 2006.

The second largest amusement park after Disney is Six Flags, Inc., based in Oklahoma City, Oklahoma, with 32 parks, with more than $1 billion in revenue (2005). Due to demographic changes and increase in aging population, Viacom Inc. has started opening adult playgrounds offering virtual reality games.

Hong Kong's oldest amusement park, Ocean Park, has been doing much better than Disney's Hong Kong Disneyland. *USA Today* (June 15, 2007, p. 9A) reported that Hong Kong Disneyland has been struggling and based on the company's report to the Securities and Exchange Commission (SEC), the company might have to persuade lenders to refinance the debt. Ocean Park has been having the advantage of understanding the local market since they have been around for more than 30 years. It also seems that Hong Kong residents are not very impressed with the small version of Disneyland built there since many have visited Disneyland in Tokyo or Anaheim, California. Comprising over 215 acres, Ocean Park's annual attendance in 2004, 2005, and 2006 has been 3.7 million, 4.0 million, and 4.4 million with profits growing also to an annual high of $20.1 million in 2006. At 310 acres, Hong Kong Disneyland is the smallest Disney theme park.

Competition — Studio Entertainment

The success of Studio Entertainment operations fluctuate due to the timing and performance of releases in the theatrical, home entertainment, and television markets. Release dates are determined by several factors, including competition and the timing of vacation and holiday periods. This segment of Disney competes with all forms of entertainment. A significant number of companies produce and/or distribute theatrical and television films, exploit products in the home entertainment market, provide pay television programming services, and sponsor live theater. The company also competes to obtain creative and performing talents, story properties, advertiser support, broadcast rights, and market share.

For years, movies have been a reasonably priced entertainment for many individuals, couples, and families. A geographic breakdown of movie revenues are United States (49.8 percent), Europe (33 percent), and Asia and developed countries (14 percent). A few companies dominate the industry and control the production and distribution of most movies. Some key competitors in this segment along with their 2007 forecast (% of industry revenue) are: Warner Brothers (17.10 percent), Walt Disney (11.70 percent), Twentieth Century Fox (10.3 percent), Viacom (6.3 percent), and other (54.6 percent).

Competition — Consumer Products

The leading competitors to Disney in this segment are Warner Brothers, Fox, Sony, Marvel, and Nickelodeon. Disney competes in its character merchandising and other licensing, publishing, interactive, and retail activities with other licensors, publishers, and retailers of character, brand, and celebrity names. Disney is perhaps the largest worldwide licensor of character-based merchandise and producer/distributor of children's film-related products based on retail sales. Operating results for the licensing and retail distribution business are influenced by seasonal consumer purchasing behavior and by the timing and performance of animated theatrical releases.

Conclusion

As a content-oriented company, Walt Disney's strategy for many years has been to match creativity and innovation with international expansion and leveraging of new technologies. Disney continuously has to adapt to demographic changes in order to deliver products and services that match changing consumer preferences across countries. Although Disney under CEO Iger has had positive growth in both revenue and earnings, there are still strong competitors and substantial risks in the entertainment industry. Competitors are consolidating and spending aggressively to promote new hit movies and TV shows.

It is difficult to manage a firm as diversified as Disney. CEO Iger has delegated accountability and responsibility much more so, however, than former CEO Eisner and this is good for the company. The Internet, however, is a threat to Disney as consumers of all ages use the Internet more and more for entertainment. Consumer preferences are shifting to more on-demand movies and shows. There is a growing risk of copyright infringements and unauthorized sharing of movies, DVDs, and other digital products. Companies such as Walt Disney spend millions of dollars to protect their intellectual property worldwide in order to maintain their competitive edge.

Increases in unemployment, interest rates, and fuel costs limit consumers' disposable income for entertainment expenses. These threats vary across continents and countries where Disney operates and oftentimes force consumers to other low-cost entertainment activities. Disney is performing well, but analysts are concerned about its level of goodwill, long-term debt, and its weak performance in the Studio Entertainment segment.

Prepare a three-year strategic plan with supporting analyses and recommendations for CEO Iger to present to his board of directors.

References

Datamonitor Industry Market Research

finance.yahoo.com

Investor's Business Daily

Multichannel News — www.multichannel.com

News Corporation — www.newscorp.com

Wall Street Journal — www.wsj.com

The Walt Disney Company — www.disney.com

TheStreet.com — www.thestreet.com

Time Warner Company — www.timewarner.com

Standard & Poor's — www.standardandpoors.com

USAtoday.com — www.usatoday.com

• **EXPERIENTIAL EXERCISES**

Experiential Exercise 1A

Getting Familiar with Strategy Terms

Purpose

The purpose of this exercise is to get you familiar with strategy terms introduced and defined in Chapter 1. Let's apply these terms to Walt Disney Company (stock symbol = DIS).

Instructions

Step 1   Go to http://www.disney.go.com/home/html/index.html, which is Walt Disney Company's Web site. Click on Corporate Info, then click on Investor Relations, and then click on *Form 10K*. Print a copy of the 2007 *Form 10K*. (Note: The *Form 10K* may be 100 pages so you may want to print this in your college library, but this Disney document will be used throughout this course. The *Form 10K* contains excellent information for developing a list of internal strengths and weaknesses of DIS. The 2007 *Form 10K* was not available when the case was written so it can also be used to update the case.

Step 2   Go to your college library and make a copy of Standard & Poor's Industry Surveys for two industries: (1) Broadcasting and Cable Industry and (2) Movies and Home Entertainment. These two documents will contain excellent information for developing a list of external opportunities and threats facing DIS.

Step 3   Using the Walt Disney Company Cohesion Case, the 2007 *Form 10K*, and the Industry Survey documents, on a separate sheet of paper list what you consider to be DIS's three major strengths, three major weaknesses, three major opportunities, and three major threats. Each factor listed for this exercise must include a %, #, $, or ratio to reveal some quantified fact or trend. These factors provide the underlying basis for a strategic plan because a firm strives to take advantage of strengths, improve weaknesses, avoid threats, and capitalize on opportunities.

Step 4   Through class discussion, compare your lists of external and internal factors to those developed by other students and add to your lists of factors. Keep this information for use in later exercises at the end of other chapters.

Experiential Exercise 1B

Evaluating Codes of Business Ethics

Purpose

This exercise aims to familiarize you with corporate codes of business ethics. Called Standards of Business Conduct both in the Walt Disney Company and its leading competitor, News Corporation, the business ethics statements for these two firms are provided at http://corporate.disney.go.com/corporate/conduct_standards3.html and www.newscorp.com/corp_gov/sobc.html, respectively. Headquartered in Washington, DC, News Corporation is a $27 billion global media giant that owns Fox Studios, 20th Century Fox, HarperCollins book publishing company, DirecTV, and many other segments that compete with Walt Disney. Both firms strive to operate in an ethical manner.

Instructions

Step 1   Go to the two Web sites listed above and print the Standards of Business Conduct for (1) Walt Disney Company and (2) News Corporation. Read the two statements.

Step 2   On a separate sheet of paper, list three aspects that you like most and three aspects that you like least about (1) the Walt Disney statement and (2) the News Corporation statement. In other words, compare the two Standards of Business Conduct statements. Conclude by indicating which statement of conduct you like best. Why do you think it is best?

Step 3   Explain why having a code of business ethics is not sufficient for ensuring ethical behavior in an organization. What other means are necessary to help ensure ethical behavior? Give the class an example of a breach of ethical conduct that you recall in your work experience.

Experiential Exercise 1C

The Ethics of Spying on Competitors

Purpose

This exercise gives you an opportunity to discuss in class ethical and legal issues related to methods being used by many companies to spy on competing firms. Gathering and using information about competitors is an area of strategic management that Japanese firms do more proficiently than American firms.

Instructions

On a separate sheet of paper, number from 1 to 18. For the eighteen spying activities listed as follows, indicate whether or not you believe the activity is ethical or unethical and legal or illegal. Place either an *E* for ethical or *U* for unethical, and either an *L* for legal or an *I* for illegal for each activity. Compare your answers to those of your classmates and discuss any differences.

1. Buying competitors' garbage
2. Dissecting competitors' products
3. Taking competitors' plant tours anonymously
4. Counting tractor-trailer trucks leaving competitors' loading bays
5. Studying aerial photographs of competitors' facilities
6. Analyzing competitors' labor contracts
7. Analyzing competitors' help-wanted ads
8. Quizzing customers and buyers about the sales of competitors' products
9. Infiltrating customers' and competitors' business operations
10. Quizzing suppliers about competitors' level of manufacturing
11. Using customers to buy out phony bids
12. Encouraging key customers to reveal competitive information
13. Quizzing competitors' former employees
14. Interviewing consultants who may have worked with competitors
15. Hiring key managers away from competitors
16. Conducting phony job interviews to get competitors' employees to reveal information
17. Sending engineers to trade meetings to quiz competitors' technical employees
18. Quizzing potential employees who worked for or with competitors

Experiential Exercise 1D

Strategic Planning for My University

Purpose

External and internal factors are the underlying bases of strategies formulated and implemented by organizations. Your college or university faces numerous external opportunities/threats and has many internal strengths/weaknesses. The purpose of this exercise is to illustrate the process of identifying critical external and internal factors.

External influences include trends in the following areas: economic, social, cultural, demographic, environmental, technological, political, legal, governmental, and competitive. External factors could include declining numbers of high school graduates; population shifts; community relations; increased competitiveness among colleges and universities; rising numbers of adults returning to college; decreased support from local, state, and federal agencies; increasing numbers of foreign students attending U.S. colleges; and a rising number of Internet courses.

Internal factors of a college or university include faculty, students, staff, alumni, athletic programs, physical plant, grounds and maintenance, student housing, administration, fund-raising, academic programs, food services, parking, placement, clubs, fraternities, sororities, and public relations.

Instructions

Step 1   On a separate sheet of paper, write four headings: External Opportunities, External Threats, Internal Strengths, and Internal Weaknesses.

Step 2   As related to your college or university, list five factors under each of the four headings.

Step 3   Discuss the factors as a class. Write the factors on the board.

Step 4   What new things did you learn about your university from the class discussion? How could this type of discussion benefit an organization?

Experiential Exercise 1E

Strategic Planning at a Local Company

Purpose

This activity is aimed at giving you practical knowledge about how organizations in your city or town are doing strategic planning. This exercise also will give you experience interacting on a professional basis with local business leaders.

Instructions

Step 1   Use the telephone to contact business owners or top managers. Find an organization that does strategic planning. Make an appointment to visit with the strategist (president, chief executive officer, or owner) of that business.

Step 2   Seek answers to the following questions during the interview:
- How does your firm formally conduct strategic planning? Who is involved in the process?
- Does your firm have a written mission statement? How was the statement developed? When was the statement last changed?
- What are the benefits of engaging in strategic planning?
- What are the major costs or problems in doing strategic planning in your business?
- Do you anticipate making any changes in the strategic planning process at your company? If yes, please explain.

Step 3   Report your findings to the class.

Experiential Exercise 1F

Does My University Recruit in Foreign Countries?

Purpose

A competitive climate is emerging among colleges and universities around the world. Colleges and universities in Europe and Japan are increasingly recruiting U.S. students to offset declining enrollments. Foreign students already make up more than one-third of the student body at many U.S. universities. The purpose of this exercise is to identify particular colleges and universities in foreign countries that represent a competitive threat to U.S. institutions of higher learning.

Instructions

Step 1   Select a foreign country. Conduct research to determine the number and nature of colleges and universities in that country. What are the major educational institutions in that country? What programs are those institutions recognized for offering? What percentage of undergraduate and graduate students attending those institutions are U.S. citizens? Do these institutions actively recruit U.S. students?

Step 2   Prepare a report for the class that summarizes your research findings. Present your report to the class.

Experiential Exercise 1G

Getting Familiar with SMCO

Purpose

This exercise is designed to get you familiar with the Strategic Management Club Online (SMCO), which offers many benefits for the strategy student. The SMCO site also offers templates for doing case analyses in this course.

Instructions

Step 1   Go to the www.strategyclub.com Web site. Review the various sections of this site.

Step 2   Select a section of the SMCO site that you feel will be most useful to you in this class. Write a one-page summary of that section and describe why you feel it will benefit you most.

Part 2 • Strategy Formulation

2 | The Business Vision and Mission

University Case Competition Gala: *Source:* Bruce Williams

chapter objectives

After studying this chapter, you should be able to do the following:

1. Describe the nature and role of vision and mission statements in strategic management.

2. Discuss why the process of developing a mission statement is as important as the resulting document.

3. Identify the components of mission statements.

4. Discuss how clear vision and mission statements can benefit other strategic-management activities.

5. Evaluate mission statements of different organizations.

6. Write good vision and mission statements.

This chapter focuses on the concepts and tools needed to evaluate and write business vision and mission statements. A practical framework for developing mission statements is provided. Actual mission statements from large and small organizations and for-profit and nonprofit enterprises are presented and critically examined. The process of creating a vision and mission statement is discussed.

We can perhaps best understand vision and mission by focusing on a business when it is first started. In the beginning, a new business is simply a collection of ideas. Starting a new business rests on a set of beliefs that the new organization can offer some product or service to some customers, in some geographic area, using some type of technology, at a profitable price. A new business owner typically believes that the management philosophy of the new enterprise will result in a favorable public image and that this concept of the business can be communicated to, and will be adopted by, important constituencies. When the set of beliefs about a business at its inception is put into writing, the resulting document mirrors the same basic ideas that underlie the vision and mission statements. As a business grows, owners or managers find it necessary to revise the founding set of beliefs, but those original ideas usually are reflected in the revised statements of vision and mission.

Vision and mission statements often can be found in the front of annual reports. They often are displayed throughout a firm's premises and are distributed with company information sent to constituencies. The statements are part of numerous internal reports, such as loan requests, supplier agreements, labor relations contracts, business plans, and customer service agreements. In a recent study, researchers concluded that 90 percent of all companies have used a mission statement sometime in the previous five years.[1]

VISIT THE NET

Gives an introduction to the vision concept. (www.csuchico.edu/mgmt/strategy/module1/sld007.htm)

What Do We Want to Become?

It is especially important for managers and executives in any organization to agree upon the basic vision that the firm strives to achieve in the long term. A vision statement should answer the basic question, "What do we want to become?" A clear vision provides the foundation for developing a comprehensive mission statement. Many organizations have both a vision and mission statement, but the vision statement should be established first and foremost. The vision statement should be short, preferably one sentence, and as many managers as possible should have input into developing the statement.

Several example vision statements are provided in Table 2-1.

TABLE 2-1   Vision Statement Examples

Tyson Foods' vision is to be the world's first choice for protein solutions while maximizing shareholder value. *(Author comment: Good statement, unless Tyson provides nonprotein products)*

General Motors' vision is to be the world leader in transportation products and related services. *(Author comment: Good statement)*

PepsiCo's responsibility is to continually improve all aspects of the world in which we operate—environment, social, economic—creating a better tomorrow than today. *(Author comment: Statement is too vague; it should reveal beverage and food business)*

Dell's vision is to create a company culture where environmental excellence is second nature. *(Author comment: Statement is too vague; it should reveal computer business in some manner; the word environmental is generally used to refer to natural environment so is unclear in its use here)*

The vision of First Reliance Bank is to be recognized as the largest and most profitable bank in South Carolina. *(Author comment: This is a very small, new bank headquartered in Florence, South Carolina, so this goal is not achievable in five years; the statement is too futuristic)*

Samsonite's vision is to provide innovative solutions for the traveling world. *(Author comment: Statement needs to be more specific, perhaps mention luggage; statement as is could refer to air carriers or cruise lines, which is not good)*

Royal Caribbean's vision is to empower and enable our employees to deliver the best vacation experience for our guests, thereby generating superior returns for our shareholders and enhancing the well-being of our communities. *(Author comment: Statement is good, but could end after the word "guests")*

Procter & Gamble's vision is to be, and be recognized as, the best consumer products company in the world. *(Author comment: Statement is too vague and readability is not that good)*

What Is Our Business?

Current thought on mission statements is based largely on guidelines set forth in the mid-1970s by Peter Drucker, who is often called "the father of modern management" for his pioneering studies at General Motors Corporation and for his 22 books and hundreds of articles. *Harvard Business Review* has called Drucker "the preeminent management thinker of our time."

VISIT THE NET

Gives an introduction to the mission concept. (www.csuchico.edu/mgmt/ strategy/module1/sld008.htm)

Drucker says that asking the question "What is our business?" is synonymous with asking the question "What is our mission?" An enduring statement of purpose that distinguishes one organization from other similar enterprises, the *mission statement* is a declaration of an organization's "reason for being." It answers the pivotal question "What is our business?" A clear mission statement is essential for effectively establishing objectives and formulating strategies.

Sometimes called a *creed statement,* a statement of purpose, a statement of philosophy, a statement of beliefs, a statement of business principles, or a statement "defining our business," a mission statement reveals what an organization wants to be and whom it wants to serve. All organizations have a reason for being, even if strategists have not consciously transformed this reason into writing. As illustrated in Figure 2-1, carefully prepared statements of vision and mission are widely recognized by both practitioners and academicians as the first step in strategic management.

Some example mission statements are provided in Table 2-2.

TABLE 2-2   Example Mission Statements

Fleetwood Enterprises will lead the recreational vehicle and manufactured housing industries (2, 7) in providing quality products, with a passion for customer-driven innovation (1). We will emphasize training, embrace diversity and provide growth opportunities for our associates and our dealers (9). We will lead our industries in the application of appropriate technologies (4). We will operate at the highest levels of ethics and compliance with a focus on exemplary corporate governance (6). We will deliver value to our shareholders, positive operating results and industry-leading earnings (5). *(Author comment: Statement lacks two components: Markets and Concern for Public Image)*

We aspire to make PepsiCo the world's (3) premier consumer products company, focused on convenient foods and beverages (2). We seek to produce healthy financial rewards for investors (5) as we provide opportunities for growth and enrichment to our employees (9), our business partners and the communities (8) in which we operate. And in everything we do, we strive to act with honesty, openness, fairness and integrity (6). *(Author comment: Statement lacks three components: Customers, Technology, and Self-Concept)*

We are loyal to Royal Caribbean and Celebrity and strive for continuous improvement in everything we do. We always provide service with a friendly greeting and a smile (7). We anticipate the needs of our customers and make all efforts to exceed our customers' expectations (1). We take ownership of any problem that is brought to our attention. We engage in conduct that enhances our corporate reputation and employee morale (9). We are committed to act in the highest ethical manner and respect the rights and dignity of others (6). *(Author comment: Statement lacks five components: Products/Services, Markets, Technology, Concern for Survival/Growth/Profits, Concern for Public Image)*

Dell's mission is to be the most successful computer company (2) in the world (3) at delivering the best customer experience in markets we serve (1). In doing so, Dell will meet customer expectations of highest quality; leading technology (4); competitive pricing; individual and company accountability (6); best-in-class service and support (7); flexible customization capability (7); superior corporate citizenship (8); financial stability (5). *(Author comment: Statement lacks only one component: Concern for Employees)*

Procter & Gamble will provide branded products and services of superior quality and value (7) that improve the lives of the world's (3) consumers. As a result, consumers (1) will reward us with industry leadership in sales, profit (5), and value creation, allowing our people (9), our shareholders, and the communities (8) in which we live and work to prosper. *(Author comment: Statement lacks three components: Products/Services, Technology, and Philosophy)*

At L'Oreal, we believe that lasting business success is built upon ethical (6) standards which guide growth and on a genuine sense of responsibility to our employees (9), our consumers, our environment and to the communities in which we operate (8). *(Author comment: Statement lacks six components: Customers, Products/Services, Markets, Technology, Concern for Survival/Growth/Profits, Concern for Public Image)*

Note: The numbers in parentheses correspond to the nine components listed on page 61; author comment also refers to those components.

FIGURE 2-1

A Comprehensive Strategic-Management Model

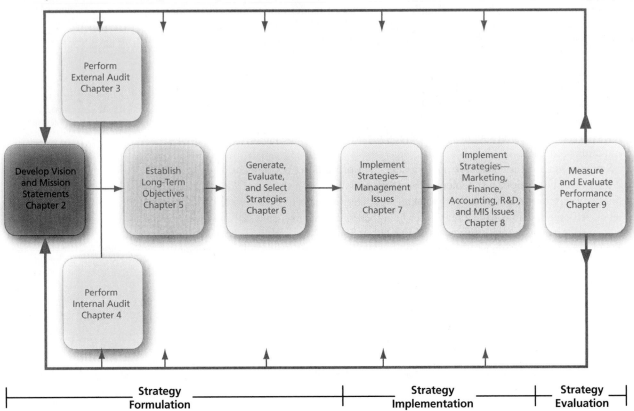

Source: Fred R. David, "How Companies Define Their Mission," *Long Range Planning* 22, no. 3 (June 1988): 40.

A business mission is the foundation for priorities, strategies, plans, and work assignments. It is the starting point for the design of managerial jobs and, above all, for the design of managerial structures. Nothing may seem simpler or more obvious than to know what a company's business is. A steel mill makes steel, a railroad runs trains to carry freight and passengers, an insurance company underwrites fire risks, and a bank lends money. Actually, "What is our business?" is almost always a difficult question and the right answer is usually anything but obvious. The answer to this question is the first responsibility of strategists. Only strategists can make sure that this question receives the attention it deserves and that the answer makes sense and enables the business to plot its course and set its objectives.[2]

Some strategists spend almost every moment of every day on administrative and tactical concerns, and strategists who rush quickly to establish objectives and implement strategies often overlook the development of a vision and mission statement. This problem is widespread even among large organizations. Many corporations in America have not yet developed a formal vision or mission statement.[3] An increasing number of organizations are developing these statements.

Some companies develop mission statements simply because they feel it is fashionable, rather than out of any real commitment. However, as will be described in this chapter, firms that develop and systematically revisit their vision and mission statements, treat them as living documents, and consider them to be an integral part of the firm's culture realize great benefits. Johnson & Johnson (J&J) is an example firm. J&J managers meet regularly with employees to review, reword, and reaffirm the firm's vision and mission. The entire

J&J workforce recognizes the value that top management places on this exercise, and these employees respond accordingly.

Vision versus Mission

Many organizations develop both a mission statement and a vision statement. Whereas the mission statement answers the question "What is our business," the *vision statement* answers the question "What do we want to become?" Many organizations have both a mission and vision statement.

It can be argued that profit, not mission or vision, is the primary corporate motivator. But profit alone is not enough to motivate people.[4] Profit is perceived negatively by some employees in companies. Employees may see profit as something that they earn and management then uses and even gives away to shareholders. Although this perception is undesired and disturbing to management, it clearly indicates that both profit and vision are needed to effectively motivate a workforce.

When employees and managers together shape or fashion the vision and mission statements for a firm, the resultant documents can reflect the personal visions that managers and employees have in their hearts and minds about their own futures. Shared vision creates a commonality of interests that can lift workers out of the monotony of daily work and put them into a new world of opportunity and challenge.

The Process of Developing Vision and Mission Statements

As indicated in the strategic-management model, clear vision and mission statements are needed before alternative strategies can be formulated and implemented. It is important to involve as many managers as possible in the process of developing these statements, because through involvement, people become committed to an organization.

A widely used approach to developing a vision and mission statement is first to select several articles about these statements and ask all managers to read these as background information. Then ask managers themselves to prepare a vision and mission statement for the organization. A facilitator, or committee of top managers, should then merge these statements into a single document and distribute the draft statements to all managers. A request for modifications, additions, and deletions is needed next, along with a meeting to revise the document. To the extent that all managers have input into and support the final documents, organizations can more easily obtain managers' support for other strategy formulation, implementation, and evaluation activities. Thus, the process of developing a vision and mission statement represents a great opportunity for strategists to obtain needed support from all managers in the firm.

During the process of developing vision and mission statements, some organizations use discussion groups of managers to develop and modify existing statements. Some organizations hire an outside consultant or facilitator to manage the process and help draft the language. Sometimes an outside person with expertise in developing such statements, who has unbiased views, can manage the process more effectively than an internal group or committee of managers. Decisions on how best to communicate the vision and mission to all managers, employees, and external constituencies of an organization are needed when the documents are in final form. Some organizations even develop a videotape to explain the statements, and how they were developed.

An article by Campbell and Yeung emphasizes that the process of developing a mission statement should create an "emotional bond" and "sense of mission" between the organization and its employees.[5] Commitment to a company's strategy and intellectual agreement on the strategies to be pursued do not necessarily translate into an emotional bond; hence, strategies that have been formulated may not be implemented. These researchers stress that an emotional bond comes when an individual personally identifies with the underlying values and behavior of a firm, thus turning intellectual agreement and commitment to strategy into a sense of mission. Campbell and Yeung also differentiate between the terms *vision* and *mission,* saying that vision is "a possible and desirable future state of an organization" that includes specific goals, whereas mission is more associated with behavior and the present.

VISIT THE NET

Gives questions that help form an effective vision and mission statement. (www.csuchico.edu/ mgmt/strategy/module1/ sld009.htm)

Importance (Benefits) of Vision and Mission Statements

The importance (benefits) of vision and mission statements to effective strategic management is well documented in the literature, although research results are mixed. Rarick and Vitton found that firms with a formalized mission statement have twice the average return on shareholders' equity than those firms without a formalized mission statement have; Bart and Baetz found a positive relationship between mission statements and organizational performance; *BusinessWeek* reports that firms using mission statements have a 30 percent higher return on certain financial measures than those without such statements; however, some studies have found that having a mission statement does not directly contribute positively to financial performance.[6] The extent of manager and employee involvement in developing vision and mission statements can make a difference in business success. This chapter provides guidelines for developing these important documents. In actual practice, wide variations exist in the nature, composition, and use of both vision and mission statements. King and Cleland recommend that organizations carefully develop a written mission statement in order to keep the following benefits:

VISIT THE NET

(http://sbinformation.about.com/cs/businessplans/a/mission.htm)

1. To ensure unanimity of purpose within the organization
2. To provide a basis, or standard, for allocating organizational resources
3. To establish a general tone or organizational climate
4. To serve as a focal point for individuals to identify with the organization's purpose and direction, and to deter those who cannot from participating further in the organization's activities
5. To facilitate the translation of objectives into a work structure involving the assignment of tasks to responsible elements within the organization
6. To specify organizational purposes and then to translate these purposes into objectives in such a way that cost, time, and performance parameters can be assessed and controlled.[7]

Reuben Mark, former CEO of Colgate, maintains that a clear mission increasingly must make sense internationally. Mark's thoughts on vision are as follows:

> When it comes to rallying everyone to the corporate banner, it's essential to push one vision globally rather than trying to drive home different messages in different cultures. The trick is to keep the vision simple but elevated: "We make the world's fastest computers" or "Telephone service for everyone." You're never going to get anyone to charge the machine guns only for financial objectives. It's got to be something that makes people feel better, feel a part of something.[8]

A Resolution of Divergent Views

Another benefit of developing a comprehensive mission statement is that divergent views among managers can be revealed and resolved through the process. The question "What is our business?" can create controversy. Raising the question often reveals differences among strategists in the organization. Individuals who have worked together for a long time and who think they know each other suddenly may realize that they are in fundamental disagreement. For example, in a college or university, divergent views regarding the relative importance of teaching, research, and service often are expressed during the mission statement development process. Negotiation, compromise, and eventual agreement on important issues are needed before people can focus on more specific strategy formulation activities.

> "What is our mission?" is a genuine decision; and a genuine decision must be based on divergent views to have a chance to be a right and effective decision. Developing a business mission is always a choice between alternatives, each of which rests on different assumptions regarding the reality of the business and its environment. It is always a high-risk decision. A change in mission always leads to

changes in objectives, strategies, organization, and behavior. The mission decision is far too important to be made by acclamation. Developing a business mission is a big step toward management effectiveness. Hidden or half-understood disagreements on the definition of a business mission underlie many of the personality problems, communication problems, and irritations that tend to divide a top-management group. Establishing a mission should never be made on plausibility alone, should never be made fast, and should never be made painlessly.[9]

Considerable disagreement among an organization's strategists over vision and mission statements can cause trouble if not resolved. For example, unresolved disagreement over the business mission was one of the reasons for W. T. Grant's bankruptcy and eventual liquidation. As one executive reported:

There was a lot of dissension within the company whether we should go the Kmart route or go after the Montgomery Ward and JCPenney position. Ed Staley and Lou Lustenberger (two top executives) were at loggerheads over the issue, with the upshot being we took a position between the two and that consequently stood for nothing.[10]

Too often, strategists develop vision and business mission statements only when the organization is in trouble. Of course, it is needed then. Developing and communicating a clear mission during troubled times indeed may have spectacular results and even may reverse decline. However, to wait until an organization is in trouble to develop a vision and mission statement is a gamble that characterizes irresponsible management. According to Drucker, the most important time to ask seriously, "What do we want to become?" and "What is our business?" is when a company has been successful:

Success always obsoletes the very behavior that achieved it, always creates new realities, and always creates new and different problems. Only the fairy tale story ends, "They lived happily ever after." It is never popular to argue with success or to rock the boat. The ancient Greeks knew that the penalty of success can be severe. The management that does not ask "What is our mission?" when the company is successful is, in effect, smug, lazy, and arrogant. It will not be long before success will turn into failure. Sooner or later, even the most successful answer to the question "What is our business?" becomes obsolete.[11]

In multidivisional organizations, strategists should ensure that divisional units perform strategic-management tasks, including the development of a statement of vision and mission. Each division should involve its own managers and employees in developing a vision and mission statement that is consistent with and supportive of the corporate mission.

An organization that fails to develop a vision statement as well as a comprehensive and inspiring mission statement loses the opportunity to present itself favorably to existing and potential stakeholders. All organizations need customers, employees, and managers, and most firms need creditors, suppliers, and distributors. The vision and mission statements are effective vehicles for communicating with important internal and external stakeholders. The principal benefit of these statements as tools of strategic management is derived from their specification of the ultimate aims of a firm:

They provide managers with a unity of direction that transcends individual, parochial, and transitory needs. They promote a sense of shared expectations among all levels and generations of employees. They consolidate values over time and across individuals and interest groups. They project a sense of worth and intent that can be identified and assimilated by company outsiders. Finally, they affirm the company's commitment to responsible action, which is symbiotic with its need to preserve and protect the essential claims of insiders for sustained survival, growth, and profitability of the firm.[12]

Characteristics of a Mission Statement

A Declaration of Attitude

A mission statement is more than a statement of specific details; it is a declaration of attitude and outlook. It usually is broad in scope for at least two major reasons. First, a good mission statement allows for the generation and consideration of a range of feasible alternative objectives and strategies without unduly stifling management creativity. Excess specificity would limit the potential of creative growth for the organization. On the other hand, an overly general statement that does not exclude any strategy alternatives could be dysfunctional. Apple Computer's mission statement, for example, should not open the possibility for diversification into pesticides—or Ford Motor Company's into food processing.

Second, a mission statement needs to be broad to effectively reconcile differences among, and appeal to, an organization's diverse *stakeholders,* the individuals and groups of individuals who have a special stake or claim on the company. Stakeholders include employees, managers, stockholders, boards of directors, customers, suppliers, distributors, creditors, governments (local, state, federal, and foreign), unions, competitors, environmental groups, and the general public. Stakeholders affect and are affected by an organization's strategies, yet the claims and concerns of diverse constituencies vary and often conflict. For example, the general public is especially interested in social responsibility, whereas stockholders are more interested in profitability. Claims on any business literally may number in the thousands, and they often include clean air, jobs, taxes, investment opportunities, career opportunities, equal employment opportunities, employee benefits, salaries, wages, clean water, and community services. All stakeholders' claims on an organization cannot be pursued with equal emphasis. A good mission statement indicates the relative attention that an organization will devote to meeting the claims of various stakeholders. Many firms are environmentally proactive in response to the concerns of stakeholders, as indicated in the "Natural Environment Perspective" box.

The fine balance between specificity and generality is difficult to achieve, but it is well worth the effort. George Steiner offers the following insight on the need for a mission statement to be broad in scope:

> Most business statements of mission are expressed at high levels of abstraction. Vagueness nevertheless has its virtues. Mission statements are not designed to express concrete ends, but rather to provide motivation, general direction, an image, a tone, and a philosophy to guide the enterprise. An excess of detail could prove counterproductive since concrete specification could be the base for rallying opposition. Precision might stifle creativity in the formulation of an acceptable mission or purpose. Once an aim is cast in concrete, it creates a rigidity in an organization and resists change. Vagueness leaves room for other managers to fill in the details, perhaps even to modify general patterns. Vagueness permits more flexibility in adapting to changing environments and internal operations. It facilitates flexibility in implementation.[13]

In addition to being broad in scope, an effective mission statement should not be too lengthy; recommended length is less than 250 words. An effective mission statement should arouse positive feelings and emotions about an organization; it should be inspiring in the sense that it motivates readers to action. A mission statement should be enduring. All of the above are desired characteristics of a statement. An effective mission statement generates the impression that a firm is successful, has direction, and is worthy of time, support, and investment—from all socioeconomic groups of people.

It reflects judgments about future growth directions and strategies that are based upon forward-looking external and internal analyses. A business mission should provide useful criteria for selecting among alternative strategies. A clear mission statement provides a basis for generating and screening strategic options. The statement of mission should be dynamic in orientation, allowing judgments about the most promising growth directions and those considered less promising.

NATURAL ENVIRONMENT PERSPECTIVE
Is Your Firm Environmentally Proactive?

Conducting business in a way that preserves the natural environment is more than just good public relations; it is good business. Preserving the environment is a permanent part of doing business for the following reasons:

1. Consumer demand for environmentally safe products and packages is high.
2. Public opinion demanding that firms conduct business in ways that preserve the natural environment is strong.
3. Environmental advocacy groups now have over 20 million Americans as members.
4. Federal and state environmental regulations are changing rapidly and becoming more complex.
5. More lenders are examining the environmental liabilities of businesses seeking loans.
6. Many consumers, suppliers, distributors, and investors shun doing business with environmentally weak firms.
7. Liability suits and fines against firms having environmental problems are on the rise.

More firms are becoming environmentally proactive, which means they are taking the initiative to develop and implement strategies that preserve the environment while enhancing their efficiency and effectiveness. The old undesirable alternative is to be environmentally reactive—waiting until environmental pressures are thrust upon a firm by law or consumer pressure. A reactive environmental policy often leads to high cleanup costs, numerous liability suits, loss in market share, reduced customer loyalty, and higher medical costs. In contrast, a proactive policy views environmental pressures as opportunities and includes such actions as developing green products and packages, conserving energy, reducing waste, recycling, and creating a corporate culture that is environmentally sensitive.

A proactive policy forces a company to innovate and upgrade processes; this leads to reduced waste, improved efficiency, better quality, and greater profits. Successful firms today assess "the profit in preserving the environment" in decisions ranging from developing a mission statement to determining plant location, manufacturing technology, design, products, packaging, and consumer relations. A proactive environmental policy is simply good business.

For example, more than 373,000 big-rig trucks were produced in North America in 2006, a record, but new federal regulations on big truck emissions have dropped that number to about 220,000 in 2007. New required diesel technology has reduced emissions by up to 98 percent in all new big trucks, at an average cost increase of $12,000 per truck. "Clean air is not free," says Rich Moskowitz, who handles regulatory affairs for the American Trucking Association, which supports the transition.

Sources: Adapted from "The Profit in Preserving America," *Forbes* (November 11, 1991): 181–189; Forest Beinhardt, "Bringing the Environment Down to Earth," *Harvard Business Review* (July–August 1999): 149–158; Christine Rosen; "Environmental Strategy and Competitive Advantage," *California Management Review* 43, 3 (Spring 2001): 8–15; and Chris Woodyard, "Cleaner Diesel Engine Rules Take Effect," *USA Today* (December 29, 2006): 1B.

Yellowstone River in Billings, Montana. *Source:* Andy Holligan (c) Dorling Kindersley

A Customer Orientation

A good mission statement describes an organization's purpose, customers, products or services, markets, philosophy, and basic technology. According to Vern McGinnis, a mission statement should (1) define what the organization is and what the organization aspires to be, (2) be limited enough to exclude some ventures and broad enough to allow for creative growth, (3) distinguish a given organization from all others, (4) serve as a framework for evaluating both current and prospective activities, and (5) be stated in terms sufficiently clear to be widely understood throughout the organization.[14]

A good mission statement reflects the anticipations of customers. Rather than developing a product and then trying to find a market, the operating philosophy of organizations should be to identify customers' needs and then provide a product or service to fulfill those needs.

Good mission statements identify the utility of a firm's products to its customers. This is why AT&T's mission statement focuses on communication rather than on telephones; it is why ExxonMobil's mission statement focuses on energy rather than on oil and gas; it is why Union Pacific's mission statement focuses on transportation rather than on railroads; it is why Universal Studio's mission statement focuses on entertainment rather than on movies. The following utility statements are relevant in developing a mission statement:

Do not offer me things.

Do not offer me clothes. Offer me attractive looks.

Do not offer me shoes. Offer me comfort for my feet and the pleasure of walking.

Do not offer me a house. Offer me security, comfort, and a place that is clean and happy.

Do not offer me books. Offer me hours of pleasure and the benefit of knowledge.

Do not offer me records. Offer me leisure and the sound of music.

Do not offer me tools. Offer me the benefits and the pleasure that come from making beautiful things.

Do not offer me furniture. Offer me comfort and the quietness of a cozy place.

Do not offer me things. Offer me ideas, emotions, ambience, feelings, and benefits.

Please, do not offer me *things*.

A major reason for developing a business mission statement is to attract customers who give meaning to an organization. Hotel customers today want to use the Internet, so more and more hotels are providing Internet service. A classic description of the purpose of a business reveals the relative importance of customers in a statement of mission:

It is the customer who determines what a business is. It is the customer alone whose willingness to pay for a good or service converts economic resources into wealth and things into goods. What a business thinks it produces is not of first importance, especially not to the future of the business and to its success. What the customer thinks he/she is buying, what he/she considers value, is decisive—it determines what a business is, what it produces, and whether it will prosper. And what the customer buys and considers value is never a product. It is always utility, meaning what a product or service does for him or her. The customer is the foundation of a business and keeps it in existence.[15]

A Declaration of Social Policy

As indicated in Table 2-3, another characteristic of mission statements is that they shoud reveal that the firm is socially responsible. The term *social policy* embraces managerial philosophy and thinking at the highest levels of an organization. For this reason, social policy affects the development of a business mission statement. Social issues mandate that strategists consider not only what the organization owes its various stakeholders but also what responsibilities the firm has to consumers, environmentalists, minorities, communities, and other groups. After decades of debate on the topic of social responsibility, many firms still struggle to determine appropriate social policies.

The issue of social responsibility arises when a company establishes its business mission. The impact of society on business and vice versa is becoming more pronounced each year. Social policies directly affect a firm's customers, products and services, markets, technology, profitability, self-concept, and public image. An organization's social policy should be integrated into all strategic-management activities, including the development of a mission statement. Corporate social policy should be designed and articulated during strategy formulation, set and administered during strategy implementation, and reaffirmed or changed during strategy evaluation.[16] The emerging view of social responsibility holds that social issues should be attended to both directly and indirectly in determining strategies. In 2007, the most admired companies for social responsibility were as follows:

1. CHS
2. United Parcel Service
3. Whole Foods Market
4. McDonald's
5. Alcan
6. YRC Worldwide
7. Starbucks
8. International Paper
9. Vulcan Materials
10. Walt Disney

From a social responsibility perspective, the least admired companies in 2007 were:

1. Visteon
2. Dana
3. CA
4. Delphi
5. Federal-Mogul
6. ArvinMeritor
7. Huntsman
8. Navistar International
9. Lyondell Chemical
10. Toys "R" Us [17]

Firms should strive to engage in social activities that have economic benefits. For example, Merck & Co. recently developed the drug ivermectin for treating river blindness, a disease caused by a fly-borne parasitic worm endemic in poor, tropical areas of Africa, the Middle East, and Latin America. In an unprecedented gesture that reflected its corporate commitment to social responsibility, Merck then made ivermectin available at no cost to medical personnel throughout the world. Merck's action highlights the dilemma of orphan drugs, which offer pharmaceutical companies no economic incentive for development and distribution.

Despite differences in approaches, most U.S. companies try to ensure outsiders that they conduct their businesses in socially responsible ways. As indicated in the Global Perspective, an increasing number of Japanese firms are embracing the notion of equal employment opportunity for women. The mission statement is an effective instrument for conveying this message.

Some strategists agree with Ralph Nader, who proclaims that organizations have tremendous social obligations. Others agree with Milton Friedman, the economist, who maintains that organizations have no obligation to do any more for society than is legally required. Most strategists agree that the first social responsibility of any business must be to make enough profit to cover the costs of the future, because if this is not achieved, no other social responsibility can be met. Strategists should examine social problems in terms of potential costs and benefits to the firm, and they should address social issues that could benefit the firm most.

VISIT THE NET

Provides example mission and vision statements that can be critiqued. (www.csuchico.edu/mgmt/strategy/module1/sld015.htm; www.csuchico.edu/mgmt/strategy/module1/sld014.htm; www.csuchico.edu/mgmt/strategy/module1/sld017.htm)

GLOBAL PERSPECTIVE
Social Policies on Retirement: Japan Versus the World

Some countries around the world are facing severe workforce shortages associated with their aging populations. The percentage of persons age 65 or older reached 20 percent in 2006 in both Japan and Italy, and will reach 20 percent in 2036 in China and the United States. Persons age 65 and older will reach 20 percent of the population in Germany and France in 2009 and 2018 respectively. Unlike the United States, Japan is reluctant to rely on large-scale immigration to bolster its workforce. Instead, Japan is providing incentives for its elderly to work until ages 65 to 75. Western European countries are doing the opposite, providing incentives for its elderly to retire at ages 55 to 60. The International Labor Organization says 71 percent of Japanese men ages 60 to 64 work, compared to 57 percent of American men and just 17 percent of French men in the same age group.

Mr. Sachiko Ichioka, a typical 67-year-old man in Japan, says, "I want to work as long as I'm healthy. The extra money means I can go on trips, and I'm not a burden on my children." Better diet and health care have raised Japan's life expectancy now to 82, the highest in the world. Japanese women are having on average only 1.28 children compared to 2.04 in the United States. Keeping the elderly at work, coupled with reversing the old-fashioned trend of keeping women at home, are

Japan's two key remedies for sustaining its workforce in factories and businesses. This prescription for dealing with problems associated with an aging society should be considered by many countries around the world. The Japanese government is phasing in a shift from ages 60 to 65 as the date when a person may begin receiving a pension, and premiums paid by Japanese employees are rising while payouts are falling. Unlike the United States, Japan has no law against discrimination based on age.

Japan's huge national debt, 175 percent of GDP compared to 65 percent for the United States, is difficult to lower with a falling population because Japan has fewer taxpaying workers. Worker productivity increases in Japan are not able to offset declines in number of workers, thus resulting in a decline in overall economic production. Like many countries, Japan does not view immigration as a good means to solve this problem. A leading Japanese economist and high government official, Ms. Hiroko Ota, says, "I would like to bring about a labor big bang. We need women to work while bringing up children. I want to make Japan an open country that grows along with the rest of Asia."

Japan's shrinking workforce has become such a concern that the government has just recently allowed an unspecified number of Indonesian and Filipino nurses

Wedding participants in Rajpipla, Gujarat wearing traditional clothing.
Source: Christopher and Sally Gable (c) Dorling Kindersley

and caregivers to work in Japan for two years. The number of working-age Japanese—those between ages 15 and 64—is projected to shrink to 70 million by 2030, from 83 million in 2007. For many years, Japan has been known for its resistance to mass immigration, but the country is now starting to use more foreigners—known as *gaikokujin roudousha* in Japanese. Foreign workers, especially Filipinos, are being hired now to work in agriculture and factories throughout Japan.

From 1639 to 1854, Japan banned nearly all foreigners from entering the country. The percentage of foreign workers to the total population is 20 percent in the United States, nearly 10 percent in Germany, 5 percent in the United Kingdom, and less than 1 percent in Japan. But most Japanese now acknowledge that this percentage must move upward and perhaps quickly for their nation's economy to prosper.

Source: Adapted from Sebastian Moffett, "Fat-Aging Japan Keeps Its Elders on the Job Longer," *Wall Street Journal* (June 15, 2005): A1, A8; Sebastian Moffett, "Japan Seeks More Efficiency as Population Drops," *Wall Street Journal* (December 12, 2006): A2; Yuka Hayashi, "Japan Turns to Foreign Workers Amid Labor Crunch," *Wall Street Journal* (November 30, 2006): A10; and Yuka Hayashi and Sebastian Moffett, "Cautiously, an Aging Japan Warms to Foreign Workers," *Wall Street Journal* (May 25, 2007): A1, A12.

Mission Statement Components

Mission statements can and do vary in length, content, format, and specificity. Most practitioners and academicians of strategic management feel that an effective statement exhibits nine characteristics or components. Because a mission statement is often the most visible and public part of the strategic-management process, it is important that it includes all of these essential components:

1. *Customers*—Who are the firm's customers?
2. *Products or services*—What are the firm's major products or services?
3. *Markets*—Geographically, where does the firm compete?
4. *Technology*—Is the firm technologically current?
5. *Concern for survival, growth, and profitability*—Is the firm committed to growth and financial soundness?
6. *Philosophy*—What are the basic beliefs, values, aspirations, and ethical priorities of the firm?
7. *Self-concept*—What is the firm's distinctive competence or major competitive advantage?
8. *Concern for public image*—Is the firm responsive to social, community, and environmental concerns?
9. *Concern for employees*—Are employees a valuable asset of the firm?

Excerpts from the mission statements of different organizations are provided in Table 2-4 to exemplify the nine essential mission statement components.

TABLE 2-3 **Characteristics of a Mission Statement**

- Broad in scope
- Less than 250 words in length
- Inspiring
- Identify the utility of a firm's products
- Reveal that the firm is socially responsible
- Reveal that the firm is environmentally responsible
- Include nine components
    customers, products or services, markets, technology, concern for survival/growth/profits, philosophy, self-concept, concern for public image, concern for employees
- Enduring

TABLE 2-4 Examples of the Nine Essential Components of a Mission Statement

1. Customers

We believe our first responsibility is to the doctors, nurses, patients, mothers, and all others who use our products and services. (Johnson & Johnson)

To earn our customers' loyalty, we listen to them, anticipate their needs, and act to create value in their eyes. (Lexmark International)

2. Products or Services

AMAX's principal products are molybdenum, coal, iron ore, copper, lead, zinc, petroleum and natural gas, potash, phosphates, nickel, tungsten, silver, gold, and magnesium. (AMAX Engineering Company)

Standard Oil Company (Indiana) is in business to find and produce crude oil, natural gas, and natural gas liquids; to manufacture high-quality products useful to society from these raw materials; and to distribute and market those products and to provide dependable related services to the consuming public at reasonable prices. (Standard Oil Company)

3. Markets

We are dedicated to the total success of Corning Glass Works as a worldwide competitor. (Corning Glass Works)

Our emphasis is on North American markets, although global opportunities will be explored. (Blockway)

4. Technology

Control Data is in the business of applying micro-electronics and computer technology in two general areas: computer-related hardware; and computing-enhancing services, which include computation, information, education, and finance. (Control Data)

We will continually strive to meet the preferences of adult smokers by developing technologies that have the potential to reduce the health risks associated with smoking. (RJ Reynolds)

5. Concern for Survival, Growth, and Profitability

In this respect, the company will conduct its operations prudently and will provide the profits and growth which will assure Hoover's ultimate success. (Hoover Universal)

To serve the worldwide need for knowledge at a fair profit by adhering, evaluating, producing, and distributing valuable information in a way that benefits our customers, employees, other investors, and our society. (McGraw-Hill)

6. Philosophy

Our world-class leadership is dedicated to a management philosophy that holds people above profits. (Kellogg)

It's all part of the Mary Kay philosophy—a philosophy based on the golden rule. A spirit of sharing and caring where people give cheerfully of their time, knowledge, and experience. (Mary Kay Cosmetics)

7. Self-Concept

Crown Zellerbach is committed to leapfrogging ongoing competition within 1,000 days by unleashing the constructive and creative abilities and energies of each of its employees. (Crown Zellerbach)

8. Concern for Public Image

To share the world's obligation for the protection of the environment. (Dow Chemical)

To contribute to the economic strength of society and function as a good corporate citizen on a local, state, and national basis in all countries in which we do business. (Pfizer)

9. Concern for Employees

To recruit, develop, motivate, reward, and retain personnel of exceptional ability, character, and dedication by providing good working conditions, superior leadership, compensation on the basis of performance, an attractive benefit program, opportunity for growth, and a high degree of employment security. (The Wachovia Corporation)

To compensate its employees with remuneration and fringe benefits competitive with other employment opportunities in its geographical area and commensurate with their contributions toward efficient corporate operations. (Public Service Electric & Gas Company)

VISIT THE NET

Provides mission statement information on nonprofit firms. (http://www.nonprofits.org/npofaq/03/21.html)

Writing and Evaluating Mission Statements

Perhaps the best way to develop a skill for writing and evaluating mission statements is to study actual company missions. Therefore, the mission statements presented on page 61 are evaluated based on the nine desired components.

There is no one best mission statement for a particular organization, so good judgment is required in evaluating mission statements. Note earlier in Table 2-2 on page 51 that numbers provided in each statement reveal what components are included in the respective documents. Among the statements in Table 2-2, note that the Dell mission statement is the best because it lacks only one component, whereas the L'Oreal statement is the worst, lacking six of the nine recommended components. Realize that some individuals are more demanding than others in assessing mission statements in this manner. For example, if a statement merely includes the word "customers" without specifying who the customers are, is that satisfactory? Ideally a statement would provide more than simply inclusion of a single word such as "products" or "employees" regarding a respective component. Why? Because the statement should be informative, inspiring, enduring, and serve to motivate stakeholders to action. Evaluation of a mission statement regarding inclusion of the nine components is just the beginning of the process to assess a statement's overall effectiveness.

Conclusion

Every organization has a unique purpose and reason for being. This uniqueness should be reflected in vision and mission statements. The nature of a business vision and mission can represent either a competitive advantage or disadvantage for the firm. An organization achieves a heightened sense of purpose when strategists, managers, and employees develop and communicate a clear business vision and mission. Drucker says that developing a clear business vision and mission is the "first responsibility of strategists."

A good mission statement reveals an organization's customers; products or services; markets; technology; concern for survival, growth, and profitability; philosophy; self-concept; concern for public image; and concern for employees. These nine basic components serve as a practical framework for evaluating and writing mission statements. As the first step in strategic management, the vision and mission statements provide direction for all planning activities.

Well-designed vision and mission statements are essential for formulating, implementing, and evaluating strategy. Developing and communicating a clear business vision and mission are the most commonly overlooked tasks in strategic management. Without clear statements of vision and mission, a firm's short-term actions can be counterproductive to long-term interests. Vision and mission statements always should be subject to revision, but, if carefully prepared, they will require infrequent major changes. Organizations usually reexamine their vision and mission statements annually. Effective mission statements stand the test of time.

Vision and mission statements are essential tools for strategists, a fact illustrated in a short story told by Porsche former CEO Peter Schultz:

Three people were at work on a construction site. All were doing the same job, but when each was asked what his job was, the answers varied: "Breaking rocks," the first replied; "Earning a living," responded the second; "Helping to build a cathedral," said the third. Few of us can build cathedrals. But to the extent we can see the cathedral in whatever cause we are following, the job seems more worthwhile. Good strategists and a clear mission help us find those cathedrals in what otherwise could be dismal issues and empty causes.[18]

We invite you to visit the David page on the Prentice Hall Companion Web site at www.prenhall.com/david for this chapter's review quiz.

Key Terms and Concepts

Concern for Employees (p. 61)
Concern for Public Image (p. 61)
Concern for Survival, Growth, and Profitability (p. 61)
Creed Statement (p. 51)
Customers (p. 61)
Markets (p. 61)
Mission Statement (p. 51)

Issues for Review and Discussion

1. Compare and contrast vision statements with mission statements in terms of composition and importance.
2. Do local service stations need to have written vision and mission statements? Why or why not?
3. Why do you think organizations that have a comprehensive mission tend to be high performers? Does having a comprehensive mission cause high performance?
4. Explain why a mission statement should not include strategies and objectives.
5. What is your college or university's self-concept? How would you state that in a mission statement?
6. Explain the principal value of a vision and a mission statement.
7. Why is it important for a mission statement to be reconciliatory?
8. In your opinion, what are the three most important components that should be included when writing a mission statement? Why?
9. How would the mission statements of a for-profit and a nonprofit organization differ?
10. Write a vision and mission statement for an organization of your choice.
11. Conduct a search on the Internet with the keywords *vision statement* and *mission statement.* Find various company vision and mission statements, and evaluate the documents. Write a one-page single-spaced report on your findings.
12. Who are the major stakeholders of the bank that you locally do business with? What are the major claims of those stakeholders?
13. How could a strategist's attitude toward social responsibility affect a firm's strategy? What is your attitude toward social responsibility?
14. List seven characteristics of a mission statement.
15. List eight benefits of a having a clear mission statement.
16. How often do you think a firm's vision and mission statements should be changed?

Notes

1. Barbara Bartkus, Myron Glassman, and Bruce McAfee, "Mission Statements: Are They Smoke and Mirrors?" *Business Horizons* (November–December 2000): 23.
2. Peter Drucker, *Management: Tasks, Responsibilities, and Practices* (New York: Harper & Row, 1974): 61.
3. Fred David, "How Companies Define Their Mission," *Long Range Planning* 22, no. 1 (February 1989): 90–92; John Pearce II and Fred David, "Corporate Mission Statements: The Bottom Line," *Academy of Management Executive* 1, no. 2 (May 1987): 110.
4. Joseph Quigley, "Vision: How Leaders Develop It, Share It and Sustain It," *Business Horizons* (September–October 1994): 39.
5. Andrew Campbell and Sally Yeung, "Creating a Sense of Mission," *Long Range Planning* 24, no. 4 (August 1991): 17.
6. Charles Rarick and John Vitton, "Mission Statements Make Cents," *Journal of Business Strategy* 16 (1995): 11. Also, Christopher Bart and Mark Baetz, "The Relationship Between Mission Statements and Firm Performance: An Exploratory Study," *Journal of Management Studies* 35 (1998): 823; "Mission Possible," *BusinessWeek* (August 1999): F12.
7. W. R. King and D. I. Cleland, *Strategic Planning and Policy* (New York: Van Nostrand Reinhold, 1979): 124.
8. Brian Dumaine, "What the Leaders of Tomorrow See," *Fortune* (July 3, 1989): 50.
9. Drucker, 78, 79.
10. "How W. T. Grant Lost $175 Million Last Year," *BusinessWeek* (February 25, 1975): 75.
11. Drucker, 88.
12. John Pearce II, "The Company Mission as a Strategic Tool," *Sloan Management Review* 23, no. 3 (Spring 1982): 74.

13. George Steiner, *Strategic Planning: What Every Manager Must Know* (New York: The Free Press, 1979): 160.

14. Vern McGinnis, "The Mission Statement: A Key Step in Strategic Planning," *Business* 31, no. 6 (November–December 1981): 41.

15. Drucker, 61.

16. Archie Carroll and Frank Hoy, "Integrating Corporate Social Policy into Strategic Management," *Journal of Business Strategy* 4, no. 3 (Winter 1984): 57.

17. http://money.cnn.com/magazines/fortune/mostadmired/2007/best_worst/best4.html.

18. Robert Waterman, Jr., *The Renewal Factor: How the Best Get and Keep the Competitive Edge* (New York: Bantam, 1987); *BusinessWeek* (September 14, 1987): 120.

Current Readings

Aguilera,, Ruth V., Deborah E. Rupp, Cynthia A. Williams, and Ganapathi. "Corporate Social Responsibility and Firm Performance: Investor Preferences and Corporate Strategies." *The Academy of Management Review* 32, no. 3 (July 2007): 836.

Baetz, Mark C., and Christopher K. Bart. "Developing Mission Statements Which Work." *Long Range Planning* 29, no. 4 (August 1996): 526–533.

Barnett, M. L., and R. M. Salomon. "Beyond Dichotomy: The Curvilinear Relationship Between Social Responsibility and Financial Performance." *Strategic Management Journal* 27, no. 11 (November 2006): 1101.

Bartkus, Barbara, Myron Glassman, and R. Bruce McAfee. "Mission Statements: Are They Smoke and Mirrors?" *Business Horizons* 43, no. 6 (November–December 2000): 23.

Bloom, M., P. David, and A. J. Hillman. "Investor Activism, Managerial Responsiveness, and Corporate Social Performance." *Strategic Management Journal* 28, no. 1 (January 2007): 91.

Brabet, Julienne, and Mary Klemm. "Sharing the Vision: Company Mission Statements in Britain and France." *Long Range Planning* (February 1994): 84–94.

Collins, James C., and Jerry I. Porras. "Building a Visionary Company." *California Management Review* 37, no. 2 (Winter 1995): 80–100.

Collins, James C., and Jerry I. Porras. "Building Your Company's Vision." *Harvard Business Review* (September–October 1996): 65–78.

Cummings, Stephen, and John Davies. "Brief Case—Mission, Vision, Fusion." *Long Range Planning* 27, no. 6 (December 1994): 147–150.

Dalton, Catherine M. "When Organizational Values Are Mere Rhetoric." *Business Horizons* 49, no. 5 (September–October 2006): 345.

Davies, Stuart W., and Keith W. Glaister. "Business School Mission Statements—The Bland Leading the Bland?" *Long Range Planning* 30, no. 4 (August 1997): 594–604.

Day, George S., and Paul Schoemaker, "Peripheral Vision: Sensing and Acting on Weak Signals." *Long Range Planning* 37, no. 2 (April 2004): 117.

Dowling, Grahame R. "Corporate Reputations: Should You Compete on Yours?" *California Management Review* 46, no. 3 (Spring 2004): 19.

Gietzmann, Miles. "Disclosure of Timely and Forward-Looking Statements and Strategic Management of Major Institutional Ownership." *Long Range Planning* 39, no. 4 (August 2006): 409.

Gratton, Lynda. "Implementing a Strategic Vision—Key Factors for Success." *Long Range Planning* 29, no. 3 (June 1996): 290–303.

Greenfield, W. M. "In the Name of Corporate Social Responsibility." *Business Horizons* 47, no. 1 (January–February 2004): 19.

Hollender, Jeffery. "What Matters Most: Corporate Values and Social Responsibility." *California Management Review* 46, no. 4 (Summer 2004): 111.

Larwood, Laurie, Cecilia M. Falbe, Mark P. Kriger, and Paul Miesing. "Structure and Meaning of Organizational Vision." *Academy of Management Journal* 38, no. 3 (June 1995): 740–769.

Lissak, Michael, and Johan Roos. "Be Coherent, Not Visionary." *Long Range Planning* 34, no. 1 (February 2001): 53.

Mackey, Alison, Tyson B. Mackey, and Jay Barney. "Corporate Social Responsibility and Firm Performance: Investor Preferences and Corporate Strategies." *The Academy of Management Review* 32, no. 3 (July 2007): 817.

McTavish, Ron. "One More Time: What Business Are You In?" *Long Range Planning* 28, no. 2 (April 1995): 49–60.

Perrini, Francesco. "Corporate Social Responsibility: Doing the Most Good for Your Company and Your Cause." *The Academy of Management Perspectives* 20, no. 2 (May 2006): 90.

Experiential Exercise 2A

Evaluating Mission Statements

Purpose

A business mission statement is an integral part of strategic management. It provides direction for formulating, implementing, and evaluating strategic activities. This exercise will give you practice evaluating mission statements, a skill that is a prerequisite to writing a good mission statement.

Instructions

Step 1   On a clean sheet of paper, prepare a 9 × 3 matrix. Place the nine mission statement components down the left column and the following three companies across the top of your paper.

Step 2   Write *Yes* or *No* in each cell of your matrix to indicate whether you feel the particular mission statement has included the respective component.

Step 3   Turn your paper in to your instructor for a classwork grade.

Mission Statements

General Motors

Our mission is to be the world leader in transportation products and related services. We aim to maintain this position through enlightened customer enthusiasm and continuous improvement driven by the integrity, teamwork, innovation and individual respect and responsibility of our employees.

North Carolina Zoo

Our mission is to encourage understanding of and commitment to the conservation of the world's wildlife and wild places through recognition of the interdependence of people and

Epcot at Disney World in Orlando. *Source:* Ted Poweski

nature. We will do this by creating a sense of enjoyment, wonder and discovery throughout the Park and in our outreach programs.

Samsonite

Our mission is to be the leader in the travel industry. Samsonite's ambition is to provide unparalleled durability, security and dependability in all of its products, through leading edge functionality, features, innovation, technology, contemporary aesthetics and design. In order to fill every niche in the travel market, Samsonite will seek to create strategic alliances, combining our strengths with other partners in our brands.

Experiential Exercise 2B

Evaluating Walt Disney's Vision and Mission Statement

Purpose

There is always room for improvement in regard to an existing vision and mission statement. Currently the Walt Disney Company does not have a vision statement, so this exercise will ask you to develop one. The company does have a mission statement, but analysts feel that the statement could be improved.

> The mission of the Walt Disney Company is to be one of the world's leading producers and providers of entertainment and information. Using our portfolio of brands to differentiate our content, services and consumer products, we seek to develop the most creative, innovative and profitable entertainment experiences and related products in the world.

Instructions

Step 1	Refer back to page 31 the Cohesion Case for Walt Disney's mission statement.
Step 2	On a clean sheet of paper, write a one-sentence vision statement for the Walt Disney Company.
Step 3	On that same sheet of paper, evaluate Walt Disney's mission statement. Which of the nine recommended components are lacking in the company's current statement?
Step 4	Write an improved mission statement for Walt Disney that meets the eight characteristics summarized in Table 2-3.

Experiential Exercise 2C

Writing a Vision and Mission Statement for My University

Purpose

Most universities have a vision and mission statement. The purpose of this exercise is to give you practice writing a vision and mission statement for a nonprofit organization such as your own university.

Instructions

Step 1	Write a vision statement and a mission statement for your university. Your mission statement should meet the eight characteristics summarized in Table 2-3.
Step 2	Read your vision and mission statement to the class.
Step 3	Determine whether your institution has a vision and/or mission statement. Look in the front of the college handbook. If your institution has a written statement, contact an appropriate administrator of the institution to inquire as to how and when the statement was prepared. Share this information with the class. Analyze your college's vision and mission statement in light of the concepts presented in this chapter.

Experiential Exercise 2D

Conducting Mission Statement Research

Purpose

This exercise gives you the opportunity to study the nature and role of vision and mission statements in strategic management.

Instructions

Step 1   Call various organizations in your city or county to identify firms that have developed a formal vision and/or mission statement. Contact nonprofit organizations and government agencies in addition to small and large businesses. Ask to speak with the director, owner, or chief executive officer of each organization. Explain that you are studying vision and mission statements in class and are conducting research as part of a class activity.

Step 2   Ask several executives the following four questions, and record their answers.
1.   When did your organization first develop its vision and/or mission statement? Who was primarily responsible for its development?
2.   How long have your current statements existed? When were they last modified? Why were they modified at that time?
3.   By what process are your firm's vision and mission statements altered?
4.   How are your vision and mission statements used in the firm?

Step 3   Provide an overview of your findings to the class.

3 The External Assessment

A Retreat for Strategic Planning on the Adriatic Sea. *Source:* Forest David

chapter objectives

After studying this chapter, you should be able to do the following:

1. Describe how to conduct an external strategic-management audit.

2. Discuss 10 major external forces that affect organizations: economic, social, cultural, demographic, environmental, political, governmental, legal, technological, and competitive.

3. Identify key sources of external information, including the Internet.

4. Discuss important forecasting tools used in strategic management.

5. Discuss the importance of monitoring external trends and events.

6. Explain how to develop an EFE Matrix.

7. Explain how to develop a Competitive Profile Matrix.

8. Discuss the importance of gathering competitive intelligence.

9. Describe the trend toward cooperation among competitors.

10. Discuss the economic environment in Russia.

11. Discuss the global challenge facing American firms.

12. Discuss market commonality and resource similarity in relation to competitive analysis.

This chapter examines the tools and concepts needed to conduct an external strategic management audit (sometimes called *environmental scanning* or *industry analysis*). An *external audit* focuses on identifying and evaluating trends and events beyond the control of a single firm, such as increased foreign competition, population shifts to the Sunbelt, an aging society, consumer fear of traveling, and stock market volatility. An external audit reveals key opportunities and threats confronting an organization so that managers can formulate strategies to take advantage of the opportunities and avoid or reduce the impact of threats. This chapter presents a practical framework for gathering, assimilating, and analyzing external information. The Industrial Organization (I/O) view of strategic management is introduced.

The Nature of an External Audit

VISIT THE NET

Reveals how strategic planning evolved from long-range planning and environmental scanning (external audit or assessment). (horizon.unc.edu/projects/ seminars/futuresresearch/strategic. asp#planning)

The purpose of an *external audit* is to develop a finite list of opportunities that could benefit a firm and threats that should be avoided. As the term *finite* suggests, the external audit is not aimed at developing an exhaustive list of every possible factor that could influence the business; rather, it is aimed at identifying key variables that offer actionable responses. Firms should be able to respond either offensively or defensively to the factors by formulating strategies that take advantage of external opportunities or that minimize the impact of potential threats. Figure 3-1 illustrates how the external audit fits into the strategic-management process.

Key External Forces

External forces can be divided into five broad categories: (1) economic forces; (2) social, cultural, demographic, and environmental forces; (3) political, governmental, and legal forces; (4) technological forces; and (5) competitive forces. Relationships among these

FIGURE 3-1

A Comprehensive Strategic-Management Model

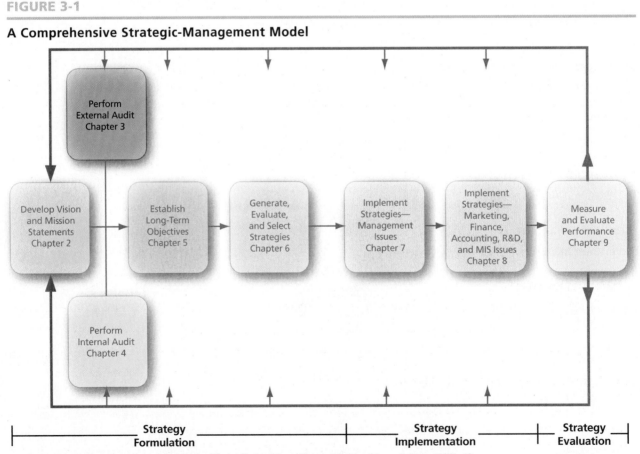

Source: Fred R. David, "How Companies Define Their Mission," *Long Range Planning* 22, no. 3 (June 1988): 40.

FIGURE 3-2

Relationships Between Key External Forces and an Organization

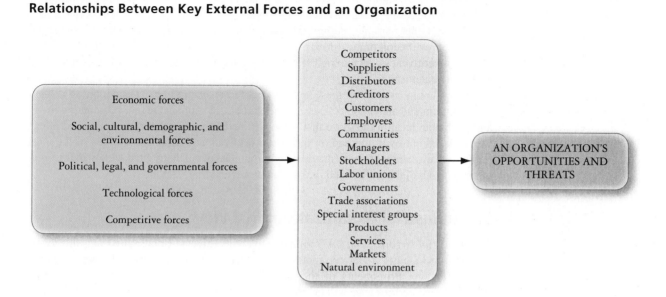

forces and an organization are depicted in Figure 3-2. External trends and events significantly affect all products, services, markets, and organizations in the world.

Changes in external forces translate into changes in consumer demand for both industrial and consumer products and services. External forces affect the types of products developed, the nature of positioning and market segmentation strategies, the type of services offered, and the choice of businesses to acquire or sell. External forces directly affect both suppliers and distributors. Identifying and evaluating external opportunities and threats enables organizations to develop a clear mission, to design strategies to achieve long-term objectives, and to develop policies to achieve annual objectives.

The increasing complexity of business today is evidenced by more countries developing the capacity and will to compete aggressively in world markets. Foreign businesses and countries are willing to learn, adapt, innovate, and invent to compete successfully in the marketplace. There are more competitive new technologies in Europe and Asia today than ever before. U.S. businesses can no longer beat foreign competitors with ease.

The Process of Performing an External Audit

The process of performing an external audit must involve as many managers and employees as possible. As emphasized in earlier chapters, involvement in the strategic-management process can lead to understanding and commitment from organizational members. Individuals appreciate having the opportunity to contribute ideas and to gain a better understanding of their firms' industry, competitors, and markets.

To perform an external audit, a company first must gather competitive intelligence and information about economic, social, cultural, demographic, environmental, political, governmental, legal, and technological trends. Individuals can be asked to monitor various sources of information, such as key magazines, trade journals, and newspapers. These persons can submit periodic scanning reports to a committee of managers charged with performing the external audit. This approach provides a continuous stream of timely strategic information and involves many individuals in the external-audit process. The Internet provides another source for gathering strategic information, as do corporate, university, and public libraries. Suppliers, distributors, salespersons, customers, and competitors represent other sources of vital information.

Once information is gathered, it should be assimilated and evaluated. A meeting or series of meetings of managers is needed to collectively identify the most important opportunities and threats facing the firm. These key external factors should be listed on flip charts or a chalkboard. A prioritized list of these factors could be obtained by requesting that all managers rank the factors identified, from 1 for the most important opportunity/threat to 20 for the least important opportunity/threat. These key external factors can vary over time and by industry. Relationships with suppliers or distributors are often a critical success factor. Other variables commonly used include market share, breadth of competing products, world economies, foreign affiliates, proprietary and key account advantages, price competitiveness, technological advancements, population shifts, interest rates, and pollution abatement.

Freund emphasized that these key external factors should be (1) important to achieving long-term and annual objectives, (2) measurable, (3) applicable to all competing firms, and (4) hierarchical in the sense that some will pertain to the overall company and others will be more narrowly focused on functional or divisional areas.[1] A final list of the most important key external factors should be communicated and distributed widely in the organization. Both opportunities and threats can be key external factors.

The Industrial Organization (I/O) View

The *Industrial Organization (I/O)* approach to competitive advantage advocates that external (industry) factors are more important than internal factors in a firm achieving competitive advantage. Proponents of the I/O view, such as Michael Porter, contend that organizational performance will be primarily determined by industry forces. Porter's Five-Forces Model, presented later in this chapter, is an example of the I/O perspective, which focuses upon analyzing external forces and industry variables as a basis for getting and keeping competitive advantage. Competitive advantage is determined largely by competitive positioning within an industry, according to I/O advocates. Managing strategically from the I/O perspective entails firms striving to compete in attractive industries, avoiding weak or faltering industries, and gaining a full understanding of key external factor relationships within that attractive industry. I/O research was mainly conducted from the 1960s to the 1980s and provided important contributions to our understanding of how to gain competitive advantage.

I/O theorists contend that the industry in which a firm chooses to compete has a stronger influence on the firm's performance than do the internal functional decisions managers make in marketing, finance, and the like. Firm performance, they contend, is primarily based more on industry properties, such as economies of scale, barriers to market entry, product differentiation, and level of competitiveness than on internal resources, capabilities, structure, and operations. Research findings suggest that approximately 20 percent of a firm's profitability can be explained by the industry, whereas 36 percent of the variance in profitability is attributed to the firm's internal factors (see the RBV discussion in the next chapter).[2]

The I/O view has enhanced our understanding of strategic management. However, it is not a question of whether external or internal factors are more important in gaining and maintaining competitive advantage. Effective integration and understanding of *both* external and internal factors is the key to securing and keeping a competitive advantage. In fact, as will be discussed in Chapter 6, matching key external opportunities/threats with key internal strengths/weaknesses provides the basis for successful strategy formulation.

Economic Forces

Increasing numbers of two-income households is an economic trend in the United States. Individuals place a premium on time. Improved customer service, immediate availability, trouble-free operation of products, and dependable maintenance and repair services are becoming more important. People today are more willing than ever to pay for good service if it limits inconvenience.

Economic factors have a direct impact on the potential attractiveness of various strategies. For example, when interest rates rise, funds needed for capital expansion become more costly or unavailable. Also, when interest rates rise, discretionary income declines, and the demand for discretionary goods falls. When stock prices increase, the desirability of equity as a source of capital for market development increases. Also, when the market rises, consumer and business wealth expands. A summary of economic variables that often represent opportunities and threats for organizations is provided in Table 3-1.

Trends in the dollar's value have significant and unequal effects on companies in different industries and in different locations. For example, the pharmaceutical, tourism, entertainment, motor vehicle, aerospace, and forest products industries benefit greatly when the dollar falls against the yen and euro. Agricultural and petroleum industries are hurt by the dollar's rise against the currencies of Mexico, Brazil, Venezuela, and Australia. Generally, a strong or high dollar makes U.S. goods more expensive in overseas markets. This worsens the U.S. trade deficit. When the value of the dollar falls, tourism-oriented firms benefit because Americans do not travel abroad as much when the value of the dollar is low; rather, foreigners visit and vacation more in the United States.

A low value of the dollar means lower imports and higher exports; it helps U.S. companies' competitiveness in world markets. The dollar has fallen to five-year lows against the euro and yen, which makes U.S. goods cheaper to foreign consumers and combats deflation by pushing up prices of imports. However, European firms such as Volkswagen AG, Nokia Corp., and Michelin complain that the strong euro hurts their financial performance. The low value of the dollar benefits the U.S. economy in many ways. First, it helps to stave off the risks of deflation in the United States and also reduces the U.S. trade deficit. In addition, the low value of the dollar raises the foreign sales and profits of domestic firms, thanks to dollar-induced gains, and encourages foreign countries to lower interest rates and loosen fiscal policy, which stimulates worldwide economic expansion. Some sectors, such as consumer staples, energy, materials, technology, and health care, especially benefit from a low value of the dollar. Manufacturers in many domestic industries in fact benefit because of a weak dollar, which forces foreign rivals to raise prices and extinguish discounts. Domestic firms with big overseas sales, such as McDonald's, greatly benefit from a weak dollar.

The country of Slovenia, just east of Italy, adopted the euro in 2007, in what Prime Minister Janez Jansa called the "biggest national achievement" since the country joined the European Union in 2004. Adoption of the common currency is expected to bring macroeconomic stability to the country, increase its exports, and yield productivity gains. A downside, however, is that adoption of the euro means a country such as Slovenia gives up its ability to fix its own interest rates, which could increase inflation and prices within the country.

TABLE 3-1 Key Economic Variables to Be Monitored

Shift to a service economy in the United States	Import/export factors
Availability of credit	Demand shifts for different categories of goods and services
Level of disposable income	Income differences by region and consumer groups
Propensity of people to spend	Price fluctuations
Interest rates	Export of labor and capital from the United States
Inflation rates	Monetary policies
Money market rates	Fiscal policies
Federal government budget deficits	Tax rates
Gross domestic product trend	European Economic Community (EEC) policies
Consumption patterns	Organization of Petroleum Exporting Countries (OPEC) policies
Unemployment trends	Coalitions of Lesser Developed Countries (LDC) policies
Worker productivity levels	
Value of the dollar in world markets	
Stock market trends	
Foreign countries' economic conditions	

Social, Cultural, Demographic, and Environmental Forces

Social, cultural, demographic, and environmental changes have a major impact upon virtually all products, services, markets, and customers. Small, large, for-profit and nonprofit organizations in all industries are being staggered and challenged by the opportunities and threats arising from changes in social, cultural, demographic, and environmental variables. In every way, the United States is much different today than it was yesterday, and tomorrow promises even greater changes.

The United States is getting older and less Caucasian. The oldest members of America's 76 million baby boomers plan to retire in 2011, and this has lawmakers and younger taxpayers deeply concerned about who will pay their Social Security, Medicare, and Medicaid. Individuals age 65 and older in the United States as a percent of the population will rise to 18.5 percent by 2025. The five "oldest" states and five "youngest" states in 2007 are given in Table 3-2.

By the year 2075, the United States will have no racial or ethnic majority. This forecast is aggravating tensions over issues such as immigration and affirmative action. Hawaii, California, and New Mexico already have no majority race or ethnic group.

The seven states with the highest percentage of minorities (African-Americans, Native Americans, Asians, Hispanics, Native Hawaiians) are: Nevada (25 percent), Arizona (20 percent), Georgia (14 percent), Florida (13 percent), Idaho (13 percent), North Carolina (10 percent), and Colorado (10 percent).[3]

The population of the world surpassed 6.8 billion in 2008; the United States has just over 300 million people. That leaves billions of people outside the United States who may be interested in the products and services produced through domestic firms. Remaining solely domestic is an increasingly risky strategy, especially as the world population continues to grow to an estimated 8 billion in 2028 and 9 billion in 2054.

Social, cultural, demographic, and environmental trends are shaping the way Americans live, work, produce, and consume. New trends are creating a different type of consumer and, consequently, a need for different products, different services, and different strategies. There are now more American households with people living alone or with unrelated people than there are households consisting of married couples with children. American households are making more and more purchases online. Beer consumption in the United States is growing at only 0.5 percent per year, whereas wine consumption is growing 3.5 percent and distilled spirits consumption is growing at 2.0 percent.[4] Beer is still the most popular alcoholic beverage in the United States, but its market share has dropped from 59.5 percent in its peak year of 1995 to 56.7 percent today. For a wine company such as Gallo, this trend is an opportunity whereas for a firm such as Adolph Coors Brewing, this trend is an external threat.

The trend toward an older America is good news for restaurants, hotels, airlines, cruise lines, tours, resorts, theme parks, luxury products and services, recreational vehicles, home builders, furniture producers, computer manufacturers, travel services, pharmaceutical

TABLE 3-2 The Oldest and Youngest States by Average Age of Residents

Five Oldest States	Average Age	Five Youngest States	Average Age
Maine	41.1	Utah	28.3
Vermont	40.4	Texas	33.1
West Virginia	40.2	Alaska	33.4
Florida	39.6	Idaho	34.2
Pennsylvania	39.5	California	34.4

Source: Adapted from U.S. Census Bureau. Also, Ken Jackson, "State Population Changes by Race, Ethnicity," *USA Today* (May 17, 2007): 2A.

firms, automakers, and funeral homes. Older Americans are especially interested in health care, financial services, travel, crime prevention, and leisure. The world's longest-living people are the Japanese, with Japanese women living to 86.3 years and men living to 80.1 years on average. By 2050, the Census Bureau projects that the number of Americans age 100 and older will increase to over 834,000 from just under 100,000 centenarians in the United States in 2000. Americans age 65 and over will increase from 12.6 percent of the U.S. population in 2000 to 20.0 percent by the year 2050.

The aging American population affects the strategic orientation of nearly all organizations. Apartment complexes for the elderly, with one meal a day, transportation, and utilities included in the rent, have increased nationwide. Called *lifecare facilities,* these complexes now exceed 2 million. Some well-known companies building these facilities include Avon, Marriott, and Hyatt. Individuals age 65 and older in the United States comprise 13 percent of the total population; Japan's elderly population ratio is 17 percent, and Germany's is 19 percent.

Americans are on the move in a population shift to the South and West (Sunbelt) and away from the Northeast and Midwest (Frostbelt). The Internal Revenue Service provides the Census Bureau with massive computer files of demographic data. By comparing individual address changes from year to year, the Census Bureau publishes extensive information about population shifts across the country. All of these facts represent major opportunities and threats for some companies. For example, the four fastest growing states in rank order are Arizona, Nevada, Idaho, Georgia, and Texas, whereas four states (Louisiana, Rhode Island, New York, Michigan) and Washington, D.C. lost residents in 2006. In the Northeast, New York, New Jersey, and Massachusetts continue to lose large numbers of people to other states. In the Midwest, the big losers of residents annually are Illinois, Michigan, and Ohio. The fastest growing large metropolitan areas in the United States are Dallas–Fort Worth, Houston, Atlanta, Phoenix, Las Vegas, and Riverside, California.[5] Hard number data related to this information can represent key opportunities for many firms and thus can be essential for successful strategy formulation, including where to locate new plants and distribution centers and where to focus marketing efforts.

Except for terrorism, no greater threat to business and society exists than the voracious, continuous decimation and degradation of our natural environment. The U.S. Clean Air Act went into effect in 1994. The U.S. Clean Water Act went into effect in 1984. A summary of important social, cultural, demographic, and environmental variables that represent opportunities or threats for virtually all organizations is given in Table 3-3.

Political, Governmental, and Legal Forces

Federal, state, local, and foreign governments are major regulators, deregulators, subsidizers, employers, and customers of organizations. Political, governmental, and legal factors, therefore, can represent key opportunities or threats for both small and large organizations.

For industries and firms that depend heavily on government contracts or subsidies, political forecasts can be the most important part of an external audit. Changes in patent laws, antitrust legislation, tax rates, and lobbying activities can affect firms significantly. The U.S. Justice Department offers excellent information at its Web site (www.usdoj.gov) on such topics.

In the world of biopolitics, Americans are still deeply divided over issues such as assisted suicide, genetic testing, genetic engineering, cloning, stem-cell research, and abortion.

As indicated in the Natural Environment Perspective, American business leaders are also divided on their support for the Kyoto Protocol to cap emissions from industrialized nations. The Kyoto Protocol expires in 2012.

The increasing global interdependence among economies, markets, governments, and organizations makes it imperative that firms consider the possible impact of political variables on the formulation and implementation of competitive strategies.

In Europe, many large multinational firms such as John Deere, Polo Ralph Lauren, Gillette, Cargill, and General Mills are moving their headquarters from France,

TABLE 3-3   **Key Social, Cultural, Demographic, and Environmental Variables**

Childbearing rates	Attitudes toward retirement
Number of special-interest groups	Attitudes toward leisure time
Number of marriages	Attitudes toward product quality
Number of divorces	Attitudes toward customer service
Number of births	Pollution control
Number of deaths	Attitudes toward foreign peoples
Immigration and emigration rates	Energy conservation
Social Security programs	Social programs
Life expectancy rates	Number of churches
Per capita income	Number of church members
Location of retailing, manufacturing, and service businesses	Social responsibility
Attitudes toward business	Attitudes toward careers
Lifestyles	Population changes by race, age, sex, and level of affluence
Traffic congestion	Attitudes toward authority
Inner-city environments	Population changes by city, county, state, region, and country
Average disposable income	Value placed on leisure time
Trust in government	Regional changes in tastes and preferences
Attitudes toward government	Number of women and minority workers
Attitudes toward work	Number of high school and college graduates by geographic area
Buying habits	Recycling
Ethical concerns	Waste management
Attitudes toward saving	Air pollution
Sex roles	Water pollution
Attitudes toward investing	Ozone depletion
Racial equality	Endangered species
Use of birth control	
Average level of education	
Government regulation	

Netherlands, and Germany to Switzerland and Ireland to avoid costs associated with *tax harmonization*—a term that refers to the EU's effort to end competitive tax breaks among member countries. Although the EU strives to standardize tax breaks, member countries vigorously defend their right to politically and legally set their own tax rates. Behind Switzerland as the most attractive European location for corporations, Ireland keeps its corporate tax rates low, which is why Ingersoll-Rand recently moved much of its operations there. About 650 U.S. companies already have operations in Switzerland.

The European Union celebrated its 51st anniversary in 2008, but the 27 member countries have agreed not to allow any other countries to join until 2010. The Union desires to get all member countries on board with signing of its constitution and also desires more trade between member countries. A recent report by Bruegel, a think tank in Brussels, reveals that member EU countries still spend 86 percent of their income on goods and services made at home and just 10 percent on those from other EU countries. France wants Europe's social welfare model included in the EU constitution, others do not. Poland wants Christianity mentioned, others such as France do not. Britain says the word "constitution" cannot be used, others disagree. And Italy was voted into the EU with a public debt of more than 120 percent of gross domestic product, twice the ratio allowed under EU rules. Some countries that have petitioned to be admitted to the EU include Ukraine, Georgia, Croatia, Turkey, and Macedonia.

NATURAL ENVIRONMENT PERSPECTIVE
American Business Leaders Pushing for Legislation on Climate Change

General Electric's (GE) Jeffrey Immelt, Dupont's Chad Holliday, and Duke Energy's Jim Rogers are driving forces in Washington, D.C. behind a group of ten CEOs who are pressuring Congress, the Business Roundtable, and the government to cap greenhouse-gas emissions. Emission caps are already in place in Europe and California. American business leaders have generally come about-face and now support legislation to curb emissions and global warming, even though the coal industry, oil industry, and a few politicians still oppose such efforts. GE says it has a $20 billion backlog of orders for its "ecomagination" products, which include fuel-efficient jet engines and locomotives, wind turbines, and compact fluorescent light bulbs. Alcoa, Caterpillar, and Toyota also are companies making excellent progress on natural environment issues and lobbying other firms to do likewise.

Carbon dioxide, the main greenhouse gas, is produced when fossil fuels such as coal, oil, and natural gas are burned. However, even the Electric Power Supply Association, which represents about one-third of U.S. power generation, now lobbies legislators to enact legislation to cap emissions. Business leaders desire a single national emissions cap to take precedence over different state emission caps that are emerging. Even Exxon Mobil, a long-time opponent of government curbs on global-warming emissions, has ceased verbal and monetary opposition and now is trying to influence the nature of such curbs. Still, both Exxon and the U.S. government oppose the Kyoto Protocol, the global-warming treaty that caps emissions from industrialized nations.

Even the airline industry, including both airports and air carriers, is feeling pressure to reduce pollution. Every year the industry discards more than 6,000 tons of aluminum cans, 9,000 tons of plastic, and enough newspapers and magazines to fill a football field to a depth of 230 feet. Airport and air carrier recycling programs are generally underdeveloped because both ports and carriers are preoccupied with security and finances. Airliners emit carbon dioxide and nitrogen oxides high in the atmosphere and both gases contribute to global warming.

Among states, California leads the way in pushing for high environmental standards. New California laws mandate that 20 percent of the state's energy supply is to come from renewable resources, such as wind and solar power, by 2010. Unfortunately, however, California

The Purcell Mountains in Alberta, Canada.
Source: Peter Wilson (c) Dorling Kindersley

state law still prohibits construction of more nuclear plants even though they emit no greenhouse gases.

Among companies, the top five buyers of green power, purchased by total kilowatt hours and as a percentage of their total purchased electricity use, are PepsiCo, Wells Fargo, Whole Foods, U.S. Air Force, and Johnson & Johnson. Both PepsiCo and organic grocer Whole Foods get 100 percent of their power from green sources such as wind, solar, hydroelectric, and nuclear.

Sources: Adapted from Alan Murray, "Why Key Executives Are Warming to Legislation on Climate Change," *Wall Street Journal* (February 7, 2007): A10; Jeffrey Ball, "Electric Industry to Call for Cap on Emissions," *Wall Street Journal* (February 7, 2007): A4; Susan Carey, "Airlines Feel Pressure as Pollution Fight Takes Off," *Wall Street Journal* (December 12, 2006): A6; Rebecca Smith, "California Kindles Green Energy," *Wall Street Journal* (December 26, 2006): A2; John Fialka and Kathryn Kranhold, "GE Fights EPA's Tougher Smog Proposals," *Wall Street Journal* (February 13, 2007): A2; and Bruce Horovitz, "PepsiCo Takes Top Spot in Global Warming Battle," *USA Today* (April 30, 2007): B1.

TABLE 3-4 Some Political, Governmental, and Legal Variables

Government regulations or deregulations	Sino-American relationships
Changes in tax laws	Russian-American relationships
Special tariffs	European-American relationships
Political action committees	African-American relationships
Voter participation rates	Import–export regulations
Number, severity, and location of government protests	Government fiscal and monetary policy changes
Number of patents	Political conditions in foreign countries
Changes in patent laws	Special local, state, and federal laws
Environmental protection laws	Lobbying activities
Level of defense expenditures	Size of government budgets
Legislation on equal employment	World oil, currency, and labor markets
Level of government subsidies	Location and severity of terrorist activities
Antitrust legislation	Local, state, and national elections

Political relations between Japan and China have thawed considerably in recent years, which is good for the world economy because China's low-cost manufactured goods have become essential for the functioning of most industrialized nations. China's Premier Wen Jiabao addressed the Japanese parliament in April 2007, something no Chinese leader has done for more than twenty years, and Japanese Prime Minister Shinzo Abe has visited Beijing. Japan's largest trading partner is China, and China's third-largest trading partner is Japan—after the European Union, number one, and the United States, number two.

A world market has emerged from what previously was a multitude of distinct national markets, and the climate for international business today is much more favorable than yesterday. Mass communication and high technology are creating similar patterns of consumption in diverse cultures worldwide. This means that many companies may find it difficult to survive by relying solely on domestic markets.

> It is no exaggeration that in an industry that is, or is rapidly becoming, global, the riskiest possible posture is to remain a domestic competitor. The domestic competitor will watch as more aggressive companies use this growth to capture economies of scale and learning. The domestic competitor will then be faced with an attack on domestic markets using different (and possibly superior) technology, product design, manufacturing, marketing approaches, and economies of scale. A few examples suggest how extensive the phenomenon of world markets has already become. Hewlett-Packard's manufacturing chain reaches halfway around the globe, from well-paid, skilled engineers in California to low-wage assembly workers in Malaysia. General Electric has survived as a manufacturer of inexpensive audio products by centralizing its world production in Singapore.[6]

Local, state, and federal laws; regulatory agencies; and special-interest groups can have a major impact on the strategies of small, large, for-profit, and nonprofit organizations. Many companies have altered or abandoned strategies in the past because of political or governmental actions. A summary of political, governmental, and legal variables that can represent key opportunities or threats to organizations is provided in Table 3-4.

Technological Forces

Revolutionary technological changes and discoveries are having a dramatic impact on organizations. Superconductivity advancements alone, which increase the power of electrical products by lowering resistance to current, are revolutionizing business operations, especially in the transportation, utility, health care, electrical, and computer industries.

The *Internet* is acting as a national and global economic engine that is spurring productivity, a critical factor in a country's ability to improve living standards; and it is saving companies billions of dollars in distribution and transaction costs from direct sales to self-service systems.

The Internet is changing the very nature of opportunities and threats by altering the life cycles of products, increasing the speed of distribution, creating new products and services, erasing limitations of traditional geographic markets, and changing the historical trade-off between production standardization and flexibility. The Internet is altering economies of scale, changing entry barriers, and redefining the relationship between industries and various suppliers, creditors, customers, and competitors.

To effectively capitalize on e-commerce, a number of organizations are establishing two new positions in their firms: *chief information officer (CIO)* and *chief technology officer (CTO)*. This trend reflects the growing importance of *information technology (IT)* in strategic management. A CIO and CTO work together to ensure that information needed to formulate, implement, and evaluate strategies is available where and when it is needed. These individuals are responsible for developing, maintaining, and updating a company's information database. The CIO is more a manager, managing the overall external-audit process; the CTO is more a technician, focusing on technical issues such as data acquisition, data processing, decision-support systems, and software and hardware acquisition.

Technological forces represent major opportunities and threats that must be considered in formulating strategies. Technological advancements can dramatically affect organizations' products, services, markets, suppliers, distributors, competitors, customers, manufacturing processes, marketing practices, and competitive position. Technological advancements can create new markets, result in a proliferation of new and improved products, change the relative competitive cost positions in an industry, and render existing products and services obsolete. Technological changes can reduce or eliminate cost barriers between businesses, create shorter production runs, create shortages in technical skills, and result in changing values and expectations of employees, managers, and customers. Technological advancements can create new competitive advantages that are more powerful than existing advantages. No company or industry today is insulated against emerging technological developments. In high-tech industries, identification and evaluation of key technological opportunities and threats can be the most important part of the external strategic-management audit.

Organizations that traditionally have limited technology expenditures to what they can fund after meeting marketing and financial requirements urgently need a reversal in thinking. The pace of technological change is increasing and literally wiping out businesses every day. An emerging consensus holds that technology management is one of the key responsibilities of strategists. Firms should pursue strategies that take advantage of technological opportunities to achieve sustainable, competitive advantages in the marketplace.

> Technology-based issues will underlie nearly every important decision that strategists make. Crucial to those decisions will be the ability to approach technology planning analytically and strategically. . . . technology can be planned and managed using formal techniques similar to those used in business and capital investment planning. An effective technology strategy is built on a penetrating analysis of technology opportunities and threats, and an assessment of the relative importance of these factors to overall corporate strategy.[7]

In practice, critical decisions about technology too often are delegated to lower organizational levels or are made without an understanding of their strategic implications. Many strategists spend countless hours determining market share, positioning products in terms of features and price, forecasting sales and market size, and monitoring distributors; yet too often, technology does not receive the same respect.

Not all sectors of the economy are affected equally by technological developments. The communications, electronics, aeronautics, and pharmaceutical industries are much more volatile than the textile, forestry, and metals industries. For strategists in industries affected by rapid technological change, identifying and evaluating technological opportunities and threats can represent the most important part of an external audit.

For example, in the office supply industry, business customers find that purchasing supplies over the Internet is more convenient than shopping in a store. Office Depot was the first office supply company to establish a Web site for this purpose and remains the largest Internet office supply retailer, with close to $1 billion in sales. Staples, Inc., has recently also entered the Internet office supply business with its staples.com Web site, but it has yet to make a profit on these operations, although revenue from the site is growing dramatically.

Competitive Forces

VISIT THE NET

Provides information regarding the importance of gathering information about competitors. This Web site offers audio answers to key questions about intelligence systems. (www.fuld.com)

The top five U.S. competitors in four different industries are identified in Table 3-5. An important part of an external audit is identifying rival firms and determining their strengths, weaknesses, capabilities, opportunities, threats, objectives, and strategies.

Collecting and evaluating information on competitors is essential for successful strategy formulation. Identifying major competitors is not always easy because many firms have divisions that compete in different industries. Many multidivisional firms generally do not provide sales and profit information on a divisional basis for competitive reasons. Also, privately held firms do not publish any financial or marketing information. Addressing questions about competitors such as those presented in Table 3-6 is important in performing an external audit.

Competition in virtually all industries can be described as intense—and sometimes as cutthroat. For example, when Circuit City falters its major competitor, Best Buy, cuts prices, adds stores, and increases advertising aimed to further its rival's demise. Best Buy is opening 130 new stores in 2007, many near Circuit City stores, while Circuit City is closing underperforming stores, considering a sale of its 510-store chain in Canada, and

TABLE 3-5   The Top U.S. Five Competitors in Four Different Industries in 2006

	2006 Sales (In Millions)	% Change from 2005	2006 Profits (In Millions)	% Change from 2005
	Beverages			
Coca-Cola	24,088	+4	5,080	+4
Pepsi Bottling	12,730	+7	522	+12
Coca-Cola Enterprises	19,804	+6	(1,143)	−322
Anheuser-Busch	15,717	+5	1,965	+7
Molson Coors Brewing	5,903	+3	361	+168
	Pharmaceuticals			
Johnson & Johnson	53,324	+6	11,053	+6
Pfizer	52,415	+2	19,337	+139
Merck	22,636	+3	4,434	−4
Abbott Laboratories	22,476	+1	1,717	−49
Wyeth	20,351	+9	4,197	+15
	Industrial and Farm Equipment			
Caterpillar	41,517	+14	3,537	+24
Deere	22,769	+4	1,694	+17
Illinois Tool Works	14,055	+9	1,718	+15
Eaton	12,370	+11	950	+18
Cummins	11,362	+15	715	+30
	Computers			
Hewlett-Packard	91,658	+6	6,198	+158
IBM	91,424	+0	9,492	+20
Dell	57,095	+2	2,614	−27
Xerox	15,895	+1	1,210	+24
Apple Computer	19,315	+9	2,614	+50

Source: Adapted from *Fortune*, April 30, 2007, F50–F73.

TABLE 3-6   Key Questions About Competitors

1. What are the major competitors' strengths?

2. What are the major competitors' weaknesses?

3. What are the major competitors' objectives and strategies?

4. How will the major competitors most likely respond to current economic, social, cultural, demographic, environmental, political, governmental, legal, technological, and competitive trends affecting our industry?

5. How vulnerable are the major competitors to our alternative company strategies?

6. How vulnerable are our alternative strategies to successful counterattack by our major competitors?

7. How are our products or services positioned relative to major competitors?

8. To what extent are new firms entering and old firms leaving this industry?

9. What key factors have resulted in our present competitive position in this industry?

10. How have the sales and profit rankings of major competitors in the industry changed over recent years? Why have these rankings changed that way?

11. What is the nature of supplier and distributor relationships in this industry?

12. To what extent could substitute products or services be a threat to competitors in this industry?

laying off another 3,400 employees in fiscal 2007. Best Buy's first-quarter 2007 profits were up 18 percent, while Circuit City again lost money.

As Dollar General, based in Goodlettsville, Tennessee, falters its major competitor, Family Dollar Stores, based in Matthews, North Carolina, intensifies its efforts to cripple Dollar General. With 6,300 stores and $6.4 billion in annual sales, the smaller Family Dollar Stores is rapidly gaining on Dollar General, an 8,260-store chain with $9.2 billion in annual sales. Whereas Dollar General is closing stores, revamping inventory strategy, and laying off employees, Family Dollar is growing and practicing "zone pricing"—raising or lowering prices on given items at given stores to capitalize on competitive pressure. Dollar General uses "uniform pricing," which refers to consistent prices from store to store. Weakened, Dollar General was bought out by Kohlberg Kravis Roberts in 2007. If a firm detects weakness in a competitor, no mercy at all is shown in capitalizing on its problems.

Seven characteristics describe the most competitive companies:

1. Market share matters; the 90th share point isn't as important as the 91st, and nothing is more dangerous than falling to 89.

2. Understand and remember precisely what business you are in.

3. Whether it's broke or not, fix it—make it better; not just products, but the whole company, if necessary.

4. Innovate or evaporate; particularly in technology-driven businesses, nothing quite recedes like success.

5. Acquisition is essential to growth; the most successful purchases are in niches that add a technology or a related market.

6. People make a difference; tired of hearing it? Too bad.

7. There is no substitute for quality and no greater threat than failing to be cost-competitive on a global basis.

These are complementary concepts, not mutually exclusive ones.[8]

Competitive Intelligence Programs

What is competitive intelligence? *Competitive intelligence (CI),* as formally defined by the Society of Competitive Intelligence Professionals (SCIP), is a systematic and ethical process for gathering and analyzing information about the competition's activities and general business trends to further a business's own goals (SCIP Web site).

Good competitive intelligence in business, as in the military, is one of the keys to success. The more information and knowledge a firm can obtain about its competitors, the more likely it is that it can formulate and implement effective strategies. Major competitors' weaknesses can represent external opportunities; major competitors' strengths may represent key threats.

According to *BusinessWeek,* there are more than 5,000 corporate spies now actively engaged in intelligence activities, and 9 out of 10 large companies have employees dedicated solely to gathering competitive intelligence.[9] The article contends that many large U.S. companies spend more than $1 million annually tracking their competitors. Evidence suggests that the benefits of corporate spying include increased revenues, lower costs, and better decision making.

Unfortunately, the majority of U.S. executives grew up in times when U.S. firms dominated foreign competitors so much that gathering competitive intelligence did not seem worth the effort. Too many of these executives still cling to these attitudes—to the detriment of their organizations today. Even most MBA programs do not offer a course in competitive and business intelligence, thus reinforcing this attitude. As a consequence, three strong misperceptions about business intelligence prevail among U.S. executives today:

1. Running an intelligence program requires lots of people, computers, and other resources.
2. Collecting intelligence about competitors violates antitrust laws; business intelligence equals espionage.
3. Intelligence gathering is an unethical business practice.[10]

All three of these perceptions are totally misguided. Any discussions with a competitor about price, market, or geography intentions could violate antitrust statutes, but this fact must not lure a firm into underestimating the need for and benefits of systematically collecting information about competitors for the purpose of enhancing a firm's effectiveness. The Internet has become an excellent medium for gathering competitive intelligence. Information gathering from employees, managers, suppliers, distributors, customers, creditors, and consultants also can make the difference between having superior or just average intelligence and overall competitiveness.

Firms need an effective competitive intelligence (CI) program. The three basic missions of a CI program are (1) to provide a general understanding of an industry and its competitors, (2) to identify areas in which competitors are vulnerable and to assess the impact strategic actions would have on competitors, and (3) to identify potential moves that a competitor might make that would endanger a firm's position in the market.[11] Competitive information is equally applicable for strategy formulation, implementation, and evaluation decisions. An effective CI program allows all areas of a firm to access consistent and verifiable information in making decisions. All members of an organization—from the chief executive officer to custodians—are valuable intelligence agents and should feel themselves to be a part of the CI process. Special characteristics of a successful CI program include flexibility, usefulness, timeliness, and cross-functional cooperation.

The increasing emphasis on *competitive analysis* in the United States is evidenced by corporations putting this function on their organizational charts under job titles such as Director of Competitive Analysis, Competitive Strategy Manager, Director of Information Services, or Associate Director of Competitive Assessment. The responsibilities of a *director of competitive analysis* include planning, collecting data, analyzing data, facilitating the process of gathering and analyzing data, disseminating intelligence on a timely basis, researching special issues, and recognizing what information is important and who needs to know. Competitive intelligence is not corporate espionage because 95 percent of the information a company needs to make strategic decisions is available and accessible to the public. Sources of competitive information include trade journals, want ads, newspaper articles, and government filings, as well as customers, suppliers, distributors, competitors themselves, and the Internet.

Unethical tactics such as bribery, wiretapping, and computer break-ins should never be used to obtain information. Marriott and Motorola—two U.S. companies that do a particularly good job of gathering competitive intelligence—agree that all the information you could wish for can be collected without resorting to unethical tactics. They keep their intelligence staffs small, usually under five people, and spend less than $200,000 per year on gathering competitive intelligence.

Unilever recently sued Procter & Gamble (P&G) over that company's corporate-espionage activities to obtain the secrets of its Unilever hair-care business. After spending

VISIT THE NET

Describes the nature and role of strategic planning in a firm. (www. nonprofits.org/npofaq/03/22.html)

$3 million to establish a team to find out about competitors in the domestic hair-care industry, P&G allegedly took roughly 80 documents from garbage bins outside Unilever's Chicago offices. P&G produces Pantene and Head & Shoulders shampoos, while Unilver has hair-care brands such as ThermaSilk, Suave, Salon Selectives, and Finesse. Similarly, Oracle Corp. recently admitted that detectives it hired paid janitors to go through Microsoft Corp.'s garbage, looking for evidence to use in court.

An interesting aspect of any competitive analysis discussion is whether strategies themselves should be secret or open within firms. The Chinese warrior Sun Tzu and military leaders today strive to keep strategies secret, as war is based on deception. However, for a business organization, secrecy may not be best. Keeping strategies secret from employees and stakeholders at large could severely inhibit employee and stakeholder communication, understanding, and commitment and also forgo valuable input that these persons could have regarding formulation and/or implementation of that strategy. Thus strategists in a particular firm must decide for themselves whether the risk of rival firms easily knowing and exploiting a firm's strategies is worth the benefit of improved employee and stakeholder motivation and input. Most executives agree that some strategic information should remain confidential to top managers, and that steps should be taken to ensure that such information is not disseminated beyond the inner circle. For a firm that you may own or manage, would you advocate openness or secrecy in regard to strategies being formulated and implemented?

Cooperation Among Competitors

VISIT THE NET

Gives 30+ pages of excellent detail on "Developing a Business Strategy." (www.planware.org/strategy.htm)

Strategies that stress cooperation among competitors are being used more. For example, Lockheed teamed up with British Aerospace PLC to compete against Boeing Company to develop the next-generation U.S. fighter jet. Lockheed's cooperative strategy with a profitable partner in the Airbus Industrie consortium encourages broader Lockheed–European collaboration as Europe's defense industry consolidates. The British firm offers Lockheed special expertise in the areas of short takeoff and vertical landing technologies, systems integration, and low-cost design and manufacturing.

Cooperative agreements between competitors are even becoming popular. For collaboration between competitors to succeed, both firms must contribute something distinctive, such as technology, distribution, basic research, or manufacturing capacity. But a major risk is that unintended transfers of important skills or technology may occur at organizational levels below where the deal was signed.[12] Information not covered in the formal agreement often gets traded in the day-to-day interactions and dealings of engineers, marketers, and product developers. Firms often give away too much information to rival firms when operating under cooperative agreements! Tighter formal agreements are needed.

Perhaps the best example of rival firms in an industry forming alliances to compete against each other is the airline industry. Today there are three major alliances. The Star Alliance has 16 airlines such as Air Canada, Mexicana, Spanair, United, and Varig; the OneWorld Alliance has 8 airlines such as American, British Air, and LanChile; and finally, SkyTeam Alliance has 6 airlines such as Air France, Delta, and Korean Air. KLM is set to join SkyTeam soon, Swiss International is scheduled to join OneWorld, and USAirways is scheduled to join Star Alliance. Firms are moving to compete as groups within alliances more and more as it becomes increasingly difficult to survive alone in some industries.

The idea of joining forces with a competitor is not easily accepted by Americans, who often view cooperation and partnerships with skepticism and suspicion. Indeed, joint ventures and cooperative arrangements among competitors demand a certain amount of trust if companies are to combat paranoia about whether one firm will injure the other. However, multinational firms are becoming more globally cooperative, and increasing numbers of domestic firms are joining forces with competitive foreign firms to reap mutual benefits. Kathryn Harrigan at Columbia University says, "Within a decade, most companies will be members of teams that compete against each other." Northrop Grumman is planning to partner with Airbus parent EADS in Europe to battle Boeing for a Pentagon contract for aerial-refueling planes. These talks are ongoing at this time. EADS is a French/German company but is perceived widely as French because Airbus planes are assembled in France. Northrop is based in Los Angeles.

U.S. companies often enter alliances primarily to avoid investments, being more interested in reducing the costs and risks of entering new businesses or markets than in acquiring new skills. In contrast, *learning from the partner* is a major reason why Asian and European firms enter into cooperative agreements. U.S. firms, too, should place learning high on the list of reasons to be cooperative with competitors. U.S. companies often form alliances with Asian firms to gain an understanding of their manufacturing excellence, but Asian competence in this area is not easily transferable. Manufacturing excellence is a complex system that includes employee training and involvement, integration with suppliers, statistical process controls, value engineering, and design. In contrast, U.S. know-how in technology and related areas can be imitated more easily. U.S. firms thus need to be careful not to give away more intelligence than they receive in cooperative agreements with rival Asian firms.

Market Commonality and Resource Similarity

By definition, competitors are firms that offer similar products and services in the same market. Markets can be geographic or product areas or segments. For example, in the insurance industry the markets are broken down into commercial/consumer, health/life, and Europe/Asia. Researchers use the terms *market commonality* and *resource similarity* to study rivalry among competitors. *Market commonality* can be defined as the number and significance of markets that a firm competes in with rivals.[13] *Resource similarity* is the extent to which the type and amount of a firm's internal resources are comparable to a rival.[14] One way to analyze competitiveness between two or among several firms is to investigate market commonality and resource similarity issues while looking for areas of potential competitive advantage along each firm's value chain.

Competitive Analysis: Porter's Five-Forces Model

As illustrated in Figure 3-3, *Porter's Five-Forces Model* of competitive analysis is a widely used approach for developing strategies in many industries. The intensity of competition among firms varies widely across industries. Table 3-7 reveals the average profit margin and return on investment for firms in different industries. Note the substantial variation among industries. For example, the range in profit margin goes from 0 to 18 for food production to computer software, respectively. Intensity of competition is highest in lower-return industries. The collective impact of competitive forces is so brutal in some industries that the market is clearly "unattractive" from a profit-making standpoint. Rivalry among existing firms is severe, new rivals can enter the industry with relative

FIGURE 3-3

The Five-Forces Model of Competition

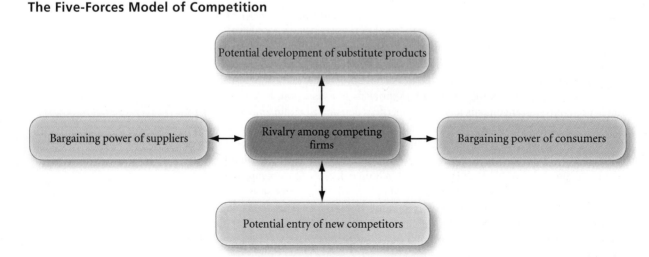

TABLE 3-7 **Intensity of Competition among Firms in Different Industries (A through H industries only)**

Industry	Profit Margin	Return on Investment
Aerospace and Defense	6	6
Airlines	2	2
Apparel	5	8
Automotive Retailing	1	3
Beverages	7	4
Building Materials, Glass	14	14
Chemicals	5	5
Commercial Banks	16	1.3
Computer Peripherals	8	7
Computer Software	18	8
Computers, Office Equipment	6	7
Diversified Financials	12	1
Diversified Outsourcing Services	4	5
Electronics, Electrical Equipment	7	8
Energy	3	3
Engineering, Construction	2	4
Entertainment	10	4
Financial Data Services	10	6
Food and Drug Stores	2	5
Food Consumer Products	5	6
Food Production	0	1
Food Services	4	7
Forest and Paper Products	3	4
Furniture	5	7
General Merchandisers	3	5
Health Care: Insurance	5	8
Health Care: Medical Facilities	4	4
Health Care: Pharmacy	3	9
Home Equipment/Furnishings	4	6
Homebuilders	6	6
Hotels, Casinos, Resorts	7	3

Source: Adapted from John Moore, "Ranked Within Industries," *Fortune* (April 30, 2007): F-50 to F-75.

ease, and both suppliers and customers can exercise considerable bargaining leverage. According to Porter, the nature of competitiveness in a given industry can be viewed as a composite of five forces:

1. Rivalry among competing firms
2. Potential entry of new competitors
3. Potential development of substitute products
4. Bargaining power of suppliers
5. Bargaining power of consumers

The following three steps for using Porter's Five-Forces Model can reveal whether competition in a given industry is such that the firm can make an acceptable profit:

1. Identify key aspects or elements of each competitive force that impact the firm.
2. Evaluate how strong and important each element is for the firm.
3. Decide whether the collective strength of the elements is worth the firm entering or staying in the industry.

VISIT THE NET

Gives good information about why employees may resist change. (http://www.mindtools.com/)

Rivalry Among Competing Firms

Rivalry among competing firms is usually the most powerful of the five competitive forces. The strategies pursued by one firm can be successful only to the extent that they provide competitive advantage over the strategies pursued by rival firms. Changes in strategy by one firm may be met with retaliatory countermoves, such as lowering prices, enhancing quality, adding features, providing services, extending warranties, and increasing advertising.

Free-flowing information on the Internet is driving down prices and inflation worldwide. The Internet, coupled with the common currency in Europe, enables consumers to make price comparisons easily across countries. Just for a moment, consider the implications for car dealers who used to know everything about a new car's pricing, while you, the consumer, knew very little. You could bargain, but being in the dark, you rarely could win. Now you can go to Web sites such as CarPoint.com or Edmunds.com and learn more about new car prices than the car salesperson, and you can even shop online in a few hours at every dealership within 500 miles to find the best price and terms. So you, the consumer, can win. This is true in many, if not most, business-to-consumer and business-to-business sales transactions today.

The intensity of rivalry among competing firms tends to increase as the number of competitors increases, as competitors become more equal in size and capability, as demand for the industry's products declines, and as price cutting becomes common. Rivalry also increases when consumers can switch brands easily; when barriers to leaving the market are high; when fixed costs are high; when the product is perishable; when consumer demand is growing slowly or declines such that rivals have excess capacity and/or inventory; when the products being sold are commodities (not easily differentiated such as gasoline); when rival firms are diverse in strategies, origins, and culture; and when mergers and acquisitions are common in the industry. As rivalry among competing firms intensifies, industry profits decline, in some cases to the point where an industry becomes inherently unattractive.

Rivalry in the automobile industry is fierce. As Ford and General Motors' market shares steadily decline, Toyota and Honda have stepped up their marketing and production efforts in the United States. Toyota is currently building its eighth North American assembly plant, in the southeast United States. Toyota's new plant starts production in 2009 and has a capacity of 200,000 vehicles annually. Ford and GM are both losing money in their North American auto operations. When rival firms sense weakness, typically they will intensify both marketing and production efforts to capitalize on the "opportunity."

Potential Entry of New Competitors

Whenever new firms can easily enter a particular industry, the intensity of competitiveness among firms increases. Barriers to entry, however, can include the need to gain economies of scale quickly, the need to gain technology and specialized know-how, the lack of experience, strong customer loyalty, strong brand preferences, large capital requirements, lack of adequate distribution channels, government regulatory policies, tariffs, lack of access to raw materials, possession of patents, undesirable locations, counterattack by entrenched firms, and potential saturation of the market.

Despite numerous barriers to entry, new firms sometimes enter industries with higher-quality products, lower prices, and substantial marketing resources. The strategist's job, therefore, is to identify potential new firms entering the market, to monitor the new rival firms' strategies, to counterattack as needed, and to capitalize on existing strengths and opportunities. When the threat of new firms entering the market is strong, incumbent firms generally fortify their positions and take actions to deter new entrants, such as lowering prices, extending warranties, adding features, or offering financing specials.

Potential Development of Substitute Products

In many industries, firms are in close competition with producers of substitute products in other industries. Examples are plastic container producers competing with glass, paperboard, and aluminum can producers, and acetaminophen manufacturers competing with other manufacturers of pain and headache remedies. The presence of substitute products puts a ceiling on the price that can be charged before consumers will switch to the substitute product. Price ceilings equate to profit ceilings and more intense competition among rivals. Producers of eyeglasses and contact lenses, for example, face increasing competitive pressures from laser eye surgery. Producers of sugar face similar pressures from artificial sweeteners. Newspapers and magazines face substitute-product competitive pressures from the Internet and 24-hour cable television. The magnitude of competitive pressure derived from development of substitute products is generally evidenced by rivals' plans for expanding production capacity, as well as by their sales and profit growth numbers.

Competitive pressures arising from substitute products increase as the relative price of substitute products declines and as consumers' switching costs decrease. The competitive strength of substitute products is best measured by the inroads into the market share those products obtain, as well as those firms' plans for increased capacity and market penetration.

Bargaining Power of Suppliers

The bargaining power of suppliers affects the intensity of competition in an industry, especially when there is a large number of suppliers, when there are only a few good substitute raw materials, or when the cost of switching raw materials is especially costly. It is often in the best interest of both suppliers and producers to assist each other with reasonable prices, improved quality, development of new services, just-in-time deliveries, and reduced inventory costs, thus enhancing long-term profitability for all concerned.

Firms may pursue a backward integration strategy to gain control or ownership of suppliers. This strategy is especially effective when suppliers are unreliable, too costly, or not capable of meeting a firm's needs on a consistent basis. Firms generally can negotiate more favorable terms with suppliers when backward integration is a commonly used strategy among rival firms in an industry.

However, in many industries it is more economical to use outside suppliers of component parts than to self-manufacture the items. This is true, for example, in the outdoor power equipment industry where producers of lawn mowers, rotary tillers, leaf blowers, and edgers such as Murray generally obtain their small engines from outside manufacturers such as Briggs & Stratton who specialize in such engines and have huge economies of scale.

In more and more industries, sellers are forging strategic partnerships with select suppliers in efforts to (1) reduce inventory and logistics costs (e.g., through just-in-time deliveries); (2) speed the availability of next-generation components; (3) enhance the quality of the parts and components being supplied and reduce defect rates; and (4) squeeze out important cost savings for both themselves and their suppliers.[15]

Bargaining Power of Consumers

When customers are concentrated or large or buy in volume, their bargaining power represents a major force affecting the intensity of competition in an industry. Rival firms may offer extended warranties or special services to gain customer loyalty whenever the bargaining power of consumers is substantial. Bargaining power of consumers also is higher when the products being purchased are standard or undifferentiated. When this is the case, consumers often can negotiate selling price, warranty coverage, and accessory packages to a greater extent.

The bargaining power of consumers can be the most important force affecting competitive advantage. Consumers gain increasing bargaining power under the following circumstances:

1. If they can inexpensively switch to competing brands or substitutes
2. If they are particularly important to the seller
3. If sellers are struggling in the face of falling consumer demand
4. If they are informed about sellers' products, prices, and costs
5. If they have discretion in whether and when they purchase the product[16]

Sources of External Information

A wealth of strategic information is available to organizations from both published and unpublished sources. Unpublished sources include customer surveys, market research, speeches at professional and shareholders' meetings, television programs, interviews, and conversations with stakeholders. Published sources of strategic information include periodicals, journals, reports, government documents, abstracts, books, directories, newspapers, and manuals. The Internet has made it easier for firms to gather, assimilate, and evaluate information.

The Internet offers consumers and businesses a widening range of services and information resources from all over the world. Interactive services offer users not only access to information worldwide but also the ability to communicate with the person or company that created the information. Historical barriers to personal and business success—time zones and diverse cultures—are being eliminated. The Internet has become as important to our society as television and newspapers.

VISIT THE NET

Gives an extensive slide show presentation about strategic management, from beginning to the end of the process. (www.csuchico.edu/mgmt/strategy/)

Forecasting Tools and Techniques

Forecasts are educated assumptions about future trends and events. Forecasting is a complex activity because of factors such as technological innovation, cultural changes, new products, improved services, stronger competitors, shifts in government priorities, changing social values, unstable economic conditions, and unforeseen events. Managers often must rely upon published forecasts to effectively identify key external opportunities and threats.

A sense of the future permeates all action and underlies every decision a person makes. People eat expecting to be satisfied and nourished—in the future. People sleep assuming that in the future they will feel rested. They invest energy, money, and time because they believe their efforts will be rewarded in the future. They build highways assuming that automobiles and trucks will need them in the future. Parents educate children on the basis of forecasts that they will need certain skills, attitudes, and knowledge when they grow up. The truth is we all make implicit forecasts throughout our daily lives. The question, therefore, is not whether we should forecast but rather how we can best forecast to enable us to move beyond our ordinarily unarticulated assumptions about the future. Can we obtain information and then make educated assumptions (forecasts) to better guide our current decisions to achieve a more desirable future state of affairs? We should go into the future with our eyes and our minds open, rather than stumble into the future with our eyes closed.[17]

Many publications and sources on the Internet forecast external variables. Several published examples include *Industry Week*'s "Trends and Forecasts," *BusinessWeek*'s "Investment Outlook," and Standard & Poor's *Industry Survey.* The reputation and continued success of these publications depend partly on accurate forecasts, so published sources of information can offer excellent projections. An especially good Web site for industry forecasts is finance.yahoo.com. Just insert a firm's stock symbol and go from there.

Sometimes organizations must develop their own projections. Most organizations forecast (project) their own revenues and profits annually. Organizations sometimes forecast market share or customer loyalty in local areas. Because forecasting is so important in strategic management and because the ability to forecast (in contrast to the ability to use a forecast) is essential, selected forecasting tools are examined further here.

Forecasting tools can be broadly categorized into two groups: quantitative techniques and qualitative techniques. Quantitative forecasts are most appropriate when historical data are available and when the relationships among key variables are expected to remain the same in the future. *Linear regression,* for example, is based on the assumption that the future will be just like the past—which, of course, it never is. As historical relationships become less stable, quantitative forecasts become less accurate.

No forecast is perfect, and some forecasts are even wildly inaccurate. This fact accents the need for strategists to devote sufficient time and effort to study the underlying bases for published forecasts and to develop internal forecasts of their own. Key external opportunities and threats can be effectively identified only through good forecasts. Accurate forecasts can provide major competitive advantages for organizations. Forecasts are vital to the strategic-management process and to the success of organizations.

Making Assumptions

Planning would be impossible without assumptions. McConkey defines assumptions as the "best present estimates of the impact of major external factors, over which the manager has little if any control, but which may exert a significant impact on performance or the ability to achieve desired results."[18] Strategists are faced with countless variables and imponderables that can be neither controlled nor predicted with 100 percent accuracy. Wild guesses should never be made in formulating strategies, but reasonable assumptions based on available information must always be made.

By identifying future occurrences that could have a major effect on the firm and by making reasonable assumptions about those factors, strategists can carry the strategic-management process forward. Assumptions are needed only for future trends and events that are most likely to have a significant effect on the company's business. Based on the best information at the time, assumptions serve as checkpoints on the validity of strategies. If future occurrences deviate significantly from assumptions, strategists know that corrective actions may be needed. Without reasonable assumptions, the strategy-formulation process could not proceed effectively. Firms that have the best information generally make the most accurate assumptions, which can lead to major competitive advantages.

The Global Challenge

Foreign competitors are battering U.S. firms in many industries. In its simplest sense, the international challenge faced by U.S. business is twofold: (1) how to gain and maintain exports to other nations and (2) how to defend domestic markets against imported goods. Few companies can afford to ignore the presence of international competition. Firms that seem insulated and comfortable today may be vulnerable tomorrow; for example, foreign banks do not yet compete or operate in most of the United States but this too is changing.

America's economy is becoming much less American. A world economy and monetary system are emerging. Corporations in every corner of the globe are taking advantage of the opportunity to share in the benefits of worldwide economic development. Markets are shifting rapidly and in many cases converging in tastes, trends, and prices. Innovative transport systems are accelerating the transfer of technology. Shifts in the nature and location of production systems, especially to China and India, are reducing the response time to changing market conditions.

More and more countries around the world are welcoming foreign investment and capital. As a result, labor markets have steadily become more international. East Asian countries have become market leaders in labor-intensive industries, Brazil offers abundant natural resources and rapidly developing markets, and Germany offers skilled labor and technology. The drive to improve the efficiency of global business operations is leading to greater functional specialization. This is not limited to a search for the familiar low-cost labor in Latin America or Asia. Other considerations include the cost of energy, availability of resources, inflation rates, existing tax rates, and the nature of trade regulations.

When it joined the World Trade Organization in 2001, China agreed to respect copyright protections and liberalize restrictions on the import and distribution of foreign-made goods. However, in 2008 Chinese counterfeiters still can be criminally prosecuted for commercial piracy only when caught in possession of at least 500 counterfeit items.[19] Pirated goods such as Nike running shoes, new Hollywood movies on DVD, and Microsoft software can be purchased for a fraction of their actual prices on many streets in China. And China still has substantial barriers to sales of authentic U.S.-made copyrighted products. U.S. Trade Representative Susan Schwab says, "This is more than a handbag here or a logo item there; it is often theft on a grand scale." China's counterfeit trade practices contribute to an annual bilateral trade deficit of about $250 billion with the United States. Chinese pirating of products is an external threat facing many firms.

Multinational Corporations

Multinational corporations (MNCs) face unique and diverse risks, such as expropriation of assets, currency losses through exchange rate fluctuations, unfavorable foreign court interpretations of contracts and agreements, social/political disturbances, import/export restrictions, tariffs, and trade barriers. Strategists in MNCs are often confronted with the need to be globally competitive and nationally responsive at the same time. With the rise in world commerce, government and regulatory bodies are more closely monitoring foreign business practices. The United States Foreign Corrupt Practices Act, for example, defines corrupt practices in many areas of business. A sensitive issue is that some MNCs sometimes violate legal and ethical standards of the home country, but not of the host country.

Before entering international markets, firms should scan relevant journals and patent reports, seek the advice of academic and research organizations, participate in international trade fairs, form partnerships, and conduct extensive research to broaden their contacts and diminish the risk of doing business in new markets. Firms can also reduce the risks of doing business internationally by obtaining insurance from the U.S. government's Overseas Private Investment Corporation (OPIC). Note in the "Global Perspective" section that General Motors and Ford, large American MNCs, are now being challenged not only by German and Japanese auto firms but also by Chinese auto firms.

GLOBAL PERSPECTIVE
China's Automobile Producers Heading to the United States in 2008

China's auto exports doubled in 2006 from the previous year to a record 340,000 units. Vice Minister of Commerce Wei Jianguo says, "China is aiming to lift the value of its vehicle and auto parts exports to $120 billion, or 10 percent of the world's total vehicle trading volume in the next ten years." China's seven million automobiles produced in 2006 catapulted the country ahead of Germany to become the world's number three automobile producer behind the United States and Japan. DaimlerChrysler AG's Chrysler Group has recently agreed to sell China's Chery Automobile Company subcompact cars in the United States in 2008.

A Chinese automaker, Changfeng Group, displayed five new vehicles at the 2007 Detroit Auto Show, marking the first Chinese autos on show in the United States. China has more than 100 automakers and the government in Beijing desires to see these firms consolidate and expand globally. The majority owner of Changfeng, Anhui Changfeng Yangzi Motor Manufacturing, is especially interested in promoting its Liebao brand in North America. Other Chinese automakers with plans to market cars in the United States for the first time next year include Great Wall Motor Company and Geely Automobile Company.

Source: Adapted from "China Auto Exports Doubled During 2006," *Wall Street Journal* (January 2, 2007): A16; and Norihiko Shirouzu, "Obscure Chinese Car Maker Seeks U.S. Presence," *Wall Street Journal* (January 3, 2007): B1.

1971 Chevrolet Nova ss. Courtesy of Tallahassee Car Museum, Mathew Ward(c) Dorling Kindersley

Globalization

Globalization is a process of worldwide integration of strategy formulation, implementation, and evaluation activities. Strategic decisions are made based on their impact upon global profitability of the firm, rather than on just domestic or other individual country considerations. A global strategy seeks to meet the needs of customers worldwide, with the highest value at the lowest cost. This may mean locating production in countries with the lowest labor costs or abundant natural resources, locating research and complex engineering centers where skilled scientists and engineers can be found, and locating marketing activities close to the markets to be served. A global strategy includes designing, producing, and marketing products with global needs in mind, instead of considering individual countries alone. A global strategy integrates actions against competitors into a worldwide plan.

Globalization of industries is occurring for many reasons, including a worldwide trend toward similar consumption patterns, the emergence of global buyers and sellers, and e-commerce and the instant transmission of money and information across continents. The Olympics, the World Bank, world trade centers, the Red Cross, the Internet, environmental conferences, telecommunications, and economic summits all contribute to global interdependencies and the emerging global marketplace.

It is clear that different industries become global for different reasons. The need to amortize massive R&D investments over many markets is a major reason why the aircraft manufacturing industry became global. Monitoring globalization in one's industry is an important strategic-management activity. Knowing how to use that information for one's competitive advantage is even more important. For example, firms may look around the world for the best technology and select one that has the most promise for the largest number of markets. When firms design a product, they design it to be marketable in as many countries as possible. When firms manufacture a product, they select the lowest-cost source, which may be Japan for semiconductors, Sri Lanka for textiles, Malaysia for simple electronics, and Europe for precision machinery. MNCs design manufacturing systems to accommodate world markets. One of the riskiest strategies for a domestic firm is to remain solely a domestic firm in an industry that is rapidly becoming global.

Industry Analysis: The External Factor Evaluation (EFE) Matrix

An *External Factor Evaluation (EFE) Matrix* allows strategists to summarize and evaluate economic, social, cultural, demographic, environmental, political, governmental, legal, technological, and competitive information. Illustrated in Table 3-8, the EFE Matrix can be developed in five steps:

1. List key external factors as identified in the external-audit process. Include a total of 10 to 20 factors, including both opportunities and threats, that affect the firm and its industry. List the opportunities first and then the threats. Be as specific as possible, using percentages, ratios, and comparative numbers whenever possible.
2. Assign to each factor a weight that ranges from 0.0 (not important) to 1.0 (very important). The weight indicates the relative importance of that factor to being successful in the firm's industry. Opportunities often receive higher weights than threats, but threats can receive high weights if they are especially severe or threatening. Appropriate weights can be determined by comparing successful with unsuccessful competitors or by discussing the factor and reaching a group consensus. The sum of all weights assigned to the factors must equal 1.0.
3. Assign a rating between 1 and 4 to each key external factor to indicate how effectively the firm's current strategies respond to the factor, where 4 = *the response is superior*, 3 = *the response is above average*, 2 = *the response is average*, and 1 = *the response is poor*. Ratings are based on effectiveness of the firm's strategies. Ratings are thus company-based, whereas the weights in Step 2 are industry-based. It is important to note that both threats and opportunities can receive a 1, 2, 3, or 4.

4. Multiply each factor's weight by its rating to determine a weighted score.
5. Sum the weighted scores for each variable to determine the total weighted score for the organization.

Regardless of the number of key opportunities and threats included in an EFE Matrix, the highest possible total weighted score for an organization is 4.0 and the lowest possible total weighted score is 1.0. The average total weighted score is 2.5. A total weighted score of 4.0 indicates that an organization is responding in an outstanding way to existing opportunities and threats in its industry. In other words, the firm's strategies effectively take advantage of existing opportunities and minimize the potential adverse effects of external threats. A total score of 1.0 indicates that the firm's strategies are not capitalizing on opportunities or avoiding external threats.

An example of an EFE Matrix is provided in Table 3-8 for a local ten-theatre cinema complex. Note that the most important factor to being successful in this business is "Trend toward healthy eating eroding concession sales" as indicated by the 0.12 weight. Also note that the local cinema is doing excellent in regard to handling two factors, "TDB University is expanding 6 percent annually" and "Trend toward healthy eating eroding concession sales." Perhaps the cinema is placing flyers on campus and also adding yogurt and healthy drinks to its concession menu. Note that you may have a 1, 2, 3, or 4 anywhere down the Rating column. Note also that the factors are stated in quantitative terms to the extent possible, rather than being stated in vague terms. Quantify the factors as much as possible in constructing an EFE Matrix. Finally, note that the total weighted score of 2.58 is above the average (midpoint) of 2.5, so this cinema business is doing pretty well, taking advantage of the external opportunities and avoiding the threats facing the firm. There is definitely room for improvement, though, because the highest total weighted score would be 4.0. As indicated by ratings of 1, this business needs to capitalize more on the "two new neighborhoods nearby" opportunity and the "movies rented from Time Warner" threat.

TABLE 3-8   EFE Matrix for a Local Ten-Theatre Cinema Complex

Key External Factors	Weight	Rating	Weighted Score
Opportunities			
1. Rowan County is growing 8% annually in population	0.05	3	0.15
2. TDB University is expanding 6% annually	0.08	4	0.32
3. Major competitor across town recently ceased operations	0.08	3	0.24
4. Demand for going to cinema growing 10% annually	0.07	2	0.14
5. Two new neighborhoods being developed within 3 miles	0.09	1	0.09
6. Disposable income among citizens grew 5% in prior year	0.06	3	0.18
7. Unemployment rate in county declined to 3.1%	0.03	2	0.06
Threats			
8. Trend toward healthy eating eroding concession sales	0.12	4	0.48
9. Demand for online movies and DVDs growing 10% annually	0.06	2	0.12
10. Commercial property adjacent to cinemas for sale	0.06	3	0.18
11. TDB University installing an on-campus movie theatre	0.04	3	0.12
12. County and city property taxes increasing 25% this year	0.08	2	0.16
13. Local religious groups object to R-rated movies being shown	0.04	3	0.12
14. Movies rented from local Blockbuster store up 12%	0.08	2	0.16
15. Movies rented last quarter from Time Warner up 15%	0.06	1	0.06
Total	**1.00**		**2.58**

Note also that there are many percentage-based factors among the group. Be quantitative to the extent possible! Note also that the ratings range from 1 to 4 on both the opportunities and threats.

The Competitive Profile Matrix (CPM)

The *Competitive Profile Matrix (CPM)* identifies a firm's major competitors and its particular strengths and weaknesses in relation to a sample firm's strategic position. The weights and total weighted scores in both a CPM and an EFE have the same meaning. However, *critical success* factors in a CPM include both internal and external issues; therefore, the ratings refer to strengths and weaknesses, where 4 = major strength, 3 = minor strength, 2 = minor weakness, and 1 = major weakness. There are some important differences between the EFE and CPM. First of all, the critical success factors in a CPM are broader, they do not include specific or factual data, and they even may focus on internal issues. The critical success factors in a CPM also are not grouped into opportunities and threats as they are in an EFE. In a CPM, the ratings and total weighted scores for rival firms can be compared to the sample firm. This comparative analysis provides important internal strategic information.

A sample Competitive Profile Matrix is provided in Table 3-9. In this example, the two most important factors to being successful in the industry are "advertising" and "global expansion," as indicated by weights of 0.20. If there were no weight column in this analysis, note that each factor then would be equally important. Thus, having a weight column makes for a more robust analysis, because it enables the analyst to assign higher and lower numbers to capture perceived or actual levels of importance. Note in Table 3-9 that Company 1 is strongest on "product quality," as indicated by a rating of 4, whereas Company 2 is strongest on "advertising." Overall, Company 1 is strongest, as indicated by the total weighted score of 3.15.

Other than the critical success factors listed in the example CPM, factors often included in this analysis include breadth of product line, effectiveness of sales distribution, proprietary or patent advantages, location of facilities, production capacity and efficiency, experience, union relations, technological advantages, and e-commerce expertise.

A word on interpretation: Just because one firm receives a 3.2 rating and another receives a 2.80 rating in a Competitive Profile Matrix, it does not follow that the first firm is 20 percent better than the second. Numbers reveal the relative strengths of firms, but their implied precision is an illusion. Numbers are not magic. The aim is not to arrive at a single number, but rather to assimilate and evaluate information in a meaningful way that aids in decision making.

TABLE 3-9   An Example Competitive Profile Matrix

Critical Success Factors	Weight	Company 1		Company 2		Company 3	
		Rating	Score	Rating	Score	Rating	Score
Advertising	0.20	1	0.20	4	0.80	3	0.60
Product Quality	0.10	4	0.40	3	0.30	2	0.20
Price Competitiveness	0.10	3	0.30	2	0.20	4	0.40
Management	0.10	4	0.40	3	0.20	3	0.30
Financial Position	0.15	4	0.60	2	0.30	3	0.45
Customer Loyalty	0.10	4	0.40	3	0.30	2	0.20
Global Expansion	0.20	4	0.80	1	0.20	2	0.40
Market Share	0.05	1	0.05	4	0.20	3	0.15
Total	**1.00**		**3.15**		**2.50**		**2.70**

Note: (1) The ratings values are as follows: 1 = major weakness, 2 = minor weakness, 3 = minor strength, 4 = major strength. (2) As indicated by the total weighted score of 2.50, Competitor 2 is weakest. (3) Only eight critical success factors are included for simplicity; this is too few in actuality.

TABLE 3-10   **Another Example of a Competitive Profile Matrix**

Critical Success Factors	Weight	Company 1		Company 2		Company 3	
		Rating	Weighted Score	Rating	Weighted Score	Rating	Weighted Score
Market share	0.15	3	0.45	2	0.30	4	0.60
Inventory system	0.08	2	0.16	2	0.16	4	0.32
Financial position	0.10	2	0.20	3	0.30	4	0.40
Product quality	0.08	3	0.24	4	0.32	3	0.24
Consumer loyalty	0.02	3	0.06	3	0.06	4	0.08
Sales distribution	0.10	3	0.30	2	0.20	3	0.30
Global expansion	0.15	3	0.45	2	0.30	4	0.60
Organization structure	0.05	3	0.15	4	0.20	2	0.10
Production capacity	0.04	3	0.12	2	0.08	4	0.16
E-commerce	0.10	3	0.30	1	0.10	4	0.40
Customer service	0.10	3	0.30	2	0.20	4	0.40
Price competitive	0.02	4	0.08	1	0.02	3	0.06
Management experience	0.01	2	0.02	4	0.04	2	0.02
Total	**1.00**		**2.83**		**2.28**		**3.68**

Another Competitive Profile Matrix is provided in Table 3-10. Note that Company 2 has the best product quality and management experience; Company 3 has the best market share and inventory system; and Company 1 has the best price as indicated by the ratings.

Conclusion

Increasing turbulence in markets and industries around the world means the external audit has become an explicit and vital part of the strategic-management process. This chapter provides a framework for collecting and evaluating economic, social, cultural, demographic, environmental, political, governmental, legal, technological, and competitive information. Firms that do not mobilize and empower their managers and employees to identify, monitor, forecast, and evaluate key external forces may fail to anticipate emerging opportunities and threats and, consequently, may pursue ineffective strategies, miss opportunities, and invite organizational demise. Firms not taking advantage of the Internet are technologically falling behind.

A major responsibility of strategists is to ensure development of an effective external-audit system. This includes using information technology to devise a competitive intelligence system that works. The external-audit approach described in this chapter can be used effectively by any size or type of organization. Typically, the external-audit process is more informal in small firms, but the need to understand key trends and events is no less important for these firms. The EFE Matrix and Porter's Five-Forces Model can help strategists evaluate the market and industry, but these tools must be accompanied by good intuitive judgment. Multinational firms especially need a systematic and effective external-audit system because external forces among foreign countries vary so greatly.

We invite you to visit the David page on the Prentice Hall Companion Web site at www.prenhall.com/david for this chapter's review quiz.

Key Terms and Concepts

Chief Information Officer (CIO) (p. 81)
Chief Technology Officer (CTO) (p. 81)
Competitive Analysis (p. 84)
Competitive Intelligence (CI) (p. 83)

Issues for Review and Discussion

1. Explain how to conduct an external strategic-management audit.
2. Identify a recent economic, social, political, or technological trend that significantly affects financial institutions.
3. Discuss the following statement: Major opportunities and threats usually result from an inter-action among key environmental trends rather than from a single external event or factor.
4. Identify two industries experiencing rapid technological changes and three industries that are experiencing little technological change. How does the need for technological forecasting differ in these industries? Why?
5. Use Porter's Five-Forces Model to evaluate competitiveness within the U.S. banking industry.
6. What major forecasting techniques would you use to identify (1) economic opportunities and threats and (2) demographic opportunities and threats? Why are these techniques most appropriate?
7. How does the external audit affect other components of the strategic-management process?
8. As the owner of a small business, explain how you would organize a strategic-information scanning system. How would you organize such a system in a large organization?
9. Construct an EFE Matrix for an organization of your choice.
10. Make an appointment with a librarian at your university to learn how to use online databases. Report your findings in class.
11. Give some advantages and disadvantages of cooperative versus competitive strategies.
12. As strategist for a local bank, explain when you would use qualitative versus quantitative forecasts.
13. What is your forecast for interest rates and the stock market in the next several months? As the stock market moves up, do interest rates always move down? Why? What are the strategic implications of these trends?
14. Explain how information technology affects strategies of the organization where you worked most recently.
15. Let's say your boss develops an EFE Matrix that includes 62 factors. How would you suggest reducing the number of factors to 20?
16. Discuss the ethics of gathering competitive intelligence.
17. Discuss the ethics of cooperating with rival firms.
18. Visit the SEC Web site at www.sec.gov, and discuss the benefits of using information provided there.
19. What are the major differences between U.S. and multinational operations that affect strategic management?
20. Why is globalization of industries a common factor today?
21. Do you agree with I/O theorists that external factors are more important than internal factors to a firm's achieving competitive advantage? Explain both your and their position.
22. Define, compare, and contrast the weights versus ratings in an EFE versus IFE Matrix.
23. Develop a Competitive Profile Matrix for your university. Include six factors.
24. List the 10 external areas that give rise to opportunities and threats.

Notes

1. York Freund, "Critical Success Factors," *Planning Review* 16, no. 4 (July–August 1988): 20.
2. A. M. McGahan, "Competition, Strategy and Business Performance," *California Management Review* 41, no. 3 (1999): 74–101; A. McGahan and M. Porter, "How Much Does Industry Matter Really?," *Strategic Management Journal* 18, no. 8 (1997): 15–30.
3. Ken Jackson, "State Population Changes by Race, Ethnicity," *USA Today* (May 17, 2007): 2A.
4. S&P Industry Surveys, Beverage Industry, 2005.
5. Ken Thurston, "Population Change in States' Top Urban Areas," *USA Today* (April 5, 2007): 13A.
6. Frederick Gluck, "Global Competition in the 1990s," *Journal of Business Strategy* (Spring 1983): 22–24.
7. John Harris, Robert Shaw, Jr., and William Sommers, "The Strategic Management of Technology," *Planning Review* 11, no. 11 (January–February 1983): 28, 35.
8. Bill Saporito, "Companies That Compete Best," *Fortune* (May 22, 1989): 36.
9. Louis Lavelle, "The Case of the Corporate Spy," *BusinessWeek* (November 26, 2001): 56–57.
10. Kenneth Sawka, "Demystifying Business Intelligence," *Management Review* (October 1996): 49.
11. John Prescott and Daniel Smith, "The Largest Survey of 'Leading-Edge' Competitor Intelligence Managers," *Planning Review* 17, no. 3 (May–June 1989): 6–13.
12. Gary Hamel, Yves Doz, and C. K. Prahalad, "Collaborate with Your Competitors—and Win," *Harvard Business Review* 67, no. 1 (January–February 1989): 133.
13. M.J. Chen. "Competitor Analysis and Interfirm Rivalry: Toward a Theoretical Integration," *Academy of Management Review* 21 (1996): 106.
14. S. Jayachandran, J. Gimeno, and P. R. Varadarajan, "Theory of Multimarket Competition: A Synthesis and Implications for Marketing Strategy," *Journal of Marketing* 63, 3 (1999): 59; and M. J. Chen. "Competitor Analysis and Interfirm Rivalry: Toward a Theoretical Integration," *Academy of Management Review* 21 (1996): 107–108.
15. Arthur Thompson, Jr., A. J. Strickland III, and John Gamble, *Crafting and Executing Strategy: Text and Readings* (New York: McGraw-Hill/Irwin, 2005): 63.
16. Michael E. Porter, *Competitive Strategy: Techniques for Analyzing Industries and Competitors* (New York: Free Press, 1980): 24–27.
17. horizon.unc.edu/projects/seminars/futuresresearch/rationale.asp.
18. Dale McConkey, "Planning in a Changing Environment," *Business Horizons* 31, no. 5 (September–October 1988): 67.
19. David Lynch, "U.S. Complains to WTO on China," *USA Today* (April 10, 2007): B1.

Current Readings

Baron, Robert A. "Opportunity Recognition as Pattern Recognition: How Entrepreneurs 'Connect the Dots' to Identify New Business Opportunities." *The Academy of Management Perspectives* 20, no. 1 (February 2006): 104.

Brews, Peter and Devararat Purohit. "Strategic Planning in Unstable Environments." *Long Range Planning* 40, no. 1 (February 2007): 64.

Gottschlag, Oliver and Maurizo Zollo. "Interest Alignment and Competitive Advantage." *The Academy of Management Review* 32, no. 2 (April 2007): 418.

Hambrick, Donald C. "Upper Echelons Theory: An Update" *The Academy of Management Review* 32, no. 2 (April 2007): 334.

Hult, G. T. M., D. J. Ketchen Jr., and T. B. Palmer. "Firm, Strategic Group, and Industry Influences on Performance." *Strategic Management Journal* 28, no. 2 (February 2007): 147.

King, Andrew. "Cooperation Between Corporations and Environmental Groups: A Transaction Cost Perspective." *The Academy of Management Perspectives* 32, no. 3 (July 2007): 889.

Rousseau, Denise M. and Rosemary Blatt. "Global Competition's Perfect Storm: Why Business and Labor Cannot Solve Their Problems Alone." *The Academy of Management Perspectives* 21, no. 2 (May 2007): 16.

Slone, Reuben E., John T. Mentzer, and Paul J. Dittmann "Are You the Weakest Link in Company's Supply Chain?" *Harvard Business Review* (September): 116.

• **EXPERIENTIAL EXERCISES**   **D**ISNEY

Experiential Exercises 3A

Developing an EFE Matrix for Walt Disney Company

Purpose

This exercise will give you practice developing an EFE Matrix. An EFE Matrix summarizes the results of an external audit. This is an important tool widely used by strategists.

Instructions

Step 1   Join with two other students in class, and jointly prepare an EFE Matrix for Walt Disney Company. Refer back to the Cohesion Case and to Experiential Exercise 1A, if necessary, to identify external opportunities and threats. Use the information in the S&P Industry Surveys that you copied as part of Experiential Exercise 1A. Be sure not to include strategies as opportunities, but do include as many $'s, %'s, #'s, and ratios as possible.

Step 2   All three-person teams participating in this exercise should record their EFE total weighted scores on the board. Put your initials after your score to identify it as your team's.

Step 3   Compare the total weighted scores. Which team's score came closest to the instructor's answer? Discuss reasons for variation in the scores reported on the board.

Experiential Exercise 3B

The External Assessment

Purpose

This exercise will help you become familiar with important sources of external information available in your college library. A key part of preparing an external audit is searching the Internet and examining published sources of information for relevant economic, social,

A pair of Mickey and Minnie Mouse painted cast phenolic napkin rings. *Source:* (c) Judith Miller / Dorling Kindersley / Wallis and Wallis

cultural, demographic, environmental, political, governmental, legal, technological, and competitive trends and events. External opportunities and threats must be identified and evaluated before strategies can be formulated effectively.

Instructions

Step 1   Select a company or business where you currently or previously have worked. Conduct an external audit for this company. Find opportunities and threats in recent issues of newspapers and magazines. Search for information using the Internet. Use the following four Web sites:

http://marketwatch.multexinvestor.com
http://moneycentral.msn.com
http://financeyahoo.com
www.clearstation.com
https://us.etrade.com/e/t/invest/markets.

Step 2   On a separate sheet of paper, list 10 opportunities and 10 threats that face this company. Be specific in stating each factor.

Step 3   Include a bibliography to reveal where you found the information.

Step 4   Write a three-page summary of your findings, and submit it to your instructor.

Experiential Exercise 3C

Developing an EFE Matrix for My University

Purpose

More colleges and universities are embarking upon the strategic-management process. Institutions are consciously and systematically identifying and evaluating external opportunities and threats facing higher education in your state, the nation, and the world.

Instructions

Step 1   Join with two other individuals in class and jointly prepare an EFE Matrix for your institution.

Step 2   Go to the board and record your total weighted score in a column that includes the scores of all three-person teams participating. Put your initials after your score to identify it as your team's.

Step 3   Which team viewed your college's strategies most positively? Which team viewed your college's strategies most negatively? Discuss the nature of the differences.

Experiential Exercise 3D

Developing a Competitive Profile Matrix for Walt Disney Company

Purpose

Monitoring competitors' performance and strategies is a key aspect of an external audit. This exercise is designed to give you practice evaluating the competitive position of organizations in a given industry and assimilating that information in the form of a Competitive Profile Matrix.

Instructions

Step 1   Turn back to the Cohesion Case and review the section on competitors (pages 39–43).

Step 2   On a separate sheet of paper, prepare a Competitive Profile Matrix that includes Walt Disney, Time Warner, and News Corporation.

Step 3   Turn in your Competitive Profile Matrix for a classwork grade.

Experiential Exercise 3E

Developing a Competitive Profile Matrix for My University

Purpose

Your college or university competes with all other educational institutions in the world, especially those in your own state. State funds, students, faculty, staff, endowments, gifts, and federal funds are areas of competitiveness. Other areas include athletic programs, dorm life, academic reputation, location, and career services. The purpose of this exercise is to give you practice thinking competitively about the business of education in your state.

Instructions

Step 1   Identify two colleges or universities in your state that compete directly with your institution for students. Interview several persons, perhaps classmates, who are aware of particular strengths and weaknesses of those universities. Record information about the two competing universities.

Step 2   Prepare a Competitive Profile Matrix that includes your institution and the two competing institutions. Include at least the following ten factors in your analysis:

1. Tuition costs
2. Quality of faculty
3. Academic reputation
4. Average class size
5. Campus landscaping
6. Athletic programs
7. Quality of students
8. Graduate programs
9. Location of campus
10. Campus culture

Step 3   Submit your Competitive Profile Matrix to your instructor for evaluation.

4 The Internal Assessment

The New York Stock Exchange. *Source:* EMGEducation Management Group

chapter objectives

After studying this chapter, you should be able to do the following:

1. Describe how to perform an internal strategic-management audit.

2. Discuss the Resource-Based View (RBV) in strategic management.

3. Discuss key interrelationships among the functional areas of business.

4. Compare and contrast culture in the United States with other countries.

5. Identify the basic functions or activities that make up management, marketing, finance/accounting, production/operations, research and development, and management information systems.

6. Explain how to determine and prioritize a firm's internal strengths and weaknesses.

7. Explain the importance of financial ratio analysis.

8. Discuss the nature and role of management information systems in strategic management.

9. Develop an Internal Factor Evaluation (IFE) Matrix.

10. Explain benchmarking as a strategic management tool.

This chapter focuses on identifying and evaluating a firm's strengths and weaknesses in the functional areas of business, including management, marketing, finance/accounting, production/operations, research and development, and management information systems. Relationships among these areas of business are examined. Strategic implications of important functional area concepts are examined. The process of performing an internal audit is described. The Resource-Based View (RBV) of strategic management is introduced as is the Value Chain Analysis (VCA) concept.

The Nature of an Internal Audit

VISIT THE NET

Excellent strategic planning quotes. (www.planware.org/quotes.htm#3)

All organizations have strengths and weaknesses in the functional areas of business. No enterprise is equally strong or weak in all areas. Maytag, for example, is known for excellent production and product design, whereas Procter & Gamble is known for superb marketing. Internal strengths/weaknesses, coupled with external opportunities/threats and a clear statement of mission, provide the basis for establishing objectives and strategies. Objectives and strategies are established with the intention of capitalizing upon internal strengths and overcoming weaknesses. The internal-audit part of the strategic-management process is illustrated in Figure 4-1.

Key Internal Forces

It is not possible in a business policy text to review in depth all the material presented in courses such as marketing, finance, accounting, management, management information systems, and production/operations; there are many subareas within these functions, such as customer service, warranties, advertising, packaging, and pricing under marketing.

For different types of organizations, such as hospitals, universities, and government agencies, the functional business areas, of course, differ. In a hospital, for example,

FIGURE 4-1

A Comprehensive Strategic-Management Model

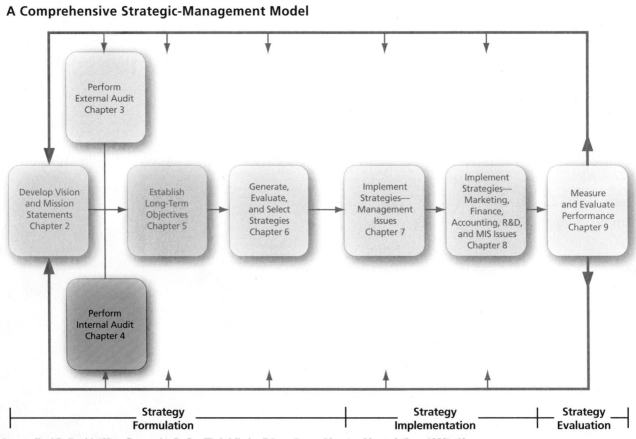

Source: Fred R. David, "How Companies Define Their Mission," *Long Range Planning* 22, no. 3 (June 1988): 40.

functional areas may include cardiology, hematology, nursing, maintenance, physician support, and receivables. Functional areas of a university can include athletic programs, placement services, housing, fundraising, academic research, counseling, and intramural programs. Within large organizations, each division has certain strengths and weaknesses.

A firm's strengths that cannot be easily matched or imitated by competitors are called *distinctive competencies*. Building competitive advantages involves taking advantage of distinctive competencies. For example, 3M exploits its distinctive competence in research and development by producing a wide range of innovative products. Strategies are designed in part to improve on a firm's weaknesses, turning them into strengths—and maybe even into distinctive competencies.

Some researchers emphasize the importance of the internal audit part of the strategic-management process by comparing it to the external audit. Robert Grant concluded that the internal audit is more important, saying:

> In a world where customer preferences are volatile, the identity of customers is changing, and the technologies for serving customer requirements are continually evolving; an externally focused orientation does not provide a secure foundation for formulating long-term strategy. When the external environment is in a state of flux, the firm's own resources and capabilities may be a much more stable basis on which to define its identity. Hence, a definition of a business in terms of what it is capable of doing may offer a more durable basis for strategy than a definition based upon the needs which the business seeks to satisfy.[1]

The Process of Performing an Internal Audit

The process of performing an *internal audit* closely parallels the process of performing an external audit. Representative managers and employees from throughout the firm need to be involved in determining a firm's strengths and weaknesses. The internal audit requires gathering and assimilating information about the firm's management, marketing, finance/accounting, production/operations, research and development (R&D), and management information systems operations. Key factors should be prioritized as described in Chapter 3 so that the firm's most important strengths and weaknesses can be determined collectively.

Compared to the external audit, the process of performing an internal audit provides more opportunity for participants to understand how their jobs, departments, and divisions fit into the whole organization. This is a great benefit because managers and employees perform better when they understand how their work affects other areas and activities of the firm. For example, when marketing and manufacturing managers jointly discuss issues related to internal strengths and weaknesses, they gain a better appreciation of the issues, problems, concerns, and needs of all the functional areas. In organizations that do not use strategic management, marketing, finance, and manufacturing managers often do not interact with each other in significant ways. Performing an internal audit thus is an excellent vehicle or forum for improving the process of communication in the organization. *Communication* may be the most important word in management.

Performing an internal audit requires gathering, assimilating, and evaluating information about the firm's operations. Critical success factors, consisting of both strengths and weaknesses, can be identified and prioritized in the manner discussed in Chapter 3. According to William King, a task force of managers from different units of the organization, supported by staff, should be charged with determining the 10 to 20 most important strengths and weaknesses that should influence the future of the organization. He says:

> The development of conclusions on the 10 to 20 most important organizational strengths and weaknesses can be, as any experienced manager knows, a difficult task, when it involves managers representing various organizational interests and points of view. Developing a 20-page list of strengths and weaknesses could be accomplished relatively easily, but a list of the 10 to 15 most important ones involves significant analysis and negotiation. This is true because of the judgments that are required and the impact which such a list will inevitably have as it is used in the formulation, implementation, and evaluation of strategies.[2]

VISIT THE NET

Provides the complete strategic plan for the Wyoming Insurance Department Agency, including its list of strengths and weaknesses. (www.state.wy.us/state/strategy/insurance.html)

Strategic management is a highly interactive process that requires effective coordination among management, marketing, finance/accounting, production/operations, R&D, and management information systems managers. Although the strategic-management process is overseen by strategists, success requires that managers and employees from all functional areas work together to provide ideas and information. Financial managers, for example, may need to restrict the number of feasible options available to operations managers, or R&D managers may develop products for which marketing managers need to set higher objectives. A key to organizational success is effective coordination and understanding among managers from all functional business areas. Through involvement in performing an internal strategic-management audit, managers from different departments and divisions of the firm come to understand the nature and effect of decisions in other functional business areas in their firm. Knowledge of these relationships is critical for effectively establishing objectives and strategies.

A failure to recognize and understand relationships among the functional areas of business can be detrimental to strategic management, and the number of those relationships that must be managed increases dramatically with a firm's size, diversity, geographic dispersion, and the number of products or services offered. Governmental and nonprofit enterprises traditionally have not placed sufficient emphasis on relationships among the business functions. Some firms place too great an emphasis on one function at the expense of others. Ansoff explained:

> During the first fifty years, successful firms focused their energies on optimizing the performance of one of the principal functions: production/operations, R&D, or marketing. Today, due to the growing complexity and dynamism of the environment, success increasingly depends on a judicious combination of several functional influences. This transition from a single function focus to a multifunction focus is essential for successful strategic management.[3]

Financial ratio analysis exemplifies the complexity of relationships among the functional areas of business. A declining return on investment or profit margin ratio could be the result of ineffective marketing, poor management policies, research and development errors, or a weak management information system. The effectiveness of strategy formulation, implementation, and evaluation activities hinges upon a clear understanding of how major business functions affect one another. For strategies to succeed, a coordinated effort among all the functional areas of business is needed. In the case of planning, George wrote:

> We may conceptually separate planning for the purpose of theoretical discussion and analysis, but in practice, neither is it a distinct entity nor is it capable of being separated. The planning function is mixed with all other business functions and, like ink once mixed with water, it cannot be set apart. It is spread throughout and is a part of the whole of managing an organization.[4]

The Resource-Based View (RBV)

Gaining in popularity in the 1990s and continuing today, the *Resource-Based View (RBV)* approach to competitive advantage contends that internal resources are more important for a firm than external factors in achieving and sustaining competitive advantage. In contrast to the I/O theory presented in the previous chapter, proponents of the RBV view contend that organizational performance will primarily be determined by internal resources that can be grouped into three all-encompassing categories: physical resources, human resources, and organizational resources.[5] Physical resources include all plant and equipment, location, technology, raw materials, machines; human resources include all employees, training, experience, intelligence, knowledge, skills, abilities; and organizational resources include firm structure, planning processes, information systems, patents, trademarks, copyrights, databases, and so on. RBV theory asserts that resources are actually what helps a firm exploit opportunities and neutralize threats.

The basic premise of the RBV is that the mix, type, amount, and nature of a firm's internal resources should be considered first and foremost in devising strategies that can lead to sustainable competitive advantage. Managing strategically according to the RBV involves developing and exploiting a firm's unique resources and capabilities, and continually maintaining and strengthening those resources. The theory asserts that it is advantageous for a firm to pursue a strategy that is not currently being implemented by any competing firm. When other firms are unable to duplicate a particular strategy, then the focal firm has a sustainable competitive advantage, according to RBV theorists. For a resource to be valuable, however, it must be either (1) rare, (2) hard to imitate, or (3) not easily substitutable. Often called *empirical indicators,* these three characteristics of resources enable a firm to implement strategies that improve its efficiency and effectiveness and lead to a sustainable competitive advantage. The more a resource(s) is rare, nonimitable, and nonsubstitutable, the stronger a firm's competitive advantage will be and the longer it will last.

Rare resources are resources that other competing firms do not possess. If many firms have the same resource, then those firms will likely implement similar strategies, thus giving no one firm a sustainable competitive advantage. This is not to say that resources that are common are not valuable; they do indeed aid the firm in its chance for economic prosperity. However, to sustain a competitive advantage, it is more advantageous if the resource(s) is also rare.

It is also important that these same resources be difficult to imitate. If firms cannot easily gain the resources, say RBV theorists, then those resources will lead to a competitive advantage more so than resources easily imitable. Even if a firm employs resources that are rare, a sustainable competitive advantage may be achieved only if other firms cannot easily obtain these resources.

The third empirical indicator that can make resources a source of competitive advantage is substitutability. Borrowing from Porter's Five-Forces Model, to the degree that there are no viable substitutes, a firm will be able to sustain its competitive advantage. However, even if a competing firm cannot perfectly imitate a firm's resource, it can still obtain a sustainable competitive advantage of its own by obtaining resource substitutes.

The RBV has continued to grow in popularity and continues to seek a better understanding of the relationship between resources and sustained competitive advantage in strategic management. However, as alluded to in Chapter 3, one cannot say with any degree of certainty that either external or internal factors will always or even consistently be more important in seeking competitive advantage. Understanding both external and internal factors, and more importantly, understanding the relationships among them, will be the key to effective strategy formulation (discussed in Chapter 6). Since both external and internal factors continually change, strategists seek to identify and take advantage of positive changes and buffer against negative changes in a continuing effort to gain and sustain a firm's competitive advantage. This is the essence and challenge of strategic management, and oftentimes survival of the firm hinges on this work.

Integrating Strategy and Culture

Relationships among a firm's functional business activities perhaps can be exemplified best by focusing on organizational culture, an internal phenomenon that permeates all departments and divisions of an organization. *Organizational culture* can be defined as "a pattern of behavior that has been developed by an organization as it learns to cope with its problem of external adaptation and internal integration, and that has worked well enough to be considered valid and to be taught to new members as the correct way to perceive, think, and feel."[6] This definition emphasizes the importance of matching external with internal factors in making strategic decisions.

Organizational culture captures the subtle, elusive, and largely unconscious forces that shape a workplace. Remarkably resistant to change, culture can represent a major strength or weakness for the firm. It can be an underlying reason for strengths or weaknesses in any of the major business functions.

Defined in Table 4-1, *cultural products* include values, beliefs, rites, rituals, ceremonies, myths, stories, legends, sagas, language, metaphors, symbols, heroes, and heroines. These products or dimensions are levers that strategists can use to influence and direct strategy formulation, implementation, and evaluation activities. An organization's culture compares to an individual's personality in the sense that no two organizations have the same culture and no two individuals have the same personality. Both culture and personality are fairly enduring and can be warm, aggressive, friendly, open, innovative, conservative, liberal, harsh, or likable.

Dimensions of organizational culture permeate all the functional areas of business. It is something of an art to uncover the basic values and beliefs that are deeply buried in an organization's rich collection of stories, language, heroes, and rituals, but cultural products can represent both important strengths and weaknesses. Culture is an aspect of an organization that can no longer be taken for granted in performing an internal strategic-management audit because culture and strategy must work together.

The strategic-management process takes place largely within a particular organization's culture. Lorsch found that executives in successful companies are emotionally committed to the firm's culture, but he concluded that culture can inhibit strategic management in two basic ways. First, managers frequently miss the significance of changing external conditions because they are blinded by strongly held beliefs. Second, when a particular culture has been effective in the past, the natural response is to stick with it in the future, even during times of major strategic change.[7] An organization's culture must support the collective commitment of its people to a common purpose. It must foster competence and enthusiasm among managers and employees.

Organizational culture significantly affects business decisions and thus must be evaluated during an internal strategic-management audit. If strategies can capitalize on cultural strengths, such as a strong work ethic or highly ethical beliefs, then management often can swiftly and easily implement changes. However, if the firm's culture is not supportive, strategic changes may be ineffective or even counterproductive. A firm's culture can become antagonistic to new strategies, with the result being confusion and disorientation.

TABLE 4-1 **Cultural Products and Associated Definitions**

Rites	Relatively elaborate, dramatic, planned sets of activities that consolidate various forms of cultural expressions into one event, carried out through social interactions, usually for the benefit of an audience
Ceremonial	A system of several rites connected with a single occasion or event
Ritual	A standardized, detailed set of techniques and behaviors that manage anxieties but seldom produce intended, technical consequences of practical importance
Myth	A dramatic narrative of imagined events, usually used to explain origins or transformations of something; also, an unquestioned belief about the practical benefits of certain techniques and behaviors that is not supported by facts
Saga	A historical narrative describing the unique accomplishments of a group and its leaders, usually in heroic terms
Legend	A handed-down narrative of some wonderful event that is based on history but has been embellished with fictional details
Story	A narrative based on true events, sometimes a combination of truth and fiction
Folktale	A completely fictional narrative
Symbol	Any object, act, event, quality, or relation that serves as a vehicle for conveying meaning, usually by representing another thing
Language	A particular form or manner in which members of a group use sounds and written signs to convey meanings to each other
Metaphors	Shorthand of words used to capture a vision or to reinforce old or new values
Values	Life-directing attitudes that serve as behavioral guidelines
Belief	An understanding of a particular phenomenon
Heroes/Heroine	Individuals whom the organization has legitimized to model behavior for others

Source: Adapted from H. M. Trice and J. M. Beyer, "Studying Organizational Cultures through Rites and Ceremonials," *Academy of Management Review* 9, no. 4 (October 1984): 655.

An organization's culture should infuse individuals with enthusiasm for implementing strategies. Allarie and Firsirotu emphasized the need to understand culture:

> Culture provides an explanation for the insuperable difficulties a firm encounters when it attempts to shift its strategic direction. Not only has the "right" culture become the essence and foundation of corporate excellence, it is also claimed that success or failure of reforms hinges on management's sagacity and ability to change the firm's driving culture in time and in time with required changes in strategies.[8]

The potential value of organizational culture has not been realized fully in the study of strategic management. Ignoring the effect that culture can have on relationships among the functional areas of business can result in barriers to communication, lack of coordination, and an inability to adapt to changing conditions. Some tension between culture and a firm's strategy is inevitable, but the tension should be monitored so that it does not reach a point at which relationships are severed and the culture becomes antagonistic. The resulting disarray among members of the organization would disrupt strategy formulation, implementation, and evaluation. On the other hand, a supportive organizational culture can make managing much easier.

Internal strengths and weaknesses associated with a firm's culture sometimes are overlooked because of the interfunctional nature of this phenomenon. It is important, therefore, for strategists to understand their firm as a sociocultural system. Success is often determined by linkages between a firm's culture and strategies. The challenge of strategic management today is to bring about the changes in organizational culture and individual mind-sets that are needed to support the formulation, implementation, and evaluation of strategies.

U.S. versus Foreign Cultures

To successfully compete in world markets, U.S. managers must obtain a better knowledge of historical, cultural, and religious forces that motivate and drive people in other countries. In Japan, for example, business relations operate within the context of *Wa,* which stresses group harmony and social cohesion. In China, business behavior revolves around *guanxi,* or personal relations. In Korea, activities involve concern for *inhwa,* or harmony based on respect of hierarchical relationships, including obedience to authority.[9]

In Europe, it is generally true that the farther north on the continent, the more participatory the management style. Most European workers are unionized and enjoy more frequent vacations and holidays than U.S. workers. A 90-minute lunch break plus 20-minute morning and afternoon breaks are common in European firms. Guaranteed permanent employment is commonly a part of employment contracts in Europe. In socialist countries such as France, Belgium, and the United Kingdom, the only ground for immediate dismissal from work is a criminal offense. A six-month trial period at the beginning of employment is usually part of the contract with a European firm. Many Europeans resent pay-for-performance, commission salaries, and objective measurement and reward systems. This is true especially of workers in southern Europe. Many Europeans also find the notion of team spirit difficult to grasp because the unionized environment has dichotomized worker–management relations throughout Europe.

A weakness that U.S. firms have in competing with Pacific Rim firms is a lack of understanding of Asian cultures, including how Asians think and behave. Spoken Chinese, for example, has more in common with spoken English than with spoken Japanese or Korean. Managers around the world face the responsibility of having to exert authority while at the same time trying to be liked by subordinates. U.S. managers consistently put more weight on being friendly and liked, whereas Asian and European managers exercise authority often without this concern. Americans tend to use first names instantly in business dealings with foreigners, but foreigners find this presumptuous. In Japan, for example, first names are used only among family members and intimate friends; even longtime business associates and coworkers shy away from the use of first names. Other cultural differences or pitfalls that U.S. managers need to know about are given in Table 4-2.

U.S. managers have a low tolerance for silence, whereas Asian managers view extended periods of silence as important for organizing and evaluating one's thoughts. U.S. managers are much more action-oriented than their counterparts around the world; they rush to appointments, conferences, and meetings—and then feel the day has been productive. But for foreign managers, resting, listening, meditating, and thinking is considered productive. Sitting through a conference without talking is unproductive in the United States, but it is viewed as positive in Japan if one's silence helps preserve unity.

U.S. managers also put greater emphasis on short-term results than foreign managers do. In marketing, for example, Japanese managers strive to achieve "everlasting customers," whereas many Americans strive to make a one-time sale. Marketing managers in Japan see making a sale as the beginning, not the end, of the selling process. This is an important distinction. Japanese managers often criticize U.S. managers for worrying more about shareholders, whom they do not know, than employees, whom they do know. Americans refer to "hourly employees," whereas many Japanese companies still refer to "lifetime employees."

Rose Knotts recently summarized some important cultural differences between U.S. and foreign managers:[10]

1. Americans place an exceptionally high priority on time, viewing time as an asset. Many foreigners place more worth on relationships. This difference results in foreign managers often viewing U.S. managers as "more interested in business than people."

2. Personal touching and distance norms differ around the world. Americans generally stand about three feet from each other when carrying on business conversations, but Arabs and Africans stand about one foot apart. Touching another person with the left hand in business dealings is taboo in some countries. American managers need to learn the personal-space rules of foreign managers with whom they interact in business.

3. People in some cultures do not place the same significance on material wealth as American managers often do. Lists of the "largest corporations" and "highest-paid" executives abound in the United States. "More is better" and "bigger is better" in the United States, but not everywhere. This can be a consideration in trying to motivate individuals in other countries.

4. Family roles and relationships vary in different countries. For example, males are valued more than females in some cultures, and peer pressure, work situations, and business interactions reinforce this phenomenon.

TABLE 4-2   Cultural Pitfalls That You Need to Know

- Waving is a serious insult in Greece and Nigeria, particularly if the hand is near someone's face.
- Making a "good-bye" wave in Europe can mean "No," but it means "Come here" in Peru.
- In China, last names are written first.
- A man named Carlos Lopez-Garcia should be addressed as Mr. Lopez in Latin America, but as Mr. Garcia in Brazil.
- Breakfast meetings are considered uncivilized in most foreign countries.
- Latin Americans are on average 20 minutes late to business appointments.
- Direct eye contact is impolite in Japan.
- Don't cross your legs in any Arab or many Asian countries—it's rude to show the sole of your shoe.
- In Brazil, touching your thumb and first finger—an American "Okay" sign—is the equivalent of raising your middle finger.
- Nodding or tossing your head back in southern Italy, Malta, Greece, and Tunisia means "No." In India, this body motion means "Yes."
- Snapping your fingers is vulgar in France and Belgium.
- Folding your arms across your chest is a sign of annoyance in Finland.
- In China, leave some food on your plate to show that your host was so generous that you couldn't finish.
- Do not eat with your left hand when dining with clients from Malaysia or India.
- One form of communication works the same worldwide. It's the smile—so take that along wherever you go.

5. Language differs dramatically across countries, even in countries where people speak the same language. Words and expressions commonly used in one country may be disrespectful in another.

6. Business and daily life in some societies are governed by religious factors. Prayer times, holidays, daily events, and dietary restrictions, for example, need to be respected by American managers not familiar with these practices in some countries.

7. Time spent with the family and the quality of relationships are more important in some cultures than the personal achievement and accomplishments espoused by the traditional U.S. manager. For example, where a person stands in the hierarchy of a firm's organizational structure, how large the firm is, and where the firm is located are much more important factors to U.S. managers than to many foreign managers.

8. Many cultures around the world value modesty, team spirit, collectivity, and patience much more than the competitiveness and individualism that are so important in the United States.

9. Punctuality is a valued personal trait when conducting business in the United States, but it is not revered in many of the world's societies. Eating habits also differ dramatically across cultures. For example, belching is acceptable in many countries as evidence of satisfaction with the food that has been prepared. Chinese culture considers it good manners to sample a portion of each food served.

10. To prevent social blunders when meeting with managers from other lands, one must learn and respect the rules of etiquette of others. Sitting on a toilet seat is viewed as unsanitary in most countries, but not in the United States. Leaving food or drink after dining is considered impolite in some countries, but not in China. Bowing instead of shaking hands is customary in many countries. Many cultures view Americans as unsanitary for locating toilet and bathing facilities in the same area, whereas Americans view people of some cultures as unsanitary for not taking a bath or shower every day.

11. Americans often do business with individuals they do not know, but this practice is not accepted in many other cultures. In Mexico and Japan, for example, an amicable relationship is often mandatory before conducting business.

In many countries, effective managers are those who are best at negotiating with government bureaucrats rather than those who inspire workers. Many U.S. managers are uncomfortable with nepotism and bribery, which are common in many countries. In almost every country except the United States, bribery is tax deductible.

The United States has gained a reputation for defending women from sexual harassment and minorities from discrimination, but not all countries embrace the same values.

American managers in China have to be careful about how they arrange office furniture because Chinese workers believe in *feng shui,* the practice of harnessing natural forces. U.S. managers in Japan have to be careful about *nemaswashio,* whereby Japanese workers expect supervisors to alert them privately of changes rather than informing them in a meeting. Japanese managers have little appreciation for versatility, expecting all managers to be the same. In Japan, "If a nail sticks out, you hit it into the wall," says Brad Lashbrook, an international consultant for Wilson Learning.

Probably the biggest obstacle to the effectiveness of U.S. managers—or managers from any country working in another—is the fact that it is almost impossible to change the attitude of a foreign workforce. "The system drives you; you cannot fight the system or culture," says Bill Parker, president of Phillips Petroleum in Norway.

Management

The *functions of management* consist of five basic activities: planning, organizing, motivating, staffing, and controlling. An overview of these activities is provided in Table 4-3.

Planning

The only thing certain about the future of any organization is change, and *planning* is the essential bridge between the present and the future that increases the likelihood of achieving desired results. Planning is the process by which one determines whether to attempt a

TABLE 4-3 **The Basic Functions of Management**

Function	Description	Stage of Strategic-Management Process When Most Important
Planning	Planning consists of all those managerial activities related to preparing for the future. Specific tasks include forecasting, establishing objectives, devising strategies, developing policies, and setting goals.	Strategy Formulation
Organizing	Organizing includes all those managerial activities that result in a structure of task and authority relationships. Specific areas include organizational design, job specialization, job descriptions, job specifications, span of control, unity of command, coordination, job design, and job analysis.	Strategy Implementation
Motivating	Motivating involves efforts directed toward shaping human behavior. Specific topics include leadership, communication, work groups, behavior modification, delegation of authority, job enrichment, job satisfaction, needs fulfillment, organizational change, employee morale, and managerial morale.	Strategy Implementation
Staffing	Staffing activities are centered on personnel or human resource management. Included are wage and salary administration, employee benefits, interviewing, hiring, firing, training, management development, employee safety, affirmative action, equal employment opportunity, union relations, career development, personnel research, discipline policies, grievance procedures, and public relations.	Strategy Implementation
Controlling	Controlling refers to all those managerial activities directed toward ensuring that actual results are consistent with planned results. Key areas of concern include quality control, financial control, sales control, inventory control, expense control, analysis of variances, rewards, and sanctions.	Strategy Evaluation

task, works out the most effective way of reaching desired objectives, and prepares to overcome unexpected difficulties with adequate resources. Planning is the start of the process by which an individual or business may turn empty dreams into achievements. Planning enables one to avoid the trap of working extremely hard but achieving little.

Planning is an up-front investment in success. Planning helps a firm achieve maximum effect from a given effort. Planning enables a firm to take into account relevant factors and focus on the critical ones. Planning helps ensure that the firm can be prepared for all reasonable eventualities and for all changes that will be needed. Planning enables a firm to gather the resources needed and carry out tasks in the most efficient way possible. Planning enables a firm to conserve its own resources, avoid wasting ecological resources, make a fair profit, and be seen as an effective, useful firm. Planning enables a firm to identify precisely what is to be achieved and to detail precisely the who, what, when, where, why, and how needed to achieve desired objectives. Planning enables a firm to assess whether the effort, costs, and implications associated with achieving desired objectives are warranted.[11] Planning is the cornerstone of effective strategy formulation. But even though it is considered the foundation of management, it is commonly the task that managers neglect most. Planning is essential for successful strategy implementation and strategy evaluation, largely because organizing, motivating, staffing, and controlling activities depend upon good planning.

The process of planning must involve managers and employees throughout an organization. The time horizon for planning decreases from two to five years for top-level to less than six months for lower-level managers. The important point is that all managers do planning and should involve subordinates in the process to facilitate employee understanding and commitment.

Planning can have a positive impact on organizational and individual performance. Planning allows an organization to identify and take advantage of external opportunities as well as minimize the impact of external threats. Planning is more than extrapolating from the past and present into the future. It also includes developing a mission, forecasting future events and trends, establishing objectives, and choosing strategies to pursue.

An organization can develop synergy through planning. *Synergy* exists when everyone pulls together as a team that knows what it wants to achieve; synergy is the 2 + 2 = 5 effect. By establishing and communicating clear objectives, employees and managers can work together toward desired results. Synergy can result in powerful competitive advantages. The strategic-management process itself is aimed at creating synergy in an organization.

Planning allows a firm to adapt to changing markets and thus to shape its own destiny. Strategic management can be viewed as a formal planning process that allows an organization to pursue proactive rather than reactive strategies. Successful organizations strive to control their own futures rather than merely react to external forces and events as they occur. Historically, organisms and organizations that have not adapted to changing conditions have become extinct. Swift adaptation is needed today more than ever because changes in markets, economies, and competitors worldwide are accelerating.

Organizing

The purpose of *organizing* is to achieve coordinated effort by defining task and authority relationships. Organizing means determining who does what and who reports to whom. There are countless examples in history of well-organized enterprises successfully competing against—and in some cases defeating—much stronger but less-organized firms. A well-organized firm generally has motivated managers and employees who are committed to seeing the organization succeed. Resources are allocated more effectively and used more efficiently in a well-organized firm than in a disorganized firm.

The organizing function of management can be viewed as consisting of three sequential activities: breaking down tasks into jobs (work specialization), combining jobs to form departments (departmentalization), and delegating authority. Breaking down tasks into jobs requires the development of job descriptions and job specifications. These tools clarify for both managers and employees what particular jobs entail. In *The Wealth of Nations*, published in 1776, Adam Smith cited the advantages of work specialization in the manufacture of pins:

> One man draws the wire, another straightens it, a third cuts it, a fourth points it, a fifth grinds it at the top for receiving the head. Ten men working in this manner can produce 48,000 pins in a single day, but if they had all wrought separately and independently, each might at best produce twenty pins in a day.[12]

Combining jobs to form departments results in an organizational structure, span of control, and a chain of command. Changes in strategy often require changes in structure because positions may be created, deleted, or merged. Organizational structure dictates how resources are allocated and how objectives are established in a firm. Allocating resources and establishing objectives geographically, for example, is much different from doing so by product or customer.

The most common forms of departmentalization are functional, divisional, strategic business unit, and matrix. These types of structure are discussed further in Chapter 7.

Delegating authority is an important organizing activity, as evidenced in the old saying "You can tell how good a manager is by observing how his or her department functions when he or she isn't there." Employees today are more educated and more capable of participating in organizational decision making than ever before. In most cases, they expect to be delegated authority and responsibility and to be held accountable for results. Delegation of authority is embedded in the strategic-management process.

Motivating

Motivating can be defined as the process of influencing people to accomplish specific objectives.[13] Motivation explains why some people work hard and others do not. Objectives, strategies, and policies have little chance of succeeding if employees and managers are not motivated to implement strategies once they are formulated. The motivating function of management includes at least four major components: leadership, group dynamics, communication, and organizational change.

When managers and employees of a firm strive to achieve high levels of productivity, this indicates that the firm's strategists are good leaders. Good leaders establish rapport with subordinates, empathize with their needs and concerns, set a good example, and are trustworthy and fair. Leadership includes developing a vision of the firm's future and inspiring people to work hard to achieve that vision. Kirkpatrick and Locke reported that certain traits also characterize effective leaders: knowledge of the business, cognitive ability, self-confidence, honesty, integrity, and drive.[14]

Research suggests that democratic behavior on the part of leaders results in more positive attitudes toward change and higher productivity than does autocratic behavior. Drucker said:

> Leadership is not a magnetic personality. That can just as well be demagoguery. It is not "making friends and influencing people." That is flattery. Leadership is the lifting of a person's vision to higher sights, the raising of a person's performance to a higher standard, the building of a person's personality beyond its normal limitations.[15]

Group dynamics play a major role in employee morale and satisfaction. Informal groups or coalitions form in every organization. The norms of coalitions can range from being very positive to very negative toward management. It is important, therefore, that strategists identify the composition and nature of informal groups in an organization to facilitate strategy formulation, implementation, and evaluation. Leaders of informal groups are especially important in formulating and implementing strategy changes.

Communication, perhaps the most important word in management, is a major component in motivation. An organization's system of communication determines whether strategies can be implemented successfully. Good two-way communication is vital for gaining support for departmental and divisional objectives and policies. Top-down communication can encourage bottom-up communication. The strategic-management process becomes a lot easier when subordinates are encouraged to discuss their concerns, reveal their problems, provide recommendations, and give suggestions. A primary reason for instituting strategic management is to build and support effective communication networks throughout the firm.

> The manager of tomorrow must be able to get his people to commit themselves to the business, whether they are machine operators or junior vice-presidents. Ah, you say, participative management. Have a cigar. But just because most managers tug a forelock at the P word doesn't mean they know how to make it work. Today, throwing together a few quality circles won't suffice. The key issue will be empowerment, a term whose strength suggests the need to get beyond merely sharing a little information and a bit of decision making.[16]

Staffing

The management function of *staffing,* also called *personnel management* or *human resource management,* includes activities such as recruiting, interviewing, testing, selecting, orienting, training, developing, caring for, evaluating, rewarding, disciplining, promoting, transferring, demoting, and dismissing employees, as well as managing union relations.

Staffing activities play a major role in strategy-implementation efforts, and for this reason, human resource managers are becoming more actively involved in the strategic-management process. It is important to identify strengths and weaknesses in the staffing area.

The complexity and importance of human resource activities have increased to such a degree that all but the smallest organizations now need a full-time human resource manager. Numerous court cases that directly affect staffing activities are decided each day. Organizations and individuals can be penalized severely for not following federal, state, and local laws and guidelines related to staffing. Line managers simply cannot stay abreast of all the legal developments and requirements regarding staffing. The human resources department coordinates staffing decisions in the firm so that an organization as a whole meets legal requirements. This department also provides needed consistency in administering company rules, wages, and policies.

Human resource management is particularly challenging for international companies. For example, the inability of spouses and children to adapt to new surroundings has become a major staffing problem in overseas transfers. The problems include premature returns, job performance slumps, resignations, discharges, low morale, marital discord, and general discontent. Firms such as Ford Motor and ExxonMobil have begun screening and interviewing spouses and children before assigning persons to overseas positions. The 3M Corporation introduces children to peers in the target country and offers spouses educational benefits.

Strategists are becoming increasingly aware of how important human resources are to effective strategic management. Human resource managers are becoming more involved and more proactive in formulating and implementing strategies. They provide leadership for organizations that are restructuring, or they allow employees to work at home.

Controlling

The *controlling* function of management includes all of those activities undertaken to ensure that actual operations conform to planned operations. All managers in an organization have controlling responsibilities, such as conducting performance evaluations and taking necessary action to minimize inefficiencies. The controlling function of management is particularly important for effective strategy evaluation. Controlling consists of four basic steps:

1. Establishing performance standards
2. Measuring individual and organizational performance
3. Comparing actual performance to planned performance standards
4. Taking corrective actions

Measuring individual performance is often conducted ineffectively or not at all in organizations. Some reasons for this shortcoming are that evaluations can create confrontations that most managers prefer to avoid, can take more time than most managers are willing to give, and can require skills that many managers lack. No single approach to measuring individual performance is without limitations. For this reason, an organization should examine various methods, such as the graphic rating scale, the behaviorally anchored rating scale, and the critical incident method, and then develop or select a performance-appraisal approach that best suits the firm's needs. Increasingly, firms are striving to link organizational performance with managers' and employees' pay. This topic is discussed further in Chapter 7.

Management Audit Checklist of Questions

The following checklist of questions can help determine specific strengths and weaknesses in the functional area of business. An answer of *no* to any question could indicate a potential weakness, although the strategic significance and implications of negative answers, of course, will vary by organization, industry, and severity of the weakness. Positive or yes answers to the checklist questions suggest potential areas of strength.

1. Does the firm use strategic-management concepts?
2. Are company objectives and goals measurable and well communicated?
3. Do managers at all hierarchical levels plan effectively?
4. Do managers delegate authority well?
5. Is the organization's structure appropriate?
6. Are job descriptions and job specifications clear?
7. Is employee morale high?
8. Are employee turnover and absenteeism low?
9. Are organizational reward and control mechanisms effective?

Marketing

Marketing can be described as the process of defining, anticipating, creating, and fulfilling customers' needs and wants for products and services. There are seven basic *functions of marketing:* (1) customer analysis, (2) selling products/services, (3) product and service planning, (4) pricing, (5) distribution, (6) marketing research, and (7) opportunity analysis.[17] Understanding these functions helps strategists identify and evaluate marketing strengths and weaknesses.

Customer Analysis

Customer analysis—the examination and evaluation of consumer needs, desires, and wants—involves administering customer surveys, analyzing consumer information, evaluating market positioning strategies, developing customer profiles, and determining optimal market segmentation strategies. The information generated by customer analysis can be essential in developing an effective mission statement. Customer profiles can reveal the demographic characteristics of an organization's customers. Buyers, sellers, distributors, salespeople, managers, wholesalers, retailers, suppliers, and creditors can all participate in gathering information to successfully identify customers' needs and wants. Successful organizations continually monitor present and potential customers' buying patterns.

Selling Products/Services

Successful strategy implementation generally rests upon the ability of an organization to sell some product or service. *Selling* includes many marketing activities, such as advertising, sales promotion, publicity, personal selling, sales force management, customer relations, and dealer relations. These activities are especially critical when a firm pursues a market penetration strategy. The effectiveness of various selling tools for consumer and industrial products varies. Personal selling is most important for industrial goods companies, and advertising is most important for consumer goods companies. During the CBS telecast of Super Bowl XXXVIX on February 4, 2007, a 30-second advertisement cost $2.6 million, up 4 percent from the prior year when ABC broadcast the game. But the Super Bowl continues to be among the few television events that draw a huge audience, about 100 million each year, according to Nielsen Media Research. Anheuser-Busch was again the biggest advertiser, with 10 advertising slots in the game.

Advertising on television is declining dramatically while Internet advertising is growing rapidly. Newspaper advertising declined 2.4 percent in 2006 while magazine advertising rose 3.8 percent.[18] The top U.S. firms in terms of spending on advertising are listed in Table 4-4. Note that Procter & Gamble, GM, and AT&T spent the most on advertising in 2006. Note also that the average total ad dollars spent is declining.

TABLE 4-4 **Which U.S. Firms Spend the Most on Advertising? (In Billions $)**

Company	2005	2006	Percent Change
P&G	3.2	3.3	+03.3
GM	3.0	2.3	−23.7
AT&T	1.7	2.2	+30.8
Verizon	1.8	1.9	+10.4
Time Warner	2.1	1.8	−12.0
Ford	1.6	1.7	+08.5
Walt Disney	1.4	1.4	+00.9
DaimlerChrysler	1.6	1.4	−10.7
Johnson & Johnson	1.6	1.3	−19.8
News Corp.	1.3	1.3	−02.4
Average			−02.8

Source: Adapted from Emily Steel, "Ad Cutbacks Likely Signal Budget Shift," *Wall Street Journal* (March 14, 2007): B3.

JCPenney Co. recently unveiled a new marketing campaign centered around the slogan "Every Day Matters," after abandoning its prior slogan, "It's All Inside." Penney's hopes the slogan will become as powerful as Nike's "Just Do It." Penney's new slogan aims to create an emotional connection between the store and its customers, rather than emphasize its broad selection of merchandise. Determining organizational strengths and weaknesses in the selling function of marketing is an important part of performing an internal strategic-management audit.

With regard to advertising products and services on the Internet, a new trend is to base advertising rates exclusively on sales rates. This new accountability contrasts sharply with traditional broadcast and print advertising, which bases rates on the number of persons expected to see a given advertisement. The new cost-per-sale online advertising rates are possible because any Web site can monitor which user clicks on which advertisement and then can record whether that consumer actually buys the product. If there are no sales, then the advertisement is free.

In a major strategic shift, pharmaceutical companies are significantly reducing the number of their salespersons who call on primary-care doctors such as internists and general practitioners. For example, drug maker Wyeth is reducing by 30 percent its sales force to less than 5,000 persons. The strategic shift among drug firms is to drastically reduce multiple salespeople calling on identical doctors. This common but costly strategy, called *mirroring,* has alienated physicians. Pfizer, which has the world's largest drug sales force, is cutting its sales force dramatically.

Product and Service Planning

Product and service planning includes activities such as test marketing; product and brand positioning; devising warranties; packaging; determining product options, product features, product style, and product quality; deleting old products; and providing for customer service. Product and service planning is particularly important when a company is pursuing product development or diversification.

One of the most effective product and service planning techniques is *test marketing.* Test markets allow an organization to test alternative marketing plans and to forecast future sales of new products. In conducting a test market project, an organization must decide how many cities to include, which cities to include, how long to run the test, what information to collect during the test, and what action to take after the test has been completed. Test marketing is used more frequently by consumer goods companies than by industrial goods companies. Test marketing can allow an organization to avoid substantial losses by revealing weak products and ineffective marketing approaches before large-scale production begins.

Pricing

Five major stakeholders affect *pricing* decisions: consumers, governments, suppliers, distributors, and competitors. Sometimes an organization will pursue a forward integration strategy primarily to gain better control over prices charged to consumers. Governments can impose constraints on price fixing, price discrimination, minimum prices, unit pricing, price advertising, and price controls. For example, the Robinson-Patman Act prohibits manufacturers and wholesalers from discriminating in price among channel member purchasers (suppliers and distributors) if competition is injured.

Competing organizations must be careful not to coordinate discounts, credit terms, or condition of sale; not to discuss prices, markups, and costs at trade association meetings; and not to arrange to issue new price lists on the same date, to rotate low bids on contracts, or to uniformly restrict production to maintain high prices. Strategists should view price from both a short-run and a long-run perspective, because competitors can copy price changes with relative ease. Often a dominant firm will aggressively match all price cuts by competitors.

With regard to pricing, as the value of the dollar increases, U.S. multinational companies have a choice. They can raise prices in the local currency of a foreign country or risk losing sales and market share. Alternatively, multinational firms can keep prices steady and face reduced profit when their export revenue is reported in the United States in dollars.

Intense price competition coupled with Internet price-comparative shopping in most industries has reduced profit margins to bare minimum levels for most companies. For example, airline tickets, rental car prices, and even computer prices are lower today than they have been in many years.

Distribution

Distribution includes warehousing, distribution channels, distribution coverage, retail site locations, sales territories, inventory levels and location, transportation carriers, wholesaling, and retailing. Most producers today do not sell their goods directly to consumers. Various marketing entities act as intermediaries; they bear a variety of names such as wholesalers, retailers, brokers, facilitators, agents, vendors—or simply distributors.

Distribution becomes especially important when a firm is striving to implement a market development or forward integration strategy. Some of the most complex and challenging decisions facing a firm concern product distribution. Intermediaries flourish in our economy because many producers lack the financial resources and expertise to carry out direct marketing. Manufacturers who could afford to sell directly to the public often can gain greater returns by expanding and improving their manufacturing operations. Even General Motors would find it very difficult to buy out its more than 18,000 independent dealers.

Successful organizations identify and evaluate alternative ways to reach their ultimate market. Possible approaches vary from direct selling to using just one or many wholesalers and retailers. Strengths and weaknesses of each channel alternative should be determined according to economic, control, and adaptive criteria. Organizations should consider the costs and benefits of various wholesaling and retailing options. They must consider the need to motivate and control channel members and the need to adapt to changes in the future. Once a marketing channel is chosen, an organization usually must adhere to it for an extended period of time.

Marketing Research

Marketing research is the systematic gathering, recording, and analyzing of data about problems relating to the marketing of goods and services. Marketing research can uncover critical strengths and weaknesses, and marketing researchers employ numerous scales, instruments, procedures, concepts, and techniques to gather information. Marketing research activities support all of the major business functions of an organization. Organizations that possess excellent marketing research skills have a definite strength in pursuing generic strategies.

> The President of PepsiCo said, "Looking at the competition is the company's best form of market research. The majority of our strategic successes are ideas that we borrow from the marketplace, usually from a small regional or local competitor. In each case, we spot a promising new idea, improve on it, and then out-execute our competitor."[19]

Opportunity Analysis

The seventh function of marketing is *opportunity analysis,* which involves assessing the costs, benefits, and risks associated with marketing decisions. Three steps are required to perform a *cost/benefit analysis:* (1) compute the total costs associated with a decision, (2) estimate the total benefits from the decision, and (3) compare the total costs with the total benefits. When expected benefits exceed total costs, an opportunity becomes more attractive. Sometimes the variables included in a cost/benefit analysis cannot be quantified or even measured, but usually reasonable estimates can be made to allow the analysis to be performed. One key factor to be considered is risk. Cost/benefit analysis should also be performed when a company is evaluating alternative ways to be socially responsible.

Marketing Audit Checklist of Questions

The following questions about marketing, much like the earlier questions for management, are pertinent:

1. Are markets segmented effectively?
2. Is the organization positioned well among competitors?
3. Has the firm's market share been increasing?
4. Are present channels of distribution reliable and cost-effective?
5. Does the firm have an effective sales organization?
6. Does the firm conduct market research?
7. Are product quality and customer service good?
8. Are the firm's products and services priced appropriately?
9. Does the firm have an effective promotion, advertising, and publicity strategy?
10. Are marketing, planning, and budgeting effective?
11. Do the firm's marketing managers have adequate experience and training?

Finance/Accounting

Financial condition is often considered the single best measure of a firm's competitive position and overall attractiveness to investors. Determining an organization's financial strengths and weaknesses is essential to effectively formulating strategies. A firm's liquidity, leverage, working capital, profitability, asset utilization, cash flow, and equity can eliminate some strategies as being feasible alternatives. Financial factors often alter existing strategies and change implementation plans.

An especially good Web site from which to obtain financial information about a company is https://us.etrade.com/e/t/invest/markets, which provides excellent financial ratio, stock, and valuation information on all publicly held companies. Simply insert the company's stock symbol when the screen first loads and a wealth of information follows. Another nice site for obtaining financial information is www.forbes.com. Be sure to access the Manufacturing and Service section of www.strategyclub.com for excellent financial-related Web sites.

Finance/Accounting Functions

According to James Van Horne, the *functions of finance/accounting* comprise three decisions: the investment decision, the financing decision, and the dividend decision.[20] Financial ratio analysis is the most widely used method for determining an organization's strengths and weaknesses in the investment, financing, and dividend areas. Because the functional areas of business are so closely related, financial ratios can signal strengths or weaknesses in management, marketing, production, research and development, and management information systems activities. It is important to note here that financial ratios are equally applicable in for-profit and nonprofit organizations. Even though nonprofit organizations obviously would not have return-on-investment or earnings-per-share ratios, they would routinely monitor many other special ratios. For example, a church would monitor the ratio of dollar contributions to number of members, while a zoo would monitor dollar food sales to number of visitors. A university would monitor number of students divided by number of professors. Therefore, be creative when performing ratio analysis for nonprofit organizations because they strive to be financially sound just as for-profit firms do.

The *investment decision,* also called *capital budgeting,* is the allocation and reallocation of capital and resources to projects, products, assets, and divisions of an organization. Once strategies are formulated, capital budgeting decisions are required to successfully implement strategies. The *financing decision* determines the best capital structure for the firm and includes examining various methods by which the firm can raise capital (for example, by issuing stock, increasing debt, selling assets, or using a combination of these approaches). The financing decision must consider both short-term and long-term needs for working capital. Two key financial ratios that indicate whether a firm's financing decisions have been effective are the debt-to-equity ratio and the debt-to-total-assets ratio.

Dividend decisions concern issues such as the percentage of earnings paid to stock-holders, the stability of dividends paid over time, and the repurchase or issuance of stock. Dividend decisions determine the amount of funds that are retained in a firm compared to the amount paid out to stockholders. Three financial ratios that are helpful in evaluating a firm's dividend decisions are the earnings-per-share ratio, the dividends-per-share ratio, and the price-earnings ratio. The benefits of paying dividends to investors must be balanced against the benefits of internally retaining funds, and there is no set formula on how to balance this trade-off. For the reasons listed here, dividends are sometimes paid out even when funds could be better reinvested in the business or when the firm has to obtain outside sources of capital:

1. Paying cash dividends is customary. Failure to do so could be thought of as a stigma. A dividend change is considered a signal about the future.
2. Dividends represent a sales point for investment bankers. Some institutional investors can buy only dividend-paying stocks.
3. Shareholders often demand dividends, even in companies with great opportunities for reinvesting all available funds.
4. A myth exists that paying dividends will result in a higher stock price.

Among Standard & Poors (S&P) 500 companies in the United States, only 295 raised their dividend payout in 2006, down from 306 in 2005. Only six S&P 500 companies began paying dividends in 2006 for the first time, down from 10 in both 2005 and 2004. Dividend-paying companies in the S&P 500 outperformed non-dividend-paying companies by 3.7 percent in 2006, but paying dividends is becoming less common than buying back one's stock (Treasury stock) as a use for net income.[21] Alcoa is in the process of buying back 10 percent of its shares outstanding, and also just approved a 13 percent increase in its dividend payout.

The largest pharmaceutical company in the world, Pfizer, in 2007 raised its dividend 21 percent to 29 cents per share on the heels of a 26 percent increased in its dividend payout the prior year. Analysts say Pfizer did this to appease investors who were restless over its sliding stock price and who no longer viewed Pfizer as a growth stock. Pfizer in 2007 is also eliminating 10,000 jobs and closing two U.S. plants and five research sites.

Wal-Mart Stores approved a 31 percent increase in the company's annual dividend, in a move to return $3.6 billion to shareholders in its 2008 fiscal year. The world's largest retailer said its annual dividend for the year ending January 31, 2008 will rise to 88 cents per share from 67 cents previously.

Maytag cut its dividend payout from 18 cents per share, which had been in place since 1998, to 9 cents per share following an 80 percent collapse in first-quarter 2005 company earnings. Maytag has been slow to move its manufacturing outside the United States to capitalize on lower labor costs. Only 12 percent of Maytag products are made outside the United States, although it just closed a refrigerator factory in Galesburg, Illinois, and reopened that factory in Reynosa, Mexico.

Basic Types of Financial Ratios

Financial ratios are computed from an organization's income statement and balance sheet. Computing financial ratios is like taking a picture because the results reflect a situation at just one point in time. Comparing ratios over time and to industry averages is more likely to result in meaningful statistics that can be used to identify and evaluate strengths and weaknesses. Trend analysis, illustrated in Figure 4-2, is a useful technique that incorporates both the time and industry average dimensions of financial ratios. Note that the dotted lines reveal projected ratios. Some Web sites, such as those provided in Table 4-5 calculate financial ratios and provide data with charts. Four major sources of industry-average financial ratios follow:

VISIT THE NET

Enter your stock symbol and then access the up-to-date financial news about the company. (http://finance.yahoo.com)

1. Dun & Bradstreet's *Industry Norms and Key Business Ratios*—Fourteen different ratios are calculated in an industry-average format for 800 different types of

FIGURE 4-2

A Financial Ratio Trend Analysis

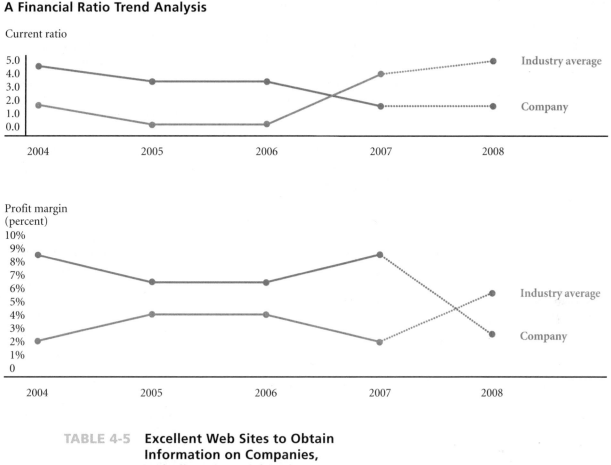

TABLE 4-5   **Excellent Web Sites to Obtain Information on Companies, Including Financial Ratios**

http://marketwatch.multexinvestor.com
http://moneycentral.msn.com
http://finance.yahoo.com
www.clearstation.com
https://us.etrade.com/e/t/invest/markets

businesses. The ratios are presented by Standard Industrial Classification (SIC) number and are grouped by annual sales into three size categories.

2. Robert Morris Associates' *Annual Statement Studies*—Sixteen different ratios are calculated in an industry-average format. Industries are referenced by SIC numbers published by the Bureau of the Census. The ratios are presented in four size categories by annual sales for all firms in the industry.

3. *Almanac of Business & Industrial Financial Ratios*—Twenty-two financial ratios and percentages are provided in an industry-average format for all major industries. The ratios and percentages are given for 12 different company-size categories for all firms in a given industry.

4. *Federal Trade Commission Reports*—The FTC publishes quarterly financial data, including ratios on manufacturing companies. FTC reports include analyses by industry group and asset size.

Table 4-6 provides a summary of key financial ratios showing how each ratio is calculated and what each ratio measures. However, all the ratios are not significant for all industries and companies. For example, accounts receivable turnover and average collection

TABLE 4-6   **A Summary of Key Financial Ratios**

Ratio	How Calculated	What It Measures
Liquidity Ratios		
Current Ratio	$\dfrac{\text{Current assets}}{\text{Current liabilities}}$	The extent to which a firm can meet its short-term obligations
Quick Ratio	$\dfrac{\text{Current assets minus inventory}}{\text{Current liabilities}}$	The extent to which a firm can meet its short-term obligations without relying upon the sale of its inventories
Leverage Ratios		
Debt-to-Total-Assets Ratio	$\dfrac{\text{Total debt}}{\text{Total assets}}$	The percentage of total funds that are provided by creditors
Debt-to-Equity Ratio	$\dfrac{\text{Total debt}}{\text{Total stockholders' equity}}$	The percentage of total funds provided by creditors versus by owners
Long-Term Debt-to-Equity Ratio	$\dfrac{\text{Long-term debt}}{\text{Total stockholders' equity}}$	The balance between debt and equity in a firm's long-term capital structure
Times-Interest-Earned Ratio	$\dfrac{\text{Profits before interest and taxes}}{\text{Total interest charges}}$	The extent to which earnings can decline without the firm becoming unable to meet its annual interest costs
Activity Ratios		
Inventory Turnover	$\dfrac{\text{Sales}}{\text{Inventory of finished goods}}$	Whether a firm holds excessive stocks of inventories and whether a firm is slowly selling its inventories compared to the industry average
Fixed Assets Turnover	$\dfrac{\text{Sales}}{\text{Fixed assets}}$	Sales productivity and plant and equipment utilization
Total Assets Turnover	$\dfrac{\text{Sales}}{\text{Total assets}}$	Whether a firm is generating a sufficient volume of business for the size of its asset investment
Accounts Receivable Turnover	$\dfrac{\text{Annual credit sales}}{\text{Accounts receivable}}$	The average length of time it takes a firm to collect credit sales (in percentage terms)
Average Collection Period	$\dfrac{\text{Accounts receivable}}{\text{Total credit sales/365 days}}$	The average length of time it takes a firm to collect on credit sales (in days)
Profitability Ratios		
Gross Profit Margin	$\dfrac{\text{Sales minus cost of goods sold}}{\text{Sales}}$	The total margin available to cover operating expenses and yield a profit
Operating Profit Margin	$\dfrac{\text{Earnings before interest and taxes (EBIT)}}{\text{Sales}}$	Profitability without concern for taxes and interest
Net Profit Margin	$\dfrac{\text{Net income}}{\text{Sales}}$	After-tax profits per dollar of sales

TABLE 4-6 A Summary of Key Financial Ratios—continued

Ratio	How Calculated	What It Measures
Profitability Ratios		
Return on Total Assets (ROA)	$\dfrac{\text{Net income}}{\text{Total assets}}$	After-tax profits per dollar of assets; this ratio is also called return on investment (ROI)
Return on Stockholders' Equity (ROE)	$\dfrac{\text{Net income}}{\text{Total stockholders' equity}}$	After-tax profits per dollar of stockholders' investment in the firm
Earnings Per Share (EPS)	$\dfrac{\text{Net income}}{\text{Number of shares of common stock outstanding}}$	Earnings available to the owners of common stock
Price-Earnings Ratio	$\dfrac{\text{Market price per share}}{\text{Earnings per share}}$	Attractiveness of firm on equity markets
Growth Ratios		
Sales	Annual percentage growth in total sales	Firm's growth rate in sales
Net Income	Annual percentage growth in profits	Firm's growth rate in profits
Earnings Per Share	Annual percentage growth in EPS	Firm's growth rate in EPS
Dividends Per Share	Annual percentage growth in dividends per share	Firm's growth rate in dividends per share

period are not very meaningful to a company that primarily does a cash receipts business. Key financial ratios can be classified into the following five types:

1. *Liquidity ratios* measure a firm's ability to meet maturing short-term obligations.
   Current ratio
   Quick (or acid-test) ratio

2. *Leverage ratios* measure the extent to which a firm has been financed by debt.
   Debt-to-total-assets ratio
   Debt-to-equity ratio
   Long-term debt-to-equity ratio
   Times-interest-earned (or coverage) ratio

3. *Activity ratios* measure how effectively a firm is using its resources.
   Inventory turnover
   Fixed assets turnover
   Total assets turnover
   Accounts receivable turnover
   Average collection period

4. *Profitability ratios* measure management's overall effectiveness as shown by the returns generated on sales and investment.
   Gross profit margin
   Operating profit margin
   Net profit margin
   Return on total assets (ROA)

      Return on stockholders' equity (ROE)
      Earnings per share (EPS)
      Price-earnings ratio

5. *Growth ratios* measure the firm's ability to maintain its economic position in the growth of the economy and industry.
      Sales
      Net income
      Earnings per share
      Dividends per share

Financial ratio analysis must go beyond the actual calculation and interpretation of ratios. The analysis should be conducted on three separate fronts:

1. *How has each ratio changed over time?* This information provides a means of evaluating historical trends. It is important to note whether each ratio has been historically increasing, decreasing, or nearly constant. For example, a 10 percent profit margin could be bad if the trend has been down 20 percent each of the last three years. But a 10 percent profit margin could be excellent if the trend has been up, up, up. Therefore, calculate the percentage change in each ratio from one year to the next to assess historical financial performance on that dimension. Identify and examine large percent changes in a financial ratio from one year to the next.

2. *How does each ratio compare to industry norms?* A firm's inventory turnover ratio may appear impressive at first glance but may pale when compared to industry standards or norms. Industries can differ dramatically on certain ratios. For example grocery companies, such as Kroger, have a high inventory turnover whereas automobile dealerships have a lower turnover. Therefore, comparison of a firm's ratios within its particular industry can be essential in determining strength/weakness.

3. *How does each ratio compare with key competitors?* Oftentimes competition is more intense between several competitors in a given industry or location than across all rival firms in the industry. When this is true, financial ratio analysis should include comparison to those key competitors. For example, if a firm's profitability ratio is trending up over time and compares favorably to the industry average, but it is trending down relative to its leading competitor, there may be reason for concern.

Financial ratio analysis is not without some limitations. First of all, financial ratios are based on accounting data, and firms differ in their treatment of such items as depreciation, inventory valuation, research and development expenditures, pension plan costs, mergers, and taxes. Also, seasonal factors can influence comparative ratios. Therefore, conformity to industry composite ratios does not establish with certainty that a firm is performing normally or that it is well managed. Likewise, departures from industry averages do not always indicate that a firm is doing especially well or badly. For example, a high inventory turnover ratio could indicate efficient inventory management and a strong working capital position, but it also could indicate a serious inventory shortage and a weak working capital position.

It is important to recognize that a firm's financial condition depends not only on the functions of finance, but also on many other factors that include (1) management, marketing, management production/operations, research and development, and management information systems decisions; (2) actions by competitors, suppliers, distributors, creditors, customers, and shareholders; and (3) economic, social, cultural, demographic, environmental, political, governmental, legal, and technological trends. Even natural environment liabilities can affect financial ratios, as indicated in the "Natural Environment Perspective." So financial ratio analysis, like all other analytical tools, should be used wisely.

NATURAL ENVIRONMENT PERSPECTIVE
European Union Countries Impose Strict Curbs on Use of Chemicals Among Manufacturers

The European Union in 2007 greatly expanded its campaign against industrial pollutants by imposing sweeping restrictions on manufacturers regarding their use of chemicals in producing products. Tough new laws to start in 2008 require all EU firms to document how some 30,000 chemicals are used in products from cleaning liquids and plastics to furniture and electronics. Europe has been a leader for a decade in requiring electronics companies, automakers, and others to clean up their acts. The new EU laws require manufacturers to cease using 1,500 of the most dangerous chemicals known or suspected to cause cancer, birth defects, and other serious illnesses. Also, the new laws require EU countries to cut their emissions in the 2008–2012 period by a collective 7 percent from the 2005 level.

Many U.S. and other global manufacturers hope to be considered so-called downstream users of such chemicals as opposed to manufacturers or importers, and thus avoid the new laws. Whereas Europe relies on government regulation, the United States relies more on lawsuits to provide a strong incentive for manufacturers to avoid endangering human health and the environment. But increasingly the corporate world in the United States is pushing federal and state governments to regulate carbon-dioxide emissions.

Source: Adapted from Mary Jacoby, "Companies Brace for EU Chemical Curbs," *Wall Street Journal* (December 13, 2006): A4.

Water Polo Match In Dubrovnik. *Source:* Fred David

Finance/Accounting Audit Checklist

The following finance/accounting questions, like the similar questions about marketing and management earlier, should be examined:

1. Where is the firm financially strong and weak as indicated by financial ratio analyses?
2. Can the firm raise needed short-term capital?
3. Can the firm raise needed long-term capital through debt and/or equity?
4. Does the firm have sufficient working capital?
5. Are capital budgeting procedures effective?

6. Are dividend payout policies reasonable?
7. Does the firm have good relations with its investors and stockholders?
8. Are the firm's financial managers experienced and well trained?

Production/Operations

The *production/operations function* of a business consists of all those activities that transform inputs into goods and services. Production/operations management deals with inputs, transformations, and outputs that vary across industries and markets. A manufacturing operation transforms or converts inputs such as raw materials, labor, capital, machines, and facilities into finished goods and services. As indicated in Table 4-7, Roger Schroeder suggested that production/operations management comprises five functions or decision areas: process, capacity, inventory, workforce, and quality.

Most automakers require a 30-day notice to build vehicles, but Toyota Motor fills a buyer's new car order in just 5 days. Honda Motor was considered the industry's fastest producer, filling orders in 15 days. Automakers have for years operated under just-in-time inventory systems, but Toyota's 360 suppliers are linked to the company via computers on a virtual assembly line. The new Toyota production system was developed in the company's Cambridge, Ontario, plant and now applies to its Solara, Camry, Corolla, and Tacoma vehicles.

Production/operations activities often represent the largest part of an organization's human and capital assets. In most industries, the major costs of producing a product or service are incurred within operations, so production/operations can have great value as a competitive weapon in a company's overall strategy. Strengths and weaknesses in the five functions of production can mean the success or failure of an enterprise. For example, the average hourly pay of employees can significantly affect total production costs—and as evidenced in the "Global Perspective," there is great variation in average employee pay among countries.

Many production/operations managers are finding that cross-training of employees can help their firms respond faster to changing markets. Cross-training of workers can increase efficiency, quality, productivity, and job satisfaction. For example, at General Motors' Detroit gear and axle plant, costs related to product defects were reduced 400 percent in two years as a result of cross-training workers. A shortage of qualified labor in the United States is another reason cross-training is becoming a common management practice.

Singapore rivals Hong Kong as an attractive site for locating production facilities in Southeast Asia. Singapore is a city-state near Malaysia. An island nation of about 4 million, Singapore is changing from an economy built on trade and services to one built on information technology. A large-scale program in computer education for older (over age 26)

TABLE 4-7 The Basic Functions of Production Management

Function	Description
1. Process	Process decisions concern the design of the physical production system. Specific decisions include choice of technology, facility layout, process flow analysis, facility location, line balancing, process control, and transportation analysis.
2. Capacity	Capacity decisions concern determination of optimal output levels for the organization—not too much and not too little. Specific decisions include forecasting, facilities planning, aggregate planning, scheduling, capacity planning, and queuing analysis.
3. Inventory	Inventory decisions involve managing the level of raw materials, work-in-process, and finished goods. Specific decisions include what to order, when to order, how much to order, and materials handling.
4. Workforce	Workforce decisions are concerned with managing the skilled, unskilled, clerical, and managerial employees. Specific decisions include job design, work measurement, job enrichment, work standards, and motivation techniques.
5. Quality	Quality decisions are aimed at ensuring that high-quality goods and services are produced. Specific decisions include quality control, sampling, testing, quality assurance, and cost control.

Source: Adapted from R. Schroeder, *Operations Management* (New York: McGraw-Hill, 1981): 12.

GLOBAL PERSPECTIVE
Automobile Industry Work Week and Hourly Pay Variation Across Countries

Employees at the giant Volkswagen plant in Wolfsburg, Germany, enjoyed the shortest work week in the global auto industry, 28.8 hours, until early 2007 when the firm bumped this number up to 33 hours at the company's German plants. Still, 33 is low compared to General Motors' 40-hour norm and even less than the 35-hour standard at other German car makers. Germany is home to the world's highest-paid auto workers, with Volkswagen paying $69 an hour, compared with the national average of $44 in Germany. The average hourly pay for auto workers in other countries is:

Germany	$44.05
United States	33.95

Canada	29.17
Japan	27.38
France	26.34
South Korea	15.82
Mexico	3.50

With unemployment running about 10 percent in Germany, companies have more leverage to demand concessions from unions and employees. Volkswagen plans to shed up to 20,000 jobs—mostly in Germany—between 2007 and 2009.

Source: Adapted from Stephen Power, "VW's 28-Hour Workweek Goes Kaputt in Wolfsburg," *Wall Street Journal* (January 5, 2007): B1.

Volkswagon Employees in Germany. *Source:* Photographer Peter Frischmuth / argus. Courtesy Peter Arnold, Inc.

residents is very popular. Singapore children receive outstanding computer training in schools. All government services are computerized nicely. Singapore lures multinational businesses with great tax breaks, world-class infrastructure, excellent courts that efficiently handle business disputes, exceptionally low tariffs, large land giveaways, impressive industrial parks, excellent port facilities, and a government very receptive to and cooperative with foreign businesses. Foreign firms now account for 70 percent of manufacturing output in Singapore.

In terms of ship container traffic processed annually, Singapore has the largest and busiest seaport in the world, followed by Hong Kong, Shanghai, Los Angeles, Busan (South Korea), Rotterdam, Hamburg, New York, and Tokyo. The Singapore seaport is five times the size of the New York City seaport.[22]

TABLE 4-8   Implications of Various Strategies on the Production/Operations Function

Various Strategies	Implications
1. Compete as low-cost provider of goods or services	Creates high barriers to entry
	Creates larger market
	Requires longer production runs and fewer product changes
	Requires special-purpose equipment and facilities
2. Compete as high-quality provider	Offers more total profit from a smaller volume of sales
	Requires more quality-assurance effort and higher operating cost
	Requires more precise equipment, which is more expensive
	Requires highly skilled workers, necessitating higher wages and greater training efforts
3. Stress customer service	Requires more service people, service parts, and equipment
	Requires rapid response to customer needs or changes in customer tastes
	Requires a higher inventory investment
4. Provide rapid and frequent introduction of new products	Requires versatile equipment and people
	Has higher research and development costs
	Has high retraining and tooling costs
	Provides lower volumes for each product and fewer opportunities for improvements due to the learning curve
5. Vertical integration	Enables company to control more of the process
	May require entry into unfamilar business areas
	May require high capital investment as well as technology and skills beyond those currently available
6. Consolidate processing (centralize)	Can result in economies of scale
	Can locate near one major customer or supplier
	Vulnerability: one strike, fire, or flood can halt the entire operation
7. Disperse processing of service (decentralize)	Can be near more customers and resources
	Requires more complex coordination and duplication of some personnel and equipment at each location
	If each location produces one product in the line, then other products still must be transported to be available at all locations
	If each location specializes in a type of component for all products, the company is vulnerable to strike, fire, flood, and so on
	If each location provides total product line, then economies of scale may not be realized
8. Stress the use of mmmechanization, automation, robots	Requires high capital investment
	Reduces flexibility
	May affect labor relations
	Makes maintenance more crucial
9. Stress stability of employment	Serves the security needs of employees and may develop employee loyalty
	Helps to attract and retain highly skilled employees
	May require revisions of make-or-buy decisions, use of idle time, inventory, and subcontractors as demand fluctuates

Source: Adapted from J. Dilworth, *Production and Operations Management: Manufacturing and Nonmanufacturing,* 2nd ed. Copyright © 1983 by Random House, Inc. Reprinted by permission of Random House, Inc.

There is much reason for concern that many organizations have not taken sufficient account of the capabilities and limitations of the production/operations function in formulating strategies. Scholars contend that this neglect has had unfavorable consequences on corporate performance in America. As shown in Table 4-8, James Dilworth outlined several types of strategic decisions that a company might make with the production/operations implications of those decisions. Production capabilities and policies can also greatly affect strategies.

Production/Operations Audit Checklist

Questions such as the following should be examined:

1. Are supplies of raw materials, parts, and subassemblies reliable and reasonable?
2. Are facilities, equipment, machinery, and offices in good condition?
3. Are inventory-control policies and procedures effective?
4. Are quality-control policies and procedures effective?
5. Are facilities, resources, and markets strategically located?
6. Does the firm have technological competencies?

Research and Development

The fifth major area of internal operations that should be examined for specific strengths and weaknesses is *research and development (R&D)*. Many firms today conduct no R&D, and yet many other companies depend on successful R&D activities for survival. Firms pursuing a product development strategy especially need to have a strong R&D orientation.

Organizations invest in R&D because they believe that such an investment will lead to a superior product or service and will give them competitive advantages. Research and development expenditures are directed at developing new products before competitors do, at improving product quality, or at improving manufacturing processes to reduce costs.

Effective management of the R&D function requires a strategic and operational partnership between R&D and the other vital business functions. A spirit of partnership and mutual trust between general and R&D managers is evident in the best-managed firms today. Managers in these firms jointly explore; assess; and decide the what, when, where, why, and how much of R&D. Priorities, costs, benefits, risks, and rewards associated with R&D activities are discussed openly and shared. The overall mission of R&D thus has become broad-based, including supporting existing businesses, helping launch new businesses, developing new products, improving product quality, improving manufacturing efficiency, and deepening or broadening the company's technological capabilities.[23]

The best-managed firms today seek to organize R&D activities in a way that breaks the isolation of R&D from the rest of the company and promotes a spirit of partnership between R&D managers and other managers in the firm. R&D decisions and plans must be integrated and coordinated across departments and divisions by having the departments share experiences and information. The strategic-management process facilitates this cross-functional approach to managing the R&D function.

Internal and External R&D

Cost distributions among R&D activities vary by company and industry, but total R&D costs generally do not exceed manufacturing and marketing start-up costs. Four approaches to determining R&D budget allocations commonly are used: (1) financing as many project proposals as possible, (2) using a percentage-of-sales method, (3) budgeting about the same amount that competitors spend for R&D, or (4) deciding how many successful new products are needed and working backward to estimate the required R&D investment.

R&D in organizations can take two basic forms: (1) internal R&D, in which an organization operates its own R&D department, and/or (2) contract R&D, in which a firm hires independent researchers or independent agencies to develop specific products. Many companies use both approaches to develop new products. A widely used approach for obtaining outside R&D assistance is to pursue a joint venture with another firm. R&D strengths (capabilities) and weaknesses (limitations) play a major role in strategy formulation and strategy implementation.

Most firms have no choice but to continually develop new and improved products because of changing consumer needs and tastes, new technologies, shortened product life cycles, and increased domestic and foreign competition. A shortage of ideas for new products, increased global competition, increased market segmentation, strong special-interest groups, and increased government regulations are several factors making the successful development of new products more and more difficult, costly, and risky. In the pharmaceutical industry, for example, only one out of every few thousand drugs created in the laboratory ends up on pharmacists' shelves. Scarpello, Boulton, and Hofer emphasized that different strategies require different R&D capabilities:

> The focus of R&D efforts can vary greatly depending on a firm's competitive strategy. Some corporations attempt to be market leaders and innovators of new products, while others are satisfied to be market followers and developers of currently available products. The basic skills required to support these strategies will vary, depending on whether R&D becomes the driving force behind competitive strategy. In cases where new product introduction is the driving force for strategy, R&D activities must be extensive. The R&D unit must then be able to advance scientific and technological knowledge, exploit that knowledge, and manage the risks associated with ideas, products, services, and production requirements.[24]

Companies in the United States are expected to spend about $219 billion on R&D in 2007, a 3.4 percent increase over 2006.[25] Analysts expect annual increases of about 3 to 4 percent in R&D spending among U.S. companies through 2010. U.S. firms on average and collectively spend more on R&D than any other country in the world, although China's R&D spending is increasing at an annual rate of about 17 percent. U.S. corporate spending alone on R&D is 64 percent more than all R&D spending in China, including corporate, government, and academia combined.

Research and Development Audit

Questions such as the following should be asked in performing an R&D audit:

1. Does the firm have R&D facilities? Are they adequate?
2. If outside R&D firms are used, are they cost-effective?
3. Are the organization's R&D personnel well qualified?
4. Are R&D resources allocated effectively?
5. Are management information and computer systems adequate?
6. Is communication between R&D and other organizational units effective?
7. Are present products technologically competitive?

Management Information Systems

Information ties all business functions together and provides the basis for all managerial decisions. It is the cornerstone of all organizations. Information represents a major source of competitive management advantage or disadvantage. Assessing a firm's internal strengths and weaknesses in information systems is a critical dimension of performing an internal audit. The company motto of Mitsui, a large Japanese trading company, is "Information is the lifeblood of the company." A satellite network connects Mitsui's 200 worldwide offices.

A management information system's purpose is to improve the performance of an enterprise by improving the quality of managerial decisions. An effective information system thus collects, codes, stores, synthesizes, and presents information in such a manner that it answers important operating and strategic questions. The heart of an information system is a database containing the kinds of records and data important to managers.

A *management information system* receives raw material from both the external and internal evaluation of an organization. It gathers data about marketing, finance, production, and personnel matters internally, and social, cultural, demographic, environmental, economic, political, governmental, legal, technological, and competitive factors externally. Data are integrated in ways needed to support managerial decision making.

There is a logical flow of material in a computer information system, whereby data are input to the system and transformed into output. Outputs include computer printouts, written reports, tables, charts, graphs, checks, purchase orders, invoices, inventory records, payroll accounts, and a variety of other documents. Payoffs from alternative strategies can be calculated and estimated. *Data* become *information* only when they are evaluated, filtered, condensed, analyzed, and organized for a specific purpose, problem, individual, or time.

An effective management information system utilizes computer hardware, software, models for analysis, and a database. Some people equate information systems with the advent of the computer, but historians have traced recordkeeping and non-computer data processing to Babylonian merchants living in 3500 B.C. Benefits of an effective information system include an improved understanding of business functions, improved communications, more informed decision making, a better analysis of problems, and improved control.

Because organizations are becoming more complex, decentralized, and globally dispersed, the function of information systems is growing in importance. Spurring this advance is the falling cost and increasing power of computers. There are costs and benefits associated with obtaining and evaluating information, just as with equipment and land. Like equipment, information can become obsolete and may need to be purged from the system. An effective information system is like a library, collecting, categorizing, and filing data for use by managers throughout the organization. Information systems are a major strategic resource, monitoring internal and external issues and trends, identifying competitive threats, and assisting in the implementation, evaluation, and control of strategy.

We are truly in an information age. Firms whose information-system skills are weak are at a competitive disadvantage. On the other hand, strengths in information systems allow firms to establish distinctive competencies in other areas. Low-cost manufacturing and good customer service, for example, can depend on a good information system.

Strategic-Planning Software

Some strategic decision support systems, however, are too sophisticated, expensive, or restrictive to be used easily by managers in a firm. This is unfortunate because the strategic-management process must be a people process to be successful. People make the difference! Strategic-planning software should thus be simple and unsophisticated. Simplicity allows wide participation among managers in a firm and participation is essential for effective strategy implementation.

One strategic-planning software product that parallels this text and offers managers and executives a simple yet effective approach for developing organizational strategies is CheckMATE. This personal computer software performs planning analyses and generates strategies a firm could pursue. CheckMATE incorporates the most modern strategic-planning techniques. No previous experience with computers or knowledge of strategic planning is required of the user. CheckMATE thus promotes communication, understanding, creativity, and forward thinking among users.

CheckMATE is not a spreadsheet program or database; it is an expert system that carries a firm through strategy formulation and implementation. A major strength of CheckMATE strategic-planning software is its simplicity and participative approach. The user is asked appropriate questions, responses are recorded, information is assimilated, and results are printed. Individuals can independently work through the software, and then the program will develop joint recommendations for the firm.

Specific analytical procedures included in the CheckMATE program are Strategic Position and Action Evaluation (SPACE) analysis, Strengths-Weaknesses-Opportunities-Threats (SWOT) analysis, Internal-External (IE) analysis, and Grand Strategy Matrix analysis. These widely used strategic-planning analyses are described in Chapter 6.

An individual license for CheckMATE costs $295. More information about CheckMATE can be obtained at www.checkmateplan.com or 910–579–5744 (phone).

Management Information Systems Audit

Questions such as the following should be asked when conducting this audit:

1. Do all managers in the firm use the information system to make decisions?
2. Is there a chief information officer or director of information systems position in the firm?

3. Are data in the information system updated regularly?
4. Do managers from all functional areas of the firm contribute input to the information system?
5. Are there effective passwords for entry into the firm's information system?
6. Are strategists of the firm familiar with the information systems of rival firms?
7. Is the information system user-friendly?
8. Do all users of the information system understand the competitive advantages that information can provide firms?
9. Are computer training workshops provided for users of the information system?
10. Is the firm's information system continually being improved in content and user-friendliness?

Value Chain Analysis (VCA)

According to Porter, the business of a firm can best be described as a *value chain,* in which total revenues minus total costs of all activities undertaken to develop and market a product or service yields value. All firms in a given industry have a similar value chain, which includes activities such as obtaining raw materials, designing products, building manufacturing facilities, developing cooperative agreements, and providing customer service. A firm will be profitable as long as total revenues exceed the total costs incurred in creating and delivering the product or service. Firms should strive to understand not only their own value chain operations but also their competitors', suppliers', and distributors' value chains.

Value chain analysis (VCA) refers to the process whereby a firm determines the costs associated with organizational activities from purchasing raw materials to manufacturing product(s) to marketing those products. VCA aims to identify where low-cost advantages or disadvantages exist anywhere along the value chain from raw material to customer service activities. VCA can enable a firm to better identify its own strengths and weaknesses, especially as compared to competitors' value chain analyses and their own data examined over time.

Substantial judgment may be required in performing a VCA because different items along the value chain may impact other items positively or negatively, so there exist complex interrelationships. For example, exceptional customer service may be especially expensive yet may reduce the costs of returns and increase revenues. Cost and price differences among rival firms can have their origins in activities performed by suppliers, distributors, creditors, or even shareholders. Despite the complexity of VCA, the initial step in implementing this procedure is to divide a firm's operations into specific activities or business processes. Then the analyst attempts to attach a cost to each discrete activity, and the costs could be in terms of both time and money. Finally, the analyst converts the cost data into information by looking for competitive cost strengths and weaknesses that may yield competitive advantage or disadvantage. Conducting a VCA is supportive of the RBV's examination of a firm's assets and capabilities as sources of distinctive competence.

When a major competitor or new market entrant offers products or services at very low prices, this may be because that firm has substantially lower value chain costs or perhaps the rival firm is just waging a desperate attempt to gain sales or market share. Thus value chain analysis can be critically important for a firm in monitoring whether its prices and costs are competitive. An example value chain is illustrated in Figure 4-3. There can be more than a hundred particular value-creating activities associated with the business of producing and marketing a product or service, and each one of the activities can represent a competitive advantage or disadvantage for the firm. The combined costs of all the various activities in a company's value chain define the firm's cost of doing business. Firms should determine where cost advantages and disadvantages in their value chain occur *relative to the value chain of rival firms.*

Value chains differ immensely across industries and firms. Whereas a paper products company, such as Stone Container, would include on its value chain timber farming, logging, pulp mills, and papermaking, a computer company such as Hewlett-Packard would

FIGURE 4-3

An Example Value Chain for a Typical Manufacturing Firm

Supplier Costs ———
     Raw materials ———
     Fuel ———
     Energy ———
     Transportation ———
     Truck drivers ———
     Truck maintenance ———
     Component parts ———
     Inspection ———
     Storing ———
     Warehouse ———
Production Costs ———
     Inventory system ———
     Receiving ———
     Plant layout ———
     Maintenance ———
     Plant location ———
     Computer ———
     R&D ———
     Cost accounting ———
Distribution Costs ———
     Loading ———
     Shipping ———
     Budgeting ———
     Personnel ———
     Internet ———
     Trucking ———
     Railroads ———
     Fuel ———
     Maintenance ———
Sales and Marketing Costs ———
     Salespersons ———
     Web site ———
     Internet ———
     Publicity ———
     Promotion ———
     Advertising ———
     Transportation ———
     Food and lodging ———
Customer Service Costs ———
     Postage ———
     Phone ———
     Internet ———
     Warranty ———
Management Costs ———
     Human resources ———
     Administration ———
     Employee benefits ———
     Labor relations ———
     Managers ———
     Employees ———
     Finance and legal ———

FIGURE 4-4

Translating Company Performance of Value Chain Activities into Competitive Advantage

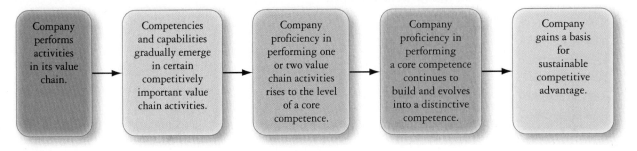

Source: Arthur Thompson, Jr., A. J. Strickland III, and John Gamble. *Crafting and Executing Strategy: Text and Readings* (New York: McGraw-Hill/Irwin, 2005): 108. Used by permission of McGraw-Hill.

include programming, peripherals, software, hardware, and laptops. A motel would include food, housekeeping, check-in and check-out operations, Web site, reservations system, and so on. However all firms should use value chain analysis to develop and nurture a core competence and convert this competence into a distinctive competence. A *core competence* is a value chain activity that a firm performs especially well. When a core competence evolves into a major competitive advantage, then it is called a *distinctive competence*. Figure 4-4 illustrates this process.

More and more companies are using VCA to gain and sustain competitive advantage by being especially efficient and effective along various parts of the value chain. For example, Wal-Mart has built powerful value advantages by focusing on exceptionally tight inventory control, volume purchasing of products, and offering exemplary customer service. Computer companies in contrast compete aggressively along the distribution end of the value chain. Of course, price competitiveness is a key component of effectiveness among both mass retailers and computer firms.

Benchmarking

Benchmarking is an analytical tool used to determine whether a firm's value chain activities are competitive compared to rivals and thus conducive to winning in the marketplace. Benchmarking entails measuring costs of value chain activities across an industry to determine "best practices" among competing firms for the purpose of duplicating or improving upon those best practices. Benchmarking enables a firm to take action to improve its competitiveness by identifying (and improving upon) value chain activities where rival firms have comparative advantages in cost, service, reputation, or operation.

The hardest part of benchmarking can be gaining access to other firms' value chain activities with associated costs. Typical sources of benchmarking information, however, include published reports, trade publications, suppliers, distributors, customers, partners, creditors, shareholders, lobbyists, and willing rival firms. Some rival firms share benchmarking data. However, the International Benchmarking Clearinghouse provides guidelines to help ensure that restraint of trade, price fixing, bid rigging, bribery, and other improper business conduct do not arise between participating firms.

Due to the popularity of benchmarking today, numerous consulting firms such as Accenture, AT Kearney, Best Practices Benchmarking & Consulting, as well as the Strategic Planning Institute's Council on Benchmarking, gather benchmarking data, conduct benchmarking studies, and distribute benchmark information without identifying the sources.

The Internal Factor Evaluation (IFE) Matrix

A summary step in conducting an internal strategic-management audit is to construct an *Internal Factor Evaluation (IFE) Matrix.* This strategy-formulation tool summarizes and evaluates the major strengths and weaknesses in the functional areas of a business, and it also provides a basis for identifying and evaluating relationships among those areas. Intuitive judgments are required in developing an IFE Matrix, so the appearance of a scientific approach should not be interpreted to mean this is an all-powerful technique. A thorough understanding of the factors included is more important than the actual numbers. Similar to the EFE Matrix and Competitive Profile Matrix described in Chapter 3, an IFE Matrix can be developed in five steps:

1. List key internal factors as identified in the internal-audit process. Use a total of from 10 to 20 internal factors, including both strengths and weaknesses. List strengths first and then weaknesses. Be as specific as possible, using percentages, ratios, and comparative numbers.
2. Assign a weight that ranges from 0.0 (not important) to 1.0 (all-important) to each factor. The weight assigned to a given factor indicates the relative importance of the factor to being successful in the firm's industry. Regardless of whether a key factor is an internal strength or weakness, factors considered to have the greatest effect on organizational performance should be assigned the highest weights. The sum of all weights must equal 1.0.
3. Assign a 1-to-4 rating to each factor to indicate whether that factor represents a major weakness (rating = 1), a minor weakness (rating = 2), a minor strength (rating = 3), or a major strength (rating = 4). Note that strengths must receive a 3 or 4 rating and weaknesses must receive a 1 or 2 rating. Ratings are thus company-based, whereas the weights in step 2 are industry-based.
4. Multiply each factor's weight by its rating to determine a weighted score for each variable.
5. Sum the weighted scores for each variable to determine the total weighted score for the organization.

Regardless of how many factors are included in an IFE Matrix, the total weighted score can range from a low of 1.0 to a high of 4.0, with the average score being 2.5. Total weighted scores well below 2.5 characterize organizations that are weak internally, whereas scores significantly above 2.5 indicate a strong internal position. Like the EFE Matrix, an IFE Matrix should include from 10 to 20 key factors. The number of factors has no effect upon the range of total weighted scores because the weights always sum to 1.0.

When a key internal factor is both a strength and a weakness, the factor should be included twice in the IFE Matrix, and a weight and rating should be assigned to each statement. For example, the Playboy logo both helps and hurts Playboy Enterprises; the logo attracts customers to *Playboy* magazine, but it keeps the Playboy cable channel out of many markets. Be as quantitative as possible when stating factors. Use $'s, %'s, #'s, and ratios to the extent possible.

An example of an IFE Matrix is provided in Table 4-9 for a retail computer store. Note that the two most important factors to be successful in the retail computer store business are "revenues from repair/service in the store" and "location of the store." Also note that the store is doing best on "average customer purchase amount" and "in-store technical support." The store is having major problems with its carpet, bathroom, paint, and checkout procedures. Note also that the matrix contains substantial quantitative data rather than vague statements; this is excellent. Overall, this store receives a 2.5 total weighted score, which on a 1-to-4 scale is exactly average/halfway, indicating there is definitely room for improvement in store operations, strategies, policies, and procedures.

The IFE Matrix provides important information for strategy formulation. For example, this retail computer store might want to hire another checkout person and repair its carpet, paint, and bathroom problems. Also, the store may want to increase advertising for its repair/services, because that is a really important (weight 0.15) factor to being successful in this business.

In multidivisional firms, each autonomous division or strategic business unit should construct an IFE Matrix. Divisional matrices then can be integrated to develop an overall corporate IFE Matrix.

TABLE 4-9   **A Sample Internal Factor Evaluation Matrix for a Retail Computer Store**

Key Internal Factors	Weight	Rating	Weighted Score
Strengths			
1. Inventory turnover increased from 5.8 to 6.7	0.05	3	0.15
2. Average customer purchase increased from $97 to $128	0.07	4	0.28
3. Employee morale is excellent	0.10	3	0.30
4. In-store promotions resulted in 20 percent increase in sales	0.05	3	0.15
5. Newspaper advertising expenditures increased 10 percent	0.02	3	0.06
6. Revenues from repair/service segment of store up 16 percent	0.15	3	0.45
7. In-store technical support personnel have MIS college degrees	0.05	4	0.20
8. Store's debt-to-total assets ratio declined to 34 percent	0.03	3	0.09
9. Revenues per employee up 19 percent	0.02	3	0.06
Weaknesses			
1. Revenues from software segment of store down 12 percent	0.10	2	0.20
2. Location of store negatively impacted by new Highway 34	0.15	2	0.30
3. Carpet and paint in store somewhat in disrepair	0.02	1	0.02
4. Bathroom in store needs refurbishing	0.02	1	0.02
5. Revenues from businesses down 8 percent	0.04	1	0.04
6. Store has no Web site	0.05	2	0.10
7. Supplier on-time delivery increased to 2.4 days	0.03	1	0.03
8. Often customers have to wait to check out	0.05	1	0.05
Total	**1.00**		**2.50**

Conclusion

Management, marketing, finance/accounting, production/operations, research and development, and management information systems represent the core operations of most businesses. A strategic-management audit of a firm's internal operations is vital to organizational health. Many companies still prefer to be judged solely on their bottom-line performance. However, an increasing number of successful organizations are using the internal audit to gain competitive advantages over rival firms.

Systematic methodologies for performing strength-weakness assessments are not well developed in the strategic-management literature, but it is clear that strategists must identify and evaluate internal strengths and weaknesses in order to effectively formulate and choose among alternative strategies. The EFE Matrix, Competitive Profile Matrix, IFE Matrix, and clear statements of vision and mission provide the basic information needed to successfully formulate competitive strategies. The process of performing an internal audit represents an opportunity for managers and employees throughout the organization to participate in determining the future of the firm. Involvement in the process can energize and mobilize managers and employees.

We invite you to visit the David page on the Prentice Hall Companion Web site at www.prenhall.com/david for this chapter's review quiz.

Key Terms and Concepts

Activity Ratios (p. 123)
Benchmarking (p. 134)
Capital Budgeting (p. 119)
Communication (p. 105)
Controlling (p. 115)

Issues for Review and Discussion

1. Explain why prioritizing the relative importance of strengths and weaknesses in an IFE Matrix is an important strategic-management activity.
2. How can delegation of authority contribute to effective strategic management?
3. Diagram a formal organizational chart that reflects the following positions: a president, 2 executive officers, 4 middle managers, and 18 lower-level managers. Now, diagram three overlapping and hypothetical informal group structures. How can this information be helpful to a strategist in formulating and implementing strategy?
4. Which of the three basic functions of finance/accounting do you feel is most important in a small electronics manufacturing concern? Justify your position.
5. Do you think aggregate R&D expenditures for U.S. firms will increase or decrease next year? Why?
6. Explain how you would motivate managers and employees to implement a major new strategy.
7. Why do you think production/operations managers often are not directly involved in strategy-formulation activities? Why can this be a major organizational weakness?
8. Give two examples of staffing strengths and two examples of staffing weaknesses of an organization with which you are familiar.

9. Would you ever pay out dividends when your firm's annual net profit is negative? Why? What effect could this have on a firm's strategies?

10. If a firm has zero debt in its capital structure, is that always an organizational strength? Why or why not?

11. Describe the production/operations system in a police department.

12. After conducting an internal audit, a firm discovers a total of 100 strengths and 100 weaknesses. What procedures then could be used to determine the most important of these? Why is it important to reduce the total number of key factors?

13. Why do you believe cultural products affect all the functions of business?

14. Do you think cultural products affect strategy formulation, implementation, or evaluation the most? Why?

15. Identify cultural products at your college or university. Do these products, viewed collectively or separately, represent a strength or weakness for the organization?

16. Describe the management information system at your college or university.

17. Explain the difference between data and information in terms of each being useful to strategists.

18. What are the most important characteristics of an effective management information system?

19. Compare and contrast U.S. versus foreign cultures in terms of doing business.

20. Do you agree or disagree with the RBV theorists that internal resources are more important for a firm than external factors in achieving and sustaining competitive advantage? Explain your and their position.

21. Define and discuss "empirical indicators."

22. Define and discuss the "spam" problem in the United States.

23. Define and explain value chain analysis (VCA).

24. List five financial ratios that may be used by your university to monitor operations.

25. Explain benchmarking.

Notes

1. Robert Grant, "The Resource-Based Theory of Competitive Advantage: Implications for Strategy Formulation," *California Management Review* (Spring 1991): 116.

2. Reprinted by permission of the publisher from "Integrating Strength–Weakness Analysis into Strategic Planning," by William King, *Journal of Business Research* 2, no. 4: p. 481. Copyright 1983 by Elsevier Science Publishing Co., Inc.

3. Igor Ansoff, "Strategic Management of Technology" *Journal of Business Strategy* 7, no. 3 (Winter 1987): 38.

4. Claude George, Jr., *The History of Management Thought*, 2nd ed. (Upper Saddle River, N.J.: Prentice-Hall, 1972): 174.

5. J. B. Barney, "Firm Resources and Sustained Competitive Advantage," *Journal of Management* 17 (1991): 99–120; J.B. Barney, "The Resource-Based Theory of the Firm," *Organizational Science* 7 (1996): 469; J.B. Barney, "Is the Resource-Based 'View' a Useful Perspective for Strategic Management Research? Yes." *Academy of Management Review* 26, no. 1 (2001): 41–56.

6. Edgar Schein, *Organizational Culture and Leadership* (San Francisco: Jossey-Bass, 1985): 9.

7. John Lorsch, "Managing Culture: The Invisible Barrier to Strategic Change," *California Management Review* 28, no. 2 (1986): 95–109.

8. Y. Allarie and M. Firsirotu, "How to Implement Radical Strategies in Large Organizations," *Sloan Management Review* (Spring 1985): 19.

9. Jon Alston, "Wa, Guanxi, and Inhwa: Managerial Principles in Japan, China and Korea," *Business Horizons* 32, no. 2 (March–April 1989): 26.

10. Rose Knotts, "Cross-Cultural Management: Transformations and Adaptations," *Business Horizons* (January–February 1989): 29–33.

11. www.mindtools.com/plfailpl.html.

12. Adam Smith, *The Wealth of Nations* (New York: Modern Library, 1937): 3–4.

13. Richard Daft, *Management*, 3rd ed. (Orlando, FL: Dryden Press, 1993): 512.

14. Shelley Kirkpatrick and Edwin Locke, "Leadership: Do Traits Matter?" *Academy of Management Executive* 5, no. 2 (May 1991): 48.

15. Peter Drucker, *Management Tasks, Responsibilities, and Practice* (New York: Harper & Row, 1973): 463.

16. Brian Dumaine, "What the Leaders of Tomorrow See," *Fortune* (July 3, 1989): 51.

17. J. Evans and B. Bergman, *Marketing* (New York: Macmillan, 1982): 17.

18. Emily Steel, "Ad Cutbacks Likely Signal Budget Shift," *Wall Street Journal* (March 14, 2007): B3.

19. Quoted in Robert Waterman, Jr., "The Renewal Factor," *BusinessWeek* (September 14, 1987): 108.

20. J. Van Horne, *Financial Management and Policy* (Upper Saddle River, N.J.: Prentice-Hall, 1974): 10.

21. Matt Krantz, "Dividend Payouts Grow Less Richly," *USA Today* (December 27, 2006): B1.

22. Kevin Klowden, "The Quiet Revolution in Transportation," *Wall Street Journal* (April 24, 2007): A14.

23. Philip Rousebl, Kamal Saad, and Tamara Erickson, "The Evolution of Third Generation R&D,"*Planning Review* 19, no. 2 (March–April 1991): 18–26.

24. Vida Scarpello, William Boulton, and Charles Hofer, "Reintegrating R&D into Business Strategy," *Journal of Business Strategy* 6, no. 4 (Spring 1986): 50–51.

25. Gautam Naik, "U.S. Companies Are Poised to Ramp Up R&D Spending," *Wall Street Journal* (January 25, 2007):A14.

Current Readings

Acedo, F. J., C. Barroso, and J. L. Galan. "The Resource-Based Theory: Dissemination and Main Trends." *Strategic Management Journal* 27, no. 7 (July 2006): 621.

Campbell, John L., "Why Would Corporation Behave in Socially Responsible Ways?" *The Academy of Management Perspective* 32, no. 3 (July 2007): 946.

Fang, Y., M. Wade, A. Delios, and P.W. Beamish, "International Diversification, Subsidiary Performance, and the Mobility of Knowledge Resources." *Strategic Management Journal* 28, no. 10 (October 2007): 1053.

Hitt, Michael A., and Jamie D. Collins, "Business Ethics, Strategic Decision Making, and Firm Performance." *Business Horizon* 50, no. 5 (September–October 2007): 353.

Lepak, David P., Ken G. Smith, and M. Susan Taylor. "Value Creation and Value Capture: A Multilevel Perspective." *Academy of Management Review* 32, no. 1 (January 2007): 180.

Ling Yan, Hao Zhao and Robert A. Baron. "Influence of Founder-CEO's Personal Values on Firm Performance: Moderating Effects of Firm Age and Size." *Journal of Management* 33, no. 5 (October 2007): 673.

Jiang, Bin and Patrick J. Murphy. "Do Business School Professors Make Good Executive Managers." *The Academy of Management Perspective* 21, no. 3 (August 2007): 29.

Newbert, S. L. "Empirical Research on the Resource-Based View of the Firm: An Assessment and Suggestions for Future Research." *Strategic Management Journal* 28, no. 2 (February 2007): 121.

Ployhart, Robert E. "Staffing in the 21st Century: New Challenges and Strategic Opportunities." *Journal of Management* 32, no. 6 (December 2006): 868.

Priem, Richard L. "A Consumer Perspective on Value Creation." *Academy of Management Review* 32, no. 1 (January 2007): 219.

Schreyogg, G., and M. Kliesh–Eberl. "How Dynamic Can Organizational Capabilities Be? Towards a Dual-Process Model of Capability Dynamization." *Strategic Management Journal* 28, no. 9 (September 2007): 913.

Sidle, Stuart D. "The Danger of Do Nothing Leaders." *The Academy of Management Perspective* 21, no. 2 (May 2007): 75.

Experiential Exercise 4A

Performing a Financial Ratio Analysis for Walt Disney Company (DIS)

Purpose

Financial ratio analysis is one of the best techniques for identifying and evaluating internal strengths and weaknesses. Potential investors and current shareholders look closely at firms' financial ratios, making detailed comparisons to industry averages and to previous periods of time. Financial ratio analyses provide vital input information for developing an IFE Matrix.

Instructions

Step 1	On a separate sheet of paper, number from 1 to 20. Referring to Walt Disney's income statement and balance sheet (pp. 32–33), calculate 20 financial ratios for 2007 for the company. Use Table 4-6 as a reference.
Step 2	In a second column, indicate whether you consider each ratio to be a strength, a weakness, or a neutral factor for Walt Disney.
Step 3	Go to the Web sites in Table 4-5 that calculate Disney's financial ratios, without your having to pay a subscription (fee) for the service. Make a copy of the ratio information provided and record the source. Report this research to your classmates and your professor.

A 1970s painted bisque Walt Disney Productions Donald Duck figurine.
Source: (c) Judith Miller / Dorling Kindersley / Three Sisters

Experiential Exercise 4B

Constructing an IFE Matrix for Walt Disney Company

Purpose

This exercise will give you experience in developing an IFE Matrix. Identifying and prioritizing factors to include in an IFE Matrix fosters communication among functional and divisional managers. Preparing an IFE Matrix allows human resource, marketing, production/operations, finance/accounting, R&D, and management information systems managers to articulate their concerns and thoughts regarding the business condition of the firm. This results in an improved collective understanding of the business.

Instructions

Step 1	Join with two other individuals to form a three-person team. Develop a team IFE Matrix for Walt Disney.
Step 2	Compare your team's IFE Matrix to other teams' IFE Matrices. Discuss any major differences.
Step 3	What strategies do you think would allow Walt Disney to capitalize on its major strengths? What strategies would allow Walt Disney to improve upon its major weaknesses?

Experiential Exercise 4C

Constructing an IFE Matrix for My University

Purpose

This exercise gives you the opportunity to evaluate your university's major strengths and weaknesses. As will become clearer in the next chapter, an organization's strategies are largely based upon striving to take advantage of strengths and improving upon weaknesses.

Instructions

Step 1	Join with two other individuals to form a three-person team. Develop a team IFE Matrix for your university. You may use the strengths/weaknesses determined in Experimental Exercise 1D.
Step 2	Go to the board and diagram your team's IFE Matrix.
Step 3	Compare your team's IFE Matrix to other teams' IFE Matrices. Discuss any major differences.
Step 4	What strategies do you think would allow your university to capitalize on its major strengths? What strategies would allow your university to improve upon its major weaknesses?

5 Strategies in Action

Strategic Management Students

chapter objectives

After studying this chapter, you should be able to do the following:

1. Discuss the value of establishing long-term objectives.

2. Identify 16 types of business strategies.

3. Identify numerous examples of organizations pursuing different types of strategies.

4. Discuss guidelines when particular strategies are most appropriate to pursue.

5. Discuss Porter's five generic strategies.

6. Describe strategic management in nonprofit, governmental, and small organizations.

7. Discuss joint ventures as a way to enter the Russian market.

8. Discuss the Balanced Scorecard.

9. Compare and contrast financial with strategic objectives.

10. Discuss the levels of strategies in large versus small firms.

11. Explain the First Mover Advantages concept.

12. Discuss recent trends in outsourcing.

13. Discuss strategies for competing in turbulent, high-velocity markets.

Hundreds of companies today, including Sears, IBM, Searle, and Hewlett-Packard, have embraced strategic planning fully in their quest for higher revenues and profits. Kent Nelson, former chair of UPS, explains why his company has created a new strategic-planning department: "Because we're making bigger bets on investments in technology, we can't afford to spend a whole lot of money in one direction and then find out five years later it was the wrong direction."[1]

This chapter brings strategic management to life with many contemporary examples. Sixteen types of strategies are defined and exemplified, including Michael Porter's generic strategies: cost leadership, differentiation, and focus. Guidelines are presented for determining when it is most appropriate to pursue different types of strategies. An overview of strategic management in nonprofit organizations, governmental agencies, and small firms is provided.

Long-Term Objectives

Long-term objectives represent the results expected from pursuing certain strategies. Strategies represent the actions to be taken to accomplish long-term objectives. The time frame for objectives and strategies should be consistent, usually from two to five years.

The Nature of Long-Term Objectives

Objectives should be quantitative, measurable, realistic, understandable, challenging, hierarchical, obtainable, and congruent among organizational units. Each objective should also be associated with a timeline. Objectives are commonly stated in terms such as growth in assets, growth in sales, profitability, market share, degree and nature of diversification, degree and nature of vertical integration, earnings per share, and social responsibility. Clearly established objectives offer many benefits. They provide direction, allow synergy, aid in evaluation, establish priorities, reduce uncertainty, minimize conflicts, stimulate exertion, and aid in both the allocation of resources and the design of jobs.

Long-term objectives are needed at the corporate, divisional, and functional levels of an organization. They are an important measure of managerial performance. Many practitioners and academicians attribute a significant part of U.S. industry's competitive decline to the short-term, rather than long-term, strategy orientation of managers in the United States. Arthur D. Little argues that bonuses or merit pay for managers today must be based to a greater extent on long-term objectives and strategies. A general framework for relating objectives to performance evaluation is provided in Table 5-1. A particular organization could tailor these guidelines to meet its own needs, but incentives should be attached to both long-term and annual objectives.

Clearly stated and communicated objectives are vital to success for many reasons. First, objectives help stakeholders understand their role in an organization's future. They also provide a basis for consistent decision making by managers whose values and attitudes differ. By reaching a consensus on objectives during strategy-formulation activities, an organization can minimize potential conflicts later during implementation. Objectives set forth organizational priorities and stimulate exertion and accomplishment. They serve as standards by which individuals, groups, departments, divisions, and entire organizations can be evaluated. Objectives provide the basis for designing jobs and organizing activities

TABLE 5-1   **Varying Performance Measures by Organizational Level**

Organizational Level	Basis for Annual Bonus or Merit Pay
Corporate	75% based on long-term objectives
	25% based on annual objectives
Division	50% based on long-term objectives
	50% based on annual objectives
Function	25% based on long-term objectives
	75% based on annual objectives

to be performed in an organization. They also provide direction and allow for organizational synergy.

Without long-term objectives, an organization would drift aimlessly toward some unknown end. It is hard to imagine an organization or individual being successful without clear objectives. Success only rarely occurs by accident; rather, it is the result of hard work directed toward achieving certain objectives.

Financial versus Strategic Objectives

Two types of objectives are especially common in organizations: financial and strategic objectives. Financial objectives include those associated with growth in revenues, growth in earnings, higher dividends, larger profit margins, greater return on investment, higher earnings per share, a rising stock price, improved cash flow, and so on; while strategic objectives include things such as a larger market share, quicker on-time delivery than rivals, shorter design-to-market times than rivals, lower costs than rivals, higher product quality than rivals, wider geographic coverage than rivals, achieving ISO 14001 certification, achieving technological leadership, consistently getting new or improved products to market ahead of rivals, and so on.

Although financial objectives are especially important in firms, oftentimes there is a trade-off between financial and strategic objectives such that crucial decisions have to be made. For example, a firm can do certain things to maximize short-term financial objectives that would harm long-term strategic objectives. To improve financial position in the short run through higher prices may, for example, jeopardize long-term market share. The dangers associated with trading off long-term strategic objectives with near-term bottom-line performance are especially severe if competitors relentlessly pursue increased market share at the expense of short-term profitability. And there are other trade-offs between financial and strategic objectives, related to riskiness of actions, concern for business ethics, need to preserve the natural environment, and social responsibility issues. Both financial and strategic objectives should include both annual and long-term performance targets. Ultimately, the best way to sustain competitive advantage over the long run is to relentlessly pursue strategic objectives that strengthen a firm's business position over rivals. Financial objectives can best be met by focusing first and foremost on achievement of strategic objectives that improve a firm's competitiveness and market strength.

Not Managing by Objectives

An unknown educator once said, "If you think education is expensive, try ignorance." The idea behind this saying also applies to establishing objectives. Strategists should avoid the following alternative ways to "not managing by objectives."

VISIT THE NET

Provides a short essay about the resurgence of strategic planning in companies. (www.businessweek.com/1996/35/b34901.htm)

- *Managing by Extrapolation*—adheres to the principle "If it ain't broke, don't fix it." The idea is to keep on doing about the same things in the same ways because things are going well.
- *Managing by Crisis*—based on the belief that the true measure of a really good strategist is the ability to solve problems. Because there are plenty of crises and problems to go around for every person and every organization, strategists ought to bring their time and creative energy to bear on solving the most pressing problems of the day. Managing by crisis is actually a form of reacting rather than acting and of letting events dictate the what and when of management decisions.
- *Managing by Subjectives*—built on the idea that there is no general plan for which way to go and what to do; just do the best you can to accomplish what you think should be done. In short, "Do your own thing, the best way you know how" (sometimes referred to as *the mystery approach to decision making* because subordinates are left to figure out what is happening and why).
- *Managing by Hope*—based on the fact that the future is laden with great uncertainty and that if we try and do not succeed, then we hope our second (or third) attempt will succeed. Decisions are predicted on the hope that they will work and the good times are just around the corner, especially if luck and good fortune are on our side![2]

The Balanced Scorecard

Developed in 1993 by Harvard Business School professors Robert Kaplan and David Norton, and refined continually through today, the Balanced Scorecard is a strategy evaluation and control technique.[3] Balanced Scorecard derives its name from the perceived need of firms to "balance" financial measures that are oftentimes used exclusively in strategy evaluation and control with nonfinancial measures such as product quality and customer service. An effective Balanced Scorecard contains a carefully chosen combination of strategic and financial objectives tailored to the company's business. As a tool to manage and evaluate strategy, the Balanced Scorecard is currently in use at Sears, United Parcel Service, 3M Corporation, Heinz, and hundreds of other firms. For example, 3M Corporation has a financial objective to achieve annual growth in earnings per share of 10 percent or better, as well as a strategic objective to have at least 30 percent of sales come from products introduced in the past four years. The overall aim of the Balanced Scorecard is to "balance" shareholder objectives with customer and operational objectives. Obviously, these sets of objectives interrelate and many even conflict. For example, customers want low price and high service, which may conflict with shareholders' desire for a high return on their investment. The Balanced Scorecard concept is consistent with the notions of continuous improvement in management (CIM) and total quality management (TQM).

Although the Balanced Scorecard concept will be covered in more detail in Chapter 9 as it relates to evaluating strategies, it should be noted here that firms should establish objectives and evaluate strategies on items other than financial measures. This is the basic tenet of the Balanced Scorecard. Financial measures and ratios are vitally important. However, of equal importance are factors such as customer service, employee morale, product quality, pollution abatement, business ethics, social responsibility, community involvement, and other such items. In conjunction with financial measures, these "softer" factors comprise an integral part of both the objective-setting process and the strategy-evaluation process. These factors can vary by organization, but such items, along with financial measures, comprise the essence of a Balanced Scorecard. A Balanced Scorecard for a firm is simply a listing of all key objectives to work toward, along with an associated time dimension of when each objective is to be accomplished, as well as a primary responsibility or contact person, department, or division for each objective.

Types of Strategies

The model illustrated in Figure 5-1 provides a conceptual basis for applying strategic management. Defined and exemplified in Table 5-2, alternative strategies that an enterprise could pursue can be categorized into 11 actions—forward integration, backward integration, horizontal integration, market penetration, market development, product development, related diversification, unrelated diversification, retrenchment, divestiture, and liquidation. Each alternative strategy has countless variations. For example, market penetration can include adding salespersons, increasing advertising expenditures, couponing, and using similar actions to increase market share in a given geographic area.

Many, if not most, organizations simultaneously pursue a combination of two or more strategies, but a *combination strategy* can be exceptionally risky if carried too far. No organization can afford to pursue all the strategies that might benefit the firm. Difficult decisions must be made. Priority must be established. Organizations, like individuals, have limited resources. Both organizations and individuals must choose among alternative strategies and avoid excessive indebtedness.

Hansen and Smith explain that strategic planning involves "choices that risk resources" and "trade-offs that sacrifice opportunity." In other words, if you have a strategy to go north, then you must buy snowshoes and warm jackets (spend resources) and forgo the opportunity of "faster population growth in southern states." You cannot have a strategy to go north and then take a step east, south, or west "just to be on the safe side." Firms spend resources and focus on a finite number of opportunities in pursuing strategies to achieve an uncertain outcome in the future. Strategic planning is much more than a roll of the dice; it is a wager based on predictions and hypotheses that are continually tested and refined by knowledge, research, experience, and learning. Survival of the firm itself may hinge on your strategic plan.[4]

FIGURE 5-1

A Comprehensive Strategic-Management Model

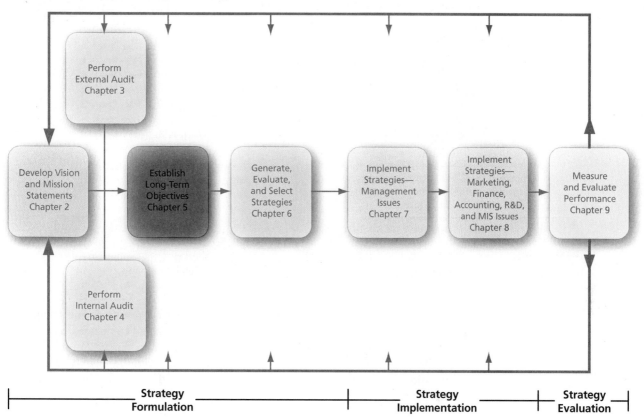

Source: Fred R. David, "How Companies Define Their Mission," *Long Range Planning* 22, no. 3 (June 1988): 40.

TABLE 5-2 Alternative Strategies Defined and Exemplified

Strategy	Definition	2007 Examples
Forward Integration	Gaining ownership or increased control over distributors or retailers	Southwest Airlines just began selling tickets through Galileo
Backward Integration	Seeking ownership or increased control of a firm's suppliers	Hilton Hotels could acquire a large furniture manufacturer
Horizontal Integration	Seeking ownership or increased control over competitors	Huntington Bancshares and Sky Financial Group in Ohio merged
Market Penetration	Seeking increased market share for present products or services in present markets through greater marketing efforts	McDonald's is spending millions on its "Shrek the Third" promotions aimed at convincing consumers it offers healthy items
Market Development	Introducing present products or services into new geographic area	Burger King opened its first restaurant in Japan
Product Development	Seeking increased sales by improving present products or services or developing new ones	Google introduced "Google Presents" to compete with Microsoft's PowerPoint
Related Diversification	Adding new but related products or services	MGM Mirage is opening its first noncasino luxury hotel
Unrelated Diversification	Adding new, unrelated products or services	Ford Motor Company entered the industrial bank business
Retrenchment	Regrouping through cost and asset reduction to reverse declining sales and profit	Discovery Channel closed its 103 mall-based and stand-alone stores to focus on the Internet—and laid off 25% of its workforce
Divestiture	Selling a division or part of an organization	Whirlpool sold its struggling Hoover floor-care business to Techtronic Industries
Liquidation	Selling all of a company's assets, in parts, for their tangible worth	Follow Me Charters sold all of its assets and ceased doing business

FIGURE 5-2

Levels of Strategies with Persons Most Responsible

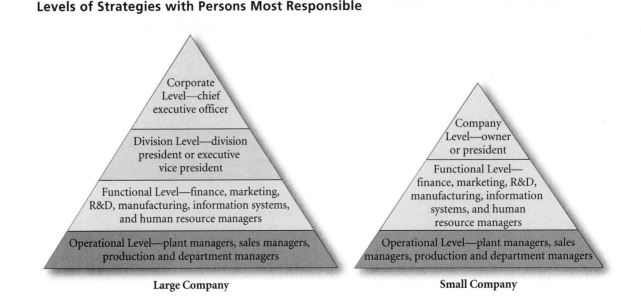

Large Company   **Small Company**

Organizations cannot do too many things well because resources and talents get spread thin and competitors gain advantage. In large diversified companies, a combination strategy is commonly employed when different divisions pursue different strategies. Also, organizations struggling to survive may simultaneously employ a combination of several defensive strategies, such as divestiture, liquidation, and retrenchment.

Levels of Strategies

Strategy making is not just a task for top executives. As discussed in Chapter 1, middle-and lower-level managers too must be involved in the strategic-planning process to the extent possible. In large firms, there are actually four levels of strategies: corporate, divisional, functional, and operational—as illustrated in Figure 5-2. However, in small firms, there are actually three levels of strategies: company, functional, and operational.

In large firms, the persons primarily responsible for having effective strategies at the various levels include the CEO at the corporate level; the president or executive vice president at the divisional level; the respective chief finance officer (CFO), chief information officer (CIO), human resource manager (HRM), chief marketing officer (CMO), and so on, at the functional level; and the plant manager, regional sales manager, and so on, at the operational level. In small firms, the persons primarily responsible for having effective strategies at the various levels include the business owner or president at the company level and then the same range of persons at the lower two levels, as with a large firm.

It is important to note that all persons responsible for strategic planning at the various levels ideally participate and understand the strategies at the other organizational levels to help ensure coordination, facilitation, and commitment while avoiding inconsistency, inefficiency, and miscommunication. Plant managers, for example, need to understand and be supportive of the overall corporate strategic plan (game plan) while the president and the CEO need to be knowledgeable of strategies being employed in various sales territories and manufacturing plants.

Integration Strategies

Forward integration, backward integration, and horizontal integration are sometimes collectively referred to as *vertical integration* strategies. Vertical integration strategies allow a firm to gain control over distributors, suppliers, and/or competitors.

Forward Integration

Forward integration involves gaining ownership or increased control over distributors or retailers. Increasing numbers of manufacturers (suppliers) today are pursuing a forward integration strategy by establishing Web sites to directly sell products to consumers. This strategy is causing turmoil in some industries. For example, Dell Computer recently began pursuing forward integration by establishing its own stores-within-a-store in Sears. This strategy supplements Dell's mall-based kiosks, which enable customers to see and try Dell computers before they purchase one. Neither the Dell kiosks nor the Dell stores-within-a-store stock computers. Customers still will order Dells exclusively by phone or over the Internet, which historically differentiated Dell from other computer firms.

An effective means of implementing forward integration is *franchising*. Approximately 2,000 companies in about 50 different industries in the United States use franchising to distribute their products or services. Businesses can expand rapidly by franchising because costs and opportunities are spread among many individuals. Total sales by franchises in the United States are annually about $1 trillion.

However, a growing trend is for franchisees, who for example may operate 10 franchised restaurants, stores, or whatever, to buy out their part of the business from their franchiser (corporate owner). There is a growing rift between franchisees and franchisers as the segment often outperforms the parent. For example, McDonald's today owns less than 23 percent of its 32,000 restaurants, down from 26 percent in 2006. Restaurant chains are increasingly being pressured to own fewer of their locations. McDonald's recently sold 1,600 of its Latin America and Caribbean restaurants to Woods Staton, a former McDonald's executive. Companies such as McDonald's are using proceeds from the sale of company stores/restaurants to franchisees to buy back company stock, pay higher dividends, and make other investments to benefit shareholders.

The huge forest products firm Boise Cascade, which owns 2.3 million acres of timberlands and more than two dozen paper and building-products mills, continues to pursue forward integration, as evidenced by its recent acquisition of OfficeMax, the third-largest retail-office-products company after Staples and Office Depot. OfficeMax has more than 1,000 superstores and has lately focused on boosting domestic sales and on remodeling stores, rather than expanding internationally. A risk to Boise Cascade in making this acquisition is that Staples and Office Depot could drop the Boise Cascade line of products, viewing the company now to be more a competitor than a supplier.

Amway and Mary Kay in 2007 were granted licenses to sell products in China, ending years of waiting by the two U.S. companies and a relaxation of curbs on direct sales that Beijing began as part of its obligations in joining the World Trade Organization. Other direct sales firms, including Nu Skin Enterprises and Avon Products, also were granted approval. These firms almost all have stores in China but only in 2007 were finally given permission to use the door-to-door sales techniques. Many direct sales firms have jumped on this opportunity by extending their forward integration strategy of adding distributorships and salespersons in China.

Six guidelines for when forward integration may be an especially effective strategy are:[5]

- When an organization's present distributors are especially expensive, or unreliable, or incapable of meeting the firm's distribution needs.
- When the availability of quality distributors is so limited as to offer a competitive advantage to those firms that integrate forward.
- When an organization competes in an industry that is growing and is expected to continue to grow markedly; this is a factor because forward integration reduces an organization's ability to diversify if its basic industry falters.
- When an organization has both the capital and human resources needed to manage the new business of distributing its own products.
- When the advantages of stable production are particularly high; this is a consideration because an organization can increase the predictability of the demand for its output through forward integration.
- When present distributors or retailers have high profit margins; this situation suggests that a company profitably could distribute its own products and price them more competitively by integrating forward.

Backward Integration

Both manufacturers and retailers purchase needed materials from suppliers. *Backward integration* is a strategy of seeking ownership or increased control of a firm's suppliers. This strategy can be especially appropriate when a firm's current suppliers are unreliable, too costly, or cannot meet the firm's needs.

When you buy a box of Pampers diapers at Wal-Mart, a scanner at the store's checkout counter instantly zaps an order to Procter & Gamble Company. In contrast, in most hospitals, reordering supplies is a logistical nightmare. Inefficiency caused by lack of control of suppliers in the health care industry is, however, rapidly changing as many giant health care purchasers, such as the U.S. Defense Department and Columbia/HCA Healthcare Corporation, move to require electronic bar codes on every supply item purchased. This allows instant tracking and recording without invoices and paperwork. Of the estimated $83 billion spent annually on hospital supplies, industry reports indicate that $11 billion can be eliminated through more effective backward integration.

Some industries in the United States, such as the automotive and aluminum industries, are reducing their historical pursuit of backward integration. Instead of owning their suppliers, companies negotiate with several outside suppliers. Ford and DaimlerChrysler buy over half of their component parts from outside suppliers such as TRW, Eaton, General Electric, and Johnson Controls. *De-integration* makes sense in industries that have global sources of supply. Companies today shop around, play one seller against another, and go with the best deal. Global competition is also spurring firms to reduce their number of suppliers and to demand higher levels of service and quality from those they keep. Although traditionally relying on many suppliers to ensure uninterrupted supplies and low prices, American firms now are following the lead of Japanese firms, which have far fewer suppliers and closer, long-term relationships with those few. "Keeping track of so many suppliers is onerous," says Mark Shimelonis, formerly of Xerox.

Seven guidelines for when backward integration may be an especially effective strategy are:[6]

- When an organization's present suppliers are especially expensive, or unreliable, or incapable of meeting the firm's needs for parts, components, assemblies, or raw materials.
- When the number of suppliers is small and the number of competitors is large.
- When an organization competes in an industry that is growing rapidly; this is a factor because integrative-type strategies (forward, backward, and horizontal) reduce an organization's ability to diversify in a declining industry.
- When an organization has both capital and human resources to manage the new business of supplying its own raw materials.
- When the advantages of stable prices are particularly important; this is a factor because an organization can stabilize the cost of its raw materials and the associated price of its product(s) through backward integration.
- When present supplies have high profit margins, which suggests that the business of supplying products or services in the given industry is a worthwhile venture.
- When an organization needs to quickly acquire a needed resource.

Horizontal Integration

Horizontal integration refers to a strategy of seeking ownership of or increased control over a firm's competitors. One of the most significant trends in strategic management today is the increased use of horizontal integration as a growth strategy. Mergers, acquisitions, and takeovers among competitors allow for increased economies of scale and enhanced transfer of resources and competencies. Kenneth Davidson makes the following observation about horizontal integration:

> The trend towards horizontal integration seems to reflect strategists' misgivings about their ability to operate many unrelated businesses. Mergers between direct competitors are more likely to create efficiencies than mergers between unrelated businesses, both because there is a greater potential for eliminating duplicate facilities and

because the management of the acquiring firm is more likely to understand the business of the target.[7]

The Chicago Mercantile Exchange (CME) acquired the CBOT Holdings exchange in mid-2007 for about $8 billion, creating the world's largest derivatives exchange, with dominant positions in several futures markets from soybeans to eurodollars. There is rapid consolidation among exchanges worldwide. For example, the New York Stock Exchange recently acquired the pan-European exchange Euronext NV.

Five guidelines for when horizontal integration may be an especially effective strategy are:[8]

- When an organization can gain monopolistic characteristics in a particular area or region without being challenged by the federal government for "tending substantially" to reduce competition.
- When an organization competes in a growing industry.
- When increased economies of scale provide major competitive advantages.
- When an organization has both the capital and human talent needed to successfully manage an expanded organization.
- When competitors are faltering due to a lack of managerial expertise or a need for particular resources that an organization possesses; note that horizontal integration would not be appropriate if competitors are doing poorly, because in that case overall industry sales are declining.

Intensive Strategies

Market penetration, market development, and product development are sometimes referred to as *intensive strategies* because they require intensive efforts if a firm's competitive position with existing products is to improve.

Market Penetration

A *market penetration* strategy seeks to increase market share for present products or services in present markets through greater marketing efforts. This strategy is widely used alone and in combination with other strategies. Market penetration includes increasing the number of salespersons, increasing advertising expenditures, offering extensive sales promotion items, or increasing publicity efforts.

Five guidelines for when market penetration may be an especially effective strategy are:[9]

- When current markets are not saturated with a particular product or service.
- When the usage rate of present customers could be increased significantly.
- When the market shares of major competitors have been declining while total industry sales have been increasing.
- When the correlation between dollar sales and dollar marketing expenditures historically has been high.
- When increased economies of scale provide major competitive advantages.

Market Development

Market development involves introducing present products or services into new geographic areas. For example, Chicago-based United Airlines in 2007 won a four-way contest to provide new service to China. Air service between the United States and China is restricted to a negotiated number of flights and through 2007, United rather than American, Continental, or Northwest will be providing this service. The world's largest trans-Pacific passenger carrier, United has served China for 20 years and is adding new nonstop flights from the United States to both Beijing and Shanghai.

General Motors sold more cars outside the United States in both 2005 and 2006 than inside the United States. Ford Motor and many other domestic firms have greater revenue and profits from business outside the United States than here at home. Dunkin' Donuts has more than 1,700 restaurants outside the United States in 30 countries and opened its first store in Taiwan in 2007. Starbucks plans to eventually have thousands of stores in China, making that country the chain's largest market outside the United States. Best Buy Company opened its first store in China in 2007.

Wal-Mart plans to open its first stores in Russia and India in 2007. Wal-Mart's international division is growing faster than the firm's flagship U.S. business. Four non-Chinese banks began operations in China in 2007: Citigroup Inc., HSBC Holdings PLC, Standard Chartered Bank PLC, and Bank of East Asia Ltd.

Polo Ralph Lauren recently expanded its presence in Japan by acquiring Impact 21 Company, a licensee for men's and women's jeans, apparel, and accessories. Japan is now Ralph Lauren's second largest market at 10 percent of revenues. Ralph Lauren paid 2,600 yen ($21.82) per share for Impact 21.

Toyota announced in mid-2007 that its five-year strategy to build manufacturing plants in the United States (market development) was misguided and is being replaced now by "build plants in Japan and export to the USA." This new strategy reveals a rare misstep for Toyota, which has surpassed General Motors as the largest auto firm by anticipating the desires of U.S. car buyers better than its Detroit competitors.

Six guidelines for when market development may be an especially effective strategy are:[10]

- When new channels of distribution are available that are reliable, inexpensive, and of good quality.
- When an organization is very successful at what it does.
- When new untapped or unsaturated markets exist.
- When an organization has the needed capital and human resources to manage expanded operations.
- When an organization has excess production capacity.
- When an organization's basic industry is becoming rapidly global in scope.

Product Development

Product development is a strategy that seeks increased sales by improving or modifying present products or services. Product development usually entails large research and development expenditures. For example, Apple Computer in 2007 introduced the media-playing cell phone, called the iPhone, after working with Cingular Wireless for over a year to develop the phone, which is being sold in both Apple and Cingular stores. The iPhone is the latest example of how lines between the entertainment and telecom industries are becoming blurred, with cable companies developing phone products and phone companies developing cable products. Examples of such competing products that were recently released are SonyEricsson's Walkman phone, Motorola's RAZR handset, Research in Motion's BlackBerry Pearl, and Palm Inc.'s Treo 750.

Five guidelines for when product development may be an especially effective strategy to pursue are:[11]

- When an organization has successful products that are in the maturity stage of the product life cycle; the idea here is to attract satisfied customers to try new (improved) products as a result of their positive experience with the organization's present products or services.
- When an organization competes in an industry that is characterized by rapid technological developments.
- When major competitors offer better-quality products at comparable prices.
- When an organization competes in a high-growth industry.
- When an organization has especially strong research and development capabilities.

Diversification Strategies

There are two general types of *diversification strategies*: related and unrelated. Businesses are said to be *related* when their value chains posses competitively valuable cross-business strategic fits; businesses are said to be *unrelated* when their value chains are so dissimilar that no competitively valuable cross-business relationships exist.[12] Most companies favor related diversification strategies in order to capitalize on synergies as follows:

- Transferring competitively valuable expertise, technological know-how, or other capabilities from one business to another.
- Combining the related activities of separate businesses into a single operation to achieve lower costs.
- Exploiting common use of a well-known brand name.
- Cross-business collaboration to create competitively valuable resource strengths and capabilities[13].

Diversification strategies are becoming less popular as organizations are finding it more difficult to manage diverse business activities. In the 1960s and 1970s, the trend was to diversify so as not to be dependent on any single industry, but the 1980s saw a general reversal of that thinking. Diversification is now on the retreat. Michael Porter, of the Harvard Business School, says, "Management found it couldn't manage the beast." Hence, businesses are selling, or closing, less profitable divisions in order to focus on core businesses.

The greatest risk of being in a single industry is having all of the firm's eggs in one basket. Although many firms are successful operating in a single industry, new technologies, new products, or fast-shifting buyer preferences can decimate a particular business. For example, digital cameras are decimating the film and film processing industry, and cell phones have permanently altered the long-distance telephone calling industry.

Diversification must do more than simply spread business risk across different industries, however, because shareholders could accomplish this by simply purchasing equity in different firms across different industries or by investing in mutual funds. Diversification makes sense only to the extent the strategy adds more to shareholder value than what shareholders could accomplish acting individually. Thus, the chosen industry for diversification must be attractive enough to yield consistently high returns on investment and offer potential across the operating divisions for synergies greater than those entities could achieve alone.

A few companies today, however, pride themselves on being conglomerates, from small firms such as Pentair Inc., and Blount International to huge companies such as Textron, Allied Signal, Emerson Electric, General Electric, Viacom, and Samsung. Samsung, for example, now has global market share leadership in many diverse areas, including cell phones (10 percent), big-screen televisions (32 percent), MP3 players (13 percent), DVD players (11 percent), and microwave ovens (25 percent).[14] Similarly, Textron, through numerous diverse acquisitions, now produces and sells Cessna airplanes, Bell helicopters, Jacobsen lawn mowers, golf products, transmissions, consumer loans, and telescopic machinery. Conglomerates prove that focus and diversity are not always mutually exclusive.

Many strategists contend that firms should "stick to the knitting" and not stray too far from the firm's basic areas of competence. However, diversification is still sometimes an appropriate strategy, especially when the company is competing in an unattractive industry. For example, United Technologies is diversifying away from its core aviation business due to the slumping airline industry. Most recently, United Technologies acquired British electronic-security company Chubb PLC, which follows up its acquisition of Otis Elevator Company and Carrier air conditioning to reduce its dependence on the volatile airline industry. Hamish Maxwell, Philip Morris's former CEO, says, "We want to become a consumer-products company." Diversification makes sense for Philip Morris because cigarette consumption is declining, product liability suits are a risk, and some investors reject tobacco stocks on principle.

Related Diversification

An example of related diversification is the AT&T acquisition of BellSouth in 2007, which was the largest telecommunications acquisition ever approved in the United States and represented AT&T's entry (diversification) into Internet video service. AT&T and Verizon Communications, its major competitor, are adding television to the roster of services they offer consumers so they can better compete with cable companies that already offer bundles of television, phone, and Internet service.

Google's stated strategy is to organize all the world's information into searchable form, diversifying the firm beyond its roots as a Web search engine that sells advertising. The Google acquisition of YouTube was an example of a related diversification strategy because YouTube contains so many video clips from television shows and commercials. Google wants to diversify further into the television and cablevision business. Google plans to scan millions of books from university and public libraries into a database. Google's acquisition of DoubleClick, also in 2007, was further diversification into the business of placing, or "serving," the electronic advertisements that dot Web sites.

Seagate Technology pursued related diversification recently when it acquired EVault because this moved the company from disk drives to data-storage services. Now Seagate is a major provider of data backup and archival services for small and mid-size businesses. Similarly, Cisco Systems recently diversified with its acquisition of Web Ex Communications because it moved Cisco from manufacturing computer routers, switches, and network gear into online conferencing services.

When diversifying away from familiar products/services, firms must be careful to enter new areas mindful of environmental concerns. The "Natural Environment Perspective" reveals two animal species at risk because of weak corporate environmental policies/operations.

Six guidelines for when related diversification may be an effective strategy are as follows.[15]

- When an organization competes in a no-growth or a slow-growth industry.
- When adding new, but related, products would significantly enhance the sales of current products.
- When new, but related, products could be offered at highly competitive prices.
- When new, but related, products have seasonal sales levels that counterbalance an organization's existing peaks and valleys.
- When an organization's products are currently in the declining stage of the product's life cycle.
- When an organization has a strong management team.

NATURAL ENVIRONMENT PERSPECTIVE
Songbirds and Coral Reefs in Trouble

Songbirds

Bluebirds are one of 76 songbird species in the United States that have dramatically declined in numbers in the last two decades. Not all birds are considered songbirds, and why birds sing is not clear. Some scientists say they sing when calling for mates or warning of danger, but many scientists now contend that birds sing for sheer pleasure. Songbirds include chickadees, orioles, swallows, mockingbirds, warblers, sparrows, vireos, and the wood thrush. "These birds are telling us there's a problem, something's out of balance in our environment," says Jeff Wells, bird conservation director for the National Audubon Society. Songbirds may be telling us that their air or water is too dirty or that we are destroying too much of their habitat. People collect Picasso paintings and save historic buildings. "Songbirds are part of our natural heritage. Why

should we be willing to watch songbirds destroyed any more than allowing a great work of art to be destroyed?" asks Wells. Whatever message songbirds are singing to us today about their natural environment, the message is becoming less and less heard nationwide. Listen when you go outside today. Each of us as individuals, companies, states, and countries should do what we reasonably can to help improve the natural environment for songbirds.

Coral Reefs

The ocean covers more than 71 percent of the Earth. The destructive effect of commercial fishing on ocean habitats coupled with increasing pollution runoff into the ocean and global warming of the ocean have decimated fisheries, marine life, and coral reefs around the world. The unfortunate consequence of fishing over the last century has been *overfishing*—with the principal reasons being politics and greed. Trawl fishing with nets destroys coral reefs and has been compared to catching squirrels by cutting down forests, because bottom nets scour and destroy vast areas of the ocean. The great proportion of marine life caught in a trawl is "by-catch" juvenile fish and other life that are killed and discarded. Warming of the ocean due to CO_2 emissions also kills thousands of acres of coral reefs annually. The total area of fully protected marine habitats in the United States is only about 50 square miles, compared to some 93 million acres of national wildlife refuges and national parks on the nation's land. A healthy ocean is vital to the economic and social future of the nation—and, indeed, all countries of the world. Everything we do on land ends up in the ocean, so we all must become better stewards of this last frontier on Earth in order to sustain human survival and the quality of life.

Sources: Adapted from Tom Brook, "Declining Numbers Mute Many Birds' Songs," *USA Today* (September 11, 2001): 4A. Also adapted from John Ogden, "Maintaining Diversity in the Oceans," *Environment* (April 2001): 29–36.

Sailing Over a Coral Reef. *Source:* Fred David

Unrelated Diversification

An unrelated diversification strategy favors capitalizing upon a portfolio of businesses that are capable of delivering excellent financial performance in their respective industries, rather than striving to capitalize on value chain strategic fits among the businesses. Firms that employ unrelated diversification continually search across different industries for companies that can be acquired for a deal and yet have potential to provide a high return on investment. Pursuing unrelated diversification entails being on the hunt to acquire companies whose assets are undervalued, or companies that are financially distressed, or companies that have high growth prospects but are short on investment capital. An obvious drawback of unrelated diversification is that the parent firm must have an excellent top management team that plans, organizes, motivates, delegates, and controls effectively. It is much more difficult to manage businesses in many industries than in a single industry. However, some firms are successful pursuing unrelated diversification, such as Walt Disney that owns ABC, Viacom that owns CBS, and General Electric that owns NBC. Thus the three major television networks are all owned by diversified firms.

Many more firms have failed at unrelated diversification than have succeeded due to immense management challenges. However, unrelated diversification can be good, as it is for Cendant Corp., which owns the real-estate firm Century 21, the car-rental agency Avis, the travel-booking sites Orbitz and Flairview Travel, and the hotel brands Days Inn and

Howard Johnson. The brokerage firm Morgan Stanley is pursuing unrelated diversification by building a $1 billion casino in Atlantic City. In addition, Morgan Stanley recently obtained an 18 percent stake in Trump Entertainment Resorts. Also in 2007, Morgan Stanley acquired 13 luxury hotels in Japan for $2.4 billion from All Nippon Airways, further diversifying the firm into hotel management.

Best known for its thermostats and aircraft engines, Honeywell International in 2007 began producing flat-panel television sets. This was Honeywell's first foray into consumer electronics. There is speculation that Honeywell will soon diversify further and enter the computer monitor and display business. Regarding consumer electronics, the largest such retailer, Best Buy, in 2007 paid $97 million to buy a Seattle-based company called Speakeasy, which provides broadband Internet and Internet-based phone services to small businesses across the country. This was an unrelated diversification move by Best Buy.

Wal-Mart recently renegotiated the terms of leases with a number of banks operating in its stores, giving the company itself the explicit right to offer mortgages, home-equity lines of credit, and consumer loans. In some locations, Wal-Mart also may offer debit cards and investment and insurance products either directly or through a third-party vendor. Wal-Mart's desire to enter the banking business has drawn fierce opposition from the banking industry, some members of Congress, and activist groups. There are currently 300 different banks with 1,200 branches inside Wal-Mart stores across the United States, and Wal-Mart plans to add 200 more by 2009. Fifteen commercial firms already own banks, including Harley-Davidson and Target Corp.[16]

An increasing number of hospitals are creating miniature malls by offering banks, bookstores, coffee shops, restaurants, drugstores, and other retail stores within their buildings. Many hospitals previously had only cafeterias, gift shops, and maybe a pharmacy, but the movement into malls and retail stores is aimed at improving the ambiance for patients and their visitors. The new University Pointe Hospital in West Chester, Ohio, has 75,000 square feet of retail space. The CEO says, "Unless we diversify our revenue, we won't be able to fulfill our mission of providing health care. We want our hospital to be a place that people want to go to."[17]

Another example of unrelated diversification strategy would be the recent General Electric (GE) acquisition of Vivendi Universal Entertainment (VUE). VUE is a television and theme park empire, while GE is a highly diversified conglomerate. VUE owns and operates Universal Studios theme parks. GE owns National Broadcasting Corporation (NBC) and also produces home appliances and scores of other products. General Electric is a classic firm that is highly diversified. GE makes locomotives, lightbulbs, power plants, and refrigerators; GE manages more credit cards than American Express; GE owns more commercial aircraft than American Airlines.

Ten guidelines for when unrelated diversification may be an especially effective strategy are:[18]

- When revenues derived from an organization's current products or services would increase significantly by adding the new, unrelated products.
- When an organization competes in a highly competitive and/or a no-growth industry, as indicated by low industry profit margins and returns.
- When an organization's present channels of distribution can be used to market the new products to current customers.
- When the new products have countercyclical sales patterns compared to an organization's present products.
- When an organization's basic industry is experiencing declining annual sales and profits.
- When an organization has the capital and managerial talent needed to compete successfully in a new industry.
- When an organization has the opportunity to purchase an unrelated business that is an attractive investment opportunity.
- When there exists financial synergy between the acquired and acquiring firm. (Note that a key difference between related and unrelated diversification is that the former should be based on some commonality in markets, products, or technology, whereas the latter should be based more on profit considerations.)

- When existing markets for an organization's present products are saturated.
- When antitrust action could be charged against an organization that historically has concentrated on a single industry.

Defensive Strategies

In addition to integrative, intensive, and diversification strategies, organizations also could pursue retrenchment, divestiture, or liquidation.

Retrenchment

Retrenchment occurs when an organization regroups through cost and asset reduction to reverse declining sales and profits. Sometimes called a *turnaround* or *reorganizational strategy,* retrenchment is designed to fortify an organization's basic distinctive competence. During retrenchment, strategists work with limited resources and face pressure from shareholders, employees, and the media. Retrenchment can entail selling off land and buildings to raise needed cash, pruning product lines, closing marginal businesses, closing obsolete factories, automating processes, reducing the number of employees, and instituting expense control systems.

The telecommunications equipment vendor, Nortel, cut another 2,900 jobs in 2007, bringing its workforce to about 31,000, down from 95,000 in 2001. The retrenchment strategy is part of CEO Mike Zafirovski's strategy to stay only in businesses in which Nortel has a 20 percent global market share. Chief Strategy Officer George Riedel of Nortel says, "In the past, we were trying to be all things to all people. Now we're focused on doing a few things that matter."

Circuit City is closing 62 stores in Canada in 2007 and 7 stores in the U.S. as the firm continues to struggle against fierce rival Best Buy. Circuit City also is laying off employees and shuffling its top manager team in restructuring moves aimed to reverse declining sales and margins.

Eastman Kodak completed a three-year retrenchment strategy in 2007 during which the firm laid off 30,000 employees and incurred $3.8 billion in restructuring costs. Kodak's workforce declined to about 28,000 at year-end 2007, down from 40,000 at the end of 2006, and down from its peak of 145,000 in 1984. Kodak rolled out a new inkjet printer in 2007 and does well in motion-picture film for movies, but continues to struggle in consumer film and disposable cameras. Kodak's new inkjet printers scan and copy documents, Web pages, and photos using cartridges priced far less than those of its competitors.

DaimlerChrysler AG is cutting 10,000 jobs and closing factories in Newark, Delaware, and St. Louis as part of a retrenchment strategy that also includes turning away from big pickups and sport-utility vehicles. Chrysler's goal now is not to get bigger but rather to make money.

La-Z-Boy in 2007 is closing three plants, consolidating three others into one facility, and eliminating 500 jobs, or 4.4 percent of its overall workforce of 11,300 employees. The company expects to save $11 million annually by restructuring, closing its Lincolnton and North Wilkesboro, North Carolina facilities as well as its plant in Iuka, Mississippi.

Citigroup is in the midst of a major retrenchment/restructuring whereby the firm is laying off 15,000 employees or 5 percent of the bank's global workforce of 327,000. An additional 10,000 or more U.S. jobs are moving to cheaper overseas locations such as India. Citigroup is the world's largest bank.

In some cases, *bankruptcy* can be an effective type of retrenchment strategy. Bankruptcy can allow a firm to avoid major debt obligations and to void union contracts. There are five major types of bankruptcy: Chapter 7, Chapter 9, Chapter 11, Chapter 12, and Chapter 13.

Chapter 7 bankruptcy is a liquidation procedure used only when a corporation sees no hope of being able to operate successfully or to obtain the necessary creditor agreement. All the organization's assets are sold in parts for their tangible worth.

Chapter 9 bankruptcy applies to municipalities. A municipality that successfully declared bankruptcy is Camden, New Jersey, the state's poorest city and the fifth-poorest city in the United States. A crime-ridden city of 87,000, Camden received $62.5 million in state aid and has withdrawn its bankruptcy petition. Between 1980 and 2000, only 18 U.S. cities declared bankruptcy. Some states do not allow municipalities to declare bankruptcy.

Chapter 11 bankruptcy allows organizations to reorganize and come back after filing a petition for protection. Business bankruptcy filings dropped to a 10-year-low in fiscal 2006, reflecting the easy access to capital that troubled companies had enjoyed. Chapter 11 filings dropped by 20 percent to 27, 333 in the 12 months ending September 30, according to the Administrative Office of the U.S. Courts. However, analysts expect a surge in bankruptcy filings in 2007–2008 due to tightening credit markets and greater price competitiveness among firms.

New Century Financial, the nation's second-largest subprime mortgage lender, filed for Chapter 11 bankruptcy in April 2007 and laid off more than one half of its workforce. The company at the same time divested its mortgage-servicing assets to Carrington Capital Management, which provided $150 million to New Century to allow the firm to stay in business during bankruptcy reorganization.

Northwest Airlines emerged from bankruptcy in mid-2007 after two years of regrouping under that protection. Northwest is stronger on exit than entry, but the air carrier still has to contend with rising and high fuel costs, unhappy employees, intense competition, and slowing domestic demand. Other airlines still operating under Chapter 11 bankruptcy are UAL Corp, Delta Air Lines, and US Airways.

Startup wireless carrier Amp'dMobile filed for Chaper 11 bankruptcy in June 2007 after it ran out of cash. The company has assets of less than $100 million but is more than that amount in debt.

Chapter 12 bankruptcy was created by the Family Farmer Bankruptcy Act of 1986. This law became effective in 1987 and provides special relief to family farmers with debt equal to or less than $1.5 million.

Chapter 13 bankruptcy is a reorganization plan similar to Chapter 11, but it is available only to small businesses owned by individuals with unsecured debts of less than $100,000 and secured debts of less than $350,000. The Chapter 13 debtor is allowed to operate the business while a plan is being developed to provide for the successful operation of the business in the future.

Five guidelines for when retrenchment may be an especially effective strategy to pursue are as follows:[19]

- When an organization has a clearly distinctive competence but has failed consistently to meet its objectives and goals over time.
- When an organization is one of the weaker competitors in a given industry.
- When an organization is plagued by inefficiency, low profitability, poor employee morale, and pressure from stockholders to improve performance.
- When an organization has failed to capitalize on external opportunities, minimize external threats, take advantage of internal strengths, and overcome internal weaknesses over time; that is, when the organization's strategic managers have failed (and possibly will be replaced by more competent individuals).
- When an organization has grown so large so quickly that major internal reorganization is needed.

Divestiture

Selling a division or part of an organization is called *divestiture*. Divestiture often is used to raise capital for further strategic acquisitions or investments. Divestiture can be part of an overall retrenchment strategy to rid an organization of businesses that are unprofitable, that require too much capital, or that do not fit well with the firm's other activities. Divestiture has also become a popular strategy for firms to focus on their core businesses and become less diversified. For example, Germany's Merck KGaA is selling its generic-drug division in order to focus on branded drugs and chemicals. Merck also is trying to sell its consumer health care business for the same reason. Akzo Nobel NV of the Netherlands is trying to sell its pharmaceuticals division, Organon BioSciences, in order to focus on its chemicals and paint operations. Switzerland's Norvartis AG recently sold its medical-nutrition division to focus on drugs and vaccines. Siemens AG has been divesting its telecommunications businesses to focus on medical diagnostics.

International Paper is selling its beverage-packaging and chemical operations so it can focus on uncoated paper and packaging. Morgan Stanley plans to jettison its Discover credit-card business to focus on its brokerage business. Even Time Warner recently divested the Atlanta Braves baseball team to Liberty Media Corp. for $460 million. Ford Motor Company recently divested Aston Martin, the British brand of car most famous for its association with the James Bond films.

Headquartered in Birmingham, Alabama, HealthSouth Corporation sold its surgery division to private-investment partnership TPG Inc. in 2007. Formerly Texas Pacific Group, TPG now manages more than $30 billion in assets. HealthSouth also divested its outpatient rehabilitation centers in 35 states as the firm strives to refocus on its inpatient-rehabilitation business. Refocusing by divesting has thus become a very common strategy being employed by firms in many industries in 2006–2008. Table 5-3 provides a list of some recent divestitures.

Six guidelines for when divestiture may be an especially effective strategy to pursue follows:[20]

- When an organization has pursued a retrenchment strategy and failed to accomplish needed improvements.
- When a division needs more resources to be competitive than the company can provide.
- When a division is responsible for an organization's overall poor performance.
- When a division is a misfit with the rest of an organization; this can result from radically different markets, customers, managers, employees, values, or needs.

TABLE 5-3   Recent Divestitures

Parent Company	Part Being Divested	Acquiring Company
San Miguel Corp.	Soft drink bottling	Coca-Cola Co.
CBS	Seven TV stations	Cerberus Capital Mgt.
Lacofinance SA	Svedka Vodka	Constellation Brands
Polish Government	PZL Mielec	Sikorsky Aircraft
Delphi Corp.	Vehicle interiors	Renco Group Inc.
International Paper	Beverage packing	Carter Holt Harvey Ltd.
International Paper	Chemical operations	Rhone Capital LLC
American Skiing Co.	Steamboat Ski & Resort	Intrawest Corp.
Novartis AG	Medical nutrition	Nestle SA
Genworth Financial	Life and health insurance	Sun Life Financial
Ingersoll-Rand Co.	Road development	Volvo AB
Lyondell Chemical	Inorganic chemicals	National Industrialization
Colgate-Palmolive	Latin American bleach	Clorox
Lafarge SA	Roofing unit	PAI Partners
Ford Motor Company	Climate control	Valeo SA
Ahold NV	Polish grocery stores	Carrefour SA
Mirant Corp.	Mirant Asia Pacific	Marubeni Corp.
Dubai Ports World	U.S. assets	AIG Global Investment
Polaris Financial Group	Bank of Overseas China	Citigroup Inc.
Raytheon Co.	Aircraft manufacturing	Hawker Beechcraft
McClatchy Company	Minneapolis Star Tribune	Avista Capital Partners
Alliant Energy	Interstate Power & Light	ITC Holdings
Kraft Foods	Hot cereals	B&G Foods
Kraft Foods	Minute Rice	Ebro Puleva
Gordon Gaming Corp.	Sahara Hotel & Casino	SBE Entertainment
Accor SA	30 hotels	Land Securities Group PLC

- When a large amount of cash is needed quickly and cannot be obtained reasonably from other sources.
- When government antitrust action threatens an organization.

Liquidation

Selling all of a company's assets, in parts, for their tangible worth is called *liquidation*. Liquidation is a recognition of defeat and consequently can be an emotionally difficult strategy. However, it may be better to cease operating than to continue losing large sums of money. For example, Canadian discount airline, Jetsgo, in 2005, halted operations, filed for bankruptcy, and then liquidated. Canada's third-largest airline, Jetsgo was launched three years earlier from Montreal. Jetsgo competed against WestJet, based in Calgary, Alberta, and Air Canada, based in Montreal. Analysts had long predicted that Jetsgo would fail, given the company's rock-bottom ticket prices and aggressive expansion.

Thousands of small businesses in the United States liquidate annually without ever making the news. It is tough to start and successfully operate a small business. In China and Russia, thousands of government-owned businesses liquidate annually as those countries try to privatize and consolidate industries.

Three guidelines for when liquidation may be an especially effective strategy to pursue are:[21]

- When an organization has pursued both a retrenchment strategy and a divestiture strategy, and neither has been successful.
- When an organization's only alternative is bankruptcy. Liquidation represents an orderly and planned means of obtaining the greatest possible cash for an organization's assets. A company can legally declare bankruptcy first and then liquidate various divisions to raise needed capital.
- When the stockholders of a firm can minimize their losses by selling the organization's assets.

Michael Porter's Five Generic Strategies

Probably the three most widely read books on competitive analysis in the 1980s were Michael Porter's *Competitive Strategy* (Free Press, 1980), *Competitive Advantage* (Free Press, 1985), and *Competitive Advantage of Nations* (Free Press, 1989). According to Porter, strategies allow organizations to gain competitive advantage from three different bases: cost leadership, differentiation, and focus. Porter calls these bases *generic strategies*. *Cost leadership* emphasizes producing standardized products at a very low per-unit cost for consumers who are price-sensitive. Two alternative types of cost leadership strategies can be defined. Type 1 is a *low-cost* strategy that offers products or services to a wide range of customers at the lowest price available on the market. Type 2 is a *best-value* strategy that offers products or services to a wide range of customers at the best price-value available on the market; the best-value strategy aims to offer customers a range of products or services at the lowest price available compared to a rival's products with similar attributes. Both Type 1 and Type 2 strategies target a large market.

Porter's Type 3 generic strategy is *differentiation*. *Differentiation* is a strategy aimed at producing products and services considered unique industrywide and directed at consumers who are relatively price-insensitive.

Focus means producing products and services that fulfill the needs of small groups of consumers. Two alternative types of focus strategies are Type 4 and Type 5. Type 4 is a *low-cost focus* strategy that offers products or services to a small range (niche group) of customers at the lowest price available on the market. Examples of firms that use the Type 4 strategy include Jiffy Lube International and Pizza Hut, as well as local used car dealers and hot dog restaurants. Type 5 is a *best-value focus* strategy that offers products or services to a small range of customers at the best price-value available on the market. Sometimes called "focused differentiation," the best-value focus strategy aims to offer a niche group of customers products or services that meet their tastes and requirements better than rivals' products do. Both

Type 4 and Type 5 focus strategies target a small market. However, the difference is that Type 4 strategies offer products services to a niche group at the lowest price, whereas Type 5 offers products/services to a niche group at higher prices but loaded with features so the offerings are perceived as the best value. Examples of firms that use the Type 5 strategy include Cannondale (top-of-the-line mountain bikes), Maytag (washing machines), and Lone Star Restaurants (steak house), as well as bed-and-breakfast inns and local retail boutiques.

Porter's five strategies imply different organizational arrangements, control procedures, and incentive systems. Larger firms with greater access to resources typically compete on a cost leadership and/or differentiation basis, whereas smaller firms often compete on a focus basis. Porter's five generic strategies are illustrated in Figure 5-3. Note that a differentiation strategy (Type 3) can be pursued with either a small target market or a large target market. However, it is not effective to pursue a cost leadership strategy in a small market because profits margins are generally too small. Likewise, it is not effective to pursue a focus strategy in a large market because economies of scale would generally favor a low-cost or best-value cost leaderships strategy to gain and/or sustain competitive advantage.

Porter stresses the need for strategists to perform cost-benefit analyses to evaluate "sharing opportunities" among a firm's existing and potential business units. Sharing activities and resources enhances competitive advantage by lowering costs or increasing differentiation. In addition to prompting sharing, Porter stresses the need for firms to effectively "transfer" skills and expertise among autonomous business units in order to gain competitive advantage. Depending upon factors such as type of industry, size of firm, and nature of competition, various strategies could yield advantages in cost leadership, differentiation, and focus.

Cost Leadership Strategies (Type 1 and Type 2)

A primary reason for pursuing forward, backward, and horizontal integration strategies is to gain low-cost or best-value cost leadership benefits. But cost leadership generally must be pursued in conjunction with differentiation. A number of cost elements affect the relative attractiveness of generic strategies, including economies or diseconomies of scale achieved, learning and experience curve effects, the percentage of capacity utilization achieved, and linkages with suppliers and distributors. Other cost elements to consider in choosing among alternative strategies include the potential for sharing costs and knowledge

FIGURE 5-3

Porter's Five Generic Strategies

Type 1: Cost Leadership—Low Cost
Type 2: Cost Leadership—Best Value
Type 3: Differentiation
Type 4: Focus—Low Cost
Type 5: Focus—Best Value

GENERIC STRATEGIES

	Cost Leadership	Differentiation	Focus
Large	Type 1 Type 2	Type 3	—
Small	—	Type 3	Type 4 Type 5

SIZE OF MARKET

Source: Adapted from Michael E. Porter, *Competitive Strategy: Techniques for Analyzing Industries and Competitors* (New York: Free Press, 1980): 35–40.

within the organization, R&D costs associated with new product development or modification of existing products, labor costs, tax rates, energy costs, and shipping costs.

Striving to be the low-cost producer in an industry can be especially effective when the market is composed of many price-sensitive buyers, when there are few ways to achieve product differentiation, when buyers do not care much about differences from brand to brand, or when there are a large number of buyers with significant bargaining power. The basic idea is to underprice competitors and thereby gain market share and sales, entirely driving some competitors out of the market. Companies employing a low-cost (Type 1) or best-value (Type 2) cost leadership strategy must achieve their competitive advantage in ways that are difficult for competitors to copy or match. If rivals find it relatively easy or inexpensive to imitate the leader's cost leadership methods, the leaders' advantage will not last long enough to yield a valuable edge in the marketplace. Recall that for a resource to be valuable, it must be either rare, hard to imitate, or not easily substitutable. To successfully employ a cost leadership strategy, a firm must ensure that its total costs across its overall value chain are lower than competitors' total costs. There are two ways to accomplish this:[22]

1. Perform value chain activities more efficiently than rivals and control the factors that drive the costs of value chain activities. Such activities could include altering the plant layout, mastering newly introduced technologies, using common parts or components in different products, simplifying product design, finding ways to operate close to full capacity year-round, and so on.
2. Revamp the firm's overall value chain to eliminate or bypass some cost-producing activities. Such activities could include securing new suppliers or distributors, selling products online, relocating manufacturing facilities, avoiding the use of union labor, and so on.

When employing a cost leadership strategy, a firm must be careful not to use such aggressive price cuts that their own profits are low or nonexistent. Constantly be mindful of cost-saving technological breakthroughs or any other value chain advancements that could erode or destroy the firm's competitive advantage. A Type 1 or Type 2 cost leadership strategy can be especially effective under the following conditions:[23]

1. When price competition among rival sellers is especially vigorous.
2. When the products of rival sellers are essentially identical and supplies are readily available from any of several eager sellers.
3. When there are few ways to achieve product differentiation that have value to buyers.
4. When most buyers use the product in the same ways.
5. When buyers incur low costs in switching their purchases from one seller to another.
6. When buyers are large and have significant power to bargain down prices.
7. When industry newcomers use introductory low prices to attract buyers and build a customer base.

A successful cost leadership strategy usually permeates the entire firm, as evidenced by high efficiency, low overhead, limited perks, intolerance of waste, intensive screening of budget requests, wide spans of control, rewards linked to cost containment, and broad employee participation in cost control efforts. Some risks of pursuing cost leadership are that competitors may imitate the strategy, thus driving overall industry profits down; that technological breakthroughs in the industry may make the strategy ineffective; or that buyer interest may swing to other differentiating features besides price. Several example firms that are well known for their low-cost leadership strategies are Wal-Mart, BIC, McDonald's, Black and Decker, Lincoln Electric, and Briggs and Stratton.

Differentiation Strategies (Type 3)

Different strategies offer different degrees of differentiation. Differentiation does not guarantee competitive advantage, especially if standard products sufficiently meet customer needs or if rapid imitation by competitors is possible. Durable products protected by barriers to quick copying by competitors are best. Successful differentiation can mean greater product flexibility, greater compatibility, lower costs, improved service, less maintenance, greater convenience, or more features. Product development is an example of a strategy that offers the advantages of differentiation.

A differentiation strategy should be pursued only after a careful study of buyers' needs and preferences to determine the feasibility of incorporating one or more differentiating features into a unique product that features the desired attributes. A successful differentiation strategy allows a firm to charge a higher price for its product and to gain customer loyalty because consumers may become strongly attached to the differentiation features. Special features that differentiate one's product can include superior service, spare parts availability, engineering design, product performance, useful life, gas mileage, or ease of use.

A risk of pursuing a differentiation strategy is that the unique product may not be valued highly enough by customers to justify the higher price. When this happens, a cost leadership strategy easily will defeat a differentiation strategy. Another risk of pursuing a differentiation strategy is that competitors may quickly develop ways to copy the differentiating features. Firms thus must find durable sources of uniqueness that cannot be imitated quickly or cheaply by rival firms.

Common organizational requirements for a successful differentiation strategy include strong coordination among the R&D and marketing functions and substantial amenities to attract scientists and creative people. Firms can pursue a differentiation (Type 3) strategy based on many different competitive aspects. For example, Mountain Dew and root beer have a unique taste; Lowe's, Home Depot, and Wal-Mart offer wide selection and one-stop shopping; Dell Computer and FedEx offer superior service; BMW and Porsche offer engineering design and performance; IBM and Hewlett-Packard offer a wide range of products; and E*Trade and Ameritrade offer Internet convenience. Differentiation opportunities exist or can potentially be developed anywhere along the firm's value chain, including supply chain activities, product R&D activities, production and technological activities, manufacturing activities, human resource management activities, distribution activities, or marketing activities.

The most effective differentiation bases are those that are hard or expensive for rivals to duplicate. Competitors are continually trying to imitate, duplicate, and outperform rivals along any differentiation variable that has yielded competitive advantage. For example, when U.S. Airways cut its prices, Delta quickly followed suit. When Caterpillar instituted its quick-delivery-of-spare-parts policy, John Deere soon followed suit. To the extent that differentiating attributes are tough for rivals to copy, a differentiation strategy will be especially effective, but the sources of uniqueness must be time-consuming, cost prohibitive, and simply too burdensome for rivals to match. A firm, therefore, must be careful when employing a differentiation (Type 3) strategy. Buyers will not pay the higher differentiation price unless their perceived value exceeds the price they are paying.[24] Based upon such matters as attractive packaging, extensive advertising, quality of sales presentations, quality of Web site, list of customers, professionalism, size of the firm, and/or profitability of the company, perceived value may be more important to customers than actual value.

A Type 3 differentiation strategy can be especially effective under the following conditions:[25]

1. When there are many ways to differentiate the product or service and many buyers perceive these differences as having value.
2. When buyer needs and uses are diverse.
3. When few rival firms are following a similar differentiation approach.
4. When technological change is fast paced and competition revolves around rapidly evolving product features.

Focus Strategies (Type 4 and Type 5)

A successful focus strategy depends on an industry segment that is of sufficient size, has good growth potential, and is not crucial to the success of other major competitors. Strategies such as market penetration and market development offer substantial focusing advantages. Midsize and large firms can effectively pursue focus-based strategies only in conjunction with differentiation or cost leadership–based strategies. All firms in essence follow a differentiated strategy. Because only one firm can differentiate itself with the lowest cost, the remaining firms in the industry must find other ways to differentiate their products.

Focus strategies are most effective when consumers have distinctive preferences or requirements and when rival firms are not attempting to specialize in the same target segment. Starbucks, the largest U.S. coffeehouse chain, is pursuing a focus strategy as it recently acquired Seattle Coffee's U.S. and Canadian operations for $72 million. Based in Seattle, Starbucks now owns Seattle's 150 coffee shops and its wholesale contracts with about 12,000 grocery stores and food service stores that distribute Seattle coffee beans.

In the insurance industry, Safeco recently divested its life insurance and investment management divisions to focus exclusively on property casualty insurance operations. The Seattle-based company's strategy is just one of many examples of consolidation in the insurance industry where firms strive to focus on one type of insurance rather than many types.

Japan's second-largest airline by revenue, All Nippon Airways, has a stated strategy to focus on core passenger and cargo flight operations, so the firm is divesting all other assets. This strategy led to All Nippon selling its 13 luxury hotels in 2007 to Morgan Stanley.

Risks of pursuing a focus strategy include the possibility that numerous competitors will recognize the successful focus strategy and copy it or that consumer preferences will drift toward the product attributes desired by the market as a whole. An organization using a focus strategy may concentrate on a particular group of customers, geographic markets, or on particular product-line segments to serve a well-defined but narrow market better than competitors who serve a broader market.

A low-cost (Type 4) or best-value (Type 5) focus strategy can be especially attractive under the following conditions:[26]

1. When the target market niche is large, profitable, and growing.
2. When industry leaders do not consider the niche to be crucial to their own success.
3. When industry leaders consider it too costly or difficult to meet the specialized needs of the target market niche while taking care of their mainstream customers.
4. When the industry has many different niches and segments, thereby allowing a focuser to pick a competitively attractive niche suited to its own resources.
5. When few, if any, other rivals are attempting to specialize in the same target segment.

Strategies for Competing in Turbulent, High-Velocity Markets

The world is changing more and more rapidly, and consequently industries and firms themselves are changing faster than ever. Some industries are changing so fast that researchers call them *turbulent, high-velocity markets,* such as telecommunications, medical, biotechnology, pharmaceuticals, computer hardware, software, and virtually all Internet-based industries. High-velocity change is clearly becoming more and more the rule rather than the exception, even in such industries as toys, phones, banking, defense, publishing, and communication.

As illustrated in Figure 5-4, meeting the challenge of high-velocity change presents the firm with a choice of whether to react, anticipate, or lead the market in terms of its own strategies. To primarily react to changes in the industry would be a defensive strategy used to counter, for example, unexpected shifts in buyer tastes and technological breakthroughs. The react-to-change strategy would not be as effective as the anticipate-change strategy, which would entail devising and following through with plans for dealing with the expected changes. However, firms ideally strive to be in a position to lead the changes in high-velocity markets, whereby they pioneer new and better technologies and products and set industry standards. As illustrated, being the leader or pioneer of change in a high-velocity market is an aggressive, offensive strategy that includes rushing next-generation products to market ahead of rivals and being continually proactive in shaping the market to one's own benefit. Although a lead-change strategy is best whenever the firm has the resources to pursue this

FIGURE 5-4

Meeting the Challenge of High-Velocity Change

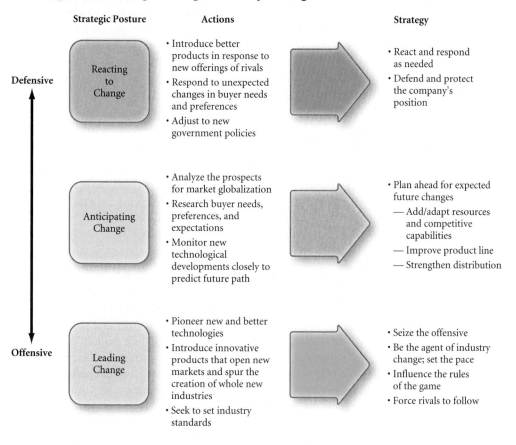

approach, on occasion even the strongest firms in turbulent industries have to employ the react-to-the-market strategy and the anticipate-the-market strategy.

Means for Achieving Strategies

Joint Venture/Partnering

Joint venture is a popular strategy that occurs when two or more companies form a temporary partnership or consortium for the purpose of capitalizing on some opportunity. Often, the two or more sponsoring firms form a separate organization and have shared equity ownership in the new entity. Other types of *cooperative arrangements* include research and development partnerships, cross-distribution agreements, cross-licensing agreements, cross-manufacturing agreements, and joint-bidding consortia. Burger King recently formed a "conceptual agreement" with its fierce rival, Hungry Jacks, in Australia, whereby the two firms will join forces against market leader McDonald's. All Burger Kings in Australia are being renamed Hungry Jacks, but Burger King retains ownership under the unusual agreement. With this agreement, Australia becomes Burger King's fourth-largest country market, tied with Spain.

U.S. regional airline operator Mesa Air Group, based in Phoenix, Arizona, recently formed a joint venture with Chinese carrier Shenzhen Airlines, based in Shenzhen, China, to create China's first commuter airline. The first joint venture ever between U.S. and Chinese passenger airlines, Bejing Airlines now links Beijing with many poorly or nonserved cities in China and Southeast Asia. One of China's largest privately owned carriers, Shenzhen Airlines aims to expand its fleet to 80 planes by 2008 and 160 planes by 2015.

Joint ventures and cooperative arrangements are being used increasingly because they allow companies to improve communications and networking, to globalize operations, and to minimize risk. Joint ventures and partnerships are often used to pursue an opportunity that is too complex, uneconomical, or risky for a single firm to pursue alone. Such business creations also are used when achieving and sustaining competitive advantage when an industry requires a broader range of competencies and know-how than any one firm can marshal. Armani's joint venture is with Emaar Hotels & Resorts LLC to create, among others, the tallest building in the world in 2008: a 2,000-foot-tall hotel in Dubai's Burj Dubai. Kathryn Rudie Harrigan, professor of strategic management at Columbia University, summarizes the trend toward increased joint venturing:

> In today's global business environment of scarce resources, rapid rates of technological change, and rising capital requirements, the important question is no longer "Shall we form a joint venture?" Now the question is "Which joint ventures and cooperative arrangements are most appropriate for our needs and expectations?" followed by "How do we manage these ventures most effectively?"[27]

In a global market tied together by the Internet, joint ventures, and partnerships, alliances are proving to be a more effective way to enhance corporate growth than mergers and acquisitions.[28] Strategic partnering takes many forms, including outsourcing, information sharing, joint marketing, and joint research and development. Many companies, such as Eli Lilly, now host partnership training classes for their managers and partners. There are today more than 10,000 joint ventures formed annually, more than all mergers and acquisitions. There are countless examples of successful strategic alliances, such as Starbucks' recent joint venture with China's President Coffee to open hundreds of new Starbuck coffee shops in China. For 4,500 years, China has been a country of tea drinkers, but Seattle-based Starbucks is having success building Chinese taste for coffee. Microsoft's online-services division recently formed a joint venture with Shanghai Alliance Investment to launch MSN China throughout China. The new company, Shanghai MSN Network Communications Technology, serves China's online consumers: 100 million (and growing) at that time. As evidence of Microsoft's determination to enter the telecom market, the firm has formed a partnership with France Telecom SA, one of the world's largest telecommunications operators. Since people increasingly interact with the Internet using either a cell phone or television, Microsoft is using the alliance to push its voice-over-Internet protocol (VOIP), which is a handheld device that combines cell phone usage with Internet coverage.

A major reason why firms are using partnering as a means to achieve strategies is globalization. Wal-Mart's successful joint venture with Mexico's Cifra is indicative of how a domestic firm can benefit immensely by partnering with a foreign company to gain substantial presence in that new country. Technology also is a major reason behind the need to form strategic alliances, with the Internet linking widely dispersed partners. The Internet paved the way and legitimized the need for alliances to serve as the primary means for corporate growth.

Evidence is mounting that firms should use partnering as a means for achieving strategies. However, the sad fact is that most U.S. firms in many industries—such as financial services, forest products, metals, and retailing—still operate in a merger or acquire mode to obtain growth. Partnering is not yet taught at most business schools and is often viewed within companies as a financial issue rather than a strategic issue. However, partnering has become a core competency, a strategic issue of such importance that top management involvement initially and throughout the life of an alliance is vital.[29]

Joint ventures among once rival firms are commonly being used to pursue strategies ranging from retrenchment to market development.

Although ventures and partnerships are preferred over mergers as a means for achieving strategies, certainly they are not all successful. The good news is that joint ventures and partnerships are less risky for companies than mergers, but the bad news is that many alliances fail. *Forbes* has reported that about 30 percent of all joint ventures and partnership alliances are outright failures, while another 17 percent have limited success and then dissipate due to problems.[30] There are countless examples of failed joint ventures. A few common problems that cause joint ventures to fail are as follows:

1. Managers who must collaborate daily in operating the venture are not involved in forming or shaping the venture.
2. The venture may benefit the partnering companies but may not benefit customers, who then complain about poorer service or criticize the companies in other ways.
3. The venture may not be supported equally by both partners. If supported unequally, problems arise.
4. The venture may begin to compete more with one of the partners than the other.[31]

Six guidelines for when a joint venture may be an especially effective strategy to pursue are:[32]

- When a privately-owned organization is forming a joint venture with a publicly owned organization; there are some advantages to being privately held, such as closed ownership; there are some advantages of being publicly held, such as access to stock issuances as a source of capital. Sometimes, the unique advantages of being privately and publicly held can be synergistically combined in a joint venture.
- When a domestic organization is forming a joint venture with a foreign company; a joint venture can provide a domestic company with the opportunity for obtaining local management in a foreign country, thereby reducing risks such as expropriation and harassment by host country officials.
- When the distinct competencies of two or more firms complement each other especially well.
- When some project is potentially very profitable but requires overwhelming resources and risks; the Alaskan pipeline is an example.
- When two or more smaller firms have trouble competing with a large firm.
- When there exists a need to quickly introduce a new technology.

Merger/Acquisition

Merger and acquisition are two commonly used ways to pursue strategies. A *merger* occurs when two organizations of about equal size unite to form one enterprise. An *acquisition* occurs when a large organization purchases (acquires) a smaller firm, or vice versa. When a merger or acquisition is not desired by both parties, it can be called a *takeover* or *hostile takeover*. In contrast, if the acquisition is desired by both firms, it is termed a *friendly merger*. Most mergers are friendly.

There were numerous examples in 2007 of hostile takeover attempts. For example, Orlando-based AirTran Airways launched a $345 million tender offer to acquire Milwaukee-based Midwest Airlines' shares directly from shareholders in hopes of forcing the Midwest board to sell the firm. AirTran has even offered to keep serving free chocolate chip cookies on all Midwest flights if the board will sell. Delta Airlines recently fended off a $9.75 billion hostile takeover bid made by U.S. Airways although industry analysts thought the takeover would succeed. Delta CEO Gerald Grinstein rallied employees, shareholders, and creditors around his "Keep Delta My Delta" campaign.

There are numerous and powerful forces driving once-fierce rivals to merge around the world. Some of these forces are deregulation, technological change, excess capacity, inability to boost profits through price increases, a depressed stock market, and the need to gain economies of scale. Other forces spurring acquisitions include increased market power, reduced entry barriers, reduced cost of new product development, increased speed of products to market, lowered risk compared to developing new products, increased diversification, avoidance of excessive competition, and opportunity to learn and develop new capabilities.

The year 2006 witnessed more mergers than ever both in the United States and worldwide, and analysts predict that the 2007 dollar volume of transactions will exceed $4 trillion for the first time ever. Merger mania is being fueled by robust stock markets, cheap and available debt, and firms desiring to expand globally. The total of $3.79 trillion in merger transactions worldwide in 2006 beat the previous record of $3.4 trillion in 2000, and was a whopping 38 percent higher than in 2005. There were 55 merger transactions in 2006 valued at more than $10 billion apiece with the AT&T acquisition of BellSouth topping the list at $72.7 billion. Across the globe, $1.1 trillion of companies traded hands in the first quarter of 2007, 27 percent higher than the same period in 2006. The 2007 figures were more startling in the United States, where the volume of deals surged 32 percent from 2006 to $439 billion.[33]

Private-equity firms played a bigger-than-ever role in the merger frenzy, with a hand in 20 percent of the world's acquisitions, and 27 percent in the United States.[34] Mergers in Europe rose 39 percent in 2006 to $1.43 trillion, compared with a 36 percent increase to $1.56 trillion in the United States. The world's five largest merger advisor/transaction firms are Goldman Sachs, Citigroup, Morgan Stanley, J.P. Morgan, and Merrill Lynch.

In China, there were 2,263 acquisitions in 2006, up from 1,786 in 2005.[35] The 2006 dollar total of acquisitions reached $103.8 billion, up 68 percent from 2005. Through mergers, the Chinese central government wants to reduce the number of state-owned companies from 161 in 2007 to 80 in 2010. Stephen Green, an economist with Standard Chartered, commented regarding the surge in acquisitions in China: "It should make things more efficient. You're looking for economies of scale, horizontal and vertical integration, improving quality of management, and also the ability to wipe out your competitors and gain pricing power." This comment reveals the motivation for most acquisitions in the United States and Europe.

In Japan, companies in 2006–2008 start acquiring other firms worldwide after a lull in this activity in 2000–2005. Japanese firms bought more than 300 foreign companies for a total exceeding $20 billion in 2006, double the figure in 2004. For example, Japan's largest tobacco company, Japan Tobacco Inc., is acquiring Gallaher Group PLC of Britain in the largest Japanese deal ever for a foreign company. Unheard of prior to 2006 in Japan, hostile takeovers are also being tried. Oji Paper recently launched an unsolicited $1.4 billion bid for rival Hokuetsu Paper Mills. This was the first hostile takeover battle between two Japanese blue-chip companies.

In Japan, new guidelines in 2007 make it much easier and actually encourage Japanese firms to merge. The value of merger/acquisition deals among Japanese companies has steadily risen over the past five years, hitting 15 trillion yen ($124 billion) in 2006. There were 2,775 deals in 2006, up 1.8 percent from 2005 and much higher than the 1,752 in 2002.

Sirius and XM Satellite Radio, two fierce rival firms in the satellite radio business, merged in 2007, creating a company valued at more than $13 billion. Neither company had a made a profit prior to the merger, and each firm's satellite radios were designed for it and cannot receive the other's signal. General Motors, Toyota, and Honda were big XM subscribers, while Ford, DaimlerChrylser, and VW/Audi were exclusive Sirius customers. The combined company is developing radio receivers that receive input from both XM and Sirius satellites.

Private-Equity Acquisitions

Private-equity firms such as Kohlberg Kravis Roberts (KKR) have made many if not most of the acquisitions in recent years. The pace and number of private-equity acquisitions was a key new trend in 2006–2007 in the merger world. Cheap and plentiful debt has propelled private-equity firms to be the most active acquirer's in today's business marketplace. These firms acquire companies and then sell them at premium prices. That is the intent of virtually all private-equity acquisitions—buy low and sell high later—which is arguably just good business.

Two private-equity firms, Apollo Management and Texas Pacific, recently paid $16.7 billion to acquire Harrah's Entertainment, the world's largest casino company. Another private-equity group, Colony Capital LLC, recently acquired Station Casinos Inc. Another,

Apax Partners, just acquired Chicago insurance brokerage Hub International. Perseus LLC recently acquired Avalon Publishing Group and Consortium Book Sales & Distribution. The recent $32 billion purchase of the largest electric company in Texas, TXU, was by two private-equity firms, KKR and Texas Pacific Group. Goodyear Tire & Rubber just divested its engineered-products division to a private-equity firm Carlyle Partners for $1.48 billion. Home-services operator ServiceMaster Company was recently acquired by private-equity firm Clayton, Dubilier & Rice for $4.8 billion.

The proliferation of private-equity deals has resulted in union leaders worldwide lobbying governments to impose restrictions on this activity. Union leaders argue that such deals suppress the bargaining power of unions and also promote widening income disparity between corporate executives and workers, despite growth in profits and productivity. Hundreds of private-equity investors such as Darby Overseas Investments Ltd., Cerberus Capital Management LP, and Blackstone Group are acquiring small firms in Asia, capitalizing on rapid growth there.

A recent article reveals that in 2006 private-equity firms launched 14 hostile or unsolicited takeover bids in Europe and this continued in 2007.[36] Three private-equity firms recently made an unsolicited bid for J Sainsbury PLC, a British grocery chain, in what would be Europe's largest private-equity deal. Countrywide PLC was recently acquired by private-equity company 3i Group PLC for 551 pence a share, which was a premium of 90 pence to the 461 pence that Countrywide PLC's shares were trading.

Blackstone Group, which had acquired Celanese, Vanguard Health, Nielsen, SunGard, TRW Automotive, Travelport, and Naico in recent years, is trying to go public, which could alter the private-equity business model. Generally these firms avoid SEC disclosure rules regarding executive pay and other matters by staying private. Going public would require Blackstone to reveal some of its secrets for wresting huge profits from the companies it acquires and thus expose the firm to criticism.

Not all mergers are effective and successful. Pricewaterhouse Coopers LLP recently researched mergers and found that the average acquirer's stock was 3.7 percent lower than its industry peer group a year later. *BusinessWeek* and the *Wall Street Journal* studied mergers and concluded that about half produced negative returns to shareholders. Warren Buffett once said in a speech that "too-high purchase price for the stock of an excellent company can undo the effects of a subsequent decade of favorable business developments." Research suggests that perhaps 20 percent of all mergers and acquisitions are successful, approximately 60 percent produce disappointing results, and the last 20 percent are clear failures.[37] So a merger between two firms can yield great benefits, but the price and reasoning must be right.

Some key reasons why many mergers and acquisitions fail are:

- Integration difficulties
- Inadequate evaluation of target
- Large or extraordinary debt
- Inability to achieve synergy
- Too much diversification
- Managers overly focused on acquisitions
- Too large an acquisition
- Difficult to integrate different organizational cultures
- Reduced employee morale due to layoffs and relocations

Among mergers, acquisitions, and takeovers in recent years, same-industry combinations have predominated. A general market consolidation is occurring in many industries, especially banking, insurance, defense, and health care, but also in pharmaceuticals, food, airlines, accounting, publishing, computers, retailing, financial services, and biotechnology. For example, SXR Uranium One Inc. recently purchased rival uranium miner UrAsia Energy Ltd, creating the world's second-largest uranium company after Cameco Corp. Similarly, Tenaris SA, based in Luxembourg and the world's biggest maker of steel tubes used in oil exploration and production, recently acquired rival Hydril Company, based in Houston, Texas.

Table 5-4 shows some mergers and acquisitions completed in 2007. There are many reasons for mergers and acquisitions, including the following:

- To provide improved capacity utilization
- To make better use of the existing sales force
- To reduce managerial staff
- To gain economies of scale
- To smooth out seasonal trends in sales
- To gain access to new suppliers, distributors, customers, products, and creditors
- To gain new technology
- To reduce tax obligations

TABLE 5-4   The Largest Mergers Completed Globally in 2007

Acquiring Firm	Acquired Firm	Price (In Billions)
AT&T (U.S.)	BellSouth Corp. (U.S.)	72.7
E.On (Germany)	Endesa (Spain)	46.9
Suez (France)	Gaz de France (France)	39.5
Banca Intesa (Italy)	SanPaolo IMI (Italy)	37.6
Porsche (Germany)	Volkswagen (Germany)	36.8
Mittal Steel (Netherlands)	Arcelor (Luxembourg)	33.8
Investor Group (U.S.)	TXU (U.S.)	32.1
Statoil (Norway)	Norsk Hydro (Norway)	30.8
America Movil (Mexico)	America Telecom (Mexico)	30.5
Freeport-McMoran (U.S.)	Phelps Dodge (U.S.)	25.8
Wachovia (U.S.)	Golden West Financial (U.S.)	25.5
CVS (U.S.)	Caremark Rx (U.S.)	23.0
Iberdrola (Spain)	Scottish Power (U.K.)	22.2
Airport Develop (Spain)	BAA (U.K.)	21.8
Investor Group (U.S.)	HCA (U.S.)	21.2
Bayer (Germany)	Schering (Germany)	20.6
Investor Group (U.S.)	Clear Channel Communications (U.S.)	18.7
Cia Vale do Rio Doce (Brazil)	Inco (Canada)	18.0
Blackstone Group (U.S.)	Equity Office Properties (U.S.)	18.0
Firestone Holdings (U.S.)	Freescale Semiconductor (U.S)	17.7
Xstrata (Switzerland)	Falconbridge (Canada)	17.4
Investor Group (U.S.)	Harrah's Entertainment (U.S.)	17.2
Investor Group (U.S.)	Alliance Boots (U.K.)	16.8
Johnson & Johnson (U.S.)	Pfizer Consumer Healthcare (U.S.)	16.6
Penn National Gaming (U.S.)	Harrah's Entertainment (U.S.)	16.5
Vodafone (U.K.)	Hutchison Essar (India)	16.5
Anadarko Petroleum (U.S.)	Kerr-McGee (U.S.)	16.1
Bank of New York (U.S.)	Mellon Financial (U.S.)	15.7
Imperial Tobacco (U.K.)	Altadis (Spain)	15.4
Capital One Financial (U.S.)	North Fork Bancorp (U.S.)	15.1
JTI Management (U.K.)	Gallaher Group (U.K.)	14.7
Investor Group (U.S.)	Kinder Morgan (U.S.)	14.6
Schering-Plough (U.S)	Organon Biosci (Netherlands)	14.4
BB Mobile (Japan)	Vodafone KK (Japan)	14.3
Linde (Germany)	BOC Group (U.K.)	14.1

Source: Adapted from Dennis Berman, "Can M&A's 'Best of Times' Get Better?" *Wall Street Journal* (January 2, 2007): R5; and Dennis Berman, "Mergers Hit Record, with Few Stop Signs," *Wall Street Journal* (April 2, 2007): C11.

The volume of mergers completed annually worldwide is growing dramatically and exceeds $1 trillion. There are annually more than 10,000 mergers in the United States that total more than $700 billion. The proliferation of mergers is fueled by companies' drive for market share, efficiency, and pricing power, as well as by globalization, the need for greater economies of scale, reduced regulation and antitrust concerns, the Internet, and e-commerce.

A *leveraged buyout* (LBO) occurs when a corporation's shareholders are bought (hence *buyout*) by the company's management and other private investors using borrowed funds (hence *leverage*).[38] Besides trying to avoid a hostile takeover, other reasons for initiating an LBO are senior management decisions that particular divisions do not fit into an overall corporate strategy or must be sold to raise cash, or receipt of an attractive offering price. An LBO takes a corporation private.

First Mover Advantages

First mover advantages refer to the benefits a firm may achieve by entering a new market or developing a new product or service prior to rival firms.[39] Some advantages of being a first mover include securing access to rare resources, gaining new knowledge of key factors and issues, and carving out market share and a position that is easy to defend and costly for rival firms to overtake. First mover advantages are analogous to taking the high ground first, which puts one in an excellent strategic position to launch aggressive campaigns and to defend territory. Being the first mover can be especially wise when such actions (1) build a firm's image and reputation with buyers, (2) produce cost advantages over rivals in terms of new technologies, new components, new distribution channels, and so on, (3) create strongly loyal customers, and (4) make imitation or duplication by a rival hard or unlikely.[40] To sustain the competitive advantage gained by being the first mover, such a firm also needs to be a fast learner. There would, however, be risks associated with being the first mover, such as unexpected and unanticipated problems and costs that occur from being the first firm doing business in the new market. Therefore, being a slow mover (also called *fast follower* or *late mover*) can be effective when a firm can easily copy or imitate the lead firm's products or services. If technology is advancing rapidly, slow movers can often leapfrog a first mover's products with improved second-generation products. However, slow movers often are relegated to relying on the first mover being a slow mover and making strategic and tactical mistakes. This situation does not occur often, so first mover advantages clearly offset the first mover disadvantages most of the time.

Strategic-management research indicates that first mover advantages tend to be greatest when competitors are roughly the same size and possess similar resources. If competitors are not similar in size, then larger competitors can wait while others make initial investments and mistakes, and then respond with greater effectiveness and resources.

Verizon, along with five Asian partner firms, expects to complete in 2008 the first high-speed optical cable directly linking the United States and China. Existing cables between the two countries go through Japan, slowing down service. China has 449 million cell phone users, making it the largest cellular market in the world. Verizon says this "first mover" cable will be able to support up to 62 million phone calls simultaneously, and the firm expects to see a positive return on its investment in the first year.

Not being the first mover can sometimes result in failure. For example, eBay expanded into Japan in 1999 but was five months behind rival Yahoo, which launched its own auction site that year in partnership with Japan's Softbank Corp. eBay never caught up with Yahoo. It exited Japan in 2002 and has not returned. Similarly, eBay was second getting into China behind YaoBao of Alibaba.com Corp. eBay is now struggling in China, and Yahoo has obtained a 40 percent stake in Alibaba. Martin Wu, chief executive of eBay's Chinese division, recently resigned abruptly.

Outsourcing

Business-process outsourcing (BPO) is a rapidly growing new business that involves companies taking over the functional operations, such as human resources, information systems, payroll, accounting, customer service, and even marketing of other firms.

Companies are choosing to outsource their functional operations more and more for several reasons: (1) it is less expensive, (2) it allows the firm to focus on its core businesses, and (3) it enables the firm to provide better services. Other advantages of outsourcing are that the strategy (1) allows the firm to align itself with "best-in-world" suppliers who focus on performing the special task, (2) provides the firm flexibility should customer needs shift unexpectedly, and (3) allows the firm to concentrate on other internal value chain activities critical to sustaining competitive advantage. BPO is a means for achieving strategies that are similar to partnering and joint venturing. The worldwide BPO market exceeded $173 billion in 2007.

Many firms, such as Dearborn, Michigan-based Visteon Corp. and J. P. Morgan Chase & Co., outsource their computer operations to IBM, which competes with firms such as Electronic Data Systems and Computer Sciences Corp., in the computer outsourcing business. 3M Corp. is outsourcing all of its manufacturing operations to Flextronics International Ltd. of Singapore or Jabil Circuit in Florida. 3M is also outsourcing all design and manufacturing of low-end standardized volume products by building a new design center in Taiwan.

U.S. and European companies for more than a decade have been outsourcing their manufacturing, tech support, and back-office work, but most insisted on keeping research and development activities in-house. However, an ever-growing number of firms today are outsourcing their product design to Asian developers. China and India are becoming increasingly important suppliers of intellectual property. For companies that include Hewlett-Packard, PalmOne, Dell, Sony, Apple, Kodak, Motorola, Nokia, Ericsson, Lucent, Cisco, and Nortel, the design of personal computers and cameras is mostly outsourced to China and India.

Companies in 2007 paid about $68 billion in outsourcing operations to other firms, but the details of what work to outsource, to whom, where, and for how much can challenge even the biggest, most sophisticated companies.[41] And some outsourcing deals do not work out, such as the J.P. Morgan Chase deal with IBM and Dow Chemical's deal with Electronic Data Systems. Both outsourcing deals were abandoned after several years. Lehman Brothers Holdings and Dell Inc. both recently reversed decisions to move customer call centers to India after a customer rebellion. As indicated in the "Global Perspective," India has become a booming place for outsourcing. According to Michael Corbett, chairman of the International Association of Outsourcing Professionals, India commands 45 percent of all back-office outsourcing, 29 percent of all call centers, 48 percent of all information technology outsourcing, 29 percent of all procurement outsourcing, and 45 percent of all product development outsourcing.[42]

GLOBAL PERSPECTIVE
Joint Ventures Mandatory for All Foreign Firms in India

India's economy (gross domestic product/GDP) expanded 9.2 percent in fiscal year ending March 31, 2007, up from 9 percent a year earlier. This is the fastest annual expansion India has seen in 18 years, and ranks India slightly below China's world-leading annual economic growth rate of 10.7 percent. This rapid growth is transforming the lives of many of India's one billion people. India's manufacturing sector grew 11.3 percent this fiscal year, up from 9.1 percent a year earlier. India's rapid growth has greatly increased wages, stocks, land prices, and interest rates.

Amid fast growth has come a 6.6 percent inflation rate, which is hurting the poor, especially in urban areas, as prices of food and staples have skyrocketed. Millions of people in India live on the margins of subsistence, so even small price increases on food and staples are painful. The government of India is highly in debt, 80 percent of GDP, and is cutting expenses to curtail spending, so the gap between rich and poor is widening further. (The U.S. federal debt is about 65 percent of GDP) But India's middle class is growing, so foreign firms continue to invest. Nissan Motor is building a factory in

Chennai in conjunction with Mahindra & Mahindra Ltd., India's largest maker of jeeps and tractors. The factory will start operating in 2009. And General Motors is expected to launch its compact Chevrolet Spark in India in 2008.

Joint ventures remain mandatory for foreign companies doing business in India. Verizon Business India, a joint venture between Verizon and Videocon Group of Mumbai, is rapidly expanding its phone and Internet services in India to compete more fiercely with AT&T and other telecom companies. Almost 20 million new cell phone customers are added in India every quarter, about the same rate of increase as in China—compared with only about 2.8 million new cell phone customers added in the United States quarterly. India's Reliance Communications Ltd. is in a battle with Britain's Vodafone Group PLC for control of India's fourth-largest cellular service, Hutchison Essar. But Vodafone must find a local partner because Indian law restricts foreign firms to 74 percent ownership of any India-based firm.

Most joint ventures among firms in India and foreign firms fail. Of 25 major joint ventures between foreign and Indian companies between 1993 and 2003, only three survive today. The Indian government has eased the joint venture restriction in the investment-banking industry, but not in other areas. Even Wal-Mart has an Indian partner, Bharti Enterprises Ltd. Heavy friction exists in virtually all joint ventures in India. John Band, president of Zoom Cortex in Mumbai, says, "Anyone that gets into a joint venture in India should assume it will fail and should be comfortable with the terms of what happens when it does fail."

Due to tourism growing 12 percent annually, hotel chains are scrambling to get established in India. Hilton Hotels just established a joint venture with New Delhi–based DLF Ltd. to develop 75 hotels in India in 2007–2010. Marriott, Four Seasons, and Carlson Companies are also establishing joint ventures in India and building hotels rapidly.

Source: Adapted from Eric Bellman and P. R. Venkat, "India's Growth Raises Fears Rates May Rise," *Wall Street Journal* (February 8, 2007): A6; Dionne Searcey, "Verizon Targets Business in India," *Wall Street Journal* (February 6, 2007): A7; Peter Wonacott, "India Faces Dark Side of Its Boom," *Wall Street Journal* (February 27, 2007): A10; Amy Chozick, "Nissan Enters Venture to Build Indian Plant," *Wall Street Journal* (February 27, 2007): A4; Cassell Bryan and Eric Bellman, "Vodafone, Reliance Gear Up for Battle in India," *Wall Street Journal* (December 22, 2006): B4; Peter Wonacott and Eric Bellman, "Foreign Firms Find Rough Passage to India," *Wall Street Journal* (February 1, 2007): A6; and Binny Sabharwal, "Hilton Expands in India as Market Demand Soars," *Wall Street Journal* (May 10, 2007): D6.

Downtown traffic in India. *Source:* Andy Crawford (c) Dorling Kindersley

Strategic Management in Nonprofit and Governmental Organizations

The strategic-management process is being used effectively by countless nonprofit and governmental organizations, such as the Girl Scouts, Boy Scouts, the Red Cross, chambers of commerce, educational institutions, medical institutions, public utilities, libraries, government agencies, and churches. The nonprofit sector, surprisingly, is by far America's largest employer. Many nonprofit and governmental organizations outperform private firms and corporations on innovativeness, motivation, productivity, and strategic management. For many nonprofit examples of strategic planning in practice, click on Strategic Planning Links found at the www.strategyclub.com Web site.

Compared to for-profit firms, nonprofit and governmental organizations may be totally dependent on outside financing. Especially for these organizations, strategic management provides an excellent vehicle for developing and justifying requests for needed financial support.

Educational Institutions

Educational institutions are more frequently using strategic-management techniques and concepts. Richard Cyert, former president of Carnegie Mellon University said "I believe we do a far better job of strategic management than any company I know." Population shifts nationally from the Northeast and Midwest to the Southeast and West are but one factor causing trauma for educational institutions that have not planned for changing enrollments. Ivy League schools in the Northeast are recruiting more heavily in the Southeast and West. This trend represents a significant change in the competitive climate for attracting the best high school graduates each year.

Online college degrees are becoming common and represent a threat to traditional colleges and universities. "You can put the kids to bed and go to law school," says Andrew Rosen, chief operating officer of Kaplan Education Centers, a subsidiary of the Washington Post Company.

For a list of college strategic plans, click on Strategic Planning Links found at the www.strategyclub.com Web site, and scroll down through the academic sites.

Medical Organizations

The $200 billion U.S. hospital industry is experiencing declining margins, excess capacity, bureaucratic overburdening, poorly planned and executed diversification strategies, soaring health care costs, reduced federal support, and high administrator turnover. The seriousness of this problem is accented by a 20 percent annual decline in use by inpatients nationwide. Declining occupancy rates, deregulation, and accelerating growth of health maintenance organizations, preferred provider organizations, urgent care centers, outpatient surgery centers, diagnostic centers, specialized clinics, and group practices are other major threats facing hospitals today. Many private and state-supported medical institutions are in financial trouble as a result of traditionally taking a reactive rather than a proactive approach in dealing with their industry.

Hospitals—originally intended to be warehouses for people dying of tuberculosis, smallpox, cancer, pneumonia, and infectious diseases—are creating new strategies today as advances in the diagnosis and treatment of chronic diseases are undercutting that earlier mission. Hospitals are beginning to bring services to the patient as much as bringing the patient to the hospital; health care is more and more being concentrated in the home and in the residential community, not on the hospital campus. Chronic care will require day-treatment facilities, electronic monitoring at home, user-friendly ambulatory services, decentralized service networks, and laboratory testing. A successful hospital strategy for the future will require renewed and deepened collaboration with physicians, who are central to hospitals' well-being, and a reallocation of resources from acute to chronic care in home and community settings.

Current strategies being pursued by many hospitals include creating home health services, establishing nursing homes, and forming rehabilitation centers. Backward integration strategies that some hospitals are pursuing include acquiring ambulance services, waste disposal services, and diagnostic services. Millions of persons annually research medical ailments online, which is causing a dramatic shift in the balance of power between doctor, patient, and hospitals. The number of persons using the Internet to obtain medical information is skyrocketing. A motivated patient using the Internet can gain knowledge on a particular subject far beyond his or her doctor's knowledge, because no person can keep up with the results and implications of billions of dollars' worth of medical research reported weekly. Patients today often walk into the doctor's office with a file folder of the latest articles detailing research and treatment options for their ailments.

Governmental Agencies and Departments

Federal, state, county, and municipal agencies and departments, such as police departments, chambers of commerce, forestry associations, and health departments, are responsible for formulating, implementing, and evaluating strategies that use taxpayers' dollars in the most cost-effective way to provide services and programs. Strategic-management concepts are generally required and thus widely used to enable governmental organizations to be more effective and efficient. For a list of government agency strategic plans, click on Strategic Planning Links found at the www.strategyclub.com Web site, and scroll down through the government sites.

Strategists in governmental organizations operate with less strategic autonomy than their counterparts in private firms. Public enterprises generally cannot diversify into unrelated businesses or merge with other firms. Governmental strategists usually enjoy little freedom in altering the organizations' missions or redirecting objectives. Legislators and politicians often have direct or indirect control over major decisions and resources. Strategic issues get discussed and debated in the media and legislatures. Issues become politicized, resulting in fewer strategic choice alternatives. There is now more predictability in the management of public sector enterprises.

Government agencies and departments are finding that their employees get excited about the opportunity to participate in the strategic-management process and thereby have an effect on the organization's mission, objectives, strategies, and policies. In addition, government agencies are using a strategic-management approach to develop and substantiate formal requests for additional funding.

Strategic Management in Small Firms

A record number of Americans started companies in 2006 and again in 2007. The reason why "becoming your own boss" has become a national obsession is that entrepreneurs are America's role models. Almost everyone wants to own a business—from teens and college students, who are signing up for entrepreneurial courses in record numbers, to those over age 65, who are forming more companies every year, to recent immigrants, who in 2005 started 25 percent more companies per capita than native-born citizens did.

America is seeing the largest entrepreneurial surge ever. According to Small Business Administration (SBA) projections, nearly 672,000 new companies with employees were created in 2005. That is the biggest business birthrate in U.S. history: 30,000 more startups than in 2004, and 12 percent more than at the height of dot-com hysteria in 1996. The Bureau of Labor Statistics reports that more businesses are being started in America every quarter of the year. Not only are more Americans launching small businesses, but most others are dreaming about it. Sixty-six percent of respondents in a 2006 Yahoo Small Business and Harris Interactive survey said they wanted to start a company someday; 37 percent of those said they hoped to do so within the next five years.

It is arguably less risky to create a business now than ever before. Interest rates are low and venture capital funds and other private-equity investors are once again pouring money into young companies. "We are figuring out new ways to bring increasingly huge amounts of capital to startups," says Carl Schramm, head of the Kauffman Foundation and author of *The Entrepreneurial Imperative*. Schramm also points out that plummeting technology costs make it less necessary now to go in debt to start a business. And many if not most entrepreneurs start new companies without quitting their day jobs. According to the SBA, the total number of firms with no employees grew by 26 percent from 1997 to 2004, to 19 million. A little more than half of those companies are run by workers with another primary source of income.

Strategic management is vital for large firms' success, but what about small firms? The strategic-management process is just as vital for small companies. From their inception, all organizations have a strategy, even if the strategy just evolves from day-to-day operations. Even if conducted informally or by a single owner/entrepreneur, the strategic-management process can significantly enhance small firms' growth and prosperity. Because an ever-increasing number of men and women in the United States are starting their own businesses, more individuals are becoming strategists. Widespread corporate layoffs have contributed to an explosion in small businesses and new ideas.

Numerous magazine and journal articles have focused on applying strategic-management concepts to small businesses.[43] A major conclusion of these articles is that a lack of strategic-management knowledge is a serious obstacle for many small business owners. Other problems often encountered in applying strategic-management concepts to small businesses are a lack of both sufficient capital to exploit external opportunities and a day-to-day cognitive frame of reference. Research also indicates that strategic management in small firms is more informal than in large firms, but small firms that engage in strategic management outperform those that do not.[44]

VISIT THE NET

Site provides 60 sample business plans for small businesses. (www.bplans.com/sp/index.cfm?a=bc)

Conclusion

The main appeal of any managerial approach is the expectation that it will enhance organizational performance. This is especially true of strategic management. Through involvement in strategic-management activities, managers and employees achieve a better understanding of an organization's priorities and operations. Strategic management allows organizations to be efficient, but more important, it allows them to be effective. Although strategic management does not guarantee organizational success, the process allows proactive rather than reactive decision making. Strategic management may represent a radical change in philosophy for some organizations, so strategists must be trained to anticipate and constructively respond to questions and issues as they arise. The 16 strategies discussed in this chapter can represent a new beginning for many firms, especially if managers and employees in the organization understand and support the plan for action.

We invite you to visit the David page on the Prentice Hall Companion Web site at www.prenhall.com/david for this chapter's review quiz.

Key Terms and Concepts

Acquisition (p. 167)
Backward Integration (p. 150)
Bankruptcy (p. 157)
Business-Processing Outsourcing (BPO) (p. 171)
Combination Strategy (p. 146)
Cooperative Arrangements (p. 165)
Cost Leadership (p. 160)
De-integration (p. 150)
Differentiation (p. 160)
Diversification Strategies (p. 152)
Divestiture (p. 158)
First Mover Advantages (p. 171)
Focus (p. 160)
Forward Integration (p. 149)
Franchising (p. 149)
Friendly Merger (p. 167)
Generic Strategies (p. 160)

Issues for Review and Discussion

1. How does strategy formulation differ for a small versus a large organization? How does it differ for a for-profit versus a nonprofit organization?
2. Give recent examples of market penetration, market development, and product development.
3. Give recent examples of forward integration, backward integration, and horizontal integration.
4. Give recent examples of related and unrelated diversification.
5. Give recent examples of joint venture, retrenchment, divestiture, and liquidation.
6. Do you think hostile takeovers are unethical? Why or why not?
7. What are the major advantages and disadvantages of diversification?
8. What are the major advantages and disadvantages of an integrative strategy?
9. How does strategic management differ in for-profit and nonprofit organizations?
10. Why is it not advisable to pursue too many strategies at once?
11. Consumers can purchase tennis shoes, food, cars, boats, and insurance on the Internet. Are there any products today than cannot be purchased online? What is the implication for traditional retailers?
12. What are the pros and cons of a firm merging with a rival firm?
13. Visit the CheckMATE strategic-planning software Web site at www.checkmateplan.com, and discuss the benefits offered.
14. Compare and contrast financial objectives with strategic objectives. Which type is more important in your opinion? Why?
15. Diagram a two-division organizational chart that includes a CEO, COO, CIO, CSO, CFO, CMO, HRM, R&D, and two division presidents. *Hint:* Division presidents report to the COO.
16. How do the levels of strategy differ in a large firm versus a small firm?
17. List 11 types of strategies. Give a hypothetical example of each strategy listed.
18. Discuss the nature of as well as the pros and cons of a "friendly merger" versus "hostile takeover" in acquiring another firm. Give an example of each.
19. Define and explain "first mover advantages."
20. Define and explain "outsourcing."
21. Discuss the business of offering a BBA or MBA degree online.
22. What strategies are best for turbulent, high-velocity markets?

Notes

1. John Byrne, "Strategic Planning—It's Back," *BusinessWeek* (August 26, 1996): 46.
2. Steven C. Brandt, *Strategic Planning in Emerging Companies* (Reading, MA: Addison-Wesley, 1981). Reprinted with permission of the publisher.
3. R. Kaplan and D. Norton, "Putting the Balanced Scorecard to Work," *Harvard Business Review* (September–October, 1993): 147.

4. F. Hansen and M. Smith, "Crisis in Corporate America: The Role of Strategy," *Business Horizons* (January–February 2003): 9.

5. Adapted from F. R. David, "How Do We Choose Among Alternative Growth Strategies?" *Managerial Planning* 33, no. 4 (January–February 1985): 14–17, 22.

6. Ibid.

7. Kenneth Davidson, "Do Megamergers Make Sense?" *Journal of Business Strategy* 7, no. 3 (Winter 1987): 45.

8. Op. cit., David.

9. Ibid.

10. Op. cit., David.

11. Ibid.

12. Arthur Thompson, Jr., A. J. Strickland III, and John Gamble. *Crafting and Executing Strategy: Text and Readings* (New York: McGraw-Hill/Irwin, 2005): 241.

13. Michael E. Porter, *Competitive Strategy: Techniques for Analyzing Industries and Competitors* (New York: Free Press, 1980): 53–57, 318–319.

14. "The Samsung Way," *BusinessWeek* (June 16, 2003): 56–60.

15. Sheila Muto, "Seeing a Boost, Hospitals Turn to Retail Stores," *Wall Street Journal* (November 7, 2001): B1, B8.

16. Damian Paletta, "Wal-Mart, in New Leases, Frees Itself for Banking Push," *Wall Street Journal* (March 15, 2007): A2.

17. Op. cit., David.

18. Op. cit., David.

19. Op. cit., David.

20. Ibid.

21. Ibid.

22. Michael Porter, *Competitive Advantage* (New York: Free Press, 1985): 97. Also, Arthur Thompson, Jr., A. J. Strickland III, and John Gamble, *Crafting and Executing Strategy: Text and Readings* (New York: McGraw-Hill/Irwin, 2005): 117.

23. Arthur Thompson, Jr., A. J. Strickland III, and John Gamble, *Crafting and Executing Strategy: Text and Readings* (New York: McGraw-Hill/Irwin, 2005): 125–126.

24. Porter, *Competitive Advantage,* pp. 160–162.

25. Thompson, Strickland, and Gamble: 129–130.

26. Ibid., 134.

27. Kathryn Rudie Harrigan, "Joint Ventures: Linking for a Leap Forward," *Planning Review* 14, no. 4 (July–August 1986): 10.

28. Matthew Schifrin, "Partner or Perish," *Forbes* (May 21, 2001): 26.

29. Ibid., p. 28.

30. Nikhil Hutheesing, "Marital Blisters," *Forbes* (May 21, 2001): 32.

31. Ibid., p. 32.

32. Steven Rattner, "Mergers: Windfalls or Pitfalls?" *Wall Street Journal* (October 11, 1999): A22; Nikhil Deogun, "Merger Wave Spurs More Stock Wipeouts," *Wall Street Journal* (November 29, 1999): C1.

33. Dennis Berman, "Mergers Hit Record, with Few Stop Signs," *Wall Street Journal* (April 2, 2007): C11.

34. Dennis Berman, "Can M&A's 'Best of Times' Get Better?" *Wall Street Journal* (January 2, 2007): R5.

35. Andrew Batson, "Merger Mania Strikes China," *Wall Street Journal* (January 12, 2007): C5.

36. Henny Sender, "New Predator in Takeovers," *Wall Street Journal* (February 26, 2007): C1.

37. J. A. Schmidt, "Business Perspective on Mergers and Acquisitions," in J. A. Schmidt, ed., *Making Mergers Work,* Alexandria, VA: Society for Human Resource Management, (2002): 23–46.

38. Joel Millman, "Mexican Mergers/Acquisitions Triple from 2001," *Wall Street Journal* (December 27, 2002): A2.

39. Robert Davis, "Net Empowering Patients," *USA Today* (July 14, 1999): 1A.

40. M. J. Gannon, K. G. Smith, and C. Grimm, "An Organizational Information-Processing Profile of First Movers," *Journal of Business Research* 25 (1992): 231–241; M. B. Lieberman and D. B. Montgomery, "First Mover Advantages," *Strategic Management Journal* 9 (Summer 1988): 41–58.

41. Scott Thurm, "Behind Outsourcing: Promise and Pitfalls," *Wall Street Journal* (February 26, 2007): B3.

42. www.fortune.com/sections.

43. Some articles are Keith D. Brouthers, Floris Andriessen, and Igor Nicolaes, "Driving Blind: Strategic Decision-Making in Small Companies," *Long Range Planning* 31 (1998): 130–138; Javad Kargar, "Strategic Planning System Characteristics and Planning Effectiveness in Small Mature Firms," *Mid-Atlantic Journal of Business* 32, no. 1 (1996): 19–35; Michael J. Peel and John Bridge, "How Planning and Capital Budgeting Improve SME Performance," *Long Range Planning* 31, no. 6 (1998): 848–856; Larry R. Smeltzer, Gail L. Fann, and V. Neal Nikolaisen, "Environmental Scanning Practices in Small Business," *Journal of Small Business Management* 26, no. 3 (1988): 55–63; and Michael P. Steiner and Olaf Solem, "Factors for Success in Small Manufacturing Firms," *Journal of Small Business Management* 26, no. 1 (1988): 51–57.

44. Anne Carey and Grant Jerding, "Internet's Reach on Campus," *USA Today* (August 26, 1999): A1; Bill Meyers, "It's a Small-Business World," *USA Today* (July 30, 1999): B1–2.

Current Readings

Barney, Jay B., Seung-Hyun Lee, and Mike W. Peng. "Bankruptcy Law and Entrepreneurship Development: A Real Options Perspective." *The Academy of Management Review* 32, no. 1 (January 2007): 257.

Brauer, Matthias. "What Have We Acquired and What Should We Acquire in Divestiture Research? A Review and Research Agenda." *Journal of Management* 32, no. 6 (December 2006): 751.

Bucerius, M., and C. Homburg. "Is Speed of Integration Really a Success Factor of Mergers and Acquisitions? An Analysis of the Role of Internal and External Relatedness." *Strategic Management Journal* 27, no. 4 (April 2006): 347.

Chakrabarti, A., I. Mahmood, and K. Singh. "Diversification and Performance: Evidence from East Asian Firms." *Strategic Management Journal* 28, no. 2 (February 2007): 101.

Connelly, Brian, Michael A. Hitt, and Laszlo Tihanyi. "International Diversification: Antecedents, Outcomes, and Moderators." *Journal of Management* 32, no. 6 (December 2006): 831.

Dacin, M. T., C. Oliver, and J. P. Roy. "The Legitimacy of Strategic Alliances: An Institutional Perspective." *Strategic Management Journal* 28, no. 2 (February 2007): 169.

Deutsch, Yuval, Thomas Keil, and Tomi Laamanen. "Decision Making in Acquisitions: The Effect of Outside Directors' Compensation on Acquisition Patterns." *Journal of Management* 33, no. 1 (February 2007): 30.

Frynas, J. G., K. Mellahi, and G. A. Pigman. "First Mover Advantages in International Business and Firm-Specific Political Resources." *Strategic Management Journal* 27, no. 4 (April 2006): 321.

Fuentelsaz, L., and J. Gómez. "Multipoint Competition, Strategic Similarity and Entry to Geographic Markets." *Strategic Management Journal* 27, no. 5 (May 2006): 477.

Hipkin, Ian, and Pete Naudé, "Developing Effective Alliance Partnerships." *Long Range Planning* 39, no. 1 (February 2006): 51.

Hitt, M. A., L. A. Jobe, and F. T. Rothaermel. "Balancing Vertical Integration and Strategic Outsourcing: Effects on Product Portfolio, Product Success, and Firm Performance." *Strategic Management Journal* 27, no. 11 (November 2006): 1033.

Hyland, MaryAnne, and Monica Yang. "Who Do Firms Imitate? A Multilevel Approach to Examining Sources of Imitation in the Choice of Mergers and Acquisitions." *Journal of Management* 32, no. 3 (June 2006): 381.

Iverson, Roderick D., and Christopher D. Zatzick. "High Involvement Management and Workforce Reduction: Competitive Advantage or Disadvantage?" *Academy of Management Journal* 49, no. 5 (October 2006): 999.

Krishnan, Rekha, Xavier Martin, and Niels G. Noorderhaven. "When Does Trust Matter to Alliance Performance?" *Academy of Management Journal* 49, no. 5 (October 2006): 894.

Lavie, Dovev, and Lori Rosenkopf. "Balancing Exploration and Exploitation in Alliance Formation." *Academy of Management Journal* 49, no. 4 (August 2006): 797.

Luo, Y. "Are Joint Venture Partners More Opportunistic in a More Volatile Environment?" *Strategic Management Journal* 28, no. 1 (January 2007): 39.

Meyer, Klaus E., and Yen Thi Thu Tran. "Market Penetration and Acquisition Strategies for Emerging Economics." *Long Range Planning* 39, no. 2 (April 2006): 177.

Michael, Steven C., and John A. Pearce II. "Strategies to Prevent Economic Recessions from Causing Business Failure." *Business Horizons* 49, no. 3 (May–June 2006): 201.

Miller, D. J. "Technological Diversity, Related Diversification, and Firm Performance." *Strategic Management Journal* 27, no. 7 (July 2006): 601.

Pehrsson, A. "Business Relatedness and Performance: A Study of Managerial Perceptions." *Strategic Management Journal* 27, no. 3 (March 2006): 265.

Suarez, Fernando F. and Gianvito Lanzolla. "The Role of Environmental Dynamics in Building a First Mover Advantage Theory." *The Academy of Management Review* 32, no. 2 (April 2007): 377.

Wirtz, Bernd W., Alexander Mathieu, and Oliver Schilke. "Strategy in High-Velocity Environments." *Long Range Planning* 40, no. 3 (June 2007): 295.

• EXPERIENTIAL EXERCISES

DISNEY

Experiential Exercise 5A

What Strategies Should Walt Disney Pursue in 2008–2009?

Purpose

In performing business policy case analysis, you can find information about the respective company's actual and planned strategies. Comparing what is planned versus *what you recommend* is an important part of case analysis. Do not recommend what the firm actually plans, unless in-depth analysis of the situation reveals those strategies to be best among all feasible alternatives. This exercise gives you experience conducting library and Internet research to determine what Walt Disney should do in 2008.

Instructions

Step 1	Look up Walt Disney and News Corporation using the Web sites provided in Table 4-5. Find some recent articles about firms in this industry. Scan Moody's, Dun & Bradstreet, and Standard & Poor's publications for information.
Step 2	Summarize your findings in a three-page report entitled "Strategies Being Pursued by Walt Disney in 2008."

Source: (c) Judith Miller / Dorling Kindersley / Three Sisters

Experiential Exercise 5B

Examining Strategy Articles

Purpose

Strategy articles can be found weekly in journals, magazines, and newspapers. By reading and studying strategy articles, you can gain a better understanding of the strategic-management process. Several of the best journals in which to find corporate strategy articles are *Advanced Management Journal, Business Horizons, Long Range Planning, Journal of Business Strategy,* and *Strategic Management Journal.* These journals are devoted to reporting the results of empirical research in management. They apply strategic-management concepts to specific organizations and industries. They introduce new strategic-management techniques and provide short case studies on selected firms.

Other good journals in which to find strategic-management articles are *Harvard Business Review, Sloan Management Review, California Management Review, Academy of Management Review, Academy of Management Journal, Academy of Management Executive, Journal of Management,* and *Journal of Small Business Management.*

In addition to journals, many magazines regularly publish articles that focus on business strategies. Several of the best magazines in which to find applied strategy articles are *Dun's Business Month, Fortune, Forbes, BusinessWeek, Inc.,* and *Industry Week.* Newspapers such as *USA Today, Wall Street Journal, New York Times,* and *Barrons* cover strategy events when they occur—for example, a joint venture announcement, a bankruptcy declaration, a new advertising campaign start, acquisition of a company, divestiture of a division, a chief executive officer's hiring or firing, or a hostile takeover attempt.

In combination, journal, magazine, and newspaper articles can make the strategic-management course more exciting. They allow current strategies of for-profit and non-profit organizations to be identified and studied.

Instructions

Step 1　　Go to your college library and find a recent journal article that focuses on a strategic-management topic. Select your article from one of the journals listed previously, not from a magazine. Copy the article and bring it to class.

Step 2　　Give a 3-minute oral report summarizing the most important information in your article. Include comments giving your personal reaction to the article. Pass your article around in class.

Experiential Exercise 5C

Classifying Some Year 2007 Strategies

Purpose

This exercise can improve your understanding of various strategies by giving you experience classifying strategies. This skill will help you use the strategy-formulation tools presented later. Consider the following 12 (actual or possible) year-2007 strategies by various firms:

1. Dunkin' Donuts is increasing the number of its U.S. stores from 5,500 to 15,000.
2. Brown-Forman Corp. sold its Hartmann luggage and leather-goods business.
3. Motorola, which makes TVs, acquired Terayon Communication, a supplier of TV equipment.
4. Macy's department stores is adding bistros and Starbucks coffee shops at many of its stores.
5. Dell just allowed Wal-Mart to begin selling its computers. This was its first move away from direct mail order selling of computers.
6. Motorola cut 7,500 additional jobs in 2007–2008.
7. Hilton Hotels is building 55 new properties in Russia, the United Kingdom, and Central America in 2007–2008.
8. Video-sharing Web site YouTube in mid-2007 launched its services into nine new countries.
9. Cadbury Schweppes PLC is slashing 7,500 jobs, shedding product variations, and closing factories globally to cut costs in 2007–2008.

10. General Electric sold its plastics division for $11.6 million to Saudi Basic Industries Corp. of Saudi Arabia.
11. Cadbury Schweppes PLC, the maker of Trident gum, just bought Turkish gum maker Intergum.
12. Limited Brands is selling its Express and Limited divisions to focus on its Victoria's Secret and Bath & Body Works divisions.

Instructions

Step 1   On a separate sheet of paper, number from 1 to 12. These numbers correspond to the strategies described.

Step 2   What type of strategy best describes the 12 actions cited? Indicate your answers.

Step 3   Exchange papers with a classmate, and grade each other's paper as your instructor gives the right answers.

Experiential Exercise 5D

How Risky Are Various Alternative Strategies?

Purpose

This exercise focuses on how risky various alternative strategies are for organizations to pursue. Different degrees of risk are based largely on varying degrees of *externality*, defined as movement away from present business into new markets and products. In general, the greater the degree of externality, the greater the probability of loss resulting from unexpected events. High-risk strategies generally are less attractive than low-risk strategies.

Instructions

Step 1   On a separate sheet of paper, number vertically from 1 to 10. Think of 1 as "most risky," 2 as "next most risky," and so forth to 10, "least risky."

Step 2   Write the following strategies beside the appropriate number to indicate how risky you believe the strategy is to pursue: horizontal integration, related diversification, liquidation, forward integration, backward integration, product development, market development, market penetration, retrenchment, and unrelated diversification.

Step 3   Grade your paper as your teacher gives you the right answers and supporting rationale. Each correct answer is worth 10 points.

Experiential Exercise 5E

Developing Alternative Strategies for My University

Purpose

It is important for representatives from all areas of a college or university to identify and discuss alternative strategies that could benefit faculty, students, alumni, staff, and other constituencies. As you complete this exercise, notice the learning and understanding that occurs as people express differences of opinion. Recall that *the process of planning is more important than the document.*

Instructions

Step 1   Recall or locate the external opportunity/threat and internal strength/weakness factors that you identified as part of Experiential Exercise 1D. If you did not do that exercise, discuss now as a class important external and internal factors facing your college or university.

Step 2   Identify and put on the chalkboard alternative strategies that you feel could benefit your college or university. Your proposed actions should allow the institution to capitalize on particular strengths, improve upon certain weaknesses, avoid external threats, and/or take advantage of particular external opportunities. List 12 possible strategies on the board. Number the strategies as they are written on the board.

Step 3   On a separate sheet of paper, number from 1 to 12. Everyone in class individually should rate the strategies identified, using a 1 to 3 scale, where 1 = *I do not support implementation*, 2 = *I am neutral about implementation*, and 3 = *I strongly support implementation*. In rating the strategies, recognize that your institution cannot do everything desired or potentially beneficial.

Step 4   Go to the board and record your ratings in a row beside the respective strategies. Everyone in class should do this, going to the board perhaps by rows in the class.

Step 5   Sum the ratings for each strategy so that a prioritized list of recommended strategies is obtained. This prioritized list reflects the collective wisdom of your class. Strategies with the highest score are deemed best.

Step 6   Discuss how this process could enable organizations to achieve understanding and commitment from individuals.

Step 7   Share your class results with a university administrator, and ask for comments regarding the process and top strategies recommended.

Experiential Exercise 5F

Lessons in Doing Business Globally

Purpose

The purpose of this exercise is to discover some important lessons learned by local businesses that do business internationally.

Instructions

Contact several local business leaders by phone. Find at least three firms that engage in international or export operations. Visit the owner or manager of each business in person. Ask the businessperson to give you several important lessons that his or her firm has learned in globally doing business. Record the lessons on paper, and report your findings to the class.

6 Strategy Analysis and Choice

"notable quotes"

Strategic management is not a box of tricks or a bundle of techniques. It is analytical thinking and commitment of resources to action. But quantification alone is not planning. Some of the most important issues in strategic management cannot be quantified at all.

PETER DRUCKER

Objectives are not commands; they are commitments. They do not determine the future; they are the means to mobilize resources and energies of an organization for the making of the future.

PETER DRUCKER

Life is full of lousy options.

GENERAL P. X. KELLEY

When a crisis forces choosing among alternatives, most people will choose the worst possible one.

RUDIN'S LAW

Strategy isn't something you can nail together in slapdash fashion by sitting around a conference table.

TERRY HALLER

Planning is often doomed before it ever starts, either because too much is expected of it or because not enough is put into it.

T. J. CARTWRIGHT

Whether it's broke or not, fix it—make it better. Not just products, but the whole company if necessary.

BILL SAPORITO

College Student Athlete. *Source:* David Cannon (c) Dorling Kindersley

chapter objectives

After studying this chapter, you should be able to do the following:

1. Describe a three-stage framework for choosing among alternative strategies.

2. Explain how to develop a SWOT Matrix, SPACE Matrix, BCG Matrix, IE Matrix, and QSPM.

3. Identify important behavioral, political, ethical, and social responsibility considerations in strategy analysis and choice.

4. Discuss the role of intuition in strategic analysis and choice.

5. Discuss the role of organizational culture in strategic analysis and choice.

6. Discuss the role of a board of directors in choosing among alternative strategies.

Strategy analysis and choice largely involve making subjective decisions based on objective information. This chapter introduces important concepts that can help strategists generate feasible alternatives, evaluate those alternatives, and choose a specific course of action. Behavioral aspects of strategy formulation are described, including politics, culture, ethics, and social responsibility considerations. Modern tools for formulating strategies are described, and the appropriate role of a board of directors is discussed.

The Nature of Strategy Analysis and Choice

As indicated by Figure 6-1, this chapter focuses on generating and evaluating alternative strategies, as well as selecting strategies to pursue. Strategy analysis and choice seek to determine alternative courses of action that could best enable the firm to achieve its mission and objectives. The firm's present strategies, objectives, and mission, coupled with the external and internal audit information, provide a basis for generating and evaluating feasible alternative strategies.

Unless a desperate situation confronts the firm, alternative strategies will likely represent incremental steps that move the firm from its present position to a desired future position. Alternative strategies do not come out of the wild blue yonder; they are derived from the firm's vision, mission, objectives, external audit, and internal audit; they are consistent with, or build on, past strategies that have worked well. Note from the "Natural Environment Perspective" box that the strategies of both companies and countries are increasingly scrutinized and evaluated from a natural environment perspective. Companies such as Wal-Mart now monitor not only the price its vendors offer for products, but also how those products are made in terms of environmental practices. A growing number of business schools offer separate courses and even a concentration in environmental management or *sustainability,* the idea that a business can meet its financial goals without hurting the environment.

FIGURE 6-1

A Comprehensive Strategic-Management Model

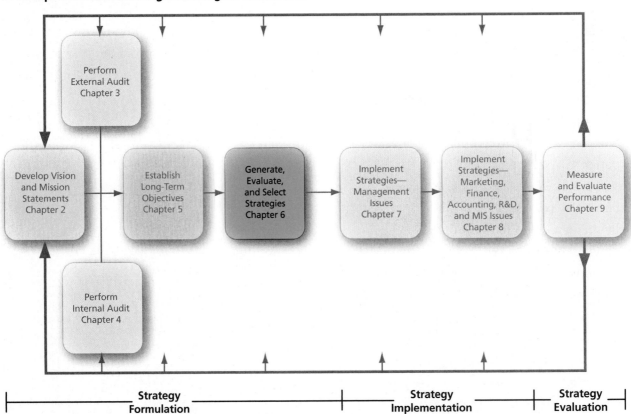

No business wants a reputation as being a big polluter; that could hurt it in the marketplace, jeopardize its standing in the community, and invite scrutiny by regulators, investors, and environmentalists. Accordingly, governments increasingly encourage businesses to behave responsibly. Various governments mandate that businesses publicly report the pollutants and wastes their facilities produce.

Wal-Mart Stores is one among many companies today that annually provide a report on the firm's social-responsibility practices. Called "sustainability" or "corporate social-responsibility" reports, these documents disclose to shareholders information about the firm's labor practices, product sourcing, energy efficiency, environmental impact, and business ethics practices. It is just good business today for a business to provide a Sustainability Report annually to the public. With 60,000 suppliers and $350 billion in annual sales, Wal-Mart "works with its suppliers to take nonrenewable energy off our shelves and out of the lives of our customers," says Wal-Mart CEO Lee Scott. Many firms use the Wal-Mart Sustainability Report as a benchmark, guideline, and model to follow in preparing their own report.

The Global Reporting Initiative has issued a set of detailed reporting guidelines specifying what information should go into sustainability reports. Wal-Mart now monitors not only prices its vendors offer for products, but also how those products are made and the vendor's social-responsibility and environmental practices. The proxy advisory firm Institutional Shareholder Services reports that an increasing number of shareholder groups are pushing firms to provide sustainability information annually. Wal-Mart also now encourages and expects its 1.35 million U.S. employees to adopt what it calls Personal Sustainability Projects, which include such measures as organizing weight-loss or smoking-cessation support groups, biking to work, or starting recycling programs.

Wal-Mart is installing solar panels in its stores in California and Hawaii, providing as much as 30 percent of the power in some stores. Wal-Mart may go national with solar power if this test works well. Also moving to solar energy is department-store chain Kohl's Corp., which is converting 64 of its 80 California stores to using solar power. There are big subsidies for solar installations in some states.

The world's second largest retailer behind Wal-Mart, Home Depot, recently more than doubled its offering of environmentally friendly products such as all-natural insect repellent. Home Depot has made it much easier for consumers to find its organic products by using special labels similar to Timberland's (the outdoor company) Green Index tags. Another huge retailer, Target, now offers more than 500 choices of organic certified food and has 18 buildings in California alone powered only by solar energy. The largest solar power plant in North America is the one in Nevada that powers Nellis Air Force Base outside Las Vegas.

Source: Antonie Boessenkool, "Activists Push More Firms on Social Responsibility," *Wall Street Journal* (January 31, 207): B13; Kris Hudson, "Wal-Mart Wants Supplies, Workers to Join Green Effort," *Wall Street Journal* (February 2, 2007): A14; and Jayne O'Donnell and Christine Dugas, "More Retailers Go for Green—The Eco Kind," *USA Today* (April 18, 2007): 3B.

Some Organic Certified Food. *Source:* Ian O'Leary (c) Dorling Kindersley

VISIT THE NET

Cautions that planners must not usurp the responsibility of line managers in strategic planning. (www.csuchico.edu/mgmt/ strategy/module1/sld050.htm)

The Process of Generating and Selecting Strategies

Strategists never consider all feasible alternatives that could benefit the firm because there are an infinite number of possible actions and an infinite number of ways to implement those actions. Therefore, a manageable set of the most attractive alternative strategies must be developed. The advantages, disadvantages, trade-offs, costs, and benefits of these strategies should be determined. This section discusses the process that many firms use to determine an appropriate set of alternative strategies.

Identifying and evaluating alternative strategies should involve many of the managers and employees who earlier assembled the organizational vision and mission statements, performed the external audit, and conducted the internal audit. Representatives from each department and division of the firm should be included in this process, as was the case in previous strategy-formulation activities. Recall that involvement provides the best opportunity for managers and employees to gain an understanding of what the firm is doing and why and to become committed to helping the firm accomplish its objectives.

All participants in the strategy analysis and choice activity should have the firm's external and internal audit information by their sides. This information, coupled with the firm's mission statement, will help participants crystallize in their own minds particular strategies that they believe could benefit the firm most. Creativity should be encouraged in this thought process.

Alternative strategies proposed by participants should be considered and discussed in a meeting or series of meetings. Proposed strategies should be listed in writing. When all feasible strategies identified by participants are given and understood, the strategies should be ranked in order of attractiveness by all participants, with 1 = should not be implemented, 2 = possibly should be implemented, 3 = probably should be implemented, and 4 = definitely should be implemented. This process will result in a prioritized list of best strategies that reflects the collective wisdom of the group.

A Comprehensive Strategy-Formulation Framework

Important strategy-formulation techniques can be integrated into a three-stage decision-making framework, as shown in Figure 6-2. The tools presented in this framework are applicable to all sizes and types of organizations and can help strategists identify, evaluate, and select strategies.

Stage 1 of the formulation framework consists of the EFE Matrix, the IFE Matrix, and the Competitive Profile Matrix (CPM). Called the *Input Stage*, Stage 1 summarizes the basic input information needed to formulate strategies. Stage 2, called the *Matching Stage*, focuses upon generating feasible alternative strategies by aligning key external and internal

FIGURE 6-2

The Strategy-Formulation Analytical Framework

STAGE 1: THE INPUT STAGE		
External Factor Evaluation (EFE) Matrix	Competitive Profile Matrix (CPM)	Internal Factor Evaluation (IFE) Matrix

STAGE 2: THE MATCHING STAGE				
Strengths-Weaknesses-Opportunities-Threats (SWOT) Matrix	Strategic Position and Action Evaluation (SPACE) Matrix	Boston Consulting Group (BCG) Matrix	Internal-External (IE) Matrix	Grand Strategy Matrix

STAGE 3: THE DECISION STAGE
Quantitative Strategic Planning Matrix (QSPM)

factors. Stage 2 techniques include the Strengths-Weaknesses-Opportunities-Threats (SWOT) Matrix, the Strategic Position and Action Evaluation (SPACE) Matrix, the Boston Consulting Group (BCG) Matrix, the Internal-External (IE) Matrix, and the Grand Strategy Matrix. Stage 3, called the *Decision Stage*, involves a single technique, the Quantitative Strategic Planning Matrix (QSPM). A QSPM uses input information from Stage 1 to objectively evaluate feasible alternative strategies identified in Stage 2. A QSPM reveals the relative attractiveness of alternative strategies and thus provides objective basis for selecting specific strategies.

All nine techniques included in the *strategy-formulation framework* require the integration of intuition and analysis. Autonomous divisions in an organization commonly use strategy-formulation techniques to develop strategies and objectives. Divisional analyses provide a basis for identifying, evaluating, and selecting among alternative corporate-level strategies.

Strategists themselves, not analytic tools, are always responsible and accountable for strategic decisions. Lenz emphasized that the shift from a words-oriented to a numbers-oriented planning process can give rise to a false sense of certainty; it can reduce dialogue, discussion, and argument as a means for exploring understandings, testing assumptions, and fostering organizational learning.[1] Strategists, therefore, must be wary of this possibility and use analytical tools to facilitate, rather than to diminish, communication. Without objective information and analysis, personal biases, politics, emotions, personalities, and *halo error* (the tendency to put too much weight on a single factor) unfortunately may play a dominant role in the strategy-formulation process.

The Input Stage

Procedures for developing an EFE Matrix, an IFE Matrix, and a CPM were presented in Chapters 3 and 4. The information derived from these three matrices provides basic input information for the matching and decision stage matrices described later in this chapter.

The input tools require strategists to quantify subjectivity during early stages of the strategy-formulation process. Making small decisions in the input matrices regarding the relative importance of external and internal factors allows strategists to more effectively generate and evaluate alternative strategies. Good intuitive judgment is always needed in determining appropriate weights and ratings.

The Matching Stage

Strategy is sometimes defined as the match an organization makes between its internal resources and skills and the opportunities and risks created by its external factors.[2] The matching stage of the strategy-formulation framework consists of five techniques that can be used in any sequence: the SWOT Matrix, the SPACE Matrix, the BCG Matrix, the IE Matrix, and the Grand Strategy Matrix. These tools rely upon information derived from the input stage to match external opportunities and threats with internal strengths and weaknesses. *Matching* external and internal critical success factors is the key to effectively generating feasible alternative strategies. For example, a firm with excess working capital (an internal strength) could take advantage of the cell phone industry's 20 percent annual growth rate (an external opportunity) by acquiring Cellfone, Inc., a firm in the cell phone industry. This example portrays simple one-to-one matching. In most situations, external and internal relationships are more complex, and the matching requires multiple alignments for each strategy generated. The basic concept of matching is illustrated in Table 6-1.

Any organization, whether military, product-oriented, service-oriented, governmental, or even athletic, must develop and execute good strategies to win. A good offense without a good defense, or vice versa, usually leads to defeat. Developing strategies that use strengths to capitalize on opportunities could be considered an offense, whereas strategies designed to improve upon weaknesses while avoiding threats could be termed defensive. Every organization has some external opportunities and threats and internal strengths and weaknesses that can be aligned to formulate feasible alternative strategies.

VISIT THE NET

Gives purpose and characteristics of objectives. (www.csuchico.edu/mgmt/strategy/module1/sld022.htm)

VISIT THE NET

Gives example objectives. (www.csuchico.edu/mgmt/strategy/module1/sld024.htm)

TABLE 6-1   Matching Key External and Internal Factors to Formulate Alternative Strategies

Key Internal Factor	Key External Factor	Resultant Strategy
Excess working capacity (an internal strength)	+ 20 percent annual growth in the cell phone industry (an external opportunity)	= Acquire Cellfone, Inc.
Insufficient capacity (an internal weakness)	+ Exit of two major foreign competitors from the industry (an external opportunity)	= Pursue horizontal integration by buying competitors' facilities
Strong R&D expertise (an internal strength)	+ Decreasing numbers of younger adults (an external threat)	= Develop new products for older adults
Poor employee morale (an internal weakness)	+ Strong union activity (an external threat)	= Develop a new employee benefits package

The Strengths-Weaknesses-Opportunities-Threats (SWOT) Matrix

The *Strengths-Weaknesses-Opportunities-Threats (SWOT) Matrix* is an important matching tool that helps managers develop four types of strategies: SO (strengths-opportunities) Strategies, WO (weaknesses-opportunities) Strategies, ST (strengths-threats) Strategies, and WT (weaknesses-threats) Strategies.[3] Matching key external and internal factors is the most difficult part of developing a SWOT Matrix and requires good judgment—and there is no one best set of matches. Note in Table 6-1 that the first, second, third, and fourth strategies are SO, WO, ST, and WT strategies, respectively.

SO Strategies use a firm's internal strengths to take advantage of external opportunities. All managers would like their organizations to be in a position in which internal strengths can be used to take advantage of external trends and events. Organizations generally will pursue WO, ST, or WT strategies to get into a situation in which they can apply SO Strategies. When a firm has major weaknesses, it will strive to overcome them and make them strengths. When an organization faces major threats, it will seek to avoid them to concentrate on opportunities.

WO Strategies aim at improving internal weaknesses by taking advantage of external opportunities. Sometimes key external opportunities exist, but a firm has internal weaknesses that prevent it from exploiting those opportunities. For example, there may be a high demand for electronic devices to control the amount and timing of fuel injection in automobile engines (opportunity), but a certain auto parts manufacturer may lack the technology required for producing these devices (weakness). One possible WO Strategy would be to acquire this technology by forming a joint venture with a firm having competency in this area. An alternative WO Strategy would be to hire and train people with the required technical capabilities.

ST Strategies use a firm's strengths to avoid or reduce the impact of external threats. This does not mean that a strong organization should always meet threats in the external environment head-on. An example of ST Strategy occurred when Texas Instruments used an excellent legal department (a strength) to collect nearly $700 million in damages and royalties from nine Japanese and Korean firms that infringed on patents for semiconductor memory chips (threat). Rival firms that copy ideas, innovations, and patented products are a major threat in many industries. This is still a major problem for U.S. firms selling products in China.

WT Strategies are defensive tactics directed at reducing internal weakness and avoiding external threats. An organization faced with numerous external threats and internal weaknesses may indeed be in a precarious position. In fact, such a firm may have to fight for its survival, merge, retrench, declare bankruptcy, or choose liquidation.

A schematic representation of the SWOT Matrix is provided in Figure 6-3. Note that a SWOT Matrix is composed of nine cells. As shown, there are four key factor cells, four strategy cells, and one cell that is always left blank (the upper-left cell). The four strategy cells, labeled *SO, WO, ST,* and *WT,* are developed after completing four key factor cells, labeled *S, W, O,* and *T.* There are eight steps involved in constructing a SWOT Matrix:

1. List the firm's key external opportunities.
2. List the firm's key external threats.
3. List the firm's key internal strengths.
4. List the firm's key internal weaknesses.

VISIT THE NET

Gives a nice sample strategic plan, including the bases for developing a SWOT Matrix. (www.planware.org/strategicsample.htm) and (http://sbinformation.about.com/cs/bestpractices/a/swot.htm)

FIGURE 6-3

A SWOT Matrix for a Retail Computer Store

	Strengths	Weaknesses
	1. Inventory turnover up 5.8 to 6.7	1. Software revenues in store down 12%
	2. Average customer purchase up $97 to $128	2. Location of store hurt by new Hwy 34
	3. Employee morale is excellent	3. Carpet and paint in store in disrepair
	4. In-store promotions = 20% increase in sales	4. Bathroom in store needs refurbishing
	5. Newspaper advertising expenditures down 10%	5. Total store revenues down 8%
	6. Revenues from repair/service in-store up 16%	6. Store has no Web site
	7. In-store technical support persons have MIS degrees	7. Supplier on-time-delivery up to 2.4 days
	8. Store's debt-to-total assets ratio down 34%	8. Customer checkout process too slow
		9. Revenues per employee up 19%

Opportunities	SO Strategies	WO Strategies
1. Population of city growing 10%	1. Add 4 new in-store promotions monthly (S4,O3)	1. Purchase land to build new store (W2, O2)
2. Rival computer store opening 1 mile away		
3. Vehicle traffic passing store up 12%	2. Add 2 new repair/service persons (S6, O5)	2. Install new carpet/paint/bath (W3, W4, O1)
4. Vendors average six new products/yr	3. Send flyer to all seniors over age 55 (S5, O5)	3. Up Web site services by 50% (W6, O7, O8)
5. Senior citizen use of computers up 8%		
6. Small business growth in area up 10%		4. Launch mailout to to all Realtors in city (W5, O7)
7. Desire for Web sites up 18% by Realtors		
8. Desire for Web sites up 12% by small firms		

Threats	ST Strategies	WT Strategies
1. Best Buy opening new store in 1yr nearby	1. Hire two more repair persons and market these new services (S6, S7, T1)	1. Hire 2 new cashiers (W8, T1, T4)
2. Local university offers computer repair		
		2. Install new carpet/paint/bath (W3, W4, T1)
3. New bypass Hwy 34 in 1 yr will divert traffic		
	2. Purchase land to build new store (S8, T3)	
4. New mall being built nearby		
5. Gas prices up 14%	3. Raise out-of-store service calls from $60 to $80 (S6, T5)	
6. Vendors raising prices 8%		

5. Match internal strengths with external opportunities, and record the resultant SO Strategies in the appropriate cell.
6. Match internal weaknesses with external opportunities, and record the resultant WO Strategies.
7. Match internal strengths with external threats, and record the resultant ST Strategies.
8. Match internal weaknesses with external threats, and record the resultant WT Strategies.

There are some important aspects of a SWOT Matrix evidenced in Figure 6-3. For example, note that both the internal/external factors and the SO/ST/WO/WT Strategies are stated in quantitative terms to the extent possible. This is important. For example, regarding the second SO #2 and ST #1 strategies, if the analyst just said "Add new repair/service persons" the reader might think that 20 new repair/service persons are needed. Actually only two are needed. Always *be specific* to the extent possible in stating factors and strategies.

It is also important to include the "S1, O2" type notation after each strategy in a SWOT Matrix. This notation reveals the rationale for each alternative strategy. Strategies do not rise out of the blue. Note in Figure 6-3 how this notation reveals the internal/external factors that were matched to formulate desirable strategies. For example, note that this retail computer store business may need to "purchase land to build new store" because a new Highway 34 will make its location less desirable. The notation (W2, O2) and (S8, T3) in Figure 6-3 exemplifies this matching process.

The purpose of each Stage 2 matching tool is to generate feasible alternative strategies, not to select or determine which strategies are best. Not all of the strategies developed in the SWOT Matrix, therefore, will be selected for implementation.

The strategy-formulation guidelines provided in Chapter 5 can enhance the process of matching key external and internal factors. For example, when an organization has both the capital and human resources needed to distribute its own products (internal strength) and distributors are unreliable, costly, or incapable of meeting the firm's needs (external threat), forward integration can be an attractive ST Strategy. When a firm has excess production capacity (internal weakness) and its basic industry is experiencing declining annual sales and profits (external threat), related diversification can be an effective WT Strategy.

Although the SWOT matrix is widely used in strategic planning, the analysis does have some limitations.[4] First, SWOT does not show how to achieve a competitive advantage, so it must not be an end in itself. The matrix should be the starting point for a discussion on how proposed strategies could be implemented as well as cost-benefit considerations that ultimately could lead to competitive advantage. Second, SWOT is a static assessment (or snapshot) in time. A SWOT matrix can be like studying a single frame of a motion picture where you see the lead characters and the setting but have no clue as to the plot. As circumstances, capabilities, threats, and strategies change, the dynamics of a competitive environment may not be revealed in a single matrix. Third, SWOT analysis may lead the firm to overemphasize a single internal or external factor in formulating strategies. There are interrelationships among the key internal and external factors that SWOT does not reveal that may be important in devising strategies.

The Strategic Position and Action Evaluation (SPACE) Matrix

The *Strategic Position and Action Evaluation (SPACE) Matrix*, another important Stage 2 matching tool, is illustrated in Figure 6-4. Its four-quadrant framework indicates whether aggressive, conservative, defensive, or competitive strategies are most appropriate for a given organization. The axes of the SPACE Matrix represent two internal dimensions (*financial strength [FS]* and *competitive advantage [CA]*) and two external dimensions (*environmental stability [ES]* and *industry strength [IS]*). These four factors are perhaps the most important determinants of an organization's overall strategic position.[5]

Depending upon the type of organization, numerous variables could make up each of the dimensions represented on the axes of the SPACE Matrix. Factors that were included earlier in the firm's EFE and IFE Matrices should be considered in developing a SPACE Matrix. Other variables commonly included are given in Table 6-2. For example, return on investment, leverage, liquidity, working capital, and cash flow are commonly considered to be determining factors of an organization's financial strength. Like the SWOT Matrix, the SPACE Matrix should be both tailored to the particular organization being studied and based on factual information as much as possible.

The steps required to develop a SPACE Matrix are as follows:

1. Select a set of variables to define financial strength (FS), competitive advantage (CA), environmental stability (ES), and industry strength (IS).
2. Assign a numerical value ranging from +1 (worst) to +6 (best) to each of the variables that make up the FS and IS dimensions. Assign a numerical value ranging from −1 (best) to −6 (worst) to each of the variables that make up the ES and CA

FIGURE 6-4

The SPACE Matrix

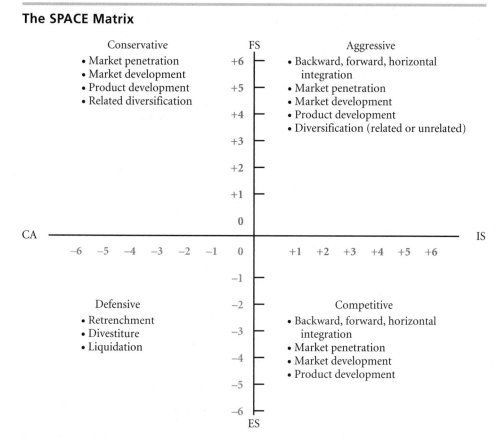

Source: H. Rowe, R. Mason, and K. Dickel, *Strategic Management and Business Policy: A Methodological Approach* (Reading, MA: Addison-Wesley Publishing Co. Inc., © 1982): 155. Reprinted with permission of the publisher.

TABLE 6-2   Example Factors That Make Up the SPACE Matrix Axes

Internal Strategic Position	External Strategic Position
Financial Strength (FS)	*Environmental Stability (ES)*
Return on investment	Technological changes
Leverage	Rate of inflation
Liquidity	Demand variability
Working capital	Price range of competing products
Cash flow	Barriers to entry into market
Inventory turnover	Competitive pressure
Earnings per share	Ease of exit from market
Price earnings ratio	Price elasticity of demand
	Risk involved in business
Competitive Advantage (CA)	*Industry Strength (IS)*
Market share	Growth potential
Product quality	Profit potential
Product life cycle	Financial stability
Customer loyalty	Technological know-how
Competition's capacity utilization	Resource utilization
Technological know-how	Ease of entry into market
Control over suppliers and distributors	Productivity, capacity utilization

Source: H. Rowe, R. Mason, and K. Dickel, *Strategic Management and Business Policy: A Methodological Approach* (Reading, MA: Addison-Wesley Publishing Co. Inc., © 1982): 155–156. Reprinted with permission of the publisher.

FIGURE 6-5

Example Strategy Profiles

Aggressive Profiles

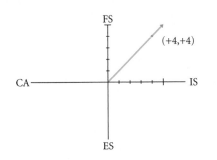

A financially strong firm that has achieved major competitive advantages in a growing and stable industry

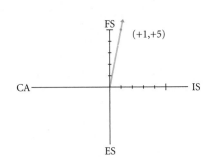

A firm whose financial strength is a dominating factor in the industry

Conservative Profiles

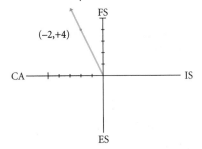

A firm that has achieved financial strength in a stable industry that is not growing; the firm has few competitive advantages

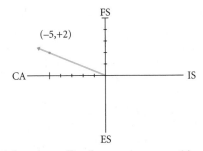

A firm that suffers from major competitive disadvantages in an industry that is technologically stable but declining in sales

Competitive Profiles

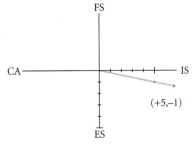

A firm with major competitive advantages in a high-growth industry

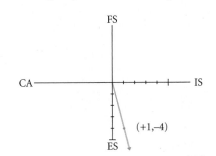

An organization that is competing fairly well in an unstable industry

Defensive Profiles

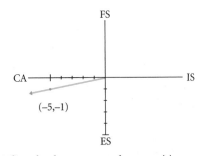

A firm that has a very weak competitive position in a negative growth, stable industry

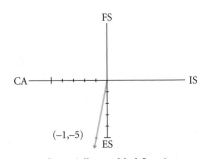

A financially troubled firm in a very unstable industry

dimensions. On the FS and CA axes, make comparison to competitors. On the IS and ES axes, make comparison to other industries.

3. Compute an average score for FS, CA, IS, and ES by summing the values given to the variables of each dimension and then by dividing by the number of variables included in the respective dimension.

4. Plot the average scores for FS, IS, ES, and CA on the appropriate axis in the SPACE Matrix.

5. Add the two scores on the *x*-axis and plot the resultant point on *X*. Add the two scores on the *y*-axis and plot the resultant point on *Y*. Plot the intersection of the new *xy* point.

6. Draw a *directional vector* from the origin of the SPACE Matrix through the new intersection point. This vector reveals the type of strategies recommended for the organization: aggressive, competitive, defensive, or conservative.

Some examples of strategy profiles that can emerge from a SPACE analysis are shown in Figure 6-5. The directional vector associated with each profile suggests the type of strategies to pursue: aggressive, conservative, defensive, or competitive. When a firm's directional vector is located in the *aggressive quadrant* (upper-right quadrant) of the SPACE Matrix, an organization is in an excellent position to use its internal strengths to (1) take advantage of external opportunities, (2) overcome internal weaknesses, and (3) avoid external threats. Therefore, market penetration, market development, product development, backward integration, forward integration, horizontal integration, diversification, or a combination strategy all can be feasible, depending on the specific circumstances that face the firm.

The directional vector may appear in the *conservative quadrant* (upper-left quadrant) of the SPACE Matrix, which implies staying close to the firm's basic competencies and not taking excessive risks. Conservative strategies most often include market penetration, market development, product development, and related diversification. The directional vector may be located in the lower-left or *defensive quadrant* of the SPACE Matrix, which suggests that the firm should focus on rectifying internal weaknesses and avoiding external threats. Defensive strategies include retrenchment, divestiture, liquidation, and related diversification. Finally, the directional vector may be located in the lower-right or *competitive quadrant* of the SPACE Matrix, indicating competitive strategies. Competitive strategies include backward, forward, and horizontal integration; market penetration; market development and product development.

A SPACE Matrix analysis for a bank is provided in Table 6-3. Note that competitive type strategies are recommended.

The Boston Consulting Group (BCG) Matrix

Autonomous divisions (or profit centers) of an organization make up what is called a *business portfolio*. When a firm's divisions compete in different industries, a separate strategy often must be developed for each business. The *Boston Consulting Group (BCG) Matrix* and the *Internal-External (IE) Matrix* are designed specifically to enhance a multidivisional firm's efforts to formulate strategies. (BCG is a private management consulting firm based in Boston. BCG employs about 1,400 consultants worldwide.)

The BCG Matrix graphically portrays differences among divisions in terms of relative market share position and industry growth rate. The BCG Matrix allows a multidivisional organization to manage its portfolio of businesses by examining the relative market share position and the industry growth rate of each division relative to all other divisions in the organization. *Relative market share position* is defined as the ratio of a division's own market share (or revenues) in a particular industry to the market share (or revenues) held by the largest rival firm in that industry. Note in Table 6-4 that Budget Rent-a-Car's relative market share position is 6.9 divided by 49.6 = 19.1 percent, which along the *x*-axis of a BCG Matrix would be pretty close to the right-hand side. Be mindful that relative market share position could also be determined by dividing Budget's revenues by the leader Enterprise's revenues.

TABLE 6-3   A SPACE Matrix for a Bank

Financial Strength	Ratings
The bank's primary capital ratio is 7.23 percent, which is 1.23 percentage points over the generally required ratio of 6 percent.	1.0
The bank's return on assets is negative 0.77, compared to a bank industry average ratio of positive 0.70.	1.0
The bank's net income was $183 million, down 9 percent from a year earlier.	3.0
The bank's revenues increased 7 percent to $3.46 billion.	4.0
	9.0

Industry Strength	
Deregulation provides geographic and product freedom.	4.0
Deregulation increases competition in the banking industry.	2.0
Pennsylvania's interstate banking law allows the bank to acquire other banks in New Jersey, Ohio, Kentucky, the District of Columbia, and West Virginia.	4.0
	10.0

Environmental Stability	
Less-developed countries are experiencing high inflation and political instability.	–4.0
Headquartered in Pittsburgh, the bank historically has been heavily dependent on the steel, oil, and gas industries. These industries are depressed.	–5.0
Banking deregulation has created instability throughout the industry.	–4.0
	–13.0

Competitive Advantage	
The bank provides data processing services for more than 450 institutions in 38 states.	–2.0
Superregional banks, international banks, and nonbanks are becoming increasingly competitive.	–5.0
The bank has a large customer base.	–2.0
	–9.0

Conclusion

ES Average is –13.0 ÷ 3 = –4.33   IS Average is + 10.0 ÷ 3 = 3.33

CA Average is –9.0 ÷ 3 = –3.00   FS Average is + 9.0 ÷ 4 = 2.25

Directional Vector Coordinates: x-axis: –3.00 + (+3.33) = +0.33

y-axis: –4.33 + (+2.25) = -2.08

The bank should pursue Competitive Strategies.

Relative market share position is given on the x-axis of the BCG Matrix. The midpoint on the x-axis usually is set at .50, corresponding to a division that has half the market share of the leading firm in the industry. The y-axis represents the industry growth rate in sales, measured in percentage terms. The growth rate percentages on the y-axis could range from –20 to +20 percent, with 0.0 being the midpoint. The average annual increase in revenues for several leading firms in the industry would be a good estimate of the value. Also, various sources such as the S&P Industry Survey would provide this value. These numerical ranges on the x- and y-axes are often used, but other numerical values could be established as deemed appropriate for particular organizations.

An example of a BCG Matrix appears in Figure 6-6. Each circle represents a separate division. The size of the circle corresponds to the proportion of corporate **revenue** generated by that business unit, and the pie slice indicates the proportion of corporate **profits** generated by that division. Divisions located in Quadrant I of the BCG Matrix are called "Question Marks," those located in Quadrant II are called "Stars," those located in Quadrant III are called "Cash Cows," and those divisions located in Quadrant IV are called "Dogs."

TABLE 6-4   Market Share Data for Selected Industries in 2007

U.S. Car Market Share (2007)	
General Motors	24.6%
Nissan	6.2%
DaimlerChrysler	14.4%
Ford	17.5%
Honda	9.2%
Toyota	15.4%

U.S. Top Banks by Domestic Deposits Market Share (2007)	
Bank of America	9.0%
J.P. Morgan Chase	6.9%
Wachovia/Golden West Financial	5.8%
Wells Fargo	4.6%
Citigroup	3.5%

U.S. Top Airlines Market Share (2007)	
American	15.7%
United	12.1%
Delta	11.8%
Southwest	11.5%
Continental	7.5%
Northwest	7.0%
U.S. Airways	4.7%
America West	3.9%

U.S. Top Rental Car Companies (2007)	
Enterprise	49.6%
Hertz	23.7%
Avis	9.9%
Budget	6.9%
Alamo National	5.2%
Dollar	4.7%

Market Share of Top Selling Vodkas Worldwide	
Smirnoff	21.4%
Absolut	9.2%
Stolichnaya	2.4%
Skyy	2.4%
Grey Goose	2.3%
Finlandia	2.1%
Ketel One	1.7%

Source: Adapted from Neal Boudette, "Big Dealer to Detroit: Fix How You Make Cars," *Wall Street Journal* (February 9, 2007): A8; Charles Fried, "Bank of America Quietly Targets a Barrier to Growth," *Wall Street Journal* (January 16, 2007): A19; Susan Carey, Melanie Trottman, and Dennis Berman, "UAL, Continental Discuss Merger as Airman Presses Bid for Midwest," *Wall Street Journal* (December 13, 2006): A1; Gary Stoller, "Enterprise Muscles Its Way onto Airport Scene," *USA Today* (December 22, 2006): B1, B2; and Deborah Ball, "As Vodka Sales Skyrocket, Many Newcomers Pour In," *Wall Street Journal* (January 26, 2007): B1.

• ***Question Marks***—Divisions in Quadrant I have a low relative market share position, yet they compete in a high-growth industry. Generally these firms' cash needs are high and their cash generation is low. These businesses are called *Question Marks* because the organization must decide whether to strengthen them by pursuing an intensive strategy (market penetration, market development, or product development) or to sell them.

FIGURE 6-6

The BCG Matrix

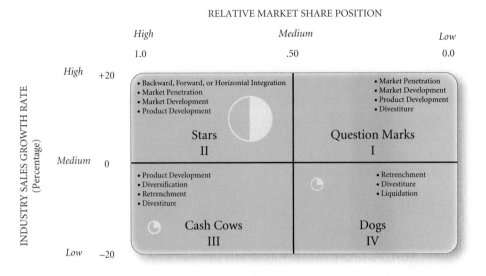

Source: Adapted from Boston Consulting Group, *Perspectives on Experience* (Boston: The Boston Consulting Group, 1974).

- *Stars*—Quadrant II businesses (*Stars*) represent the organization's best long-run opportunities for growth and profitability. Divisions with a high relative market share and a high industry growth rate should receive substantial investment to maintain or strengthen their dominant positions. Forward, backward, and horizontal integration; market penetration; market development; and product development are appropriate strategies for these divisions to consider.
- *Cash Cows*—Divisions positioned in Quadrant III have a high relative market share position but compete in a low-growth industry. Called *Cash Cows* because they generate cash in excess of their needs, they are often milked. Many of today's Cash Cows were yesterday's Stars. Cash Cow divisions should be managed to maintain their strong position for as long as possible. Product development or diversification may be attractive strategies for strong Cash Cows. However, as a Cash Cow division becomes weak, retrenchment or divestiture can become more appropriate.
- *Dogs*—Quadrant IV divisions of the organization have a low relative market share position and compete in a slow- or no-market-growth industry; they are *Dogs* in the firm's portfolio. Because of their weak internal and external position, these businesses are often liquidated, divested, or trimmed down through retrenchment. When a division first becomes a Dog, retrenchment can be the best strategy to pursue because many Dogs have bounced back, after strenuous asset and cost reduction, to become viable, profitable divisions.

The major benefit of the BCG Matrix is that it draws attention to the cash flow, investment characteristics, and needs of an organization's various divisions. The divisions of many firms evolve over time: Dogs become Question Marks, Question Marks become Stars, Stars become Cash Cows, and Cash Cows become Dogs in an ongoing counterclockwise motion. Less frequently, Stars become Question Marks, Question Marks become Dogs, Dogs become Cash Cows, and Cash Cows become Stars (in a clockwise motion). In some organizations, no cyclical motion is apparent. Over time, organizations should strive to achieve a portfolio of divisions that are Stars.

One example of a BCG Matrix is provided in Figure 6-7, which illustrates an organization composed of five divisions with annual sales ranging from $5,000 to $60,000. Division 1 has the greatest sales volume, so the circle representing that division is the largest one in the matrix. The circle corresponding to Division 5 is the smallest because its sales volume ($5,000) is least among all the divisions. The pie slices within the circles

FIGURE 6-7

An Example BCG Matrix

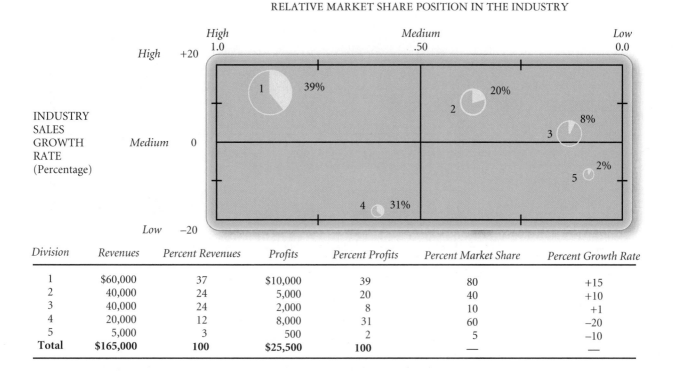

Division	Revenues	Percent Revenues	Profits	Percent Profits	Percent Market Share	Percent Growth Rate
1	$60,000	37	$10,000	39	80	+15
2	40,000	24	5,000	20	40	+10
3	40,000	24	2,000	8	10	+1
4	20,000	12	8,000	31	60	−20
5	5,000	3	500	2	5	−10
Total	$165,000	100	$25,500	100	—	—

reveal the percent of corporate profits contributed by each division. As shown, Division 1 contributes the highest profit percentage, 39 percent. Notice in the diagram that Division 1 is considered a Star, Division 2 is a Question Mark, Division 3 is also a Question Mark, Division 4 is a Cash Cow, and Division 5 is a Dog.

The BCG Matrix, like all analytical techniques, has some limitations. For example, viewing every business as either a Star, Cash Cow, Dog, or Question Mark is an oversimplification; many businesses fall right in the middle of the BCG Matrix and thus are not easily classified. Furthermore, the BCG Matrix does not reflect whether or not various divisions or their industries are growing over time; that is, the matrix has no temporal qualities, but rather it is a snapshot of an organization at a given point in time. Finally, other variables besides relative market share position and industry growth rate in sales, such as size of the market and competitive advantages, are important in making strategic decisions about various divisions.

An example BCG Matrix for Limited Brands, Inc., is provided in Figure 6-8. Headquartered in Columbus, Ohio, Limited Brands has five divisions, led by Victoria's Secret Stores, which generate nearly one-half of company profits. Also note in Figure 6-8 that the Henri Bendel division had an operating loss of $188 million. Take note how the % profit column is calculated because oftentimes a firm will have a division that incurs a loss for a year. In terms of the pie slice in circle 5 of the diagram, note that it is a *different color* from the positive profit segments in the other circles. (Note: Limited Brands' sales are 2006 actual but profits are 2006 estimate.)

The Internal-External (IE) Matrix

The *Internal-External (IE) Matrix* positions an organization's various divisions in a nine-cell display, illustrated in Figure 6-9. The IE Matrix is similar to the BCG Matrix in that both tools involve plotting organization divisions in a schematic diagram; this is why they are both called "portfolio matrices." Also, the size of each circle represents the percentage sales contribution of each division, and pie slices reveal the percentage profit contribution of each division in both the BCG and IE Matrix.

FIGURE 6-8

An Example BCG Matrix for The Limited (2006 year-end)

RELATIVE MARKET SHARE POSITION (RMSP)

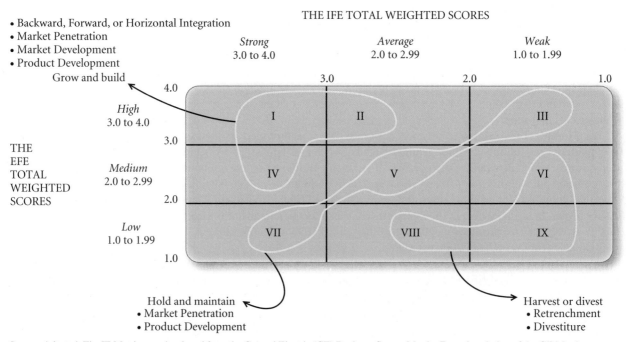

Division	$ Sales (millions)	% Sales	$ Profits (millions)	% Profits	RMSP	IG Rate %
1. Victoria's Secret	$5,139	51.5	$799	68.0	0.8	10
2. Bath & Body Works	2,556	25.6	400	39.0	0.4	05
3. Express	1,749	17.5	12	1.2	0.2	00
4. Limited Stores	493	4.9	4	0.1	0.5	−05
5. Henri Bendel & Mast Industries	42	0.5	−188	(18.3)	.02	−10
Total	**$9,979**	**100.0**	**$1,027**	**100.0**		

FIGURE 6-9

The Internal–External (IE) Matrix

- Backward, Forward, or Horizontal Integration
- Market Penetration
- Market Development
- Product Development

Grow and build

THE IFE TOTAL WEIGHTED SCORES

Strong 3.0 to 4.0   *Average* 2.0 to 2.99   *Weak* 1.0 to 1.99

THE EFE TOTAL WEIGHTED SCORES

High 3.0 to 4.0   I   II   III

Medium 2.0 to 2.99   IV   V   VI

Low 1.0 to 1.99   VII   VIII   IX

Hold and maintain
- Market Penetration
- Product Development

Harvest or divest
- Retrenchment
- Divestiture

Source: Adapted. The IE Matrix was developed from the General Electric (GE) Business Screen Matrix. For a description of the GE Matrix see Michael Allen, "Diagramming GE's Planning for What's WATT," in R. Allio and M. Pennington, eds., *Corporate Planning: Techniques and Applications* (New York: AMACOM, 1979).

But there are some important differences between the BCG Matrix and the IE Matrix. First, the axes are different. Also, the IE Matrix requires more information about the divisions than the BCG Matrix. Furthermore, the strategic implications of each matrix are different. For these reasons, strategists in multidivisional firms often develop both the BCG Matrix and the IE Matrix in formulating alternative strategies. A common practice is to develop a BCG Matrix and an IE Matrix for the present and then develop projected matrices to reflect expectations of the future. This before-and-after analysis forecasts the expected effect of strategic decisions on an organization's portfolio of divisions.

The IE Matrix is based on two key dimensions: the IFE total weighted scores on the *x*-axis and the EFE total weighted scores on the *y*-axis. Recall that each division of an organization should construct an IFE Matrix and an EFE Matrix for its part of the organization. The total weighted scores derived from the divisions allow construction of the corporate-level IE Matrix. On the *x*-axis of the IE Matrix, an IFE total weighted score of 1.0 to 1.99 represents a weak internal position; a score of 2.0 to 2.99 is considered average; and a score of 3.0 to 4.0 is strong. Similarly, on the *y*-axis, an EFE total weighted score of 1.0 to 1.99 is considered low; a score of 2.0 to 2.99 is medium; and a score of 3.0 to 4.0 is high.

The IE Matrix can be divided into three major regions that have different strategy implications. First, the prescription for divisions that fall into cells I, II, or IV can be described as *grow and build*. Intensive (market penetration, market development, and product development) or integrative (backward integration, forward integration, and horizontal integration) strategies can be most appropriate for these divisions. Second, divisions that fall into cells III, V, or VII can be managed best with *hold and maintain* strategies; market penetration and product development are two commonly employed strategies for these types of divisions. Third, a common prescription for divisions that fall into cells VI, VIII, or IX is *harvest or divest*. Successful organizations are able to achieve a portfolio of businesses positioned in or around cell I in the IE Matrix.

An example of a completed IE Matrix is given in Figure 6-10, which depicts an organization composed of four divisions. As indicated by the positioning of the circles, *grow*

FIGURE 6-10

An Example IE Matrix

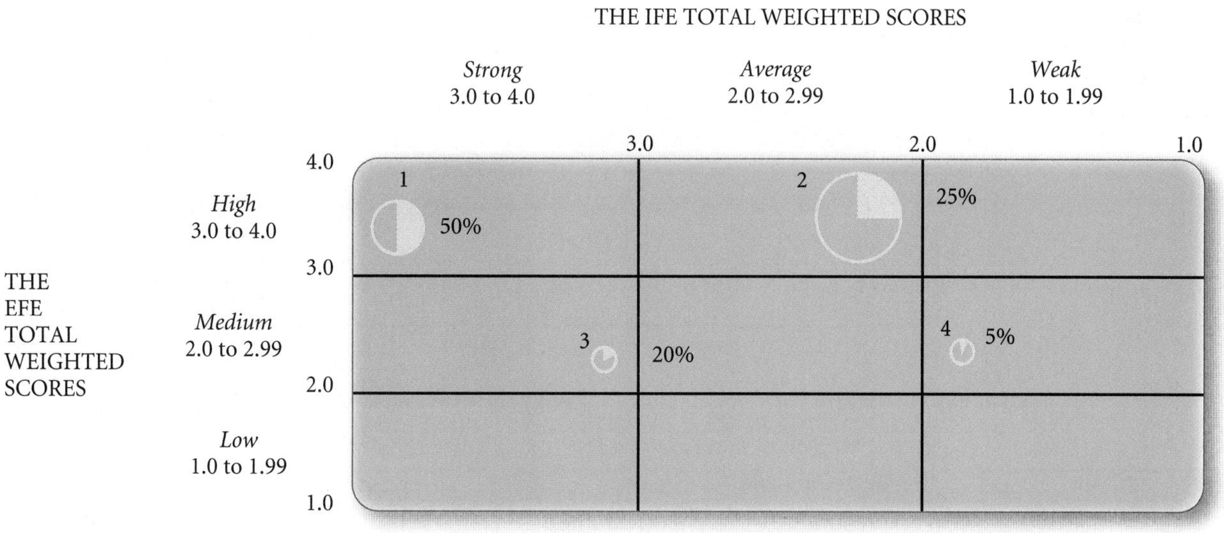

Division	Sales	Percent Sales	Profits	Percent Profits	IFE Scores	EFE Scores
1	$100	25.0	10	50	3.6	3.2
2	200	50.0	5	25	2.1	3.5
3	50	12.5	4	20	3.1	2.1
4	50	12.5	1	5	1.8	2.5
Total	**400**	**100.0**	**20**	**100**		

and build strategies are appropriate for Division 1, Division 2, and Division 3. Division 4 is a candidate for *harvest or divest*. Division 2 contributes the greatest percentage of company sales and thus is represented by the largest circle. Division 1 contributes the greatest proportion of total profits; it has the largest-percentage pie slice.

As indicated in Figure 6-11, Harrah's recently constructed an IE Matrix for its five product segments. Note that its Casino Division has the largest revenues (as indicated by the largest circle) and the largest profits (as indicated by the largest pie slice) in the matrix. Harrah's could also develop a Land-Based versus Riverboat versus Indian Gaming IE Matrix with three circles. It is common for organizations to develop both geographic and product-based IE Matrices to more effectively formulate strategies and allocate resources among divisions. In addition, firms often prepare an IE (or BCG) Matrix for competitors. Furthermore, firms will often prepare "before and after" IE (or BCG) Matrices to reveal the situation at present versus the expected situation after one year. This latter idea minimizes the limitation of these matrices being a "snapshot in time." In performing case analysis, feel free to estimate the IFE and EFE scores for the various divisions based upon your research into the company and industry—rather than preparing a separate IE Matrix for each division.

The Grand Strategy Matrix

In addition to the SWOT Matrix, SPACE Matrix, BCG Matrix, and IE Matrix, the *Grand Strategy Matrix* has become a popular tool for formulating alternative strategies. All organizations can be positioned in one of the Grand Strategy Matrix's four strategy quadrants. A firm's divisions likewise could be positioned. As illustrated in Figure 6-12, the Grand Strategy Matrix is based on two evaluative dimensions: competitive position and market (industry) growth. Any industry whose annual growth in sales exceeds 5 percent could be

---

FIGURE 6-11

The IE Matrix for Harrah's

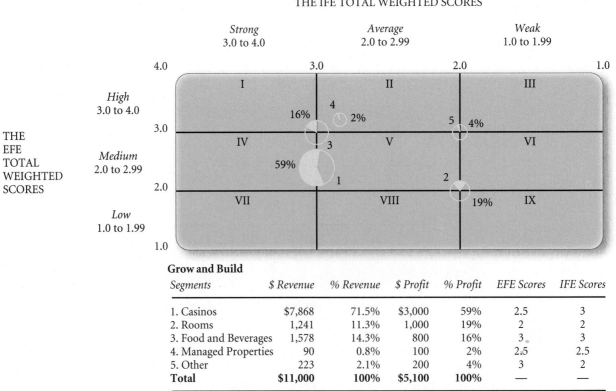

Segments	$ Revenue	% Revenue	$ Profit	% Profit	EFE Scores	IFE Scores
1. Casinos	$7,868	71.5%	$3,000	59%	2.5	3
2. Rooms	1,241	11.3%	1,000	19%	2	2
3. Food and Beverages	1,578	14.3%	800	16%	3	3
4. Managed Properties	90	0.8%	100	2%	2.5	2.5
5. Other	223	2.1%	200	4%	3	2
Total	**$11,000**	**100%**	**$5,100**	**100%**	—	—

FIGURE 6-12

The Grand Strategy Matrix

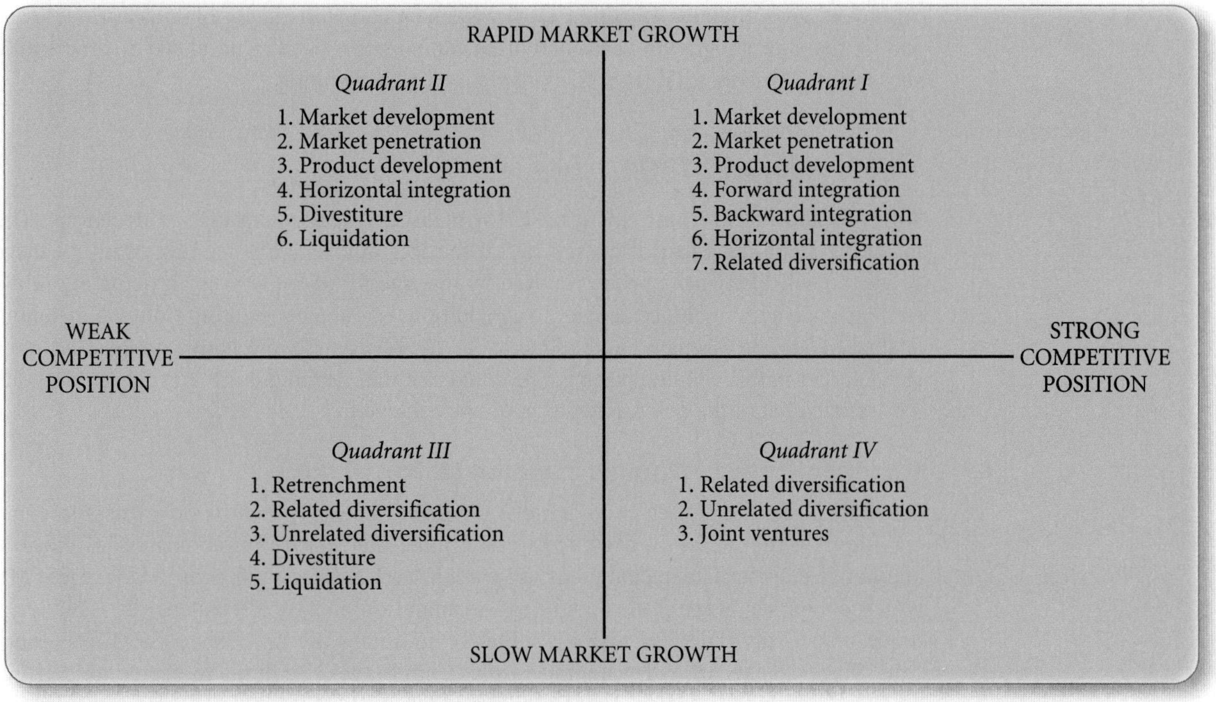

Source: Adapted from Roland Christensen, Norman Berg, and Malcolm Salter, *Policy Formulation and Administration* (Homewood, IL: Richard D. Irwin, 1976): 16–18.

considered to have rapid growth. Appropriate strategies for an organization to consider are listed in sequential order of attractiveness in each quadrant of the matrix.

Firms located in Quadrant I of the Grand Strategy Matrix are in an excellent strategic position. For these firms, continued concentration on current markets (market penetration and market development) and products (product development) is an appropriate strategy. It is unwise for a Quadrant I firm to shift notably from its established competitive advantages. When a Quadrant I organization has excessive resources, then backward, forward, or horizontal integration may be effective strategies. When a Quadrant I firm is too heavily committed to a single product, then related diversification may reduce the risks associated with a narrow product line. Quadrant I firms can afford to take advantage of external opportunities in several areas. They can take risks aggressively when necessary.

Firms positioned in Quadrant II need to evaluate their present approach to the marketplace seriously. Although their industry is growing, they are unable to compete effectively, and they need to determine why the firm's current approach is ineffective and how the company can best change to improve its competitiveness. Because Quadrant II firms are in a rapid-market-growth industry, an intensive strategy (as opposed to integrative or diversification) is usually the first option that should be considered. However, if the firm is lacking a distinctive competence or competitive advantage, then horizontal integration is often a desirable alternative. As a last resort, divestiture or liquidation should be considered. Divestiture can provide funds needed to acquire other businesses or buy back shares of stock.

Quadrant III organizations compete in slow-growth industries and have weak competitive positions. These firms must make some drastic changes quickly to avoid further decline and possible liquidation. Extensive cost and asset reduction (retrenchment) should be pursued first. An alternative strategy is to shift resources away from the current business into different areas (diversify). If all else fails, the final options for Quadrant III businesses are divestiture or liquidation.

Finally, Quadrant IV businesses have a strong competitive position but are in a slow-growth industry. These firms have the strength to launch diversified programs into more promising growth areas: Quadrant IV firms have characteristically high cash-flow levels and limited internal growth needs and often can pursue related or unrelated diversification successfully. Quadrant IV firms also may pursue joint ventures.

The Decision Stage

Analysis and intuition provide a basis for making strategy-formulation decisions. The matching techniques just discussed reveal feasible alternative strategies. Many of these strategies will likely have been proposed by managers and employees participating in the strategy analysis and choice activity. Any additional strategies resulting from the matching analyses could be discussed and added to the list of feasible alternative options. As indicated earlier in this chapter, participants could rate these strategies on a 1 to 4 scale so that a prioritized list of the best strategies could be achieved.

The Quantitative Strategic Planning Matrix (QSPM)

Other than ranking strategies to achieve the prioritized list, there is only one analytical technique in the literature designed to determine the relative attractiveness of feasible alternative actions. This technique is the *Quantitative Strategic Planning Matrix (QSPM)*, which comprises Stage 3 of the strategy-formulation analytical framework.[6] This technique objectively indicates which alternative strategies are best. The QSPM uses input from Stage 1 analyses and matching results from Stage 2 analyses to decide objectively among alternative strategies. That is, the EFE Matrix, IFE Matrix, and Competitive Profile Matrix that make up Stage 1, coupled with the SWOT Matrix, SPACE Matrix, BCG Matrix, IE Matrix, and Grand Strategy Matrix that make up Stage 2, provide the needed information for setting up the QSPM (Stage 3). The QSPM is a tool that allows strategists to evaluate alternative strategies objectively, based on previously identified external and internal critical success factors. Like other strategy-formulation analytical tools, the QSPM requires good intuitive judgment.

The basic format of the QSPM is illustrated in Table 6-5. Note that the left column of a QSPM consists of key external and internal factors (from Stage 1), and the top row consists of feasible alternative strategies (from Stage 2). Specifically, the left column of a

TABLE 6-5   The Quantitative Strategic Planning Matrix—QSPM

Key Factors	Weight	Strategic Alternatives		
		Strategy 1	Strategy 2	Strategy 3
Key External Factors				
Economy				
Political/Legal/Governmental				
Social/Cultural/Demographic/Environmental				
Technological				
Competitive				
Key Internal Factors				
Management				
Marketing				
Finance/Accounting				
Production/Operations				
Research and Development				
Management Information Systems				

QSPM consists of information obtained directly from the EFE Matrix and IFE Matrix. In a column adjacent to the critical success factors, the respective weights received by each factor in the EFE Matrix and the IFE Matrix are recorded.

The top row of a QSPM consists of alternative strategies derived from the SWOT Matrix, SPACE Matrix, BCG Matrix, IE Matrix, and Grand Strategy Matrix. These matching tools usually generate similar feasible alternatives. However, not every strategy suggested by the matching techniques has to be evaluated in a QSPM. Strategists should use good intuitive judgment in selecting strategies to include in a QSPM.

Conceptually, the QSPM determines the relative attractiveness of various strategies based on the extent to which key external and internal critical success factors are capitalized upon or improved. The relative attractiveness of each strategy within a set of alternatives is computed by determining the cumulative impact of each external and internal critical success factor. Any number of sets of alternative strategies can be included in the QSPM, and any number of strategies can make up a given set, but only strategies within a given set are evaluated relative to each other. For example, one set of strategies may include diversification, whereas another set may include issuing stock and selling a division to raise needed capital. These two sets of strategies are totally different, and the QSPM evaluates strategies only within sets. Note in Table 6-5 that three strategies are included, and they make up just one set.

A QSPM for a retail computer store is provided in Table 6-6. This example illustrates all the components of the QSPM: Strategic Alternatives, Key Factors, Weights, Attractiveness Scores (AS), Total Attractiveness Scores (TAS), and the Sum Total Attractiveness Score. The three new terms just introduced—(1) Attractiveness Scores, (2) Total Attractiveness Scores, and (3) the Sum Total Attractiveness Score—are defined and explained as the six steps required to develop a QSPM are discussed:

Step 1   *Make a list of the firm's key external opportunities/threats and internal strengths/weaknesses in the left column of the QSPM.* This information should be taken directly from the EFE Matrix and IFE Matrix. A minimum of 10 external key success factors and 10 internal key success factors should be included in the QSPM.

Step 2   *Assign weights to each key external and internal factor.* These weights are identical to those in the EFE Matrix and the IFE Matrix. The weights are presented in a straight column just to the right of the external and internal critical success factors.

Step 3   *Examine the Stage 2 (matching) matrices, and identify alternative strategies that the organization should consider implementing.* Record these strategies in the top row of the QSPM. Group the strategies into mutually exclusive sets if possible.

Step 4   *Determine the Attractiveness Scores (AS)* defined as numerical values that indicate the relative attractiveness of each strategy in a given set of alternatives. *Attractiveness Scores (AS)* are determined by examining each key external or internal factor, one at a time, and asking the question "Does this factor affect the choice of strategies being made?" If the answer to this question is *yes*, then the strategies should be compared relative to that key factor. Specifically, Attractiveness Scores should be assigned to each strategy to indicate the relative attractiveness of one strategy over others, considering the particular factor. The range for Attractiveness Scores is 1 = not attractive, 2 = somewhat attractive, 3 = reasonably attractive, and 4 = highly attractive. Work row by row in developing a QSPM. If the answer to the previous question is *no,* indicating that the respective key factor has no effect upon the specific choice being made, then do not assign Attractiveness Scores to the strategies in that set. Use a dash to indicate that the key factor does not affect the choice being made. *Note:* If you assign an AS score to one strategy, then assign AS score(s) to the other. In other words, if one strategy receives a dash, then all others must receive a dash in a given row.

Step 5   *Compute the Total Attractiveness Scores. Total Attractiveness Scores (TAS)* are defined as the product of multiplying the weights (Step 2) by the Attractiveness

TABLE 6-6 **A QSPM for a Retail Computer Store**

		STRATEGIC ALTERNATIVES			
		1		2	
		Buy New Land and Build New Larger Store		Fully Renovate Existing Store	
Key Factors	Weight	AS	TAS	AS	TAS
Opportunities					
1. Population of city growing 10%	0.10	4	0.40	2	0.20
2. Rival computer store opening 1 mile away	0.10	2	0.20	4	0.40
3. Vehicle traffic passing store up 12%	0.08	1	0.80	4	0.32
4. Vendors average six new products/year	0.05	—		—	
5. Senior citizen use of computers up 8%	0.05	—		—	
6. Small business growth in area up 10%	0.10	—		—	
7. Desire for Web sites up 18% by realtors	0.06	—		—	
8. Desire for Web sites up 12% by small firms	0.06	—		—	
Threats					
1. Best Buy opening new store nearby in 1 year	0.15	4	0.60	3	0.45
2. Local university offers computer repair	0.08	—		—	
3. New bypass for Hwy 34 in 1 year will divert traffic	0.12	4		1	
4. New mall being built nearby	0.08	2		4	
5. Gas prices up 14%	0.04	—		—	
6. Vendors raising prices 8%	0.03	—		—	
	1.00				
Strengths					
1. Inventory turnover increased from 5.8 to 6.7	0.05	—		—	
2. Average customer purchase increased from $97 to $128	0.07	2	0.14	4	0.28
3. Employee morale is excellent	0.10	—		—	
4. In-store promotions resulted in 20% increase in sales	0.05	—		—	
5. Newspaper advertising expenditures increased 10%	0.02	—		—	
6. Revenues from repair/service segment of store up 16%	0.15	4	0.60	3	0.45
7. In-store technical support personnel have MIS college degrees	0.05	—		—	
8. Store's debt-to-total assets ratio declined to 34%	0.03	4	0.12	2	0.06
9. Revenues per employee up 19%	0.02	—		—	
Weaknesses					
1. Revenues from software segment of store down 12%	0.10	—		—	
2. Location of store negatively impacted by new Highway 34	0.15	4	0.60	1	0.15
3. Carpet and paint in store somewhat in disrepair	0.02	1	0.02	4	0.08
4. Bathroom in store needs refurbishing	0.02	1	0.02	4	0.08
5. Revenues from businesses down 8%	0.04	3	0.12	4	0.16
6. Store has no Web site	0.05	—		—	
7. Supplier on-time delivery increased to 2.4 days	0.03	—		—	
8. Often customers have to wait to check out	0.05	2	0.10	4	0.20
Total	1.00		3.72		2.83

Scores (Step 4) in each row. The Total Attractiveness Scores indicate the relative attractiveness of each alternative strategy, considering only the impact of the adjacent external or internal critical success factor. The higher the Total Attractiveness Score, the more attractive the strategic alternative (considering only the adjacent critical success factor).

Step 6 *Compute the Sum Total Attractiveness Score.* Add Total Attractiveness Scores in each strategy column of the QSPM. The *Sum Total Attractiveness Scores (STAS)* reveal which strategy is most attractive in each set of alternatives. Higher scores indicate more attractive strategies, considering all the relevant external and internal factors that could affect the strategic decisions. The magnitude of the difference between the Sum Total Attractiveness Scores in a given set of strategic alternatives indicates the relative desirability of one strategy over another.

In Table 6-6, two alternative strategies—(1) buy new land and build new larger store and (2) fully renovate existing store—are being considered by a computer retail store. Note by sum total attractiveness scores of 3.72 versus 2.83 that the analysis indicates the business should buy new land and build a new larger store. Note the use of dashes to indicate which factors do not affect the strategy choice being considered. If a particular factor affects one strategy but not the other, it affects the choice being made, so attractiveness scores should be recorded for both strategies. Never rate one strategy and not the other. Note also in Table 6-6 that there are no double 1's, 2's, 3's, or 4's in a row. Never duplicate scores in a row. Never work column by column; always prepare a QSPM working row by row. If you have more than one strategy in the QSPM, then let the AS scores range from 1 to "the number of strategies being evaluated." This will enable you to have a different AS score for each strategy. These are all important guidelines to follow in developing a QSPM. In actual practice, the store did purchase the new land and build a new store; the business also did some minor refurbishing until the new store was operational.

There should be a rationale for each AS score assigned. Note in Table 6-6 in the first row that the "city population growing 10 percent annually" opportunity could be capitalized on best by strategy 1, "building the new, larger store," so an AS score of 4 was assigned to Strategy 1. AS scores, therefore, are not mere guesses; they should be rational, defensible, and reasonable.

Avoid giving each strategy the same AS score. Note in Table 6-6 that dashes are inserted all the way across the row when used. Also note that double 4's, or double 3's, or double 2's, or double 1's are never in a given row. Again work row by row, not column by column. These are important guidelines to follow in constructing a QSPM.

Positive Features and Limitations of the QSPM

A positive feature of the QSPM is that sets of strategies can be examined sequentially or simultaneously. For example, corporate-level strategies could be evaluated first, followed by division-level strategies, and then function-level strategies. There is no limit to the number of strategies that can be evaluated or the number of sets of strategies that can be examined at once using the QSPM.

Another positive feature of the QSPM is that it requires strategists to integrate pertinent external and internal factors into the decision process. Developing a QSPM makes it less likely that key factors will be overlooked or weighted inappropriately. A QSPM draws attention to important relationships that affect strategy decisions. Although developing a QSPM requires a number of subjective decisions, making small decisions along the way enhances the probability that the final strategic decisions will be best for the organization. A QSPM can be adapted for use by small and large for-profit and nonprofit organizations so can be applied to virtually any type of organization. A QSPM can especially enhance strategic choice in multinational firms because many key factors and strategies can be considered at once. It also has been applied successfully by a number of small businesses.[7]

The QSPM is not without some limitations. First, it always requires intuitive judgments and educated assumptions. The ratings and attractiveness scores require judgmental decisions, even though they should be based on objective information. Discussion among strategists, managers, and employees throughout the strategy-formulation process, including development of a QSPM, is constructive and improves strategic decisions. Constructive discussion during strategy analysis and choice may arise because of genuine differences of interpretation of information and varying opinions. Another limitation of the QSPM is that it can be only as good as the prerequisite information and matching analyses upon which it is based.

Cultural Aspects of Strategy Choice

All organizations have a culture. *Culture* includes the set of shared values, beliefs, attitudes, customs, norms, personalities, heroes, and heroines that describe a firm. Culture is the unique way an organization does business. It is the human dimension that creates solidarity and meaning, and it inspires commitment and productivity in an organization when strategy changes are made. All human beings have a basic need to make sense of the world, to feel in control, and to make meaning. When events threaten meaning, individuals react defensively. Managers and employees may even sabotage new strategies in an effort to recapture the status quo.

It is beneficial to view strategic management from a cultural perspective because success often rests upon the degree of support that strategies receive from a firm's culture. If a firm's strategies are supported by cultural products such as values, beliefs, rites, rituals, ceremonies, stories, symbols, language, heroes, and heroines, then managers often can implement changes swiftly and easily. However, if a supportive culture does not exist and is not cultivated, then strategy changes may be ineffective or even counterproductive. A firm's culture can become antagonistic to new strategies, and the result of that antagonism may be confusion and disarray.

Strategies that require fewer cultural changes may be more attractive because extensive changes can take considerable time and effort. Whenever two firms merge, it becomes especially important to evaluate and consider culture-strategy linkages.

Culture provides an explanation for the difficulties a firm encounters when it attempts to shift its strategic direction, as the following statement explains:

> Not only has the "right" corporate culture become the essence and foundation of corporate excellence, but success or failure of needed corporate reforms hinges on management's sagacity and ability to change the firm's driving culture in time and in tune with required changes in strategies.[8]

The Politics of Strategy Choice

All organizations are political. Unless managed, political maneuvering consumes valuable time, subverts organizational objectives, diverts human energy, and results in the loss of some valuable employees. Sometimes political biases and personal preferences get unduly embedded in strategy choice decisions. Internal politics affect the choice of strategies in all organizations. The hierarchy of command in an organization, combined with the career aspirations of different people and the need to allocate scarce resources, guarantees the formation of coalitions of individuals who strive to take care of themselves first and the organization second, third, or fourth. Coalitions of individuals often form around key strategy issues that face an enterprise. A major responsibility of strategists is to guide the development of coalitions, to nurture an overall team concept, and to gain the support of key individuals and groups of individuals.

In the absence of objective analyses, strategy decisions too often are based on the politics of the moment. With development of improved strategy-formation tools, political factors become less important in making strategic decisions. In the absence of objectivity, political factors sometimes dictate strategies, and this is unfortunate. Managing political relationships is an integral part of building enthusiasm and esprit de corps in an organization.

A classic study of strategic management in nine large corporations examined the political tactics of successful and unsuccessful strategists.[9] Successful strategists were found to let weakly supported ideas and proposals die through inaction and to establish additional hurdles or tests for strongly supported ideas considered unacceptable but not openly opposed. Successful strategists kept a low political profile on unacceptable proposals and strived to let most negative decisions come from subordinates or a group consensus, thereby reserving their personal vetoes for big issues and crucial moments. Successful strategists did a lot of chatting and informal questioning to stay abreast of how things were progressing and to know when to intervene. They led strategy but did not dictate it. They gave few orders, announced few decisions, depended heavily on informal questioning, and sought to probe and clarify until a consensus emerged.

Successful strategists generously and visibly rewarded key thrusts that succeeded. They assigned responsibility for major new thrusts to *champions,* the individuals most strongly identified with the idea or product and whose futures were linked to its success. They stayed alert to the symbolic impact of their own actions and statements so as not to send false signals that could stimulate movements in unwanted directions.

Successful strategists ensured that all major power bases within an organization were represented in, or had access to, top management. They interjected new faces and new views into considerations of major changes. This is important because new employees and managers generally have more enthusiasm and drive than employees who have been with the firm a long time. New employees do not see the world the same old way; nor do they act as screens against changes. Successful strategists minimized their own political exposure on highly controversial issues and in circumstances in which major opposition from key power centers was likely. In combination, these findings provide a basis for managing political relationships in an organization.

Because strategies must be effective in the marketplace and capable of gaining internal commitment, the following tactics used by politicians for centuries can aid strategists:

- *Equifinality*—It is often possible to achieve similar results using different means or paths. Strategists should recognize that achieving a successful outcome is more important than imposing the method of achieving it. It may be possible to generate new alternatives that give equal results but with far greater potential for gaining commitment.
- *Satisfying*—Achieving satisfactory results with an acceptable strategy is far better than failing to achieve optimal results with an unpopular strategy.
- *Generalization*—Shifting focus from specific issues to more general ones may increase strategists' options for gaining organizational commitment.
- *Focus on Higher-Order Issues*—By raising an issue to a higher level, many short-term interests can be postponed in favor of long-term interests. For instance, by focusing on issues of survival, the airline and automotive industries were able to persuade unions to make concessions on wage increases.
- *Provide Political Access on Important Issues*—Strategy and policy decisions with significant negative consequences for middle managers will motivate intervention behavior from them. If middle managers do not have an opportunity to take a position on such decisions in appropriate political forums, they are capable of successfully resisting the decisions after they are made. Providing such political access provides strategists with information that otherwise might not be available and that could be useful in managing intervention behavior.[10]

Governance Issues

A "director," according to Webster's Dictionary, is "one of a group of persons entrusted with the overall direction of a corporate enterprise." A *board of directors* is a group of individuals who are elected by the ownership of a corporation to have oversight and guidance over management and who look out for shareholders' interests. The act of oversight and direction is referred to as *governance*. The National Association of Corporate Directors defines governance as "the characteristic of ensuring that long-term strategic objectives and plans are established and that the proper management structure is in place to achieve those objectives, while at the same time making sure that the structure functions to maintain the corporation's integrity, reputation, and responsibility to its various constituencies." This broad scope of responsibility for the board shows how boards are being held accountable for the entire performance of the firm. In the Worldcom, Tyco, and Enron bankruptcies and scandals, the firms' boards of directors were sued by shareholders for mismanaging their interests. New accounting rules in the United States and Europe now enhance corporate-governance codes and require much more extensive financial disclosure among publicly held firms. The roles and duties of a board of directors can be divided into four broad categories, as indicated in Table 6-7.

Until recently, boards of directors did most of their work sitting around polished wooden tables. However, Hewlett-Packard's directors, among many others, now log on to

TABLE 6-7 Board of Director Duties and Responsibilities

1. CONTROL AND OVERSIGHT OVER MANAGEMENT
   a. Select the Chief Executive Officer (CEO).
   b. Sanction the CEO's team.
   c. Provide the CEO with a forum.
   d. Ensure managerial competency.
   e. Evaluate management's performance.
   f. Set management's salary levels, including fringe benefits.
   g. Guarantee managerial integrity through continuous auditing.
   h. Chart the corporate course.
   i. Devise and revise policies to be implemented by management.

2. ADHERENCE TO LEGAL PRESCRIPTIONS
   a. Keep abreast of new laws.
   b. Ensure the entire organization fulfills legal prescriptions.
   c. Pass bylaws and related resolutions.
   d. Select new directors.
   e. Approve capital budgets.
   f. Authorize borrowing, new stock issues, bonds, and so on.

3. CONSIDERATION OF STAKEHOLDERS' INTERESTS
   a. Monitor product quality.
   b. Facilitate upward progression in employee quality of work life.
   c. Review labor policies and practices.
   d. Improve the customer climate.
   e. Keep community relations at the highest level.
   f. Use influence to better governmental, professional association, and educational contacts.
   g. Maintain good public image.

4. ADVANCEMENT OF STOCKHOLDERS' RIGHTS
   a. Preserve stockholders' equity.
   b. Stimulate corporate growth so that the firm will survive and flourish.
   c. Guard against equity dilution.
   d. Ensure equitable stockholder representation.
   e. Inform stockholders through letters, reports, and meetings.
   f. Declare proper dividends.
   g. Guarantee corporate survival.

their own special board Web site twice a week and conduct business based on extensive confidential briefing information posted there by the firm's top management team. Then the board members meet face to face and fully informed every two months to discuss the biggest issues facing the firm. Even the decision of whether to locate operations in countries with low corporate tax rates would be reviewed by a board of directors—as indicated in the "Global Perspective."

GLOBAL PERSPECTIVE
Corporate Tax Rates Worldwide—Europe Is Lowest and Getting Lower

The lowest corporate tax rates among developed countries reside in Europe and European countries are lowering tax rates further to attract investment. The average corporate tax rate among European Union countries is 26 percent, compared with 30 percent in the Asia-Pacific region and nearly 40 percent in the United States and Japan. Ireland and the former Soviet-bloc nations of Eastern Europe recently slashed corporate tax rates to nearly zero, attracting substantial investment. Germany cut its corporate tax rate from 39 percent in 2007 to just under 30 percent in 2008. Great Britain cut its corporate tax rate to 28 percent from 30 percent. France plans to cut its rate from 34 percent to 27 percent in 2008.

Other factors besides the corporate tax rate obviously affect companies' decisions to locate plants and facilities. For example, the large and affluent market and efficient infrastructure in Germany and Britain attract companies, but the high labor costs and strict labor laws keep other companies away.

Ralph Gomory, president of the Alfred P. Sloan Foundation and a former top executive at IBM, warns of a growing divergence between the interests of U.S. corporations and the interests of the United States. Specifically, he says U.S. trade liberalization/globalization policies for the last two decades have encouraged corporations to seek the lowest-cost locations for their operations. The new 1,200-worker Intel semiconductor plant in Vietnam is just one example among thousands. Gomory says the United States must use the corporate income tax to greatly *reward* companies that invest in jobs here, especially high-tech jobs, and must greatly *penalize* companies that move facilities overseas. We must make it in the self-interest of companies to invest in America, Gomory says. Otherwise, living standards here will inevitably decline and America will severely weaken economically.

Source: Adapted from Marcus Walker, "Europe Competes for Investment with Lower Corporate Tax Rates," *Wall Street Journal* (April 17, 207): A12.

Source: John Heseltine (c) Dorling Kindersley

Today, boards of directors are composed mostly of outsiders who are becoming more involved in organizations' strategic management. The trend in the United States is toward much greater board member accountability with smaller boards, now averaging 12 members rather than 18 as they did a few years ago. *BusinessWeek* recently evaluated the boards of most large U.S. companies and provided the following "principles of good governance":

1. No more than two directors are current or former company executives.
2. No directors do business with the company or accept consulting or legal fees from the firm.
3. The audit, compensation, and nominating committees are made up solely of outside directors.
4. Each director owns a large equity stake in the company, excluding stock options.
5. At least one outside director has extensive experience in the company's core business and at least one has been CEO of an equivalent-size company.
6. Fully employed directors sit on no more than four boards and retirees sit on no more than seven.
7. Each director attends at least 75 percent of all meetings.
8. The board meets regularly without management present and evaluates its own performance annually.
9. The audit committee meets at least four times a year.
10. The board is frugal on executive pay, diligent in CEO succession oversight responsibilities, and prompt to act when trouble arises.
11. The CEO is not also the chairperson of the board.
12. Shareholders have considerable power and information to choose and replace directors.
13. Stock options are considered a corporate expense.
14. There are no interlocking directorships (where a director or CEO sits on another director's board).[11]

BusinessWeek identified some of the "worst" boards as those at Apple, Conseco, Gap, Kmart, Qwest, Tyson Foods, and Xerox. The "best" boards were those at 3M, Apria Healthcare, Colgate-Palmolive, General Electric, Home Depot, Intel, Johnson & Johnson, Medtronic, Pfizer, and Texas Instruments. Being a member of a board of directors today requires much more time, is much more difficult, and requires much more technical knowledge and financial commitment than in the past. Jeff Sonnerfeld, associate dean of the Yale School of Management, says, "Boards of directors are now rolling up their sleeves and becoming much more closely involved with management decision making." Since the Enron and Worldcom scandals, company CEOs and boards are required to personally certify financial statements; company loans to company executives and directors are illegal; and there is faster reporting of insider stock transactions.

Just as directors are beginning to place more emphasis on staying informed about an organization's health and operations, they are also taking a more active role in ensuring that publicly issued documents are accurate representations of a firm's status. It is becoming widely recognized that a board of directors has legal responsibilities to stockholders and society for all company activities, for corporate performance, and for ensuring that a firm has an effective strategy. Failure to accept responsibility for auditing or evaluating a firm's strategy is considered a serious breach of a director's duties. Stockholders, government agencies, and customers are filing legal suits against directors for fraud, omissions, inaccurate disclosures, lack of due diligence, and culpable ignorance about a firm's operations with increasing frequency. Liability insurance for directors has become exceptionally expensive and has caused numerous directors to resign.

More than 50 percent of outside directors at Fortune 500 firms have quit in recent years.[12] The 12 former Worldcom directors paid $25 million out of pocket to settle shareholder claims, and this has set a precedent for director liability. Among the Fortune 1,000 firms, board member average pay increased 32 percent since Sarbanes-Oxley was enacted in 2002 to $57,000 annually. This is commensurate with members' increased responsibility and liability. In the last 10 years, the percentage of those boards that include at least one woman rose from 63 to 82 percent; the percentage of those boards that have a least one member of an ethnic minority rose from 44 to 76 percent.

The Sarbanes-Oxley Act resulted in scores of boardroom overhauls among publicly traded companies. The jobs of chief executive and chairman are now held by separate persons, and board audit committees must now have at least one financial expert as a member. Board audit committees now meet 10 or more times per year, rather than 3 or 4 times as they did prior to the act. The act put an end to the "country club" atmosphere of most boards and has shifted power from CEOs to directors. Although aimed at public companies, the act has also had a similar impact on privately owned companies.[13]

In Sweden, a new law has recently been passed requiring 25 percent female representation in boardrooms. The Norwegian government has passed a similar law that requires 40 percent of corporate director seats to go to women. In the United States, women currently hold about 13 percent of board seats at S&P 500 firms and 10 percent at S&P 1,500 firms. The Investor Responsibility Research Center in Washington, D.C. reports that minorities hold just 8.8 percent of board seats of S&P 1,500 companies. Progressive firms realize that women and minorities ask different questions and make different suggestions in boardrooms than white men, which is helpful because women and minorities comprise much of the consumer base everywhere.

A direct response of increased pressure on directors to stay informed and execute their responsibilities is that audit committees are becoming commonplace. A board of directors should conduct an annual strategy audit in much the same fashion that it reviews the annual financial audit. In performing such an audit, a board could work jointly with operating management and/or seek outside counsel. Boards should play a role beyond that of performing a strategic audit. They should provide greater input and advice in the strategy-formulation process to ensure that strategists are providing for the long-term needs of the firm. This is being done through the formation of three particular board committees: nominating committees to propose candidates for the board and senior officers of the firm; compensation committees to evaluate the performance of top executives and determine the terms and conditions of their employment; and audit committees to give board-level attention to company accounting and financial policies and performance.

Conclusion

The essence of strategy formulation is an assessment of whether an organization is doing the right things and how it can be more effective in what it does. Every organization should be wary of becoming a prisoner of its own strategy, because even the best strategies become obsolete sooner or later. Regular reappraisal of strategy helps management avoid complacency. Objectives and strategies should be consciously developed and coordinated and should not merely evolve out of day-to-day operating decisions.

An organization with no sense of direction and no coherent strategy precipitates its own demise. When an organization does not know where it wants to go, it usually ends up some place it does not want to be. Every organization needs to consciously establish and communicate clear objectives and strategies.

Modern strategy-formulation tools and concepts are described in this chapter and integrated into a practical three-stage framework. Tools such as the SWOT Matrix, SPACE Matrix, BCG Matrix, IE Matrix, and QSPM can significantly enhance the quality of strategic decisions, but they should never be used to dictate the choice of strategies. Behavioral, cultural, and political aspects of strategy generation and selection are always important to consider and manage. Because of increased legal pressure from outside groups, boards of directors are assuming a more active role in strategy analysis and choice. This is a positive trend for organizations.

We invite you to visit the David page on the Prentice Hall Companion Web site at www.prenhall.com/david for this chapter's review quiz.

VISIT THE NET

Provides answers to "Frequently Asked Questions About Strategic Planning." (www.allianceonline.org/faqs.html)

Key Terms and Concepts

Aggressive Quadrant (p. 197)
Attractiveness Scores (AS) (p. 207)
Board of Directors (p. 211)
Boston Consulting Group (BCG) Matrix (p. 197)
Business Portfolio (p. 197)
Cash Cows (p. 200)
Champions (p. 211)
Competitive Advantage (CA) (p. 194)
Competitive Quadrant (p. 197)
Conservative Quadrant (p. 197)
Culture (p. 210)
Decision Stage (p. 191)
Defensive Quadrant (p. 197)
Directional Vector (p. 197)
Dogs (p. 200)
Environmental Stability (ES) (p. 194)
Financial Strength (FS) (p. 194)
Governance (p. 212)
Grand Strategy Matrix (p. 204)
Halo Error (p. 191)
Industry Strength (IS) (p. 194)
Input Stage (p. 190)
Internal-External (IE) Matrix (p. 197)
Matching (p. 191)
Matching Stage (p. 190)
Quantitative Strategic Planning Matrix (QSPM) (p. 206)
Question Marks (p. 199)
Relative Market Share Position (p. 197)
SO Strategies (p. 192)
Stars (p. 200)
Strategic Position and Action Evaluation (SPACE) Matrix (p. 194)
Strategy-Formulation Framework (p. 191)
Strengths-Weaknesses Opportunities-Threats (SWOT) Matrix (p. 192)
ST Strategies (p. 192)
Sum Total Attractiveness Scores (STAS) (p. 209)
Sustainability (p. 188)
Total Attractiveness Scores (TAS) (p. 207)
WO Strategies (p. 192)
WT Strategies (p. 192)

Issues for Review and Discussion

1. How would application of the strategy-formulation framework differ from a small to a large organization?
2. What types of strategies would you recommend for an organization that achieves total weighted scores of 3.6 on the IFE and 1.2 on the EFE Matrix?
3. Given the following information, develop a SPACE Matrix for the XYZ Corporation: FS = +2; ES = –6; CA = –2; IS = +4.
4. Given the information in the following table, develop a BCG Matrix and an IE Matrix:

Divisions	1	2	3
Profits	$10	$15	$25
Sales	$100	$50	$100
Relative Market Share	0.2	0.5	0.8
Industry Growth Rate	+.20	+.10	–.10
IFE Total Weighted Scores	1.6	3.1	2.2
EFE Total Weighted Scores	2.5	1.8	3.3

5. Explain the steps involved in developing a QSPM.
6. How would you develop a set of objectives for your school or business?
7. What do you think is the appropriate role of a board of directors in strategic management? Why?
8. Discuss the limitations of various strategy-formulation analytical techniques.
9. Explain why cultural factors should be an important consideration in analyzing and choosing among alternative strategies.
10. How are the SWOT Matrix, SPACE Matrix, BCG Matrix, IE Matrix, and Grand Strategy Matrix similar? How are they different?
11. How would for-profit and nonprofit organizations differ in their applications of the strategy-formulation framework?
12. Develop a SPACE Matrix for a company that is weak financially and is a weak competitor. The industry for this company is pretty stable, but the industry's projected growth in revenues and profits is not good. Label all axes and quadrants.
13. List four limitations of a BCG Matrix.
14. Make up an example to show clearly and completely that you can develop an IE Matrix for a three-division company, where each division has $10, $20, and $40 in revenues and $2, $4, and $1 in profits. State other assumptions needed. Label axes and quadrants.
15. What procedures could be necessary if the SPACE vector falls right on the axis between the Competitive and Defensive quadrants?
16. In a BCG Matrix or the Grand Strategy Matrix, what would you consider to be a rapid market (or industry) growth rate?
17. What are the pros and cons of a company (and country) participating in a Sustainability Report?
18. How does the Sarbanes-Oxley Act of 2002 impact boards of directors?
19. Rank *BusinessWeek*'s "principles of good governance" from 1 to 14 (1 being most important and 14 least important) to reveal your assessment of these new rules.
20. Why is it important to work row by row instead of column by column in preparing a QSPM?
21. Why should one avoid putting double 4's in a row in preparing a QSPM?
22. Envision a QSPM with no weight column. Would that still be a useful analysis? Why or why not? What do you lose by deleting the weight column?
23. Prepare a BCG Matrix for a two-division firm with sales of $5 and $8 versus profits of $3 and $1, respectively? State assumptions for the RMSP and IGR axes to enable you to construct the diagram.
24. Consider developing a before-and-after BCG or IE Matrix to reveal the expected results of your proposed strategies. What limitation of the analysis would this procedure overcome somewhat?
25. If a firm has the leading market share in its industry, where on the BCG Matrix would the circle lie?
26. If a firm competes in a very unstable industry, such as telecommunications, where on the ES axis of the SPACE Matrix would you plot the appropriate point?
27. Why do you think the SWOT Matrix is the most widely used of all strategy matrices?
28. The strategy templates described at the www.strategyclub.com Web site have templates for all of the Chapter 6 matrices. How could those templates be useful in preparing an example BCG or IE Matrix?

Notes

1. R. T. Lenz, "Managing the Evolution of the Strategic Planning Process," *Business Horizons* 30, no. 1 (January–February 1987): 37.
2. Robert Grant, "The Resource-Based Theory of Competitive Advantage: Implications for Strategy Formulation," *California Management Review* (Spring 1991): 114.
3. Heinz Weihrich, "The TOWS Matrix: A Tool for Situational Analysis," *Long Range Planning* 15, no. 2 (April 1982): 61. Note: Although Dr. Weihrich first modified SWOT analysis to form the TOWS matrix, the acronym SWOT is much more widely used than TOWS in practice, so this edition reflects a change to SWOT from the use of TOWS in previous editions.
4. Greg, Dess, G. T. Lumpkin and Alan Eisner, *Strategic Management: Text and Cases* (New York: McGraw-Hill/Irwin, 2006): 72.

5. H. Rowe, R. Mason, and K. Dickel, *Strategic Management and Business Policy: A Methodological Approach* (Reading, MA: Addison-Wesley, 1982): 155–156. Reprinted with permission of the publisher.

6. Fred David, "The Strategic Planning Matrix—A Quantitative Approach," *Long Range Planning* 19, no. 5 (October 1986): 102; Andre Gib and Robert Margulies, "Making Competitive Intelligence Relevant to the User," *Planning Review* 19, no. 3 (May–June 1991): 21.

7. Fred David, "Computer-Assisted Strategic Planning in Small Businesses," *Journal of Systems Management* 36, no. 7 (July 1985): 24–34.

8. Y. Allarie and M. Firsirotu, "How to Implement Radical Strategies in Large Organizations," *Sloan Management Review* 26, no. 3 (Spring 1985): 19. Another excellent article is P. Shrivastava, "Integrating Strategy Formulation with Organizational Culture," *Journal of Business Strategy* 5, no. 3 (Winter 1985): 103–111.

9. James Brian Quinn, *Strategies for Changes: Logical Incrementalism* (Homewood, IL: Richard D. Irwin, 1980): 128–145. These political tactics are listed in A. Thompson and A. Strickland, *Strategic Management: Concepts and Cases* (Plano, TX: Business Publications, 1984): 261.

10. William Guth and Ian MacMillan, "Strategy Implementation Versus Middle Management Self-Interest," *Strategic Management Journal* 7, no. 4 (July–August 1986): 321.

11. Louis Lavelle, "The Best and Worst Boards," *BusinessWeek* (October 7, 2002): 104–110.

12. Anne Fisher, "Board Seats Are Going Begging," *Fortune* (May 16, 2005): 204.

13. Matt Murray, "Private Companies Also Feel Pressure to Clean Up Acts," *Wall Street Journal* (July 22, 2003): B1.

Current Readings

Benz, Matthias, and Bruno S. Frey. "Corporate Governance: What Can We Learn from Public Governance?" *The Academy of Management Review* 32, no. 1 (January 2007): 92.

Dalton, Catherine M., and Dan R. Dalton "Spotlight on Corporate Governance." *Business Horizons* 49, no. 2 (March–April 2006): 91.

Drew, Stephen A., Patricia C. Kelley, and Terry Kendrick. "Class: Five Elements of Corporate Governance to Manage Strategic Risk." *Business Horizons* 49, no. 2 (March–April 2006): 127.

Gillis, William E. "How Much Is Too Much? Board of Director Responses to Shareholder Concerns About CEO Stock Options." *The Academy of Management Perspectives* 20, no. 2 (May 2006): 70.

Hillman, Amy J., Christine Shropshire, and Albert A. Cannella Jr. "Organizational Predictors of Women on Corporate Boards." *The Academy of Management Journal* 50, no. 4 (August 2007): 941.

Hoffman, W.H. "Strategies for Managing a Portfolio of Alliances." *Strategic Management Journal* 28, no. 8 (August 2007): 827.

Kor, Y. Y. "Direct and Interaction Effects of Top Management Team and Board Compositions on R&D Investment Strategy." *Strategic Management Journal* 27, no. 11 (November 2006): 1081.

Rehbein, Kathleen. "Explaining CEO Compensation: How Do Talent, Governance, and Markets Fit In?" *The Academy of Management Perspective* 21, no. 1 (February 2007): 75.

• EXPERIENTIAL EXERCISES   **D**ISNEY

Experiential Exercise 6A

Developing a SWOT Matrix for Walt Disney

Purpose

The most widely used strategy-formulation technique among U.S. firms is the SWOT Matrix. This exercise requires the development of a SWOT Matrix for Walt Disney. Matching key external and internal factors in a SWOT Matrix requires good intuitive and conceptual skills. You will improve with practice in developing a SWOT Matrix.

Instructions

Recall from Experiential Exercise 1A that you already may have determined Walt Disney's external opportunites/threats and internal strengths/weaknesses. This information could be used to complete this exercise. Follow the steps outlined as follows:

Step 1	On a separate sheet of paper, construct a large nine-cell diagram that will represent your SWOT Matrix. Appropriately label the cells.
Step 2	Appropriately record Walt Disney's opportunities/threats and strengths/weaknesses in your diagram.
Step 3	Match external and internal factors to generate feasible alternative strategies for Walt Disney. Record SO, WO, ST, and WT strategies in the appropriate cells of the SWOT Matrix. Use the proper notation to indicate the rationale for the strategies. You do not necessarily have to have strategies in all four strategy cells.
Step 4	Compare your SWOT Matrix to another student's SWOT Matrix. Discuss any major differences.

Experiential Exercise 6B

Developing a SPACE Matrix for Walt Disney

Purpose

Should Walt Disney pursue aggressive, conservative, competitive, or defensive strategies? Develop a SPACE Matrix for Walt Disney to answer this question. Elaborate on the strategic implications of your directional vector. Be specific in terms of strategies that could benefit Walt Disney.

Instructions

Step 1	Join with two other people in class and develop a joint SPACE Matrix for Walt Disney.
Step 2	Diagram your SPACE Matrix on the board. Compare your matrix with other team's matrices.
Step 3	Discuss the implications of your SPACE Matrix.

Experiential Exercise 6C

Developing a BCG Matrix for Walt Disney

Purpose

Portfolio matrices are widely used by multidivisional organizations to help identify and select strategies to pursue. A BCG analysis identifies particular divisions that should

A 1970s Walt Disney's "Goofy" Pez dispenser.
Source: (c) Judith Miller / Dorling Kindersley / Atomic Age

receive fewer resources than others. It may identify some divisions that need to be divested. This exercise can give you practice developing a BCG Matrix.

Instructions

Step 1	Place the following five column headings at the top of a separate sheet of paper: Divisions, Revenues, Profits, Relative Market Share Position, Industry Growth Rate. Down the far left of your page, list Disney's four divisions, which are (1) Studio Entertainment, (2) Parks and Resorts, (3) Media Networks, and (4) Consumer Products. Now turn back to the Cohesion Case and find information to fill in all the cells in your 4 × 5 data table.
Step 2	Complete a BCG Matrix for Walt Disney.
Step 3	Compare your BCG Matrix to other students' matrices. Discuss any major differences.

Experiential Exercise 6D

Developing a QSPM for Walt Disney

Purpose

This exercise can give you practice developing a Quantitative Strategic Planning Matrix to determine the relative attractiveness of various strategic alternatives.

Instructions

Step 1	Join with two other students in class to develop a joint QSPM for Walt Disney.
Step 2	Go to the blackboard and record your strategies and their Sum Total Attractiveness Score. Compare your team's strategies and Sum Total Attractiveness Score to those of other teams. Be sure not to assign the same AS score in a given row. Recall that dashes should be inserted all the way across a given row when used.
Step 3	Discuss any major differences.

Experiential Exercise 6E

Formulating Individual Strategies

Purpose

Individuals and organizations are alike in many ways. Each has competitors, and each should plan for the future. Every individual and organization faces some external opportunities and threats and has some internal strengths and weaknesses. Both individuals and organizations establish objectives and allocate resources. These and other similarities make it possible for individuals to use many strategic-management concepts and tools. This exercise is designed to demonstrate how the SWOT Matrix can be used by individuals to plan their futures. As one nears completion of a college degree and begins interviewing for jobs, planning can be particularly important.

Instructions

On a separate sheet of paper, construct a SWOT Matrix. Include what you consider to be your major external opportunities, your major external threats, your major strengths, and your major weaknesses. An internal weakness may be a low grade point average. An external opportunity may be that your university offers a graduate program that interests you. Match key external and internal factors by recording in the appropriate cell of the matrix alternative strategies or actions that would allow you to capitalize upon your strengths, overcome your weaknesses, take advantage of your external opportunities, and minimize the impact of external threats. Be sure to use the appropriate matching notation in the strategy cells of the matrix. Because every individual (and organization) is unique, there is no one right answer to this exercise.

Experiential Exercise 6F

The Mach Test

Purpose

The purpose of this exercise is to enhance your understanding and awareness of the impact that behavioral and political factors can have on strategy analysis and choice.

Instructions

Step 1   On a separate sheet of paper, number from 1 to 10. For each of the 10 statements given as follows, record a *1, 2, 3, 4,* or *5* to indicate your attitude, where

> 1 = I disagree a lot.
> 2 = I disagree a little.
> 3 = My attitude is neutral.
> 4 = I agree a little.
> 5 = I agree a lot.

1. The best way to handle people is to tell them what they want to hear.
2. When you ask someone to do something for you, it is best to give the real reason for wanting it, rather than a reason that might carry more weight.
3. Anyone who completely trusts anyone else is asking for trouble.
4. It is hard to get ahead without cutting corners here and there.
5. It is safest to assume that all people have a vicious streak, and it will come out when they are given a chance.
6. One should take action only when it is morally right.
7. Most people are basically good and kind.
8. There is no excuse for lying to someone else.
9. Most people forget more easily the death of their father than the loss of their property.
10. Generally speaking, people won't work hard unless they're forced to do so.

Step 2   Add up the numbers you recorded beside statements 1, 3, 4, 5, 9, and 10. This sum is Subtotal One. For the other four statements, reverse the numbers you recorded, so a *5* becomes a *1, 4* becomes *2, 2* becomes *4, 1* becomes *5,* and *3* remains *3.* Then add those four numbers to get Subtotal Two. Finally, add Subtotal One and Subtotal Two to get your Final Score.

Your Final Score

Your Final Score is your Machiavellian Score. Machiavellian principles are defined in a dictionary as "manipulative, dishonest, deceiving, and favoring political expediency over morality." These tactics are not desirable, are not ethical, and are not recommended in the strategic-management process! You may, however, encounter some highly Machiavellian individuals in your career, so beware. It is important for strategists not to manipulate others in the pursuit of organizational objectives. Individuals today recognize and resent manipulative tactics more than ever before. J. R. Ewing (on *Dallas,* a television show in the 1980s) was a good example of someone who was a high Mach (score over 30). The National Opinion Research Center used this short quiz in a random sample of U.S. adults and found the national average Final Score to be 25.[1] The higher your score, the more Machiavellian (manipulative) you tend to be. The following scale is descriptive of individual scores on this test:

- Below 16: Never uses manipulation as a tool.
- 16 to 20: Rarely uses manipulation as a tool.
- 21 to 25: Sometimes uses manipulation as a tool.
- 26 to 30: Often uses manipulation as a tool.
- Over 30: Always uses manipulation as a tool.

Test Development

The Mach (Machiavellian) test was developed by Dr. Richard Christie, whose research suggests the following tendencies:

1. Men generally are more Machiavellian than women.
2. There is no significant difference between high Machs and low Machs on measures of intelligence or ability.
3. Although high Machs are detached from others, they are detached in a pathological sense.
4. Machiavellian scores are not statistically related to authoritarian values.
5. High Machs tend to be in professions that emphasize the control and manipulation of individuals—for example, law, psychiatry, and behavioral science.
6. Machiavellianism is not significantly related to major demographic characteristics such as educational level or marital status.
7. High Machs tend to come from a city or have urban backgrounds.
8. Older adults tend to have lower Mach scores than younger adults.[2]

A classic book on power relationships, *The Prince,* was written by Niccolo Machiavelli. Several excerpts from *The Prince* follow:

Men must either be cajoled or crushed, for they will revenge themselves for slight wrongs, while for grave ones they cannot. The injury therefore that you do to a man should be such that you need not fear his revenge.

We must bear in mind . . . that there is nothing more difficult and dangerous, or more doubtful of success, than an attempt to introduce a new order of things in any state. The innovator has for enemies all those who derived advantages from the old order of things, while those who expect to be benefitted by the new institution will be but lukewarm defenders.

A wise prince, therefore, will steadily pursue such a course that the citizens of his state will always and under all circumstances feel the need for his authority, and will therefore always prove faithful to him.

A prince should seem to be merciful, faithful, humane, religious, and upright, and should even be so in reality, but he should have his mind so trained that, when occasion requires it, he may know how to change to the opposite.[3]

Notes

1. Richard Christie and Florence Geis, *Studies in Machiavellianism* (Orlando, FL: Academic Press, 1970). Material in this exercise adapted with permission of the authors and the Academic Press.
2. Ibid., 82–83.
3. Niccolo Machiavelli, *The Prince* (New York: The Washington Press, 1963).

Experiential Exercise 6G

Developing a BCG Matrix for My University

Purpose

Developing a BCG Matrix for many nonprofit organizations, including colleges and universities, is a useful exercise. Of course, there are no profits for each division or department—and in some cases no revenues. However, you can be creative in performing a BCG Matrix. For example, the pie slice in the circles can represent the number of majors receiving jobs upon graduation, the number of faculty teaching in that area, or some other variable that you believe is important to consider. The size of the circles can represent the number of students majoring in particular departments or areas.

Instructions

Step 1	On a separate sheet of paper, develop a BCG Matrix for your university. Include all academic schools, departments, or colleges.
Step 2	Diagram your BCG Matrix on the blackboard.
Step 3	Discuss differences among the BCG Matrices on the board.

Experiential Exercise 6H

The Role of Boards of Directors

Purpose

This exercise will give you a better understanding of the role of boards of directors in formulating, implementing, and evaluating strategies.

Instructions

Identify a person in your community who serves on a board of directors. Make an appointment to interview that person, and seek answers to the following questions. Summarize your findings in a five-minute oral report to the class.

- On what board are you a member?
- How often does the board meet?
- How long have you served on the board?
- What role does the board play in this company?
- How has the role of the board changed in recent years?
- What changes would you like to see in the role of the board?
- To what extent do you prepare for the board meeting?
- To what extent are you involved in strategic management of the firm?

Experiential Exercise 6I

Locating Companies in a Grand Strategy Matrix

Purpose

The Grand Strategy Matrix is a popular tool for formulating alternative strategies. All organizations can be positioned in one of the Grand Strategy Matrix's four strategy quadrants. The divisions of a firm likewise could be positioned. The Grand Strategy Matrix is based on two evaluative dimensions: competitive position and market growth. Appropriate strategies for an organization to consider are listed in sequential order of attractiveness in each quadrant of the matrix. This exercise gives you experience using a Grand Strategy Matrix.

Instructions

Using the year-end 2006 financial information provided, prepare a Grand Strategy Matrix on a separate sheet of paper. Write the respective company names in the appropriate quadrant of the matrix. Based on this analysis, what strategies are recommended for each company?

Company	Company Sales/ Profit Growth (%)	Industry	Industry Sales/ Profit Growth (%)
Ford Motor	−10% / −723%	Motor vehicles	+3% / −14%
Oshkosh Truck	+16% / +28%	Motor vehicles	+3% / −14%
International Paper	−6% / −5%	Forest/paper products	−2% / −10%
Weyerhaeuser	−3% / −38%	Forest/paper products	−2% / −10%
La-Z-Boy	−6% / −108%	Furniture	+8% / +8%
Herman Miller	+15% / +46%	Furniture	+8% / +8%
MGM Mirage	+17% / +46%	Hotels/casinos	+23% / +51%
Marriott International	+5% / −9%	Hotels/casinos	+23% / +51%

Part 3 · Strategy Implementation

7

Implementing Strategies: Management and Operations Issues

Loggers Working in the Pacific Northwest. *Source:* Peter Buckley

chapter objectives

After studying this chapter, you should be able to do the following:

1. Explain why strategy implementation is more difficult than strategy formulation.

2. Discuss the importance of annual objectives and policies in achieving organizational commitment for strategies to be implemented.

3. Explain why organizational structure is so important in strategy implementation.

4. Compare and contrast restructuring and reengineering.

5. Describe the relationships between production/operations and strategy implementation.

6. Explain how a firm can effectively link performance and pay to strategies.

7. Discuss employee stock ownership plans (ESOPs) as a strategic-management concept.

8. Describe how to modify an organizational culture to support new strategies.

9. Discuss the culture in Mexico and Japan.

10. Describe the glass ceiling in the United States.

experiential exercises

Experiential Exercise 7A
Revising Walt Disney's Organizational Chart

Experiential Exercise 7B
Do Organizations Really Establish Objectives?

Experiential Exercise 7C
Understanding My University's Culture

The strategic-management process does not end when the firm decides what strategy or strategies to pursue. There must be a translation of strategic thought into strategic action. This translation is much easier if managers and employees of the firm understand the business, feel a part of the company, and through involvement in strategy-formulation activities have become committed to helping the organization succeed. Without understanding and commitment, strategy-implementation efforts face major problems.

Implementing strategy affects an organization from top to bottom; it affects all the functional and divisional areas of a business. It is beyond the purpose and scope of this text to examine all of the business administration concepts and tools important in strategy implementation. This chapter focuses on management issues most central to implementing strategies in the year 2007, and Chapter 8 focuses on marketing, finance/accounting, R&D, and management information systems issues.

> Even the most technically perfect strategic plan will serve little purpose if it is not implemented. Many organizations tend to spend an inordinate amount of time, money, and effort on developing the strategic plan, treating the means and circumstances under which it will be implemented as afterthoughts! Change comes through implementation and evaluation, not through the plan. A technically imperfect plan that is implemented well will achieve more than the perfect plan that never gets off the paper on which it is typed.[1]

The Nature of Strategy Implementation

The strategy-implementation stage of strategic management is revealed in Figure 7-1. Successful strategy formulation does not guarantee successful strategy implementation. It is always more difficult to do something (strategy implementation) than to say you are going to do it (strategy formulation)! Although inextricably linked, strategy implementation is

VISIT THE NET

Gives a good definition of strategy implementation. (www. csuchico.edu/mgmt/strategy/ module/sld044.htm)

FIGURE 7-1

Comprehensive Strategic-Management Model

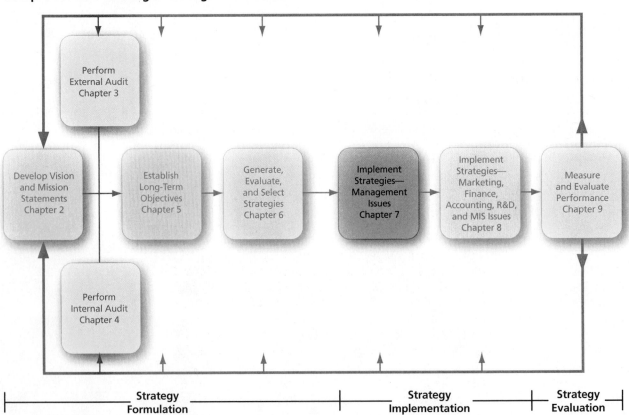

Source: Fred R. David, "How Companies Define Their Mission," *Long Range Planning* 22, no. 3 (June 1988): 40.

fundamentally different from strategy formulation. Strategy formulation and implementation can be contrasted in the following ways:

- Strategy formulation is positioning forces before the action.
- Strategy implementation is managing forces during the action.
- Strategy formulation focuses on effectiveness.
- Strategy implementation focuses on efficiency.
- Strategy formulation is primarily an intellectual process.
- Strategy implementation is primarily an operational process.
- Strategy formulation requires good intuitive and analytical skills.
- Strategy implementation requires special motivation and leadership skills.
- Strategy formulation requires coordination among a few individuals.
- Strategy implementation requires coordination among many individuals.

Strategy-formulation concepts and tools do not differ greatly for small, large, for-profit, or nonprofit organizations. However, strategy implementation varies substantially among different types and sizes of organizations. Implementing strategies requires such actions as altering sales territories, adding new departments, closing facilities, hiring new employees, changing an organization's pricing strategy, developing financial budgets, developing new employee benefits, establishing cost-control procedures, changing advertising strategies, building new facilities, training new employees, transferring managers among divisions, and building a better management information system. These types of activities obviously differ greatly between manufacturing, service, and governmental organizations.

Management Perspectives

In all but the smallest organizations, the transition from strategy formulation to strategy implementation requires a shift in responsibility from strategists to divisional and functional managers. Implementation problems can arise because of this shift in responsibility, especially if strategy-formulation decisions come as a surprise to middle- and lower-level managers. Managers and employees are motivated more by perceived self-interests than by organizational interests, unless the two coincide. Therefore, it is essential that divisional and functional managers be involved as much as possible in strategy-formulation activities. Of equal importance, strategists should be involved as much as possible in strategy-implementation activities.

Management issues central to strategy implementation include establishing annual objectives, devising policies, allocating resources, altering an existing organizational structure, restructuring and reengineering, revising reward and incentive plans, minimizing resistance to change, matching managers with strategy, developing a strategy-supportive culture, adapting production/operations processes, developing an effective human resources function, and, if necessary, downsizing. Management changes are necessarily more extensive when strategies to be implemented move a firm in a major new direction.

Managers and employees throughout an organization should participate early and directly in strategy-implementation decisions. Their role in strategy implementation should build upon prior involvement in strategy-formulation activities. Strategists' genuine personal commitment to implementation is a necessary and powerful motivational force for managers and employees. Too often, strategists are too busy to actively support strategy-implementation efforts, and their lack of interest can be detrimental to organizational success. The rationale for objectives and strategies should be understood and clearly communicated throughout an organization. Major competitors' accomplishments, products, plans, actions, and performance should be apparent to all organizational members. Major external opportunities and threats should be clear, and managers' and employees' questions should be answered. Top-down flow of communication is essential for developing bottom-up support.

Firms need to develop a competitor focus at all hierarchical levels by gathering and widely distributing competitive intelligence; every employee should be able to benchmark her or his efforts against best-in-class competitors so that the challenge becomes personal.

This is a challenge for strategists of the firm. Firms should provide training for both managers and employees to ensure that they have and maintain the skills necessary to be world-class performers.

Annual Objectives

Establishing annual objectives is a decentralized activity that directly involves all managers in an organization. Active participation in establishing annual objectives can lead to acceptance and commitment. *Annual objectives* are essential for strategy implementation because they (1) represent the basis for allocating resources; (2) are a primary mechanism

FIGURE 7-2

The Stamus Company's Hierarchy of Aims

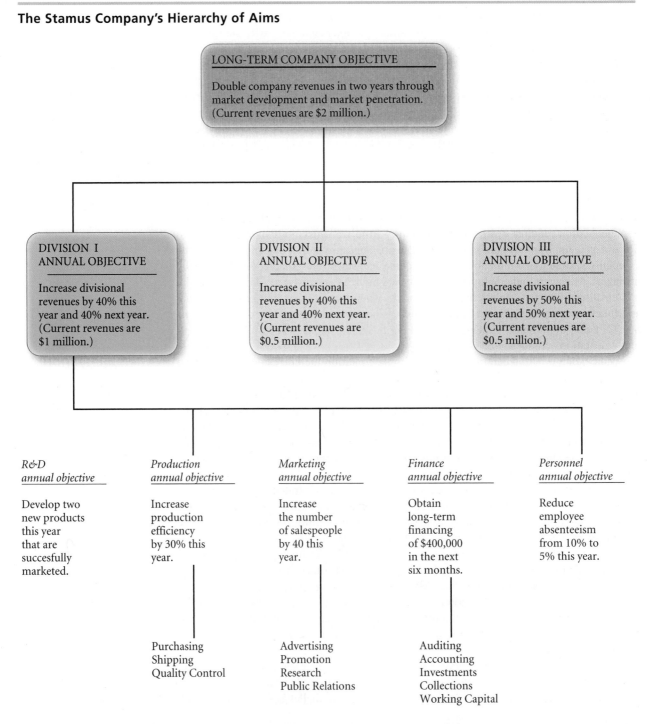

for evaluating managers; (3) are the major instrument for monitoring progress toward achieving long-term objectives; and (4) establish organizational, divisional, and departmental priorities. Considerable time and effort should be devoted to ensuring that annual objectives are well conceived, consistent with long-term objectives, and supportive of strategies to be implemented. Approving, revising, or rejecting annual objectives is much more than a rubber-stamp activity. The purpose of annual objectives can be summarized as follows:

> Annual objectives serve as guidelines for action, directing and channeling efforts and activities of organization members. They provide a source of legitimacy in an enterprise by justifying activities to stakeholders. They serve as standards of performance. They serve as an important source of employee motivation and identification. They give incentives for managers and employees to perform. They provide a basis for organizational design.[2]

Clearly stated and communicated objectives are critical to success in all types and sizes of firms. Annual objectives, stated in terms of profitability, growth, and market share by business segment, geographic area, customer groups, and product, are common in organizations. Figure 7-2 illustrates how the Stamus Company could establish annual objectives based on long-term objectives. Table 7-1 reveals associated revenue figures that correspond to the objectives outlined in Figure 7-2. Note that, according to plan, the Stamus Company will slightly exceed its long-term objective of doubling company revenues between 2008 and 2009.

Figure 7-2 also reflects how a hierarchy of annual objectives can be established based on an organization's structure. Objectives should be consistent across hierarchical levels and form a network of supportive aims. *Horizontal consistency of objectives* is as important as *vertical consistency of objectives*. For instance, it would not be effective for manufacturing to achieve more than its annual objective of units produced if marketing could not sell the additional units.

Annual objectives should be measurable, consistent, reasonable, challenging, clear, communicated throughout the organization, characterized by an appropriate time dimension, and accompanied by commensurate rewards and sanctions. Too often, objectives are stated in generalities, with little operational usefulness. Annual objectives, such as "to improve communication" or "to improve performance," are not clear, specific, or measurable. Objectives should state quantity, quality, cost, and time—and also be verifiable. Terms and phrases such as *maximize, minimize, as soon as possible,* and *adequate* should be avoided.

Annual objectives should be compatible with employees' and managers' values and should be supported by clearly stated policies. More of something is not always better. Improved quality or reduced cost may, for example, be more important than quantity. It is important to tie rewards and sanctions to annual objectives so that employees and managers understand that achieving objectives is critical to successful strategy implementation. Clear annual objectives do not guarantee successful strategy implementation, but they do increase the likelihood that personal and organizational aims can be accomplished. Overemphasis on achieving objectives can result in undesirable conduct, such as faking the numbers, distorting the records, and letting objectives become ends in themselves. Managers must be alert to these potential problems.

TABLE 7-1   **The Stamus Company's Revenue Expectations (In $Millions)**

	2008	2009	2010
Division I Revenues	1.0	1.400	1.960
Division II Revenues	0.5	0.700	0.980
Division III Revenues	0.5	0.750	1.125
Total Company Revenues	**2.0**	**2.850**	**4.065**

Policies

Changes in a firm's strategic direction do not occur automatically. On a day-to-day basis, policies are needed to make a strategy work. Policies facilitate solving recurring problems and guide the implementation of strategy. Broadly defined, *policy* refers to specific guidelines, methods, procedures, rules, forms, and administrative practices established to support and encourage work toward stated goals. Policies are instruments for strategy implementation. Policies set boundaries, constraints, and limits on the kinds of administrative actions that can be taken to reward and sanction behavior; they clarify what can and cannot be done in pursuit of an organization's objectives. For example, Carnival's *Paradise* ship has a no smoking policy anywhere, anytime aboard ship. It is the first cruise ship to comprehensively ban smoking. Another example of corporate policy relates to surfing the Web while at work. About 40 percent of companies today do not have a formal policy preventing employees from surfing the Internet, but software is being marketed now that allows firms to monitor how, when, where, and how long various employees use the Internet at work.

Policies let both employees and managers know what is expected of them, thereby increasing the likelihood that strategies will be implemented successfully. They provide a basis for management control, allow coordination across organizational units, and reduce the amount of time managers spend making decisions. Policies also clarify what work is to be done and by whom. They promote delegation of decision making to appropriate managerial levels where various problems usually arise. Many organizations have a policy manual that serves to guide and direct behavior. Wal-Mart has a policy that it calls the "10 Foot" Rule, whereby customers can find assistance within 10 feet of anywhere in the store. This is a welcomed policy in Japan where Wal-Mart is trying to gain a foothold; 58 percent of all retailers in Japan are mom-and-pop stores and consumers historically have had to pay "top yen" rather than "discounted prices" for merchandise.

Policies can apply to all divisions and departments (for example, "We are an equal opportunity employer"). Some policies apply to a single department ("Employees in this department must take at least one training and development course each year"). Whatever their scope and form, policies serve as a mechanism for implementing strategies and obtaining objectives. Policies should be stated in writing whenever possible. They represent the means for carrying out strategic decisions. Examples of policies that support a company strategy, a divisional objective, and a departmental objective are given in Table 7-2.

Some example issues that may require a management policy are as follows:

- To offer extensive or limited management development workshops and seminars
- To centralize or decentralize employee-training activities
- To recruit through employment agencies, college campuses, and/or newspapers
- To promote from within or to hire from the outside
- To promote on the basis of merit or on the basis of seniority
- To tie executive compensation to long-term and/or annual objectives
- To offer numerous or few employee benefits
- To negotiate directly or indirectly with labor unions
- To delegate authority for large expenditures or to centrally retain this authority
- To allow much, some, or no overtime work
- To establish a high- or low-safety stock of inventory
- To use one or more suppliers
- To buy, lease, or rent new production equipment
- To greatly or somewhat stress quality control
- To establish many or only a few production standards
- To operate one, two, or three shifts
- To discourage using insider information for personal gain
- To discourage sexual harassment
- To discourage smoking at work
- To discourage insider trading
- To discourage moonlighting

TABLE 7-2   A Hierarchy of Policies

Company Strategy

Acquire a chain of retail stores to meet our sales growth and profitability objectives.

Supporting Policies

1. "All stores will be open from 8 A.M. to 8 P.M. Monday through Saturday." (This policy could increase retail sales if stores currently are open only 40 hours a week.)

2. "All stores must submit a Monthly Control Data Report." (This policy could reduce expense-to-sales ratios.)

3. "All stores must support company advertising by contributing 5 percent of their total monthly revenues for this purpose." (This policy could allow the company to establish a national reputation.)

4. "All stores must adhere to the uniform pricing guidelines set forth in the Company Handbook." (This policy could help assure customers that the company offers a consistent product in terms of price and quality in all its stores.)

Divisional Objective

Increase the division's revenues from $10 million in 2007 to $15 million in 2008.

Supporting Policies

1. "Beginning in January 2008, each one of this division's salespersons must file a weekly activity report that includes the number of calls made, the number of miles traveled, the number of units sold, the dollar volume sold, and the number of new accounts opened." (This policy could ensure that salespersons do not place too great an emphasis in certain areas.)

2. "Beginning in January 2008, this division will return to its employees 5 percent of its gross revenues in the form of a Christmas bonus." (This policy could increase employee productivity.)

3. "Beginning in January 2008, inventory levels carried in warehouses will be decreased by 30 percent in accordance with a just-in-time (JIT) manufacturing approach." (This policy could reduce production expenses and thus free funds for increased marketing efforts.)

Production Department Objective

Increase production from 20,000 units in 2007 to 30,000 units in 2008.

Supporting Policies

1. "Beginning in January 2008, employees will have the option of working up to 20 hours of overtime per week." (This policy could minimize the need to hire additional employees.)

2. "Beginning in January 2008, perfect attendance awards in the amount of $100 will be given to all employees who do not miss a workday in a given year." (This policy could decrease absenteeism and increase productivity.)

3. "Beginning in January 2008, new equipment must be leased rather than purchased." (This policy could reduce tax liabilities and thus allow more funds to be invested in modernizing production processes.)

Resource Allocation

Resource allocation is a central management activity that allows for strategy execution. In organizations that do not use a strategic-management approach to decision making, resource allocation is often based on political or personal factors. Strategic management enables resources to be allocated according to priorities established by annual objectives.

Nothing could be more detrimental to strategic management and to organizational success than for resources to be allocated in ways not consistent with priorities indicated by approved annual objectives.

All organizations have at least four types of resources that can be used to achieve desired objectives: financial resources, physical resources, human resources, and technological resources. Allocating resources to particular divisions and departments does not mean that strategies will be successfully implemented. A number of factors commonly prohibit effective resource allocation, including an overprotection of resources, too great an emphasis on short-run financial criteria, organizational politics, vague strategy targets, a reluctance to take risks, and a lack of sufficient knowledge.

Below the corporate level, there often exists an absence of systematic thinking about resources allocated and strategies of the firm. Yavitz and Newman explain why:

> Managers normally have many more tasks than they can do. Managers must allocate time and resources among these tasks. Pressure builds up. Expenses are too high. The CEO wants a good financial report for the third quarter. Strategy formulation

and implementation activities often get deferred. Today's problems soak up available energies and resources. Scrambled accounts and budgets fail to reveal the shift in allocation away from strategic needs to currently squeaking wheels.[3]

The real value of any resource allocation program lies in the resulting accomplishment of an organization's objectives. Effective resource allocation does not guarantee successful strategy implementation because programs, personnel, controls, and commitment must breathe life into the resources provided. Strategic management itself is sometimes referred to as a "resource allocation process."

Managing Conflict

Interdependency of objectives and competition for limited resources often leads to conflict. *Conflict* can be defined as a disagreement between two or more parties on one or more issues. Establishing annual objectives can lead to conflict because individuals have different expectations and perceptions, schedules create pressure, personalities are incompatible, and misunderstandings between line managers (such as production supervisors) and staff managers (such as human resource specialists) occur. For example, a collection manager's objective of reducing bad debts by 50 percent in a given year may conflict with a divisional objective to increase sales by 20 percent.

Establishing objectives can lead to conflict because managers and strategists must make trade-offs, such as whether to emphasize short-term profits or long-term growth, profit margin or market share, market penetration or market development, growth or stability, high risk or low risk, and social responsiveness or profit maximization. Conflict is unavoidable in organizations, so it is important that conflict be managed and resolved before dysfunctional consequences affect organizational performance. Conflict is not always bad. An absence of conflict can signal indifference and apathy. Conflict can serve to energize opposing groups into action and may help managers identify problems.

Various approaches for managing and resolving conflict can be classified into three categories: avoidance, defusion, and confrontation. *Avoidance* includes such actions as ignoring the problem in hopes that the conflict will resolve itself or physically separating the conflicting individuals (or groups). *Defusion* can include playing down differences between conflicting parties while accentuating similarities and common interests, compromising so that there is neither a clear winner nor loser, resorting to majority rule, appealing to a higher authority, or redesigning present positions. *Confrontation* is exemplified by exchanging members of conflicting parties so that each can gain an appreciation of the other's point of view or holding a meeting at which conflicting parties present their views and work through their differences.

Matching Structure with Strategy

VISIT THE NET

Provides software to easily draw organizational charts. You may download the SmartDraw software and use it free for 30 days. (www.smartdraw.com)

Changes in strategy often require changes in the way an organization is structured for two major reasons. First, structure largely dictates how objectives and policies will be established. For example, objectives and policies established under a geographic organizational structure are couched in geographic terms. Objectives and policies are stated largely in terms of products in an organization whose structure is based on product groups. The structural format for developing objectives and policies can significantly impact all other strategy-implementation activities.

The second major reason why changes in strategy often require changes in structure is that structure dictates how resources will be allocated. If an organization's structure is based on customer groups, then resources will be allocated in that manner. Similarly, if an organization's structure is set up along functional business lines, then resources are allocated by functional areas. Unless new or revised strategies place emphasis in the same areas as old strategies, structural reorientation commonly becomes a part of strategy implementation.

Changes in strategy lead to changes in organizational structure. Structure should be designed to facilitate the strategic pursuit of a firm and, therefore, follow strategy. Without a strategy or reasons for being (mission), companies find it difficult to design an effective structure. Chandler found a particular structure sequence to be repeated often as organizations grow and change strategy over time; this sequence is depicted in Figure 7-3.

There is no one optimal organizational design or structure for a given strategy or type of organization. What is appropriate for one organization may not be appropriate for a similar firm, although successful firms in a given industry do tend to organize themselves in a similar way. For example, consumer goods companies tend to emulate the divisional structure-by-product form of organization. Small firms tend to be functionally structured (centralized). Medium-sized firms tend to be divisionally structured (decentralized). Large firms tend to use a strategic business unit (SBU) or matrix structure. As organizations grow, their structures generally change from simple to complex as a result of concatenation, or the linking together of several basic strategies.

Numerous external and internal forces affect an organization; no firm could change its structure in response to every one of these forces, because to do so would lead to chaos. However, when a firm changes its strategy, the existing organizational structure may become ineffective. Symptoms of an ineffective organizational structure include too many levels of management, too many meetings attended by too many people, too much attention being directed toward solving interdepartmental conflicts, too large a span of control, and too many unachieved objectives. Changes in structure can facilitate strategy-implementation efforts, but changes in structure should not be expected to make a bad strategy good, to make bad managers good, or to make bad products sell.

Structure undeniably can and does influence strategy. Strategies formulated must be workable, so if a certain new strategy required massive structural changes it would not be an attractive choice. In this way, structure can shape the choice of strategies. But a more important concern is determining what types of structural changes are needed to implement new strategies and how these changes can best be accomplished. We examine this issue by focusing on seven basic types of organizational structure: functional, divisional by geographic area, divisional by product, divisional by customer, divisional process, strategic business unit (SBU), and matrix.

VISIT THE NET

Lists some items that strategy implementation must include. (www.csuchico.edu/mgmt/ strategy/module1/sld045.htm)

The Functional Structure

The most widely used structure is the functional or centralized type because this structure is the simplest and least expensive of the seven alternatives. A *functional structure* groups tasks and activities by business function, such as production/operations, marketing, finance/accounting, research and development, and management information systems. A university may structure its activities by major functions that include academic affairs, student services, alumni relations, athletics, maintenance, and accounting. Besides being

FIGURE 7-3

Chandler's Strategy-Structure Relationship

Source: Adapted from Alfred Chandler, *Strategy and Structure* (Cambridge, MA: MIT Press, 1962).

simple and inexpensive, a functional structure also promotes specialization of labor, encourages efficient use of managerial and technical talent, minimizes the need for an elaborate control system, and allows rapid decision making.

Some disadvantages of a functional structure are that it forces accountability to the top, minimizes career development opportunities, and is sometimes characterized by low employee morale, line/staff conflicts, poor delegation of authority, and inadequate planning for products and markets.

A functional structure often leads to short-term and narrow thinking that may undermine what is best for the firm as a whole. For example, the research and development department may strive to overdesign products and components to achieve technical elegance, while manufacturing may argue for low-frills products that can be mass produced more easily. Thus, communication is often not as good in a functional structure. Schein gives an example of a communication problem in a functional structure:

> The word "marketing" will mean product development to the engineer, studying customers through market research to the product manager, merchandising to the salesperson, and constant change in design to the manufacturing manager. Then when these managers try to work together, they often attribute disagreements to personalities and fail to notice the deeper, shared assumptions that vary and dictate how each function thinks.[4]

Most large companies have abandoned the functional structure in favor of decentralization and improved accountability. However, two large firms that still successfully use a functional structure are Nucor Steel, based in Charlotte, North Carolina, and Sharp, the $17 billion consumer electronics firm.

The Divisional Structure

The *divisional* or *decentralized structure* is the second most common type used by U.S. businesses. As a small organization grows, it has more difficulty managing different products and services in different markets. Some form of divisional structure generally becomes necessary to motivate employees, control operations, and compete successfully in diverse locations. The divisional structure can be organized in one of four ways: *by geographic area*, *by product* or *service*, *by customer*, or *by process*. With a divisional structure, functional activities are performed both centrally and in each separate division.

Cisco Systems recently discarded its divisional structure by customer and reorganized into a functional structure. CEO John Chambers replaced the three-customer structure based on big businesses, small businesses, and telecoms, and now the company has centralized its engineering and marketing units so that they focus on technologies such as wireless networks. Chambers says the goal was to eliminate duplication, but the change should not be viewed as a shift in strategy. Chambers's span of control in the new structure is reduced from 15 to 12 managers reporting directly to him. He continues to operate Cisco without a chief operating officer or a number-two executive.

Sun Microsystems recently reduced the number of its business units from seven to four. Kodak recently reduced its number of business units from seven by-customer divisions to five by-product divisions. As consumption patterns become increasingly similar worldwide, a by-product structure is becoming more effective than a by-customer or a by-geographic type divisional structure. In the restructuring, Kodak eliminated its global operations division and distributed those responsibilities across the new by-product divisions.

A divisional structure has some clear advantages. First and perhaps foremost, accountability is clear. That is, divisional managers can be held responsible for sales and profit levels. Because a divisional structure is based on extensive delegation of authority, managers and employees can easily see the results of their good or bad performances. As a result, employee morale is generally higher in a divisional structure than it is in a centralized structure. Other advantages of the divisional design are that it creates career development opportunities for managers, allows local control of situations, leads to a competitive climate within an organization, and allows new businesses and products to be added easily.

The divisional design is not without some limitations, however. Perhaps the most important limitation is that a divisional structure is costly, for a number of reasons. First, each division requires functional specialists who must be paid. Second, there exists some duplication of staff services, facilities, and personnel; for instance, functional specialists are also needed centrally (at headquarters) to coordinate divisional activities. Third, managers must be well qualified because the divisional design forces delegation of authority; better-qualified individuals require higher salaries. A divisional structure can also be costly because it requires an elaborate, headquarters-driven control system. Fourth, competition between divisions may become so intense that it is dysfunctional and leads to limited sharing of ideas and resources for the common good of the firm. Ghoshal and Bartlett, two leading scholars in strategic management, note the following:

> As their label clearly warns, divisions divide. The divisional model fragments companies' resources; it creates vertical communication channels that insulate business units and prevents them from sharing their strengths with one another. Consequently, the whole of the corporation is often less than the sum of its parts. A final limitation of the divisional design is that certain regions, products, or customers may sometimes receive special treatment, and it may be difficult to maintain consistent, companywide practices. Nonetheless, for most large organizations and many small firms, the advantages of a divisional structure more than offset the potential limitations.[5]

A *divisional structure by geographic area* is appropriate for organizations whose strategies need to be tailored to fit the particular needs and characteristics of customers in different geographic areas. This type of structure can be most appropriate for organizations that have similar branch facilities located in widely dispersed areas. A divisional structure by geographic area allows local participation in decision making and improved coordination within a region. Hershey Foods is an example of a company organized using the divisional by geographic region type of structure. Hershey's divisions are United States, Canada, Mexico, Brazil, and Other. Analysts contend that this type of structure may not be best for Hershey because consumption patterns for candy are quite similar worldwide. An alternative—and perhaps better—type of structure for Hershey would be divisional by product because the company produces and sells three types of products worldwide: (1) chocolate, (2) nonchocolate, and (3) grocery.

The *divisional structure by product (or services)* is most effective for implementing strategies when specific products or services need special emphasis. Also, this type of structure is widely used when an organization offers only a few products or services or when an organization's products or services differ substantially. The divisional structure allows strict control over and attention to product lines, but it may also require a more skilled management force and reduced top management control. General Motors, DuPont, and Procter & Gamble use a divisional structure by product to implement strategies. Huffy, the largest bicycle company in the world, is another firm that is highly decentralized based on a divisional-by-product structure. Based in Ohio, Huffy's divisions are the Bicycle division, the Gerry Baby Products division, the Huffy Sports division, YLC Enterprises, and Washington Inventory Service. Harry Shaw, Huffy's chairman, believes decentralization is one of the keys to Huffy's success.

Eastman Chemical established a new by-product divisional organizational structure. The company's two new divisions, Eastman Company and Voridian Company, focus on chemicals and polymers, respectively. The Eastman division focuses on coatings, adhesives, inks, and plastics, whereas the Voridian division focuses on fibers, polyethylene, and other polymers. Microsoft recently reorganized the whole corporation into three large divisions-by-product. Headed by a president, the new divisions are (1) platform products and services, (2) business, and (3) entertainment and devices. The Swiss electrical-engineering company ABB Ltd. recently scrapped its two core divisions, (1) power technologies and (2) automation technologies, and replaced them with five new divisions: (1) power products, (2) power systems, (3) automation products, (4) process automation, and (5) robotics.

When a few major customers are of paramount importance and many different services are provided to these customers, then a *divisional structure by customer* can be the most effective way to implement strategies. This structure allows an organization to cater effectively to the requirements of clearly defined customer groups. For example, book publishing companies often organize their activities around customer groups, such as colleges, secondary schools, and private commercial schools. Some airline companies have two major customer divisions: passengers and freight or cargo services. Merrill Lynch is organized into separate divisions that cater to different groups of customers, including wealthy individuals, institutional investors, and small corporations. Motorola's semiconductor chip division is also organized divisionally by customer, having three separate segments that sell to (1) the automotive and industrial market, (2) the mobile phone market, and (3) the data-networking market. The automotive and industrial segment is doing well, but the other two segments are faltering, which is a reason why Motorola is trying to divest its semiconductor operations.

A *divisional structure by process* is similar to a functional structure, because activities are organized according to the way work is actually performed. However, a key difference between these two designs is that functional departments are not accountable for profits or revenues, whereas divisional process departments are evaluated on these criteria. An example of a divisional structure by process is a manufacturing business organized into six divisions: electrical work, glass cutting, welding, grinding, painting, and foundry work. In this case, all operations related to these specific processes would be grouped under the separate divisions. Each process (division) would be responsible for generating revenues and profits. The divisional structure by process can be particularly effective in achieving objectives when distinct production processes represent the thrust of competitiveness in an industry.

The Strategic Business Unit (SBU) Structure

As the number, size, and diversity of divisions in an organization increase, controlling and evaluating divisional operations become increasingly difficult for strategists. Increases in sales often are not accompanied by similar increases in profitability. The span of control becomes too large at top levels of the firm. For example, in a large conglomerate organization composed of 90 divisions, such as ConAgra, the chief executive officer could have difficulty even remembering the first names of divisional presidents. In multidivisional organizations, an SBU structure can greatly facilitate strategy-implementation efforts. ConAgra has put its many divisions into three primary SBUs: (1) food service (restaurants), (2) retail (grocery stores), and (3) agricultural products.

The SBU structure groups similar divisions into strategic business units and delegates authority and responsibility for each unit to a senior executive who reports directly to the chief executive officer. This change in structure can facilitate strategy implementation by improving coordination between similar divisions and channeling accountability to distinct business units. In a 100-division conglomerate, the divisions could perhaps be regrouped into 10 SBUs according to certain common characteristics, such as competing in the same industry, being located in the same area, or having the same customers.

Two disadvantages of an SBU structure are that it requires an additional layer of management, which increases salary expenses. Also, the role of the group vice president is often ambiguous. However, these limitations often do not outweigh the advantages of improved coordination and accountability. Another advantage of the SBU structure is that it makes the tasks of planning and control by the corporate office more manageable.

Honeywell International reorganized its aerospace division in 2005 from a products-based structure based on engines, electronics, wheels, brakes, and so on to three strategic business units: (1) air transport and regional transport, (2) business and general aviation, and (3) defense and space. Honeywell is not shedding any businesses in this reorganization. The firm wants to simplify its interactions with customers by reducing the number of layers in its organization. Atlantic Richfield and Fairchild Industries are examples of firms that successfully use an SBU-type structure.

As illustrated in Figure 7-4, Sonoco Products Corporation, based in Hartsville, South Carolina, utilizes an SBU organizational structure. Note that Sonoco's SBUs—Industrial Products and Consumer Products—each have four autonomous divisions that have their own sales, manufacturing, R&D, finance, HRM, and MIS functions.

The Matrix Structure

A *matrix structure* is the most complex of all designs because it depends upon both vertical and horizontal flows of authority and communication (hence the term *matrix*). In contrast, functional and divisional structures depend primarily on vertical flows of authority and communication. A matrix structure can result in higher overhead because it creates more management positions. Other disadvantages of a matrix structure that contribute to overall complexity include dual lines of budget authority (a violation of the unity-of-command principle), dual sources of reward and punishment, shared authority, dual reporting channels, and a need for an extensive and effective communication system.

Despite its complexity, the matrix structure is widely used in many industries, including construction, health care, research, and defense. Some advantages of a matrix structure are that project objectives are clear, there are many channels of communication, workers can see the visible results of their work, and shutting down a project can be accomplished relatively easily. Another advantage of a matrix structure is that it facilitates the use of specialized personnel, equipment, and facilities. Functional resources are shared in a matrix structure, rather than duplicated as in a divisional structure. Individuals with a high degree of expertise can divide their time as needed among projects, and they in turn develop their own skills and competencies more than in other structures. Walt Disney Corp. relies on a matrix structure.

A typical matrix structure is illustrated in Figure 7-5. Note that the letters (A through Z[4]) refer to managers. For example, if you were manager A, you would be responsible for financial aspects of Project 1, and you would have two bosses: the Project 1 Manager on site and the CFO off site.

For a matrix structure to be effective, organizations need participative planning, training, clear mutual understanding of roles and responsibilities, excellent internal communication, and mutual trust and confidence. The matrix structure is being used more frequently by U.S. businesses because firms are pursuing strategies that add new products, customer groups, and technology to their range of activities. Out of these changes are coming

FIGURE 7-4

Sonoco Products' SBU Organizational Chart

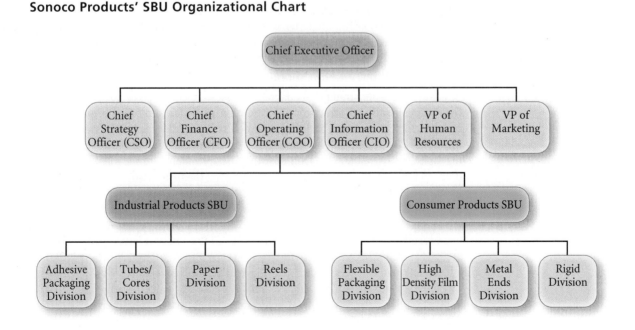

FIGURE 7-5

An Example Matrix Structure

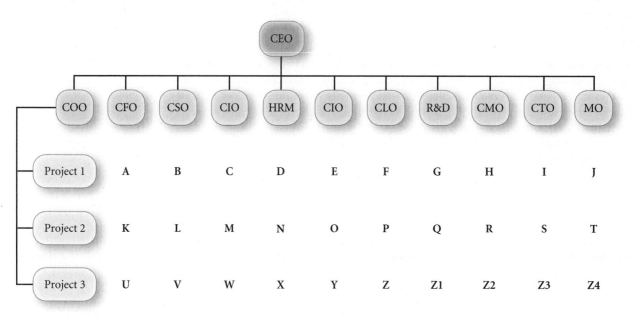

Notes: Titles spelled out as follows.

Chief Executive Officer (CEO)
Chief Finance Officer (CFO)
Chief Strategy Officer (CSO)
Chief Information Officer (CIO)
Human Resources Manager (HRM)
Chief Operating Officer (COO)
Chief Legal Officer (CLO)
Research & Development Officer (R&D)
Chief Marketing Officer (CMO)
Chief Technology Officer (CTO)
Competitive Intelligence Officer (CIO)
Maintenance Officer (MO)

product managers, functional managers, and geographic-area managers, all of whom have important strategic responsibilities. When several variables, such as product, customer, technology, geography, functional area, and line of business, have roughly equal strategic priorities, a matrix organization can be an effective structural form.

Some Do's and Don'ts in Developing Organizational Charts

Students analyzing strategic management cases are often asked to revise and develop a firm's organizational structure. This section provides some basic guidelines for this endeavor. There are some basic do's and don'ts in regard to devising or constructing organizational charts, especially for midsize to large firms. First of all, reserve the title CEO for the top executive of the firm. Don't use the title "president" for the top person; use it for the division top managers if there are divisions within the firm. Also, do not use the title "president" for functional business executives. They should have the title "chief," or "vice president," or "manager," or "officer," such as "Chief Information Officer," or "VP of Human Resources." Further, do not recommend a dual title (such as "CEO and president") for just one executive. The chairman of the board and CEO of Bristol-Myers Squibb, Peter Dolan, recently gave up his title as chairman. However, Pfizer's CEO, Jeffrey Kindler, recently added chairman of the board to his title when he succeeded Hank McKinnell as chairman of Pfizer's board. And Comverse Technology recently named Andre Dahan as its president, chief executive officer, and board director. Actually, "chairperson" is much better than "chairman" for this title.

Directly below the CEO, it is best to have a COO (chief operating officer) with any division presidents reporting directly to the COO. On the same level as the COO and also reporting to the CEO, draw in your functional business executives, such as a CFO (chief financial officer), VP of human resources, a CSO (chief strategy officer), a CIO (chief information officer), a CMO (chief marketing Officer), a VP of R&D, a VP of legal affairs, an investment relations officer, maintenance officer, and so on. Note in Figure 7-6 that these positions are labeled and placed appropriately. Note that a controller and/or treasurer would normally report to the CFO.

In developing an organizational chart, avoid having a particular person reporting to more than one person above in the chain of command. This would violate the unity-of-command principle of management that "every employee should have just one boss." Also, do not have the CFO, CIO, CSO, human resource officer, or other functional positions report to the COO. All these positions report directly to the CEO.

A key consideration in devising an organizational structure concerns the divisions. Note whether the divisions (if any) of a firm presently are established based upon geography, customer, product, or process. If the firm's organizational chart is not available, you often can devise a chart based on the titles of executives. An important case analysis activity is for you to decide how the divisions of a firm should be organized for maximum effectiveness. Even if the firm presently has no divisions, determine whether the firm would operate better with divisions. In other words, which type of divisional breakdown do you (or your group or team) feel would be best for the firm in allocating resources, establishing objectives, and devising compensation incentives? This important strategic decision faces many midsize and large firms (and teams of students analyzing a strategic-management case). As consumption patterns become more and more similar worldwide, the divisional-by-product form of structure is increasingly the most effective. Be mindful that all firms

FIGURE 7-6

Typical Top Managers of a Large Firm

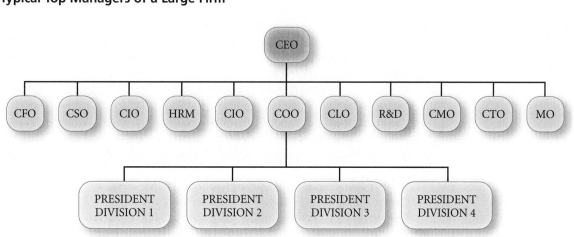

Notes: Titles spelled out as follows.

Chief Executive Officer (CEO)
Chief Finance Officer (CFO)
Chief Strategy Officer (CSO)
Chief Information Officer (CIO)
Human Resources Manager (HRM)
Chief Operating Officer (COO)
Chief Legal Officer (CLO)
Research & Development Officer (R&D)
Chief Marketing Officer (CMO)
Chief Technology Officer (CTO)
Competitive Intelligence Officer (CIO)
Maintenance Officer (MO)

have functional staff below their top executive and often readily provide this information, so be wary of concluding prematurely that a particular firm utilizes a functional structure. If you see the word "president" in the titles of executives, coupled with financial-reporting segments, such as by product or geographic region, then the firm is divisionally structured.

If the firm is large with numerous divisions, decide whether an SBU type of structure would be more appropriate to reduce the span of control reporting to the COO. Note in Figure 7-4 that the Sonoco Products' strategic business units (SBUs) are based on product groupings. An alternative SBU structure would have been to base the division groupings on location. One never knows for sure if a proposed or actual structure is indeed most effective for a particular firm. Note from Chandler's strategy-structure relationship illustrated previously in this chapter that declining financial performance signals a need for altering the structure.

Restructuring, Reengineering, and E-Engineering

Restructuring and reengineering are becoming commonplace on the corporate landscape across the United States and Europe. *Restructuring*—also called *downsizing*, *rightsizing*, or *delayering*—involves reducing the size of the firm in terms of number of employees, number of divisions or units, and number of hierarchical levels in the firm's organizational structure. This reduction in size is intended to improve both efficiency and effectiveness. Restructuring is concerned primarily with shareholder well-being rather than employee well-being.

Recessionary economic conditions have forced many European companies to downsize, laying off managers and employees. This was almost unheard of prior to the mid-1990s because European labor unions and laws required lengthy negotiations or huge severance checks before workers could be terminated. In contrast to the United States, labor union executives of large European firms sit on most boards of directors.

Job security in European companies is slowly moving toward a U.S. scenario, in which firms lay off almost at will. From banks in Milan to factories in Mannheim, European employers are starting to show people the door in an effort to streamline operations, increase efficiency, and compete against already slim and trim U.S. firms. Massive U.S.-style layoffs are still rare in Europe, but unemployment rates throughout the continent are rising quite rapidly. European firms still prefer to downsize by attrition and retirement rather than by blanket layoffs because of culture, laws, and unions.

In contrast, *reengineering* is concerned more with employee and customer well-being than shareholder well-being. Reengineering—also called process management, process innovation, or process redesign—involves reconfiguring or redesigning work, jobs, and processes for the purpose of improving cost, quality, service, and speed. Reengineering does not usually affect the organizational structure or chart, nor does it imply job loss or employee layoffs. Whereas restructuring is concerned with eliminating or establishing, shrinking or enlarging, and moving organizational departments and divisions, the focus of reengineering is changing the way work is actually carried out.

Reengineering is characterized by many tactical (short-term, business-function-specific) decisions, whereas restructuring is characterized by strategic (long-term, affecting all business functions) decisions. Developed by Motorola in 1986 and made famous by CEO Jack Welch at General Electric and more recently by Robert Nardelli, former CEO of Home Depot, *Six Sigma* is a quality-boosting process improvement technique that entails training several key persons in the firm in the techniques to monitor, measure, and improve processes and eliminate defects. Six Sigma has been widely applied across industries from retailing to financial services. CEO Dave Cote at Honeywell and CEO Jeff Immelt at General Electric spurred acceptance of Six Sigma, which aims to improve work processes and eliminate waste by training "select" employees who are given judo titles such as Master Black Belts, Black Belts, and Green Belts.

Six Sigma has been criticized in a recent *Wall Street Journal* article that cited many example firms whose stock price fell for a number of years after adoption of Six Sigma. The technique's reliance on the special group of trained employees is problematic and its use within retail firms such as Home Depot has not been as successful as in manufacturing firms.[6]

The Internet is ushering in a new wave of business transformation. No longer is it enough for companies to put up simple Web sites for customers and employees. To take full advantage of the Internet, companies must change the way they distribute goods, deal with suppliers, attract customers, and serve customers. The Internet eliminates the geographic protection/monopoly of local businesses. Basically, companies must reinvent the way they do business to take full advantage of the Internet. This whole process is being called e-engineering.[7] Dow Corning Corporation and many others have recently appointed an e-commerce top executive.

Restructuring

Firms often employ restructuring when various ratios appear out of line with competitors as determined through benchmarking exercises. Recall that *benchmarking* simply involves comparing a firm against the best firms in the industry on a wide variety of performance-related criteria. Some benchmarking ratios commonly used in rationalizing the need for restructuring are headcount-to-sales-volume, or corporate-staff-to-operating-employees, or span-of-control figures.

The primary benefit sought from restructuring is cost reduction. For some highly bureaucratic firms, restructuring can actually rescue the firm from global competition and demise. But the downside of restructuring can be reduced employee commitment, creativity, and innovation that accompanies the uncertainty and trauma associated with pending and actual employee layoffs. During 2007, Hershey Company, headquartered in Hershey, Pennsylvania, announced a three-year restructuring plan that includes 1,500 job cuts, closing certain production lines, outsourcing more activities, and building a production plant in Mexico. Hershey's financial performance of late has failed to meet Wall Street expectations.

Parent company European Aeronautic Defence & Space Company in Paris has approved a restructuring plan named Power8 for the beleaguered Airbus aircraft company. Airbus in 2007 continued to struggle to compete against rival Boeing and as part of its restructuring is cutting jobs and closing factories. But France and Germany are arguing on the best way to restructure because both countries are key underwriters of Airbus.

Another downside of restructuring is that many people today do not aspire to become managers, and many present-day managers are trying to get off the management track.[8] Sentiment against joining management ranks is higher today than ever. About 80 percent of employees say they want nothing to do with management, a major shift from just a decade ago when 60 to 70 percent hoped to become managers. Managing others historically led to enhanced career mobility, financial rewards, and executive perks; but in today's global, more competitive, restructured arena, managerial jobs demand more hours and headaches with fewer financial rewards. Managers today manage more people spread over different locations, travel more, manage diverse functions, and are change agents even when they have nothing to do with the creation of the plan or disagree with its approach. Employers today are looking for people who can do things, not for people who make other people do things. Restructuring in many firms has made a manager's job an invisible, thankless role. More workers today are self-managed, entrepreneurs, interpreneurs, or team-managed. Managers today need to be counselors, motivators, financial advisors, and psychologists. They also run the risk of becoming technologically behind in their areas of expertise. "Dilbert" cartoons commonly portray managers as enemies or as morons.

It is interesting to note that laying off employees in France is almost impossible due to labor laws that require lengthy negotiations and expensive severance packages for any individuals who are laid off. French CEOs feel that the strict layoff policies are crippling France's economy and companies. This is true because other European countries, such as Germany, have recently made it much easier for companies to lay off employees to stay competitive—and indeed to survive. Moulinex is an example of a French company that recently tried to lay off 670 employees but was denied this option, so the firm fell into bankruptcy and possible liquidation.

Reengineering

The argument for a firm engaging in reengineering usually goes as follows: Many companies historically have been organized vertically by business function. This arrangement has led over time to managers' and employees' mind-sets being defined by their particular functions rather than by overall customer service, product quality, or corporate performance. The logic is that all firms tend to bureaucratize over time. As routines become entrenched, turf becomes delineated and defended, and politics takes precedence over performance. Walls that exist in the physical workplace can be reflections of "mental" walls.

In reengineering, a firm uses information technology to break down functional barriers and create a work system based on business processes, products, or outputs rather than on functions or inputs. Cornerstones of reengineering are decentralization, reciprocal interdependence, and information sharing. A firm that exemplifies complete information sharing is Springfield Remanufacturing Corporation, which provides to all employees a weekly income statement of the firm, as well as extensive information on other companies' performances.

The *Wall Street Journal* noted that reengineering today must go beyond knocking down internal walls that keep parts of a company from cooperating effectively; it must also knock down the external walls that prohibit or discourage cooperation with other firms—even rival firms.[9] A maker of disposable diapers echoes this need differently when it says that to be successful "cooperation at the firm must stretch from stump to rump."

Hewlett-Packard is a good example of a company that has knocked down the external barriers to cooperation and practices modern reengineering. The HP of today shares its forecasts with all of its supply-chain partners and shares other critical information with its distributors and other stakeholders. HP does all the buying of resin for its many manufacturers, giving it a volume discount of up to 5 percent. HP has established many alliances and cooperative agreements of the kind discussed in Chapter 5.

A benefit of reengineering is that it offers employees the opportunity to see more clearly how their particular jobs affect the final product or service being marketed by the firm. However, reengineering can also raise manager and employee anxiety, which, unless calmed, can lead to corporate trauma.

Linking Performance and Pay to Strategies

Most companies today are practicing some form of pay-for-performance for employees and managers other than top executives. New research suggests that companies gave annual pay raises for 2007 of 3.7 percent, but performance-based pay raises and incentive bonuses are rapidly gaining in popularity.[10] About 80 percent of all companies now offer some type of bonus plan, which provides companies the flexibility to rein in costs during tight years but to share profits during abundant years. Companies are also increasingly segmenting employees based on their performance rather than job function as firms seek to attract and keep the best employees.

Staff control of pay systems often prevents line managers from using financial compensation as a strategic tool. Flexibility regarding managerial and employee compensation is needed to allow short-term shifts in compensation that can stimulate efforts to achieve long-term objectives.

How can an organization's reward system be more closely linked to strategic performance? How can decisions on salary increases, promotions, merit pay, and bonuses be more closely aligned to support the long-term strategic objectives of the organization? There are no widely accepted answers to these questions, but a dual bonus system based on both annual objectives and long-term objectives is becoming common. The percentage of a manager's annual bonus attributable to short-term versus long-term results should vary by hierarchical level in the organization. A chief executive officer's annual bonus could, for example, be determined on a 75 percent short-term and 25 percent long-term basis. It is important that bonuses not be based solely on short-term results because such a system ignores long-term company strategies and objectives.

Wal-Mart Stores in 2007 revamped its bonus program for hourly employees as the firm began paying bonuses based on sales, profit, and inventory performance at individual stores on a quarterly, rather than annual, basis. The average full-time employee at Wal-Mart in the United States is paid $10.51 per hour, but this is significantly below the $17.46 average paid to Costco Wholesale Corp. employees.[11]

Aflac, Inc. in early 2007 became the first company to give investors a nonbinding vote on executive pay starting in 2009. Shareholders at numerous other companies including Verizon, Bank of New York, and Morgan Stanley are demanding a say-so in regard to executive pay. The U.S. House of Representatives recently passed a bill to formalize this shareholder tactic, which is gaining steam across the country as a means to combat exorbitant executive pay. For example, Verizon's CEO Ivan Seidenberg's total compensation in 2006 was $21.3 million.

In an effort to cut costs and increase productivity, more and more Japanese companies are switching from seniority-based pay to performance-based approaches. Toyota has switched to a full merit system for 20,000 of its 70,000 white-collar workers. Fujitsu, Sony, Matsushita Electric Industrial, and Kao also have switched to merit pay systems. This switching is hurting morale at some Japanese companies, which have trained workers for decades to cooperate rather than to compete and to work in groups rather than individually.

Richard Brown, CEO of Electronic Data Systems (EDS), recently removed the bottom 20 percent of EDS's sales force and said,

> You have to start with an appraisal system that gives genuine feedback and differentiates performance. Some call it ranking people. That seems a little harsh. But you can't have a manager checking a box that says you're either stupendous, magnificent, very good, good, or average. Concise, constructive feedback is the fuel workers use to get better. A company that doesn't differentiate performance risks losing its best people.[12]

Profit sharing is another widely used form of incentive compensation. More than 30 percent of U.S. companies have profit sharing plans, but critics emphasize that too many factors affect profits for this to be a good criterion. Taxes, pricing, or an acquisition would wipe out profits, for example. Also, firms try to minimize profits in a sense to reduce taxes.

Still another criterion widely used to link performance and pay to strategies is gain sharing. *Gain sharing* requires employees or departments to establish performance targets; if actual results exceed objectives, all members get bonuses. More than 26 percent of U.S. companies use some form of gain sharing; about 75 percent of gain sharing plans have been adopted since 1980. Carrier, a subsidiary of United Technologies, has had excellent success with gain sharing in its six plants in Syracuse, New York; Firestone's tire plant in Wilson, North Carolina, has experienced similar success with gain sharing.

Criteria such as sales, profit, production efficiency, quality, and safety could also serve as bases for an effective *bonus system*. If an organization meets certain understood, agreed-upon profit objectives, every member of the enterprise should share in the harvest. A bonus system can be an effective tool for motivating individuals to support strategy-implementation efforts. BankAmerica, for example, recently overhauled its incentive system to link pay to sales of the bank's most profitable products and services. Branch managers receive a base salary plus a bonus based both on the number of new customers and on sales of bank products. Every employee in each branch is also eligible for a bonus if the branch exceeds its goals. Thomas Peterson, a top BankAmerica executive, says, "We want to make people responsible for meeting their goals, so we pay incentives on sales, not on controlling costs or on being sure the parking lot is swept."

Five tests are often used to determine whether a performance-pay plan will benefit an organization:

1. ***Does the plan capture attention?*** Are people talking more about their activities and taking pride in early successes under the plan?
2. ***Do employees understand the plan?*** Can participants explain how it works and what they need to do to earn the incentive?

3. ***Is the plan improving communication?*** Do employees know more than they used to about the company's mission, plans, and objectives?
4. ***Does the plan pay out when it should?*** Are incentives being paid for desired results—and being withheld when objectives are not met?
5. ***Is the company or unit performing better?*** Are profits up? Has market share grown? Have gains resulted in part from the incentives?[13]

In addition to a dual bonus system, a combination of reward strategy incentives, such as salary raises, stock options, fringe benefits, promotions, praise, recognition, criticism, fear, increased job autonomy, and awards, can be used to encourage managers and employees to push hard for successful strategic implementation. The range of options for getting people, departments, and divisions to actively support strategy-implementation activities in a particular organization is almost limitless. Merck, for example, recently gave each of its 37,000 employees a 10-year option to buy 100 shares of Merck stock at a set price of $127. Steven Darien, Merck's vice president of human resources, says, "We needed to find ways to get everyone in the workforce on board in terms of our goals and objectives. Company executives will begin meeting with all Merck workers to explore ways in which employees can contribute more."

Increasing criticism aimed at chief executive officers for their high pay has resulted in executive compensation being linked more closely than ever before to performance of their firms. Although the linkage between CEO pay and corporate performance is getting closer, CEO pay still can be astronomical. However, CEO Gerald Grinstein of Delta Airlines in 2007 agreed to accept no stock or cash bonus when his firm emerged from bankruptcy to be the second-largest U.S. airline in stock-market value, behind Southwest Airlines. In contrast among large U.S. banks, CEO Kenneth Lewis of Bank of America received pay of $27.9 million in 2006, CEO Charles Prince of Citigroup received $26 million, and CEO Kennedy Thompson of Wachovia received $23.8 million. But Yahoo's CEO Terry Semel made $71.7 million in 2006 and was the highest paid CEO, followed by XTO Energy CEO Bob Simpson, who made $59.5 million, and Occidental Petroleum CEO Ray Irani, who made $52.8 million.

Managing Resistance to Change

No organization or individual can escape change. But the thought of change raises anxieties because people fear economic loss, inconvenience, uncertainty, and a break in normal social patterns. Almost any change in structure, technology, people, or strategies has the potential to disrupt comfortable interaction patterns. For this reason, people resist change. The strategic-management process itself can impose major changes on individuals and processes. Reorienting an organization to get people to think and act strategically is not an easy task.

Resistance to change can be considered the single greatest threat to successful strategy implementation. Resistance regularly occurs in organizations in the form of sabotaging production machines, absenteeism, filing unfounded grievances, and an unwillingness to cooperate. People often resist strategy implementation because they do not understand what is happening or why changes are taking place. In that case, employees may simply need accurate information. Successful strategy implementation hinges upon managers' ability to develop an organizational climate conducive to change. Change must be viewed as an opportunity rather than as a threat by managers and employees.

Resistance to change can emerge at any stage or level of the strategy-implementation process. Although there are various approaches for implementing changes, three commonly used strategies are a force change strategy, an educative change strategy, and a rational or self-interest change strategy. A *force change strategy* involves giving orders and enforcing those orders; this strategy has the advantage of being fast, but it is plagued by low commitment and high resistance. The *educative change strategy* is one that presents information to convince people of the need for change; the disadvantage of an educative change strategy is that implementation becomes slow and difficult. However, this type of strategy evokes greater commitment and less resistance than does the force change strategy.

Finally, a *rational* or *self-interest change strategy* is one that attempts to convince individuals that the change is to their personal advantage. When this appeal is successful, strategy implementation can be relatively easy. However, implementation changes are seldom to everyone's advantage.

The rational change strategy is the most desirable, so this approach is examined a bit further. Managers can improve the likelihood of successfully implementing change by carefully designing change efforts. Jack Duncan described a rational or self-interest change strategy as consisting of four steps. First, employees are invited to participate in the process of change and in the details of transition; participation allows everyone to give opinions, to feel a part of the change process, and to identify their own self-interests regarding the recommended change. Second, some motivation or incentive to change is required; self-interest can be the most important motivator. Third, communication is needed so that people can understand the purpose for the changes. Giving and receiving feedback is the fourth step: everyone enjoys knowing how things are going and how much progress is being made.[14]

Igor Ansoff summarized the need for strategists to manage resistance to change as follows:

> Observation of the historical transitions from one orientation to another shows that, if left unmanaged, the process becomes conflict-laden, prolonged, and costly in both human and financial terms. Management of resistance involves anticipating the focus of resistance and its intensity. Second, it involves eliminating unnecessary resistance caused by misperceptions and insecurities. Third, it involves mustering the power base necessary to assure support for the change. Fourth, it involves planning the process of change. Finally, it involves monitoring and controlling resistance during the process of change.[15]

Because of diverse external and internal forces, change is a fact of life in organizations. The rate, speed, magnitude, and direction of changes vary over time by industry and organization. Strategists should strive to create a work environment in which change is recognized as necessary and beneficial so that individuals can more easily adapt to change. Adopting a strategic-management approach to decision making can itself require major changes in the philosophy and operations of a firm.

Strategists can take a number of positive actions to minimize managers' and employees' resistance to change. For example, individuals who will be affected by a change should be involved in the decision to make the change and in decisions about how to implement the change. Strategists should anticipate changes and develop and offer training and development workshops so that managers and employees can adapt to those changes. They also need to effectively communicate the need for changes. The strategic-management process can be described as a process of managing change. Robert Waterman describes how successful organizations involve individuals to facilitate change:

> Implementation starts with, not after, the decision. When Ford Motor Company embarked on the program to build the highly successful Taurus, management gave up the usual, sequential design process. Instead it showed the tentative design to the workforce and asked its help in devising a car that would be easy to build. Team Taurus came up with no less than 1,401 items suggested by Ford employees. What a contrast from the secrecy that characterized the industry before. When people are treated as the main engine rather than interchangeable parts, motivation, creativity, quality, and commitment to implementation go up.[16]

Organizational change should be viewed today as a continuous process rather than as a project or event. The most successful organizations today continuously adapt to changes in the competitive environment, which themselves continue to change at an accelerating rate. It is not sufficient today to simply react to change. Managers need to anticipate change and ideally be the creator of change. Viewing change as a continuous process is in stark contrast to an old management doctrine regarding change, which was to unfreeze behavior, change the behavior, and then refreeze the new behavior. The new "continuous organizational change" philosophy should mirror the popular "continuous quality improvement philosophy."

Managing the Natural Environment

All business functions are affected by natural environment considerations or by striving to make a profit. However, both employees and consumers are especially resentful of firms that take from more than give to the natural environment; likewise, people today are especially appreciative of firms that conduct operations in a way that mend rather than harm the environment. But a rapidly increasing number of companies are implementing tougher environmental regulation because it makes economic sense. General Electric, for example, plans to achieve $20 billion in sales by 2010 in eco-friendly technologies that include cleaner coal-fired power plants, a diesel-and-electric hybrid locomotive, and agricultural silicon that cuts the amount of water and pesticide used in spraying fields. This is double GE's sales today in "green" products.[17] GE has a goal to improve its energy efficiency by 30 percent between 2005 and 2012.

Earth itself has become a stakeholder for all business firms. Consumer interest in businesses preserving nature's ecological balance and fostering a clean, healthy environment is high. As indicated in the "Natural Environment Perspective," an increasing number of businesses today are considering the amount of formal training in environmental matters that prospective managers have received.

The ecological challenge facing all organizations requires managers to formulate strategies that preserve and conserve natural resources and control pollution. Special natural environment issues include ozone depletion, global warming, depletion of rain forests, destruction of animal habitats, protecting endangered species, developing biodegradable products and packages, waste management, clean air, clean water, erosion, destruction of natural resources, and pollution control. Firms increasingly are developing green product lines that are biodegradable and/or are made from recycled products. Green products sell well.

The Environmental Protection Agency recently reported that U.S. citizens and organizations annually spend more than about $200 billion on pollution abatement. Environmental concerns touch all aspects of a business's operations, including workplace risk exposures, packaging, waste reduction, energy use, alternative fuels, environmental cost accounting, and recycling practices.

Managing as if Earth matters requires an understanding of how international trade, competitiveness, and global resources are connected. Managing environmental affairs can no longer be simply a technical function performed by specialists in a firm; more emphasis must be placed on developing an environmental perspective among all employees and managers of the firm. Many companies are moving environmental affairs from the staff side of the organization to the line side, thus making the corporate environmental group report directly to the chief operating officer.

Societies have been plagued by environmental disasters to such an extent recently that firms failing to recognize the importance of environmental issues and challenges could suffer severe consequences. Managing environmental affairs can no longer be an incidental or secondary function of company operations. Product design, manufacturing, and ultimate disposal should not merely reflect environmental considerations, but also be driven by them. Firms that manage environmental affairs will enhance relations with consumers, regulators, vendors, and other industry players—substantially improving their prospects of success.

Firms should formulate and implement strategies from an environmental perspective. Environmental strategies could include developing or acquiring green businesses, divesting or altering environment-damaging businesses, striving to become a low-cost producer through waste minimization and energy conservation, and pursuing a differentiation strategy through green-product features. In addition to creating strategies, firms could include an environmental representative on the board of directors, conduct regular envrionmental audits, implement bonuses for favorable environmental results, become involved in environmental issues and programs, incorporate environmental values in mission statements, establish environmentally oriented objectives, acquire environmental skills, and provide environmental training programs for company employees and managers.

NATURAL ENVIRONMENT PERSPECTIVE
In Hiring, Do Companies Consider Environmental Training of Students?

The *Wall Street Journal* reports that companies actively consider environmental training in employees they hire. A recent study reported that 77 percent of corporate recruiters said "it is important to hire students with an awareness of social and environmental responsibility." According to Ford Motor Company's director of corporate governance, "We want students who will help us find solutions to societal challenges and we have trouble hiring students with such skills" (Alsop, 2001). The Aspen Institute contends that most business schools currently do not, but should, incorporate environmental training in all facets of their core curriculum, not just in special elective courses. The Institute reports that the University of Texas, the University of North Carolina, and the University of Michigan, among others, are at the cutting edge in providing environmental coverage at their respective MBA levels. Companies today do consider business schools with the best environmental programs to prepare students more effectively for the business world; companies favor hiring graduates from these universities.

Findings from research suggest that business schools at the undergraduate level are doing a poor job of educating students on environmental issues. Because business students with limited knowledge on environmental issues may make poor decisions, business schools should address environmental issues more in their curricula. Failure to do so could result in graduates making inappropriate business decisions in regard to the natural environment. Failing to provide adequate coverage of natural environment issues and decisions in their training could make those students less attractive to employers than graduates from other universities.

Sources: Adapted from R. Alsop, "Corporations Still Put Profits First, But Social Concerns Gain Ground," *Wall Street Journal* (2001): B14, Jane Kim, "Business Schools Take a Page from Kinder, Gentler Textbook," *Wall Street Journal* (October 22, 2003): B2C; and Beth Gardner, "Business Schools Going Green," *Wall Street Journal* (June 6, 2007): B5A.

Source: Tom Watson

Creating a Strategy-Supportive Culture

Strategists should strive to preserve, emphasize, and build upon aspects of an existing *culture* that support proposed new strategies. Aspects of an existing culture that are antagonistic to a proposed strategy should be identified and changed. Substantial research indicates that new strategies are often market-driven and dictated by competitive forces. For this reason, changing a firm's culture to fit a new strategy is usually more effective than changing a strategy to fit an existing culture. Numerous techniques are available to alter an organization's culture, including recruitment, training, transfer, promotion, restructure of an organization's design, role modeling, and positive reinforcement.

Jack Duncan described *triangulation* as an effective, multi-method technique for studying and altering a firm's culture.[18] Triangulation includes the combined use of obtrusive observation, self-administered questionnaires, and personal interviews to determine the nature of a firm's culture. The process of triangulation reveals changes that need to be made to a firm's culture to benefit strategy.

Schein indicated that the following elements are most useful in linking culture to strategy:

1. Formal statements of organizational philosophy, charters, creeds, materials used for recruitment and selection, and socialization
2. Designing of physical spaces, facades, buildings
3. Deliberate role modeling, teaching, and coaching by leaders
4. Explicit reward and status system, promotion criteria
5. Stories, legends, myths, and parables about key people and events
6. What leaders pay attention to, measure, and control
7. Leader reactions to critical incidents and organizational crises
8. How the organization is designed and structured
9. Organizational systems and procedures
10. Criteria used for recruitment, selection, promotion, leveling off, retirement, and "excommunication" of people[19]

In the personal and religious side of life, the impact of loss and change is easy to see.[20] Memories of loss and change often haunt individuals and organizations for years. Ibsen wrote, "Rob the average man of his life illusion and you rob him of his happiness at the same stroke."[21] When attachments to a culture are severed in an organization's attempt to change direction, employees and managers often experience deep feelings of grief. This phenomenon commonly occurs when external conditions dictate the need for a new strategy. Managers and employees often struggle to find meaning in a situation that changed many years before. Some people find comfort in memories; others find solace in the present. Weak linkages between strategic management and organizational culture can jeopardize performance and success. Deal and Kennedy emphasized that making strategic changes in an organization always threatens a culture:

> People form strong attachments to heroes, legends, the rituals of daily life, the hoopla of extravaganza and ceremonies, and all the symbols of the workplace. Change strips relationships and leaves employees confused, insecure, and often angry. Unless something can be done to provide support for transitions from old to new, the force of a culture can neutralize and emasculate strategy changes.[22]

The Mexican Culture

Mexico always has been and still is an authoritarian society in terms of schools, churches, businesses, and families. Employers seek workers who are agreeable, respectful, and obedient, rather than innovative, creative, and independent. Mexican workers tend to be activity oriented rather than problem solvers. When visitors walk into a Mexican business, they are impressed by the cordial, friendly atmosphere. This is almost always true because Mexicans desire harmony rather than conflict; desire for harmony is part of the social fabric in worker–manager relations. There is a much lower tolerance for adversarial relations or friction at work in Mexico as compared to the United States.

VISIT THE NET

Provides nice information on "What Is Culture" and also provides additional excellent links to other culture sites. (http://www.managementhelp.org/org_thry/culture/culture.htm)

Mexican employers are paternalistic, providing workers with more than a paycheck, but in return they expect allegiance. Weekly food baskets, free meals, free bus service, and free day care are often part of compensation. The ideal working condition for a Mexican worker is the family model, with people all working together, doing their share, according to their designated roles. Mexican workers do not expect or desire a work environment in which self-expression and initiative are encouraged. Whereas U.S. business embodies individualism, achievement, competition, curiosity, pragmatism, informality, spontaneity, and doing more than expected on the job, Mexican businesses stress collectivism, continuity, cooperation, belongingness, formality, and doing exactly what you're told.

In Mexico, business associates rarely entertain each other at their homes, which are places reserved exclusively for close friends and family. Business meetings and entertaining are nearly always done at a restaurant. Preserving one's honor, saving face, and looking important are also exceptionally important in Mexico. This is why Mexicans do not accept criticism and change easily; many find it humiliating to acknowledge having made a mistake. A meeting among employees and managers in a business located in Mexico is a forum for giving orders and directions rather than for discussing problems or participating in decision making. Mexican workers want to be closely supervised, cared for, and corrected in a civil manner. Opinions expressed by employees are often regarded as back talk in Mexico. Mexican supervisors are viewed as weak if they explain the rationale for their orders to workers.

Mexicans do not feel compelled to follow rules that are not associated with a particular person in authority they work for or know well. Thus, signs to wear earplugs or safety glasses, or attendance or seniority policies, and even one-way street signs are often ignored. Whereas Americans follow the rules, Mexicans often do not.

Life is slower in Mexico than in the United States. The first priority is often assigned to the last request, rather than to the first. Telephone systems break down. Banks may suddenly not have pesos. Phone repair can take months. Electricity for an entire plant or town can be down for hours or even days. Business and government offices open and close at different hours. Buses and taxis may be hours off schedule. Meeting times for appointments are not rigid. Tardiness is common everywhere. Effectively doing business in Mexico requires knowledge of the Mexican way of life, culture, beliefs, and customs.

The Japanese Culture

The Japanese place great importance upon group loyalty and consensus, a concept called *Wa*. Nearly all corporate activities in Japan encourage *Wa* among managers and employees. *Wa* requires that all members of a group agree and cooperate; this results in constant discussion and compromise. Japanese managers evaluate the potential attractiveness of alternative business decisions in terms of the long-term effect on the group's *Wa*. This is why silence, used for pondering alternatives, can be a plus in a formal Japanese meeting. Discussions potentially disruptive to *Wa* are generally conducted in very informal settings, such as at a bar, so as to minimize harm to the group's *Wa*. Entertaining is an important business activity in Japan because it strengthens *Wa*. Formal meetings are often conducted in informal settings. When confronted with disturbing questions or opinions, Japanese managers tend to remain silent, whereta tend to respond directly, defending themselves through explanation and argument.

Note in the "Global Perspective" that when negotiating orally with Japanese executives, one must periodically allow for a time of silence and must not ask, "How was your weekend?" which could be viewed as intrusive.

Most Japanese managers are reserved, quiet, distant, introspective, and other oriented, whereas most U.S. managers are talkative, insensitive, impulsive, direct, and individual oriented. Americans often perceive Japanese managers as wasting time and carrying on pointless conversations, whereas U.S. managers often use blunt criticism, ask prying questions, and make quick decisions. These kinds of cultural differences have disrupted many potentially productive Japanese–American business endeavors. Viewing the Japanese communication style as a prototype for all Asian cultures is a stereotype that must be avoided.

GLOBAL PERSPECTIVE
American versus Foreign Communication Differences

As Americans increasingly interact with managers in other countries, it is important to be sensitive to foreign business cultures. Americans too often come across as intrusive, manipulative, and garrulous, and this impression reduces their effectiveness in communication. *Forbes* recently provided the following cultural hints from Charis Intercultural Training:

1. Italians, Germans, and French generally do not soften up executives with praise before they criticize. Americans do soften up folks, and this practice seems manipulative to Europeans.
2. Israelis are accustomed to fast-paced meetings and have little patience for American informality and small talk.
3. British executives often complain that American executives chatter too much. Informality, egalitarianism, and spontaneity from Americans in business settings jolt many foreigners.

4. Europeans feel they are being treated like children when asked to wear name tags by Americans.
5. Executives in India are used to interrupting one another. Thus, when American executives listen without asking for clarification or posing questions, they are viewed by Indians as not paying attention.
6. When negotiating orally with Malaysian or Japanese executives, it is appropriate to periodically allow for a time of silence. However, no pause is needed when negotiating in Israel.

Refrain from asking foreign managers questions such as "How was your weekend?" That is intrusive to foreigners, who tend to regard their business and private lives as totally separate.

Source: Adapted from Lalita Khosla, "You Say Tomato," *Forbes* (May 21, 2001): 36.

Outside the Glass Factory In Murano/Venice, Italy.
Source: Donald A Hoffend

Americans have more freedom to control their own fates than do the Japanese. Life in the United States and life in Japan are very different; the United States offers more upward mobility to its people. This is a great strength of the United States. Sherman explained:

America is not like Japan and can never be. America's strength is the opposite: It opens its doors and brings the world's disorder in. It tolerates social change that would tear most other societies apart. This openness encourages Americans to adapt as individuals rather than as a group. Americans go west to California to get a new start; they move east to Manhattan to try to make the big time; they move to Vermont or to a farm to get close to the soil. They break away from their parents' religions or values or class; they rediscover their ethnicity. They go to night school; they change their names.[23]

Production/Operations Concerns When Implementing Strategies

Production/operations capabilities, limitations, and policies can significantly enhance or inhibit the attainment of objectives. Production processes typically constitute more than 70 percent of a firm's total assets. A major part of the strategy-implementation process takes place at the production site. Production-related decisions on plant size, plant location, product design, choice of equipment, kind of tooling, size of inventory, inventory control, quality control, cost control, use of standards, job specialization, employee training, equipment and resource utilization, shipping and packaging, and technological innovation can have a dramatic impact on the success or failure of strategy-implementation efforts.

Examples of adjustments in production systems that could be required to implement various strategies are provided in Table 7-3 for both for-profit and nonprofit organizations. For instance, note that when a bank formulates and selects a strategy to add 10 new branches, a production-related implementation concern is site location. The largest bicycle company in the United States, Huffy, recently ended its own production of bikes and now contracts out those services to Asian and Mexican manufacturers. Huffy focuses instead on the design, marketing, and distribution of bikes, but it no longer produces bikes itself. The Dayton, Ohio, company closed its plants in Ohio, Missouri, and Mississippi.

Just-in-time (JIT) production approaches have withstood the test of time. JIT significantly reduces the costs of implementing strategies. With JIT, parts and materials are delivered to a production site just as they are needed, rather than being stockpiled as a hedge against later deliveries. Harley-Davidson reports that at one plant alone, JIT freed $22 million previously tied up in inventory and greatly reduced reorder lead time.

Factors that should be studied before locating production facilities include the availability of major resources, the prevailing wage rates in the area, transportation costs related to shipping and receiving, the location of major markets, political risks in the area or country, and the availability of trainable employees.

For high-technology companies, production costs may not be as important as production flexibility because major product changes can be needed often. Industries such as biogenetics and plastics rely on production systems that must be flexible enough to allow frequent changes and the rapid introduction of new products. An article in the *Harvard Business Review* explained why some organizations get into trouble:

They too slowly realize that a change in product strategy alters the tasks of a production system. These tasks, which can be stated in terms of requirements for cost, product flexibility, volume flexibility, product performance, and product consistency,

TABLE 7-3 Production Management and Strategy Implementation

Type of Organization	Strategy Being Implemented	Production System Adjustments
Hospital	Adding a cancer center (ProductDevelopment)	Purchase specialized equipment and add specialized people.
Bank	Adding 10 new branches (Market Development)	Perform site location analysis.
Beer brewery	Purchasing a barley farm operation (Backward Integration)	Revise the inventory control system.
Steel manufacturer	Acquiring a fast-food chain (Unrelated Diversification)	Improve the quality control system.
Computer company	Purchasing a retail distribution chain (Forward Integration)	Alter the shipping, packaging, and transportation systems.

determine which manufacturing policies are appropriate. As strategies shift over time, so must production policies covering the location and scale of manufacturing facilities, the choice of manufacturing process, the degree of vertical integration of each manufacturing facility, the use of R&D units, the control of the production system, and the licensing of technology.[24]

A common management practice, cross-training of employees, can facilitate strategy implementation and can yield many benefits. Employees gain a better understanding of the whole business and can contribute better ideas in planning sessions. Production/operations managers need to realize, however, that cross-training employees can create problems related to the following issues:

1. It can thrust managers into roles that emphasize counseling and coaching over directing and enforcing.
2. It can necessitate substantial investments in training and incentives.
3. It can be very time-consuming.
4. Skilled workers may resent unskilled workers who learn their jobs.
5. Older employees may not want to learn new skills.

Human Resource Concerns When Implementing Strategies

The job of human resource manager is changing rapidly as companies continue to downsize and reorganize. Strategic responsibilities of the human resource manager include assessing the staffing needs and costs for alternative strategies proposed during strategy formulation and developing a staffing plan for effectively implementing strategies. This plan must consider how best to manage spiraling health care insurance costs. Employers' health coverage expenses consume an average 26 percent of firms' net profits, even though most companies now require employees to pay part of their health insurance premiums. The plan must also include how to motivate employees and managers during a time when layoffs are common and workloads are high.

The human resource department must develop performance incentives that clearly link performance and pay to strategies. The process of empowering managers and employees through their involvement in strategic-management activities yields the greatest benefits when all organizational members understand clearly how they will benefit personally if the firm does well. Linking company and personal benefits is a major new strategic responsibility of human resource managers. Other new responsibilities for human resource managers may include establishing and administering an *employee stock ownership plan (ESOP)*, instituting an effective child-care policy, and providing leadership for managers and employees in a way that allows them to balance work and family.

A well-designed strategic-management system can fail if insufficient attention is given to the human resource dimension. Human resource problems that arise when businesses implement strategies can usually be traced to one of three causes: (1) disruption of social and political structures, (2) failure to match individuals' aptitudes with implementation tasks, and (3) inadequate top management support for implementation activities.[25]

Strategy implementation poses a threat to many managers and employees in an organization. New power and status relationships are anticipated and realized. New formal and informal groups' values, beliefs, and priorities may be largely unknown. Managers and employees may become engaged in resistance behavior as their roles, prerogatives, and power in the firm change. Disruption of social and political structures that accompany strategy execution must be anticipated and considered during strategy formulation and managed during strategy implementation.

A concern in matching managers with strategy is that jobs have specific and relatively static responsibilities, although people are dynamic in their personal development. Commonly used methods that match managers with strategies to be implemented include transferring managers, developing leadership workshops, offering career development activities, promotions, job enlargement, and job enrichment.

A number of other guidelines can help ensure that human relationships facilitate rather than disrupt strategy-implementation efforts. Specifically, managers should do a lot of chatting and informal questioning to stay abreast of how things are progressing and to know when to intervene. Managers can build support for strategy-implementation efforts by giving few orders, announcing few decisions, depending heavily on informal questioning, and seeking to probe and clarify until a consensus emerges. Key thrusts that succeed should be rewarded generously and visibly.

It is surprising that so often during strategy formulation, individual values, skills, and abilities needed for successful strategy implementation are not considered. It is rare that a firm selecting new strategies or significantly altering existing strategies possesses the right line and staff personnel in the right positions for successful strategy implementation. The need to match individual aptitudes with strategy-implementation tasks should be considered in strategy choice.

Inadequate support from strategists for implementation activities often undermines organizational success. Chief executive officers, small business owners, and government agency heads must be personally committed to strategy implementation and express this commitment in highly visible ways. Strategists' formal statements about the importance of strategic management must be consistent with actual support and rewards given for activities completed and objectives reached. Otherwise, stress created by inconsistency can cause uncertainty among managers and employees at all levels.

Perhaps the best method for preventing and overcoming human resource problems in strategic management is to actively involve as many managers and employees as possible in the process. Although time-consuming, this approach builds understanding, trust, commitment, and ownership and reduces resentment and hostility. The true potential of strategy formulation and implementation resides in people.

Employee Stock Ownership Plans (ESOPs)

An *ESOP* is a tax-qualified, defined-contribution, employee-benefit plan whereby employees purchase stock of the company through borrowed money or cash contributions. ESOPs empower employees to work as owners; this is a primary reason why the number of ESOPs have grown dramatically to more than 10,000 firms covering more than 10 million employees. ESOPs now control more than $600 billion in corporate stock in the United States.

Besides reducing worker alienation and stimulating productivity, ESOPs allow firms other benefits, such as substantial tax savings. Principal, interest, and dividend payments on ESOP-funded debt are tax deductible. Banks lend money to ESOPs at interest rates below prime. This money can be repaid in pretax dollars, lowering the debt service as much as 30 percent in some cases. "The ownership culture really makes a difference, when management is a facilitator, not a dictator," says Corey Rosen, executive director of the National Center for Employee Ownership. The eight largest 100 percent employee-owned U.S. companies are listed in Table 7-4. Tribune, owner of the *Chicago Tribune, Los Angeles Times,* Chicago Cubs, 13 newspapers, and more, will join the ESOP list of firms in Table 7-4 in 2008.

TABLE 7-4 **The Eight Largest ESOP Firms in the USA in 2007**

Firm	Headquarters Location	Industry	Number of Employees
Publix Supermarkets	Lakeland, FL	Supermarkets	136,000
Science Applications	San Diego, CA	R&D and computers	43,000
Price Chopper	Schenectady, NY	Supermarkets	22,000
Lifetouch	Minneapolis, MN	Photography	18,000
Nypro	Clinton, MA	Plastics mfg.	13,000
Parsons	Pasadena, CA	Engineering	10,000
Houchens Industries	Bowling Green, KY	Supermarkets	9,300
Amsted Industries	Chicago, IL	Industrial mfg.	9,100

Source: Adapted from Edward Iwata, "ESOPs Can Offer Both Upsides, Drawbacks," *USA Today* (April 3, 2007): 2B.

If an ESOP owns more than 50 percent of the firm, those who lend money to the ESOP are taxed on only 50 percent of the income received on the loans. ESOPs are not for every firm, however, because the initial legal, accounting, actuarial, and appraisal fees to set up an ESOP are about $50,000 for a small or midsized firm, with annual administration expenses of about $15,000. Analysts say ESOPs also do not work well in firms that have fluctuating payrolls and profits. Human resource managers in many firms conduct preliminary research to determine the desirability of an ESOP, and then they facilitate its establishment and administration if benefits outweigh the costs.

Wyatt Cafeterias, a southwestern United States operator of 120 cafeterias, also adopted the ESOP concept to prevent a hostile takeover. Employee productivity at Wyatt greatly increased since the ESOP began, as illustrated in the following quote:

> The key employee in our entire organization is the person serving the customer on the cafeteria line. In the past, because of high employee turnover and entry-level wages for many line jobs, these employees received far less attention and recognition than managers. We now tell the tea cart server, "You own the place. Don't wait for the manager to tell you how to do your job better or how to provide better service. You take care of it." Sure, we're looking for productivity increases, but since we began pushing decisions down to the level of people who deal directly with customers, we've discovered an awesome side effect—suddenly the work crews have this "happy to be here" attitude that the customers really love.[26]

Balancing Work Life and Home Life

Work/family strategies have become so popular among companies today that the strategies now represent a competitive advantage for those firms that offer such benefits as elder care assistance, flexible scheduling, job sharing, adoption benefits, an on-site summer camp, employee help lines, pet care, and even lawn service referrals. New corporate titles such as work/life coordinator and director of diversity are becoming common.

Working Mother magazine annually published its listing of "The 100 Best Companies for Working Mothers" (www.workingmother.com). Three especially important variables used in the ranking were availability of flextime, advancement opportunities, and equitable distribution of benefits among companies. Other important criteria are compressed weeks, telecommuting, job sharing, childcare facilities, maternity leave for both parents, mentoring, career development, and promotion for women. *Working Mother's* top 10 best companies for working women in 2007 are provided in Table 7-5. *Working Mother* also conducts extensive research to determine the best U.S. firms for women of color.

Human resource managers need to foster a more effective balancing of professional and private lives because nearly 60 million people in the United States are now part of two-career families. A corporate objective to become more lean and mean must today include consideration for the fact that a good home life contributes immensely to a good work life.

TABLE 7-5 **The 10 Best Firms for Women to Work for in 2007**

1.	Abbott
2.	Bon Secours Richmond Health System
3.	Ernst & Young
4.	HSBC—North America
5.	IBM
6.	JPMorgan Chase
7.	Patagonia
8.	PricewaterhouseCoopers
9.	Principal Financial Group
10.	S. C. Johnson & Son

Source: Adapted from www.workingmother.com (2007).

The work/family issue is no longer just a women's issue. Some specific measures that firms are taking to address this issue are providing spouse relocation assistance as an employee benefit; providing company resources for family recreational and educational use; establishing employee country clubs, such as those at IBM and Bethlehem Steel; and creating family/work interaction opportunities. A study by Joseph Pleck of Wheaton College found that in companies that do not offer paternity leave for fathers as a benefit, most men take short, informal paternity leaves anyway by combining vacation time and sick days.

Some organizations have developed family days, when family members are invited into the workplace, taken on plant or office tours, dined by management, and given a chance to see exactly what other family members do each day. Family days are inexpensive and increase the employee's pride in working for the organization. Flexible working hours during the week are another human resource response to the need for individuals to balance work life and home life. The work/family topic is being made part of the agenda at meetings and thus is being discussed in many organizations.

There are now nine Fortune 500 companies with female CEOs, and four of the nine outperformed the S&P Index in 2006. Two very large firms, Archer Daniels Midland and PepsiCo, in 2006 promoted women to the position of CEO, Patricia Woertz and Indra Nooyi, respectively. eBay in 2006 became a Fortune 500 firm and its CEO, Meg Whitman, has for many years led that firm to excellence. Patricia Russ, CEO of Lucent Technologies, was selected to be CEO of Alcatel-Lucent, headquartered in Paris. Unfortunately, 48 percent of Fortune 1,000 companies still have no women in their top ranks. But firms that do promote women appear to be making it a top priority, placing women on a faster track to top management than men.[27]

Overall, women CEOs are doing very well in corporate America. For example, Mary Sammons, CEO of Rite Aid, increased the firm's stock 61 percent in 2006 versus a 13.5 percent average for all S&P 500 firms. CEO Susan Ivey of Reynolds American raised that firm's stock 37 percent. CEO Andrea Jung of Avon Products raised that firm's stock 17 percent, as did CEO Anne Mulcahy of Xerox. CEO Paula Reynolds of Safeco raised that firm's stock 12 percent. CEO Brenda Barnes of Sara Lee is leading that firm in a restructuring process.

There is great room for improvement in removing the *glass ceiling* domestically, especially considering that women make up 47 percent of the U.S. labor force. *Glass ceiling* refers to the invisible barrier in many firms that bars women and minorities from top-level management positions. The United States leads the world in promoting women and minorities into mid- and top-level managerial positions in business.

Boeing's firing of CEO Harry Stonecipher for having an extramarital affair raised public awareness of office romance. However, just 12 percent of 391 companies surveyed by the American Management Association have written guidelines on office dating.[28] The fact of the matter is that most employers in the United States turn a blind eye to marital cheating. Some employers, such as Southwest Airlines, which employs more than 1,000 married couples, explicitly allow consensual office relationships. Research suggests that more men than women engage in extramarital affairs at work, roughly 22 percent to 15 percent; however, the percentage of women having extramarital affairs is increasing steadily, whereas the percentage of men having affairs with co-workers is holding steady.[29] If an affair is disrupting your work, then "the first step is to go to the offending person privately and try to resolve the matter. If that fails, then go to the human-resources manager seeking assistance."[30] Filing a discrimination lawsuit based on the affair is recommended only as a last resort because courts generally rule that co-workers' injuries are not pervasive enough to warrant any damages.

Benefits of a Diverse Workforce

Toyota has committed almost $8 billion over 10 years to diversify its workforce and to use more minority suppliers. Hundreds of other firms, such as Ford Motor Company and Coca-Cola, are also striving to become more diversified in their workforces. TJX Companies, the parent of 1,500 T. J. Maxx and Marshall's stores, has reaped great benefits and is an exemplary company in terms of diversity. A recent *Wall Street Journal* article listed, in order of importance, the following major benefits of having a diverse workforce:[31]

1. Improves corporate culture
2. Improves employee morale
3. Leads to higher retention of employees
4. Leads to easier recruitment of new employees
5. Decreases complaints and litigation
6. Increases creativity
7. Decreases interpersonal conflict between employees
8. Enables the organization to move into emerging markets
9. Improves client relations
10. Increases productivity
11. Improves the bottom line
12. Maximizes brand identity
13. Reduces training costs

An organization can perhaps be most effective when its workforce mirrors the diversity of its customers. For global companies, this goal can be optimistic, but it is a worthwhile goal.

Conclusion

Successful strategy formulation does not at all guarantee successful strategy implementation. Although inextricably interdependent, strategy formulation and strategy implementation are characteristically different. In a single word, strategy implementation means *change*. It is widely agreed that "the real work begins after strategies are formulated." Successful strategy implementation requires the support of, as well as discipline and hard work from, motivated managers and employees. It is sometimes frightening to think that a single individual can irreparably sabotage strategy-implementation efforts.

Formulating the right strategies is not enough, because managers and employees must be motivated to implement those strategies. Management issues considered central to strategy implementation include matching organizational structure with strategy, linking performance and pay to strategies, creating an organizational climate conducive to change, managing political relationships, creating a strategy-supportive culture, adapting production/operations processes, and managing human resources. Establishing annual objectives, devising policies, and allocating resources are central strategy-implementation activities common to all organizations. Depending on the size and type of the organization, other management issues could be equally important to successful strategy implementation.

We invite you to visit the David page on the Prentice Hall Companion Web site at www.prenhall.com/david for this chapter's review quiz.

Key Terms and Concepts

Annual Objectives (p. 230)
Avoidance (p. 234)
Benchmarking (p. 243)
Bonus System (p. 245)
Conflict (p. 234)
Confrontation (p. 234)
Culture (p. 250)
Decentralized Structure (p. 236)
Defusion (p. 234)
Delayering (p. 242)
Divisional Structure by Geographic Area, Product, Customer, or Process (p. 236)

Issues for Review and Discussion

1. Allocating resources can be a political and an ad hoc activity in firms that do not use strategic management. Why is this true? Does adopting strategic management ensure easy resource allocation? Why?
2. Compare strategy formulation with strategy implementation in terms of each being an art or a science.
3. Describe the relationship between annual objectives and policies.
4. Identify a long-term objective and two supporting annual objectives for a familiar organization.
5. Identify and discuss three policies that apply to your present business policy class.
6. Explain the following statement: Horizontal consistency of goals is as important as vertical consistency.
7. Describe several reasons why conflict may occur during objective-setting activities.
8. In your opinion, what approaches to conflict resolution would be best for resolving a disagreement between a personnel manager and a sales manager over the firing of a particular salesperson? Why?
9. Describe the organizational culture of your college or university.
10. Explain why organizational structure is so important in strategy implementation.
11. In your opinion, how many separate divisions could an organization reasonably have without using an SBU-type organizational structure? Why?
12. Would you recommend a divisional structure by geographic area, product, customer, or process for a medium-sized bank in your local area? Why?
13. What are the advantages and disadvantages of decentralizing the wage and salary functions of an organization? How could this be accomplished?
14. Consider a college organization with which you are familiar. How did management issues affect strategy implementation in that organization?
15. As production manager of a local newspaper, what problems would you anticipate in implementing a strategy to increase the average number of pages in the paper by 40 percent?
16. Do you believe expenditures for child care or fitness facilities are warranted from a cost-benefit perspective? Why or why not?
17. Explain why successful strategy implementation often hinges on whether the strategy-formulation process empowers managers and employees.
18. Compare and contrast the cultures in Mexico and Japan.

19. Discuss the glass ceiling in the United States, giving your ideas and suggestions.
20. Discuss three ways discussed in this book for linking performance and pay to strategies.
21. List the different types of organizational structure. Diagram what you think is the most complex of these structures and label your chart clearly.
22. List the advantages and disadvantages of a functional versus a divisional organizational structure.
23. Compare and contrast the U.S. business culture with the Mexican business culture.
24. Discuss recent trends in women and minorities becoming top executives in the United States.
25. Discuss recent trends in firms downsizing family-friendly programs.
26. Research the latest developments in the class-action lawsuit involving women managers versus Wal-Mart Stores and report your findings to the class.
27. List seven guidelines to follow in developing an organizational chart.

Notes

1. Dale McConkey, "Planning in a Changing Environment," *Business Horizons* (September–October 1988): 66.
2. A. G. Bedeian and W. F. Glueck, *Management*, 3rd ed. (Chicago: The Dryden Press, 1983): 212.
3. Boris Yavitz and William Newman, *Strategy in Action: The Execution, Politics, and Payoff of Business Planning* (New York: The Free Press, 1982): 195.
4. Schein, E. H. "Three Cultures of Management: The Key to Organizational Learning," *Sloan Management Review* 38, 1 (1996): 9–20.
5. S. Ghoshal, and C. A. Bartlett, "Changing the Role of Management: Beyond Structure to Processes." *Harvard Business Review* 73, 1 (1995): 88.
6. Karen Richardson, "The 'Six Sigma' Factor for Home Depot," *Wall Street Journal* (January 4, 2007): C3.
7. Steve Hamm and Marcia Stepanek, "From Reengineering to E-engineering," *BusinessWeek* (March 22, 1999): EB15.
8. "Want to Be a Manager? Many People Say No, Calling Job Miserable," *Wall Street Journal* (April 4, 1997): 1; Stephanie Armour, "Management Loses Its Allure," *USA Today* (October 10, 1997): 1B.
9. Paul Carroll, "No More Business as Usual, Please. Time to Try Something Different," *Wall Street Journal* (October 23, 2001): A24.
10. Jeff Opdyke, "Companies Strive to Find True Stars for Raises, Bonus," *Wall Street Journal* (December 20, 2006): D3.
11. Kris Maher and Kris Hudson, "Wal-Mart to Sweeten Bonus Plans for Staff," *Wall Street Journal* (March 22, 2007): A11.
12. Richard Brown, "Outsider CEO: Inspiring Change with Force and Grace," *USA Today* (July 19, 1999): 3B.
13. Yavitz and Newman, 58.
14. Jack Duncan, *Management* (New York: Random House, 1983): 381–390.
15. H. Igor Ansoff, "Strategic Management of Technology," *Journal of Business Strategy* 7, no. 3 (Winter 1987): 38.
16. Robert Waterman, Jr., "How the Best Get Better," *BusinessWeek* (September 14, 1987): 104.
17. Katherine Kranhold and Jeffrey Ball, "GE to Spend More on Projects Tied to Climate Change," *Wall Street Journal* (May 9, 2005): A2.
18. Jack Duncan, "Organizational Culture: Getting a Fix on an Elusive Concept," *Academy of Management Executive* 3, no. 3 (August 1989): 229.
19. E. H. Schein, "The Role of the Founder in Creating Organizational Culture," *Organizational Dynamics* (Summer 1983): 13–28.
20. T. Deal and A. Kennedy, "Culture: A New Look Through Old Lenses," *Journal of Applied Behavioral Science* 19, no. 4 (1983): 498–504.
21. H. Ibsen, "The Wild Duck," in O. G. Brochett and L. Brochett (eds.), *Plays for the Theater* (New York: Holt, Rinehart & Winston, 1967); R. Pascale, "The Paradox of 'Corporate

Culture': Reconciling Ourselves to Socialization," *California Management Review* 28, no. 2 (1985): 26, 37–40.

22. T. Deal and A. Kennedy, *Corporate Cultures: The Rites and Rituals of Corporate Life* (Reading, MA: Addison-Wesley, 1982): 256.

23. Stratford Sherman, "How to Beat the Japanese," *Fortune* (April 10, 1989): 145.

24. Robert Stobaugh and Piero Telesio, "Match Manufacturing Policies and Product Strategy," *Harvard Business Review* 61, no. 2 (March–April 1983): 113.

25. R. T. Lenz and Marjorie Lyles, "Managing Human Resource Problems in Strategy Planning Systems," *Journal of Business Strategy* 60, no. 4 (Spring 1986): 58.

26. J. Warren Henry, "ESOPs with Productivity Payoffs," *Journal of Business Strategy* (July–August 1989): 33.

27. Del Jones, "Women-Led Firms Lift Stock Standing," *USA Today* (December 27, 2006): 3B.

28. Sue Shellenbarger, "Employers Often Ignore Office Affairs, Leaving Co-workers in Difficult Spot," *Wall Street Journal* (March 10, 2005): D1.

29. Ibid.

30. Ibid.

31. Julie Bennett, "Corporate Downsizing Doesn't Deter Search for Diversity," *Wall Street Journal* (October 23, 2001): B18.

Current Readings

Bartol, Kathryn M., Edwin A. Locke, and Abhishek Srivastava. "Empowering Leadership in Management Teams: Effects on Knowledge Sharing, Efficacy, and Performance." *Academy of Management Journal* 49, no. 6 (December 2006): 1239.

Bebchuk, Lucian A., and Jesse M. Fried. "Pay Without Performance: Overview of the Issues." *The Academy of Management Perspectives* 20, no. 1 (February 2006): 5.

Becker, Brian E., and Mark A. Huselid. "Strategic Human Resources Management: Where Do We Go from Here?" *Journal of Management* 32, no. 6 (December 2006): 898.

Bower, Joseph L., and Clark G. Gilbert. "How Managers' Everyday Decisions Create or Destroy Your Company's Strategy." *Harvard Business Review* (February 2007): 72.

Breene, Timothy R.S., Paul F. Nunes, and Walter E. Shill. "The Chief Strategy Officer." *Harvard Business Review* (October 2007) 84.

Colella, Adrienne, Ramona L. Paetzold, Michael J. Wesson, and Asghar Zardkoohi. "Exposing Pay Secrecy." *The Academy of Management Review* 32, no. 1 (January 2007): 55.

Conyon, Martin J. "Executive Compensation and Incentives." *The Academy of Management Perspectives* 20, no. 1 (February 2006): 25.

Deckop, John R., Shruti Gupta, and Kimberly K. Merriman. "The Effects of CEO Pay Structure on Coporate Social Performance." *Journal of Management* 32, no. 3 (June 2006): 329.

Harris, Dawn, Constance E. Helfat, and Paul J. Wolfson. "The Pipeline to the Top: Women and Men in the Top Executive Ranks of U.S. Corporations." *The Academy of Management Perspectives* 20, no. 4 (November 2006): 42.

Karim, S. "Modularity in Organizational Structure: The Reconfiguration of Internally Developed and Acquired Business Units." *Strategic Management Journal* 27, no. 9 (September 2006): 799.

Marler, J. H., and Y. Yanadori. "Compensation Strategy: Does Business Strategy Influence Compensation in High-Technology Firms?" *Strategic Management Journal* 27, no. 6 (June 2006): 559.

Wasserman, Noam. "Stewards, Agents, and the Founder Discount: Executive Compensation in New Ventures." *Academy of Management Journal* 49, no. 5 (October 2006): 960.

Wimbush, James C. "Spotlight on Human Resource Management." *Business Horizons* 49, no. 6 (November–December 2006): 433.

Zhang, Y. "The Presence of a Separate COO/President and Its Impact on Strategic Change and CEO Dismissal." *Strategic Management Journal* 27, no. 3 (March 2006): 283.

• EXPERIENTIAL EXERCISES

DISNEY

Three 1980s Disney themed "Viewmaster 3-D" reels, comprising Peter Pan, Cinderella, and The Little Mermaid. *Source:* (c) Judith Miller / Dorling Kindersley / Three Sisters.

Experiential Exercise 7A

Revising Walt Disney's Organizational Chart

Purpose

Developing and altering organizational charts is an important skill for strategists to possess. This exercise can improve your skill in altering an organization's hierarchical structure in response to new strategies being formulated.

Instructions

Step 1   Turn to the Walt Disney Cohesion Case (p. 30) and review the organizational chart. On a separate sheet of paper, answer the following questions:

1. What type of organizational chart is illustrated for Disney?

2. What improvements could you recommend for the Disney organizational chart? Give your reasoning for each suggestion.

3. What aspects of Disney's chart do you especially like?

4. What type of organizational chart do you believe would best suit Disney? Why?

5. What would be alternative (better) words for Disney's segment names?

6. Suppose Disney asked you to develop a different SBU-type structure for the company. Illustrate that here.

Experiential Exercise 7B

Do Organizations Really Establish Objectives?

Purpose

Objectives provide direction, allow synergy, aid in evaluation, establish priorities, reduce uncertainty, minimize conflicts, stimulate exertion, and aid in both the allocation of resources and the design of jobs. This exercise will enhance your understanding of how organizations use or misuse objectives.

Instructions

Step 1   Join with one other person in class to form a two-person team.

Step 2   Contact by telephone the owner or manager of an organization in your city or town. Request a 30-minute personal interview or meeting with that person for the purpose of discussing "business objectives." During your meeting, seek answers to the following questions:

1.   Do you believe it is important for a business to establish and clearly communicate long-term and annual objectives? Why or why not?

2.   Does your organization establish objectives? If yes, what type and how many? How are the objectives communicated to individuals? Are your firm's objectives in written form or simply communicated orally?

3.   To what extent are managers and employees involved in the process of establishing objectives?

4.   How often are your business objectives revised and by what process?

Step 3   Take good notes during the interview. Let one person be the note taker and one person do most of the talking. Have your notes typed up and ready to turn in to your professor.

Step 4   Prepare a 5-minute oral presentation for the class, reporting the results of your interview. Turn in your typed report.

Experiential Exercise 7C

Understanding My University's Culture

Purpose

It is something of an art to uncover the basic values and beliefs that are buried deeply in an organization's rich collection of stories, language, heroes, heroines, and rituals, yet culture can be the most important factor in implementing strategies.

Instructions

Step 1   On a separate sheet of paper, list the following terms: hero/heroine, belief, metaphor, language, value, symbol, story, legend, saga, folktale, myth, ceremony, rite, and ritual.

Step 2   For your college or university, give examples of each term. If necessary, speak with faculty, staff, alumni, administration, or fellow students of the institution to identify examples of each term.

Step 3   Report your findings to the class. Tell the class how you feel regarding cultural products being consciously used to help implement strategies.

8

Implementing Strategies: Marketing, Finance/Accounting, R&D, and MIS Issues

"notable quotes"

The greatest strategy is doomed if it's implemented badly.

BERNARD REIMANN

There is no "perfect" strategic decision. One always has to pay a price. One always has to balance conflicting objectives, conflicting opinions, and conflicting priorities. The best strategic decision is only an approximation—and a risk.

PETER DRUCKER

The real question isn't how well you're doing today against your own history, but how you're doing against your competitors.

DONALD KRESS

As market windows open and close more quickly, it is important that R&D be tied more closely to corporate strategy.

WILLIAM SPENSER

Most of the time, strategists should not be formulating strategy at all; they should be getting on with implementing strategies they already have.

HENRY MINTZBERG

It is human nature to make decisions based on emotion, rather than on fact. But nothing could be more illogical.

TOSHIBA CORPORATION

No business can do everything. Even if it has the money, it will never have enough good people. It has to set priorities. The worst thing to do is a little bit of everything. This makes sure that nothing is being accomplished. It is better to pick the wrong priority than none at all.

PETER DRUCKER

Weisloch, Germany: Parents of College Students. *Source:* Florian Fritsch

chapter objectives

After studying this chapter, you should be able to do the following:

1. Explain market segmentation and product positioning as strategy-implementation tools.

2. Discuss procedures for determining the worth of a business.

3. Explain why projected financial statement analysis is a central strategy-implementation tool.

4. Explain how to evaluate the attractiveness of debt versus stock as a source of capital to implement strategies.

5. Discuss the nature and role of research and development in strategy implementation.

6. Explain how management information systems can determine the success of strategy-implementation efforts.

Strategies have no chance of being implemented successfully in organizations that do not market goods and services well, in firms that cannot raise needed working capital, in firms that produce technologically inferior products, or in firms that have a weak information system. This chapter examines marketing, finance/accounting, R&D, and management information systems (MIS) issues that are central to effective strategy implementation. Special topics include market segmentation, market positioning, evaluating the worth of a business, determining to what extent debt and/or stock should be used as a source of capital, developing projected financial statements, contracting R&D outside the firm, and creating an information support system. Manager and employee involvement and participation are essential for success in marketing, finance/accounting, R&D, and MIS activities.

The Nature of Strategy Implementation

The quarterback can call the best play possible in the huddle, but that does not mean the play will go for a touchdown. The team may even lose yardage unless the play is executed (implemented) well. Less than 10 percent of strategies formulated are successfully implemented! There are many reasons for this low success rate, including failing to appropriately segment markets, paying too much for a new acquisition, and falling behind competitors in R&D.

Strategy implementation directly affects the lives of plant managers, division managers, department managers, sales managers, product managers, project managers, personnel managers, staff managers, supervisors, and all employees. In some situations, individuals may not have participated in the strategy-formulation process at all and may not appreciate, understand, or even accept the work and thought that went into strategy formulation. There may even be foot dragging or resistance on their part. Managers and employees who do not understand the business and are not committed to the business may attempt to sabotage strategy-implementation efforts in hopes that the organization will return to its old ways. The strategy-implementation stage of the strategic-management process is highlighted in Figure 8-1.

Marketing Issues

Countless marketing variables affect the success or failure of strategy implementation, and the scope of this text does not allow us to address all those issues. Some examples of marketing decisions that may require policies are as follows:

1. To use exclusive dealerships or multiple channels of distribution
2. To use heavy, light, or no TV advertising
3. To limit (or not) the share of business done with a single customer
4. To be a price leader or a price follower
5. To offer a complete or limited warranty
6. To reward salespeople based on straight salary, straight commission, or a combination salary/commission
7. To advertise online or not

A marketing issue of increasing concern to consumers today is the extent to which companies can track individuals' movements on the Internet—and even be able to identify an individual by name and e-mail address. Individuals' wanderings on the Internet are no longer anonymous, as many persons still believe. Marketing companies such as Doubleclick, Flycast, AdKnowledge, AdForce, and Real Media have sophisticated methods to identify who you are and your particular interests.[1] If you are especially concerned about being tracked, visit the www.networkadvertising.org Web site that gives details about how marketers today are identifying you and your buying habits.

FIGURE 8-1

A Comprehensive Strategic-Management Model

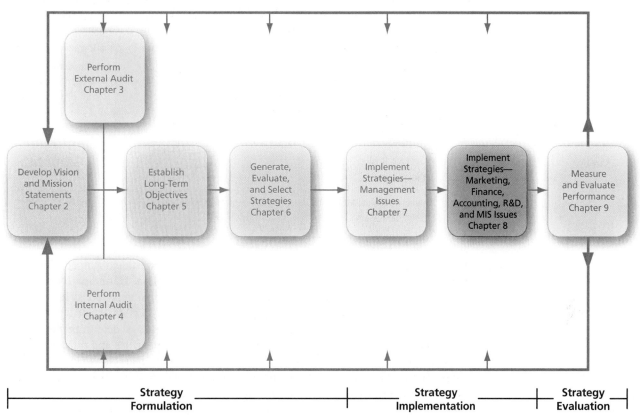

Source: Fred R. David, "How Companies Define Their Mission," *Long Range Planning* 22, no. 3 (June 1988): 40.

Two variables are of central importance to strategy implementation: *market segmentation* and *product positioning.* Market segmentation and product positioning rank as marketing's most important contributions to strategic management.

Market Segmentation

Market segmentation is widely used in implementing strategies, especially for small and specialized firms. Market segmentation can be defined as the subdividing of a market into distinct subsets of customers according to needs and buying habits.

Market segmentation is an important variable in strategy implementation for at least three major reasons. First, strategies such as market development, product development, market penetration, and diversification require increased sales through new markets and products. To successfully implement these strategies, new or improved market-segmentation approaches are required. Second, market segmentation allows a firm to operate with limited resources because mass production, mass distribution, and mass advertising are not required. Market segmentation enables a small firm to compete successfully with a large firm by maximizing per-unit profits and per-segment sales. Finally, market segmentation decisions directly affect *marketing mix variables:* product, place, promotion, and price, as indicated in Table 8-1. For example, SnackWells, a pioneer in reduced-fat snacks, has shifted its advertising emphasis from low-fat to great taste as part of its new market-segmentation strategy.

Perhaps the most dramatic new market-segmentation strategy is the targeting of regional tastes. Firms from McDonald's to General Motors are increasingly modifying their products to meet different regional preferences within the United States. Campbell's

TABLE 8–1   The Marketing Mix Component Variables

Product	Place	Promotion	Price
Quality	Distribution channels	Advertising	Level
Features and	Distribution coverage	Personal selling	Discounts and
options	Outlet location	Sales promotion	allowances
Style	Sales territories	Publicity	Payment terms
Brand name	Inventory levels		
Packaging	and locations		
Product line	Transportation		
Warranty	carriers		
Service level			
Other services			

Source: E. Jerome McCarthy, *Basic Marketing: A Managerial Approach,* 9th ed. (Homewood, IL: Richard D. Irwin, Inc., 1987): 37–44.

has a spicier version of its nacho cheese soup for the Southwest, and Burger King offers breakfast burritos in New Mexico but not in South Carolina. Geographic and demographic bases for segmenting markets are the most commonly employed, as illustrated in Table 8-2.

Evaluating potential market segments requires strategists to determine the characteristics and needs of consumers, to analyze consumer similarities and differences, and to develop consumer group profiles. Segmenting consumer markets is generally much simpler and easier than segmenting industrial markets, because industrial products, such as electronic circuits and forklifts, have multiple applications and appeal to diverse customer groups. Note in Figure 8-2 that customer age is used to segment automobile car purchases. Note that some older buyers especially like Cadillacs and Buicks.

Segmentation is a key to matching supply and demand, which is one of the thorniest problems in customer service. Segmentation often reveals that large, random fluctuations in demand actually consist of several small, predictable, and manageable patterns.

FIGURE 8-2

Average Age of Automobile Buyers, by Brand

Plymouth 38	Pontiac 42	Infiniti 45
Mitsubishi 38	Acura 42	Subaru 45
Volkswagen 38	Hyundai 42	Oldsmobile 46
Honda 41	Suzuki 42	Saturn 46
Isuzu 41	Audi 42	Chrysler 47
Kia 41	Daewoo 43	Lexus 47
Land Rover 41	Chevrolet 43	Jaguar 49
Mazda 41	Porsche 43	Mercury 50
Nissan 41	Saab 43	Lincoln 51
BMW 42	GMC 44	Cadillac 53
Dodge 42	Toyota 44	Buick 57
Jeep 42	Volvo 44	
Ford 42	Mercedes-Benz 45	

Source: Adapted from Norihiko Shirouzu, "This Is Not Your Father's Toyota," *Wall Street Journal* (March 26, 2002): B1.

TABLE 8-2 Alternative Bases for Market Segmentation

Variable	Typical Breakdowns
	Geographic
Region	Pacific, Mountain, West North Central, West South Central, East North Central, East South Central, South Atlantic, Middle Atlantic, New England
County Size	A, B, C, D
City Size	Under 5,000; 5,000–20,000; 20,001–50,000; 50,001–100,000; 100,001–250,000; 250,001–500,000; 500,001–1,000,000; 1,000,001–4,000,000; 4,000,001 or over
Density	Urban, suburban, rural
Climate	Northern, southern
	Demographic
Age	Under 6, 6–11, 12–19, 20–34, 35–49, 50–64, 65+
Gender	Male, female
Family Size	1–2, 3–4, 5+
Family Life Cycle	Young, single; young, married, no children; young, married, youngest child under 6; young, married, youngest child 6 or over; older, married, with children; older, married, no children under 18; older, single; other
Income	Under $10,000; $10,001–$15,000; $15,001–$20,000; $20,001–$30,000; $30,001–$50,000; $50,001–$70,000; $70,001–$100,000; over $100,000
Occupation	Professional and technical; managers, officials, and proprietors; clerical and sales; craftspeople; foremen; operatives; farmers; retirees; students; housewives; unemployed
Education	Grade school or less; some high school; high school graduate; some college; college graduate
Religion	Catholic, Protestant, Jewish, Islamic, other
Race	White, Asian, Hispanic, African American
Nationality	American, British, French, German, Scandinavian, Italian, Latin American, Middle Eastern, Japanese
	Psychographic
Social Class	Lower lowers, upper lowers, lower middles, upper middles, lower uppers, upper uppers
Personality	Compulsive, gregarious, authoritarian, ambitious
	Behavioral
Use Occasion	Regular occasion, special occasion
Benefits Sought	Quality, service, economy
User Status	Nonuser, ex-user, potential user, first-time user, regular user
Usage Rate	Light user, medium user, heavy user
Loyalty Status	None, medium, strong, absolute
Readiness Stage	Unaware, aware, informed, interested, desirous, intending to buy
Attitude Toward Product	Enthusiastic, positive, indifferent, negative, hostile

Source: Adapted from Philip Kotler, *Marketing Management: Analysis, Planning and Control,* © 1984: 256. Adapted by permission of Prentice-Hall, Inc., Upper Saddle River, New Jersey.

Matching supply and demand allows factories to produce desirable levels without extra shifts, overtime, and subcontracting. Matching supply and demand also minimizes the number and severity of stock-outs. The demand for hotel rooms, for example, can be dependent on foreign tourists, businesspersons, and vacationers. Focusing separately on these three market segments, however, can allow hotel firms to more effectively predict overall supply and demand.

Banks now are segmenting markets to increase effectiveness. "You're dead in the water if you aren't segmenting the market," says Anne Moore, president of a bank consulting firm in Atlanta. The Internet makes market segmentation easier today because consumers naturally form "communities" on the Web.

Does the Internet Make Market Segmentation Easier?

Yes. The segments of people whom marketers want to reach online are much more precisely defined than the segments of people reached through traditional forms of media, such as television, radio, and magazines. For example, Quepasa.com is widely visited by Hispanics. Marketers aiming to reach college students, who are notoriously difficult to reach via traditional media, focus on sites such as collegeclub.com and studentadvantage.com. The gay and lesbian population, which is estimated to comprise about 5 percent of the U.S. population, has always been difficult to reach via traditional media but now can be focused on at sites such as gay.com. Marketers can reach persons interested in specific topics, such as travel or fishing, by placing banners on related Web sites.

People all over the world are congregating into virtual communities on the Web by becoming members/customers/visitors of Web sites that focus on an endless range of topics. People in essence segment themselves by nature of the Web sites that comprise their "favorite places," and many of these Web sites sell information regarding their "visitors." Businesses and groups of individuals all over the world pool their purchasing power in Web sites to get volume discounts.

Product Positioning

After markets have been segmented so that the firm can target particular customer groups, the next step is to find out what customers want and expect. This takes analysis and research. A severe mistake is to assume the firm knows what customers want and expect. Countless research studies reveal large differences between how customers define service and rank the importance of different service activities and how producers view services. Many firms have become successful by filling the gap between what customers and producers see as good service. What the customer believes is good service is paramount, not what the producer believes service should be.

Identifying target customers upon whom to focus marketing efforts sets the stage for deciding how to meet the needs and wants of particular consumer groups. Product positioning is widely used for this purpose. Positioning entails developing schematic representations that reflect how your products or services compare to competitors' on dimensions most important to success in the industry. The following steps are required in product positioning:

1. Select key criteria that effectively differentiate products or services in the industry.
2. Diagram a two-dimensional product-positioning map with specified criteria on each axis.
3. Plot major competitors' products or services in the resultant four-quadrant matrix.
4. Identify areas in the positioning map where the company's products or services could be most competitive in the given target market. Look for vacant areas (niches).
5. Develop a marketing plan to position the company's products or services appropriately.

Because just two criteria can be examined on a single product-positioning map, multiple maps are often developed to assess various approaches to strategy implementation. Multidimensional scaling could be used to examine three or more criteria simultaneously, but this technique requires computer assistance and is beyond the scope of this text. Some examples of product-positioning maps are illustrated in Figure 8-3.

Some rules for using product positioning as a strategy-implementation tool are the following:

1. Look for the hole or *vacant niche*. The best strategic opportunity might be an unserved segment.
2. Don't squat between segments. Any advantage from squatting (such as a larger target market) is offset by a failure to satisfy one segment. In decision-theory terms, the intent here is to avoid suboptimization by trying to serve more than one objective function.

VISIT THE NET

Provides the 2007–2017 Strategic Plan of the National Archives and Records Administration, including Annual Performance Plans. (www.archives.gov/about_us/ strategic_planning_and_reporting/ 2003_strategic_plan.html)

FIGURE 8-3

Examples of Product-Positioning Maps

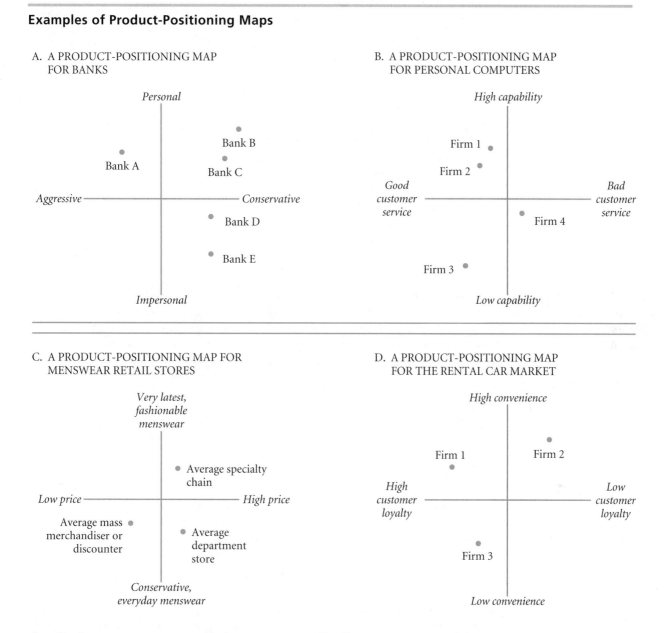

A. A PRODUCT-POSITIONING MAP FOR BANKS

B. A PRODUCT-POSITIONING MAP FOR PERSONAL COMPUTERS

C. A PRODUCT-POSITIONING MAP FOR MENSWEAR RETAIL STORES

D. A PRODUCT-POSITIONING MAP FOR THE RENTAL CAR MARKET

3. Don't serve two segments with the same strategy. Usually, a strategy successful with one segment cannot be directly transferred to another segment.

4. Don't position yourself in the middle of the map. The middle usually means a strategy that is not clearly perceived to have any distinguishing characteristics. This rule can vary with the number of competitors. For example, when there are only two competitors, as in U.S. presidential elections, the middle becomes the preferred strategic position.[2]

An effective product-positioning strategy meets two criteria: (1) it uniquely distinguishes a company from the competition, and (2) it leads customers to expect slightly less service than a company can deliver. Firms should not create expectations that exceed the service the firm can or will deliver. Network Equipment Technology is an example of a company that keeps customer expectations slightly below perceived performance. This is a constant challenge for marketers. Firms need to inform customers about what to expect and then exceed the promise. Underpromise and then overdeliver is the key!

Finance/Accounting Issues

In this section, we examine several finance/accounting concepts considered to be central to strategy implementation: acquiring needed capital, developing projected financial statements, preparing financial budgets, and evaluating the worth of a business. Some examples of decisions that may require finance/accounting policies are these:

1. To raise capital with short-term debt, long-term debt, preferred stock, or common stock
2. To lease or buy fixed assets
3. To determine an appropriate dividend payout ratio
4. To use LIFO (Last-in, First-out), FIFO (First-in, First-out), or a market-value accounting approach
5. To extend the time of accounts receivable
6. To establish a certain percentage discount on accounts within a specified period of time
7. To determine the amount of cash that should be kept on hand

NATURAL ENVIRONMENT PERSPECTIVE
Strategic Management of Your Health

The *BusinessWeek* cover story article on February 26, 2007 details how firms are striving to lower accelerating costs of employees' health care insurance premiums. Many firms such as Scotts Miracle-Gro Company, based in Marysville, Ohio; IBM; and Microsoft, are implementing wellness programs, requiring employees to get healthier or pay higher insurance premiums. Employees that do get healthier win bonuses, free trips, and pay lower premiums, while nonconforming employees pay higher premiums and receive no "healthy" benefits. Wellness of employees has become a strategic issue for many firms. Most firms require a health examination as a part of an employment application, and healthiness is more and more becoming a hiring factor. Michael Porter, co-author of *Redefining Health Care*, says: "We have this notion that you can gorge on hot dogs, be in a pie-eating contest, and drink every day, and society will take care of you. We can't afford to let individuals drive up company costs because they're not willing to address their own health problems."

Wellness programs such as the one at Scotts provide counseling to employees and seek lifestyle changes to achieve healthier living. For example, trans fats are a major cause of heart disease. Near elimination of trans fats in one's diet will reduce one's risk for heart attack by as much as 19 percent, according to a recent article. New York City now requires restaurants to inform customers about levels of trans fat being served in prepared foods. Chicago is considering a similar ban on trans fats. Denmark in 2003 became the first country to strictly regulate trans fats.

Restaurant chains are only slowly reducing trans fat levels in served foods because (1) trans fat oils make fried foods crispier, (2) trans fats give baked goods a longer shelf life, (3) trans fat oils can be used multiple times compared to other cooking oils, and (4) trans fat oils taste better. Three restaurant chains have switched to trans fat–free oils—Chili's, Ruby Tuesday, and Wendy's—but many chains still use trans fat oils, including Kentucky Fried Chicken, McDonald's, Dunkin' Donuts, Taco Bell, and Burger King. Marriott International in February 2007 eliminated trans fats from the food it serves at its 2,300 North American hotels, becoming the first big hotel chain to do so, although the 18-hotel Lowes luxury chain is close behind. Marriott's change includes its Renaissance, Courtyard, and Residence Inn brands.

Saturated fats are also bad, so one should avoid eating too much red meat and dairy products, which are high in saturated fats. The following seven lifestyle habits may significantly improve one's health and longevity:

1. Eat nutritiously—eat a variety of fruits and vegetables daily because they have ingredients that the body uses to repair and strengthen itself.

2. Stay hydrated—drink plenty of water to aid the body in eliminating toxins and to enable body organs to function efficiently; the body is mostly water.

3. Get plenty of rest—the body repairs itself during rest, so get at least seven hours of sleep nightly.

4. Get plenty of exercise—exercise vigorously at least 30 minutes daily so the body can release toxins and strengthen vital organs.

5. Reduce stress—the body's immune system is weakened when one is under stress, making the body vulnerable to many ailments, so keep stress to a minimum.

6. Do not smoke—smoking kills, no doubt about it.

7. Take vitamin supplements—consult your physician, but because it is difficult for diet alone to supply all the nutrients and vitamins needed, supplements can be helpful in achieving good health and longevity.

Source: Adapted from Michelle Conlin, "Get Healthy—or Else," *BusinessWeek* (February 26, 2007): 58–69; Lauren Etter, "Trans Fats: Will They Get Shelved?" *Wall Street Journal* (December 8, 2006): A6; and Joel Fuhrman, MD, *Eat to Live* (Boston: Little Brown, 2003).

Eating Healthy Is a Key to Success in Life. *Source:* Andy Crawford (c) Dorling Kindersley

As indicated in the "Natural Environment Perspective," employees' health is increasingly being viewed as an important financial management issue in firms. Employee wellness has become a strategic issue. As medical doctor and book author Joel Fuhrman says, we all should "Eat to Live" rather than "Live to Eat."

Acquiring Capital to Implement Strategies

Successful strategy implementation often requires additional capital. Besides net profit from operations and the sale of assets, two basic sources of capital for an organization are debt and equity. Determining an appropriate mix of debt and equity in a firm's capital structure can be vital to successful strategy implementation. An *Earnings Per Share/Earnings Before Interest and Taxes (EPS/EBIT) analysis* is the most widely used technique for determining whether debt, stock, or a combination of debt and stock is the best alternative for raising capital to implement strategies. This technique involves an examination of the impact that debt versus stock financing has on earnings per share under various assumptions as to EBIT.

Theoretically, an enterprise should have enough debt in its capital structure to boost its return on investment by applying debt to products and projects earning more than the cost of the debt. In low earning periods, too much debt in the capital structure of an organization can endanger stockholders' returns and jeopardize company survival. Fixed debt obligations generally must be met, regardless of circumstances. This does not mean that stock issuances are always better than debt for raising capital. Some special concerns with stock issuances are dilution of ownership, effect on stock price, and the need to share future earnings with all new shareholders.

Without going into detail on other institutional and legal issues related to the debt versus stock decision, EPS/EBIT may be best explained by working through an example. Let's say the Brown Company needs to raise $1 million to finance implementation of a market-development strategy. The company's common stock currently sells for $50 per share, and 100,000 shares are outstanding. The prime interest rate is 10 percent, and the company's tax rate is 50 percent. The company's earnings before interest and taxes next year are expected to be $2 million if a recession occurs, $4 million if the economy stays as is, and $8 million if the economy significantly improves. EPS/EBIT analysis can be used to determine if all stock, all debt, or some combination of stock and debt is the best capital financing alternative. The EPS/EBIT analysis for this example is provided in Table 8-3.

As indicated by the EPS values of 9.5, 19.50, and 39.50 in Table 8-3, debt is the best financing alternative for the Brown Company if a recession, boom, or normal year is expected. An EPS/EBIT chart can be constructed to determine the break-even point, where one financing alternative becomes more attractive than another. Figure 8-4 indicates that issuing common stock is the least attractive financing alternative for the Brown Company.

EPS/EBIT analysis is a valuable tool for making the capital financing decisions needed to implement strategies, but several considerations should be made whenever using this technique. First, profit levels may be higher for stock or debt alternatives when EPS levels are lower. For example, looking only at the earnings after taxes (EAT) values in Table 8-3, you can see that the common stock option is the best alternative, regardless of economic conditions. If the Brown Company's mission includes strict profit maximization, as opposed to the maximization of stockholders' wealth or some other criterion, then stock rather than debt is the best choice of financing.

Another consideration when using EPS/EBIT analysis is flexibility. As an organization's capital structure changes, so does its flexibility for considering future capital needs. Using all debt or all stock to raise capital in the present may impose fixed obligations, restrictive covenants, or other constraints that could severely reduce a firm's ability to raise additional capital in the future. Control is also a concern. When additional stock is issued to finance strategy implementation, ownership and control of the enterprise are diluted. This

TABLE 8-3   EPS/EBIT Analysis for the Brown Company (In Millions)

	Common Stock Financing			Debt Financing			Combination Financing		
	Recession	*Normal*	*Boom*	*Recession*	*Normal*	*Boom*	*Recession*	*Normal*	*Boom*
EBIT	$2.0	$ 4.0	$ 8.0	$2.0	$ 4.0	$ 8.0	$2.0	$ 4.0	$ 8.0
Interest[a]	0	0	0	.10	.10	.10	.05	.05	.05
EBT	2.0	4.0	8.0	1.9	3.9	7.9	1.95	3.95	7.95
Taxes	1.0	2.0	4.0	.95	1.95	3.95	.975	1.975	3.975
EAT	1.0	2.0	4.0	.95	1.95	3.95	.975	1.975	3.975
#Shares[b]	.12	.12	.12	.10	.10	.10	.11	.11	.11
EPS[c]	8.33	16.66	33.33	9.5	19.50	39.50	8.86	17.95	36.14

[a]The annual interest charge on $1 million at 10% is $100,000 and on $0.5 million is $50,000. This row is in $, not %.

[b]To raise all of the needed $1 million with stock, 20,000 new shares must be issued, raising the total to 120,000 shares outstanding. To raise one-half of the needed $1 million with stock, 10,000 new shares must be issued, raising the total to 110,000 shares outstanding.

[c]EPS = Earnings After Taxes (EAT) divided by shares (number of shares outstanding).

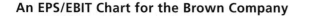

FIGURE 8-4

An EPS/EBIT Chart for the Brown Company

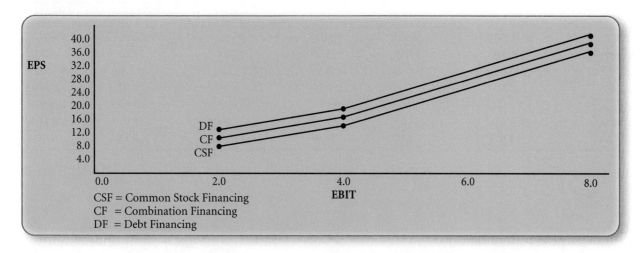

CSF = Common Stock Financing
CF = Combination Financing
DF = Debt Financing

can be a serious concern in today's business environment of hostile takeovers, mergers, and acquisitions.

Dilution of ownership can be an overriding concern in closely held corporations in which stock issuances affect the decision-making power of majority stockholders. For example, the Smucker family owns 30 percent of the stock in Smucker's, a well-known jam and jelly company. When Smucker's acquired Dickson Family, Inc., the company used mostly debt rather than stock in order not to dilute the family ownership.

When using EPS/EBIT analysis, timing in relation to movements of stock prices, interest rates, and bond prices becomes important. In times of depressed stock prices, debt may prove to be the most suitable alternative from both a cost and a demand standpoint. However, when cost of capital (interest rates) is high, stock issuances become more attractive.

Tables 8-4 and 8-5 provide EPS/EBIT analyses for two companies—Gateway and Boeing. Notice in those analyses that the combination stock/debt options vary from 30/70 to 70/30. Any number of combinations could be explored. However, sometimes in preparing the EPS/EBIT graphs, the lines will intersect, thus revealing break-even points

TABLE 8-4 **EPS/EBIT Analysis for Gateway (M = In Millions)**

Amount Needed: $1,000 M
EBIT Range: − $500 M to + $100 M to + $500 M
Interest Rate: 5%
Tax Rate: 0% (because the firm has been incurring a loss annually)
Stock Price: $6.00
# of Shares Outstanding: 371 M

	Common Stock Financing			Debt Financing		
	Recession	*Normal*	*Boom*	*Recession*	*Normal*	*Boom*
EBIT	(500.00)	100.00	500.00	(500.00)	100.00	500.00
Interest	0.00	0.00	0.00	50.00	50.00	50.00
EBT	(500.00)	100.00	500.00	(550.00)	50.00	450.00
Taxes	0.00	0.00	0.00	0.00	0.00	0.00
EAT	(500.00)	100.00	500.00	(550.00)	50.00	450.00
#Shares	537.67	537.67	537.67	371.00	371.00	371.00
EPS	**(0.93)**	**0.19**	**0.93**	**(1.48)**	**0.13**	**1.21**

(continued)

TABLE 8-4 EPS/EBIT Analysis for Gateway (M = In Millions)—continued

	70 Percent Stock—30 Percent Debt			70 Percent Debt—30 Percent Stock		
	Recession	*Normal*	*Boom*	*Recession*	*Normal*	*Boom*
EBIT	(500.00)	100.00	500.00	(500.00)	100.00	500.00
Interest	15.00	15.00	15.00	35.00	35.00	35.00
EBT	(515.00)	85.00	485.00	(535.00)	65.00	465.00
Taxes	0.00	0.00	0.00	0.00	0.00	0.00
EAT	(515.00)	85.00	485.00	(535.00)	65.00	465.00
#Shares	487.67	487.67	487.67	421.00	421.00	421.00
EPS	**(1.06)**	**0.17**	**0.99**	**(1.27)**	**0.15**	**1.10**

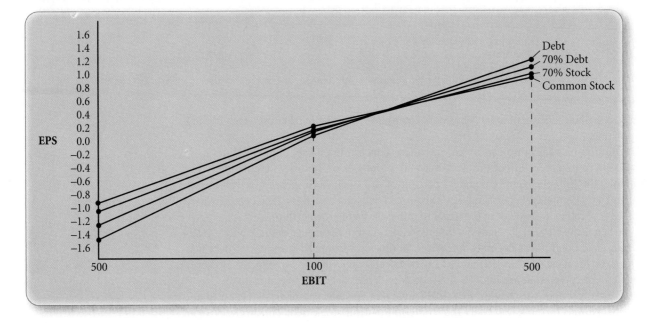

Conclusion: Gateway should use common stock to raise capital in recession or normal economic conditions but should use debt financing under boom conditions. Note that stock is the best alternative under all three conditions according to EAT (profit maximization), but EPS (maximize shareholders' wealth) is the better ratio to make this decision.

TABLE 8-5 EPS/EBIT Analysis for Boeing (M = In Millions)

Amount Needed: $10,000 M

Interest Rate: 5%

Tax Rate: 7%

Stock Price: $53.00

# of Shares Outstanding: 826 M

	Common Stock Financing			Debt Financing		
	Recession	*Normal*	*Boom*	*Recession*	*Normal*	*Boom*
EBIT	1,000.00	2,500.00	5,000.00	1,000.00	2,500.00	5,000.00
Interest	0.00	0.00	0.00	500.00	500.00	500.00
EBT	1,000.00	2,500.00	5,000.00	500.00	2,000.00	4,500.00
Taxes	70.00	175.00	350.00	35.00	140.00	315.00
EAT	930.00	2,325.00	4,650.00	465.00	1,860.00	4,185.00
# Shares	1,014.68	1,014.68	1,014.68	826.00	826.00	826.00
EPS	**0.92**	**2.29**	**4.58**	**0.56**	**2.25**	**5.07**

(*continued*)

TABLE 8-5   EPS/EBIT Analysis for Boeing (M = In Millions)—continued

	70% Stock—30% Debt			70% Debt—30% Stock		
	Recession	*Normal*	*Boom*	*Recession*	*Normal*	*Boom*
EBIT	1,000.00	2,500.00	5,000.00	1,000.00	2,500.00	5,000.00
Interest	150.00	150.00	150.00	350.00	350.00	350.00
EBT	850.00	2,350.00	4,850.00	650.00	2,150.00	4,650.00
Taxes	59.50	164.50	339.50	45.50	150.50	325.50
EAT	790.50	2,185.50	4,510.50	604.50	1,999.50	4,324.50
# Shares	958.08	958.08	958.08	882.60	882.60	882.60
EPS	**0.83**	**2.28**	**4.71**	**0.68**	**2.27**	**4.90**

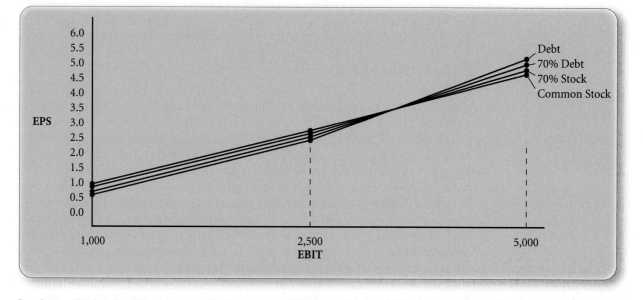

Conclusion: Boeing should use common stock to raise capital in recession (see 0.92) or normal (see 2.29) economic conditions but should use debt financing under boom conditions (see 5.07). Note that a dividends row is absent from this analysis. The more shares outstanding, the more dividends to be paid (if the firm pays dividends), which would lower the common stock EPS values.

at which one financing alternative becomes more or less attractive than another. The slope of these lines will be determined by a combination of factors including stock price, interest rate, number of shares, and amount of capital needed. Also, it should be noted here that the best financing alternatives are indicated by the highest EPS values. In Tables 8-4 and 8-5, note that the tax rates for the companies vary considerably and should be computed from the respective income statements by dividing taxes paid by income before taxes.

In Table 8-4, the higher EPS values indicate that Gateway should use stock to raise capital in recession or normal economic conditions but should use debt financing under boom conditions. Stock is the best alternative for Gateway under all three conditions if EAT (profit maximization) were the decision criteria, but EPS (maximize shareholders' wealth) is the better ratio to make this decision. Firms can do many things in the short run to maximize profits, so investors and creditors consider maximizing shareholders' wealth to be the better criteria for making financing decisions.

In Table 8-5, note that Boeing should use stock to raise capital in recession (see 0.92) or normal (see 2.29) economic conditions but should use debt financing under boom conditions (see 5.07). Let's calculate here the number of shares figure of 1014.68 given under Boeing's stock alternative. Divide $10,000 M funds needed by the stock price of $53 = 188.68 M new shares to be issued + the 826 M shares outstanding already = 1014.68 M shares under the stock scenario. Along the final row, EPS is the number of shares outstanding divided by EAT in all columns.

Note in Table 8-4 and Table 8-5 that a dividends row is absent from both the Gateway and Boeing analyses. The more shares outstanding, the more dividends to be paid (if the firm indeed pays dividends). Paying dividends lowers EAT, which lowers the stock EPS values whenever this aspect is included. To consider dividends in an EPS/EBIT analysis, simply insert another row for "Dividends" right below the "EAT" row and then insert an "Earnings After Taxes and Dividends" row. Considering dividends would make the analysis more robust.

Note in both the Gateway and Boeing graphs, there is a break-even point between the normal and boom range of EBIT where the debt option overtakes the 70% Debt/30% Stock option as the best financing alternative. A break-even point is where two lines cross each other. A break-even point is the EBIT level where various financing alternative represented by lines crossing are equally attractive in terms of EPS. Both the Gateway and Boeing graphs indicate that EPS values are highest for the 100 percent debt option at high EBIT levels. The two graphs also reveal that the EPS values for 100 percent debt increase faster than the other financing options as EBIT levels increase beyond the break-even point. At low levels of EBIT however, both the Gateway and Boeing graphs indicate that 100 percent stock is the best financing alternative because the EPS values are highest.

Projected Financial Statements

Projected financial statement analysis is a central strategy-implementation technique because it allows an organization to examine the expected results of various actions and approaches. This type of analysis can be used to forecast the impact of various implementation decisions (for example, to increase promotion expenditures by 50 percent to support a market-development strategy, to increase salaries by 25 percent to support a market-penetration strategy, to increase research and development expenditures by 70 percent to support product development, or to sell $1 million of common stock to raise capital for diversification). Nearly all financial institutions require at least three years of projected financial statements whenever a business seeks capital. A projected income statement and balance sheet allow an organization to compute projected financial ratios under various strategy-implementation scenarios. When compared to prior years and to industry averages, financial ratios provide valuable insights into the feasibility of various strategy-implementation approaches.

Primarily as a result of the Enron collapse and accounting scandal and the ensuing Sarbanes-Oxley Act, companies today are being much more diligent in preparing projected financial statements to "reasonably rather than too optimistically" project future expenses and earnings. There is much more care not to mislead shareholders and other constituencies.[3]

A 2008 projected income statement and a balance sheet for the Litten Company are provided in Table 8-6. The projected statements for Litten are based on five assumptions: (1) The company needs to raise $45 million to finance expansion into foreign markets; (2) $30 million of this total will be raised through increased debt and $15 million through common stock; (3) sales are expected to increase 50 percent; (4) three new facilities, costing a total of $30 million, will be constructed in foreign markets; and (5) land for the new facilities is already owned by the company. Note in Table 8-6 that Litten's strategies and their implementation are expected to result in a sales increase from $100 million to $150 million and in a net increase in income from $6 million to $9.75 million in the forecasted year.

There are six steps in performing projected financial analysis:

1. Prepare the projected income statement before the balance sheet. Start by forecasting sales as accurately as possible. Be careful not to blindly push historical percentages into the future with regard to revenue (sales) increases. Be mindful of what the firm did to achieve those past sales increases, which may not be appropriate for the future unless the firm takes similar or analogous actions (such as opening a similar number of stores, for example). If dealing with a manufacturing firm, also be mindful that if the firm is operating at 100 percent capacity running three eight-hour shifts per day, then probably new manufacturing facilities (land, plant, and equipment) will be needed to increase sales further.

2. Use the percentage-of-sales method to project cost of goods sold (CGS) and the expense items in the income statement. For example, if CGS is 70 percent of sales

TABLE 8-6 A Projected Income Statement and Balance Sheet for the Litten Company (In Millions)

	Prior Year 2007	Projected Year 2008	Remarks
PROJECTED INCOME STATEMENT			
Sales	$100	$150.00	50% increase
Cost of Goods Sold	70	105.00	70% of sales
Gross Margin	30	45.00	
Selling Expense	10	15.00	10% of sales
Administrative Expense	5	7.50	5% of sales
Earnings Before Interest and Taxes	15	22.50	
Interest	3	3.00	
Earnings Before Taxes	12	19.50	
Taxes	6	9.75	50% rate
Net Income	**6**	**9.75**	
Dividends	2	5.00	
Retained Earnings	4	4.75	
PROJECTED BALANCE SHEET			
Assets			
Cash	5	7.75	Plug figure
Accounts Receivable	2	4.00	100% increase
Inventory	20	45.00	
Total Current Assets	27	56.75	
Land	15	15.00	
Plant and Equipment	50	80.00	Add three new plants at $10 million each
Less Depreciation	10	20.00	
Net Plant and Equipment	40	60.00	
Total Fixed Assets	55	75.00	
Total Assets	**82**	**131.75**	
Liabilities			
Accounts Payable	10	10.00	
Notes Payable	10	10.00	
Total Current Liabilities	20	20.00	
Long-term Debt	40	70.00	Borrowed $30 million
Additional Paid-in-Capital	20	35.00	Issued 100,000 shares at $150 each
Retained Earnings	2	6.75	$2 + $4.75
Total Liabilities and Net Worth	**82**	**131.75**	

in the prior year (as it is in Table 8-6), then use that same percentage to calculate CGS in the future year—unless there is a reason to use a different percentage. Items such as interest, dividends, and taxes must be treated independently and cannot be forecasted using the percentage-of-sales method.

3. Calculate the projected net income.

4. Subtract from the net income any dividends to be paid for that year. This remaining net income is retained earnings (RE). Bring this retained earnings amount for that year (NI − DIV = RE) over to the balance sheet by adding it to the prior year's RE shown on the balance sheet. In other words, every year a firm adds its RE for that particular year (from the income statement) to its historical RE total on the balance sheet. Therefore, the RE amount on the balance sheet is a cumulative number rather than money available for strategy implementation! Note that RE is the **first** projected balance sheet item to be entered. Due to this accounting procedure in developing projected financial statements, the RE amount on the balance sheet is usually a large number. However, it also can be a low or even negative number if the firm has been

incurring losses. The only way for RE to decrease from one year to the next on the balance sheet is (1) if the firm incurred an earnings loss that year or (2) the firm had positive net income for the year but paid out dividends more than the net income. Be mindful that RE is the key link between a projected income statement and balance sheet, so be careful to make this calculation correctly.

5. Project the balance sheet items, beginning with retained earnings and then forecasting stockholders' equity, long-term liabilities, current liabilities, total liabilities, total assets, fixed assets, and current assets (in that order). Use the cash account as the plug figure—that is, use the cash account to make the assets total the liabilities and net worth. Then make appropriate adjustments. For example, if the cash needed to balance the statements is too small (or too large), make appropriate changes to borrow more (or less) money than planned.

6. List comments (remarks) on the projected statements. Any time a significant change is made in an item from a prior year to the projected year, an explanation (remark) should be provided. Remarks are essential because otherwise pro formas are meaningless.

Projected Financial Statement Analysis for Mattel, Inc.

Since so many strategic management students have limited experience developing projected financial statements, let's apply the steps outlined on the previous pages to Mattel, the huge toy company headquartered in El Segundo, California. Mattel designs, manufactures, and markets toy products from fashion dolls to children's books. The company Web site is www.mattel.com. Mattel's recent income statements and balance sheets are provided in Table 8-7 and Table 8-8 respectively.

TABLE 8-7 **Mattel's Actual Income Statements (In Thousands)**

	2006	2005	2004
Total Revenue	$5,650,156	5,179,016	5,102,786
Cost of Revenue	3,038,363	2,806,148	2,692,061
Gross Profit	2,611,793	2,372,868	2,410,725
Operating Expenses			
Research Development	-	-	-
Selling General and Administrative	1,882,975	1,708,339	1,679,908
Non-Recurring	-	-	-
Others	-	-	-
Total Operating Expenses	-	-	-
Operating Income or Loss	728,818	664,529	730,817
Income from Continuing Operations			
Total Other Income/Expenses Net	34,791	64,010	43,201
Earnings Before Interest and Taxes	763,609	728,539	774,018
Interest Expense	79,853	76,490	77,764
Income Before Tax	683,756	652,049	696,254
Income Tax Expense	90,829	235,030	123,531
Minority Interest	-	-	-
Net Income from Continuing Ops	592,927	417,019	572,723
Non-Recurring Events			
Discontinued Operations	-	-	-
Extraordinary Items	-	-	-
Effect of Accounting Changes	-	-	-
Other Items	-	-	-
Net Income	592,927	417,019	572,723
Preferred Stock and Other Adjustments	-	-	-
Net Income Applicable to Common Shares	$592,927	$417,019	$572,723

TABLE 8-8   Mattel's Actual Balance Sheets (In Thousands)

	2006	2005	2004
Assets			
Current Assets			
Cash and Cash Equivalents	$1,205,552	997,734	1,156,835
Short-Term Investments	-	-	-
Net Receivables	943,813	760,643	759,033
Inventory	383,149	376,897	418,633
Other Current Assets	317,624	277,226	302,649
Total Current Assets	2,850,138	2,412,500	2,637,150
Long-Term Investments	-	-	-
Property, Plant, and Equipment	536,749	547,104	586,526
Goodwill	845,324	718,069	735,680
Intangible Assets	70,593	20,422	22,926
Accumulated Amortization	-	-	-
Other Assets	149,912	178,304	201,836
Deferred Long-Term Asset Charges	503,168	495,914	572,374
Total Assets	$4,955,884	4,372,313	4,756,492
Liabilities			
Current Liabilities			
Accounts Payable	$1,518,234	1,245,191	1,303,822
Short/Current Long-Term Debt	64,286	217,994	423,349
Other Current Liabilities	-	-	-
Total Current Liabilities	1,582,520	1,463,185	1,727,171
Long-Term Debt	635,714	525,000	400,000
Other Liabilities	304,676	282,395	243,509
Deferred Long-Term Liability Charges	-	-	-
Minority Interest	-	-	-
Negative Goodwill	-	-	-
Total Liabilities	2,522,910	2,270,580	2,370,680
Stockholders' Equity			
Misc. Stocks, Options, Warrants	-	-	-
Redeemable Preferred Stock	-	-	-
Preferred Stock	-	-	-
Common Stock	441,369	441,369	441,369
Retained Earnings	1,652,140	1,314,068	1,093,288
Treasury Stock	(996,981)	(935,711)	(473,349)
Capital Surplus	1,613,307	1,589,281	1,594,332
Other Stockholders' Equity	(276,861)	(307,274)	(269,828)
Total Stockholders' Equity	2,432,974	2,101,733	2,385,812
Total Liabilities and SE	$4,955,884	4,372,313	4,756,492

In Tables 8-9 and 8-10, Mattel's projected income statements and balance sheets respectively for 2007, 2008, and 2009 are provided based on the following hypothetical strategies:

1. The company desires to build 20 Mattel stores annually at a cost of $1 million each.
2. The company plans to develop new toy products at an annual cost of $10 million.
3. The company plans to increase its advertising/promotion expenditures 30 percent over three years, at a cost of $30 million ($10 million per year).
4. The company plans to buy back $100 million of its own stock (called Treasury stock) annually for the next three years.

TABLE 8-9   **Mattel's Projected Income Statements (In Thousands)**

	2009	2008	2007	Author Comment
Total Revenue	$7,520,357	6,836,688	6,215,171	up 10% annually
Cost of Revenue	4,060,992	3,691,811	3,356,192	remains 54%
Gross Profit	3,459,365	3,144,877	2,858,979	subtraction
Operating Expenses				
Research Development	10,000	10,000	10,000	total $30M new
Selling General and Administrative	2,491,717	2,256,107	2,051,006	remains 33% + $10 M annually
Non-Recurring	-	-	-	
Others	-	-	-	
Total Operating Expenses	-	-	-	
Operating Income or Loss	957,648	878,770	797,973	subtraction
Income from Continuing Operations				
Total Other Income/Expenses Net	34,791	34,791	34,791	keep it the same
Earnings Before Interest and Taxes	992,439	913,561	832,764	addition
Interest Expense	97,823	91,423	85,442	up 7%; LTD up 7%
Income Before Tax	894,616	822,138	737,322	
Income Tax Expense	90,829	90,829	90,829	keep it the same
Minority Interest	-	-	-	
Net Income from Continuing Ops	803,787	731,309	646,493	subtraction
Discontinued Operations	-	-	-	
Extraordinary Items	-	-	-	
Effect of Accounting Changes	-	-	-	
Other Items	-	-	-	
Net Income	803,787	731,309	646,493	
Preferred Stock and Other Adjustments	-	-	-	
Net Income Applicable to Common Shares	$803,787	731,309	646,493	

5. The company expects revenues to increase 10 percent annually with the above strategies. Mattel can handle this increase with existing production facilities.
6. Dividend payout will be increased from 57 percent of net income to 60 percent.
7. To finance the $380 million total cost for the above strategies, Mattel plans to use long-term debt for $150 million ($50 million per year for three years) and $230 million by issuing stock ($77 million per year for three years).

The Mattel projected financial statements were prepared using the six steps outlined on prior pages and the above seven strategy statements. Note the cash account is used as the plug figure, and it is too high, so Mattel could reduce this number and concurrently reduce a liability and/or equity account the same amount to keep the statement in balance. Rarely is the cash account perfect on the first pass through, so adjustments are needed and made. However, these adjustments are *not* made on the projected statements given in Tables 8-9 and 8-10, so that the seven strategy statements above can be more readily seen on respective rows. Note the author's comments on Tables 8-9 and 8-10 that help explain changes in the numbers.

The U.S. Securities and Exchange Commission (SEC) conducts fraud investigations if projected numbers are misleading or if they omit information that's important to investors. Projected statements must conform with generally accepted accounting principles (GAAP) and must not be designed to hide poor expected results. The Sarbanes-Oxley Act requires CEOs and CFOs of corporations to personally sign their firms' financial statements attesting to their accuracy. These executives could thus be held personally liable for misleading or inaccurate statements. The collapse of the Arthur Andersen accounting firm, along with its client Enron, fostered a "zero tolerance" policy among auditors and shareholders with regard to a firm's financial statements. But plenty of firms still "inflate" their financial projections and call them "pro formas," so investors, shareholders, and other stakeholders must still be wary of different companies' financial projections.[4]

TABLE 8-10   **Mattel's Projected Balance Sheets (In Thousands)**

	2009	2008	2007	Author Comment
Assets				
Current Assets				
Cash and Cash Equivalents	$3,232,406	2,972,664	2,570,635	too high, could reduce this and pay off some LTD to keep balance
Short-Term Investments	-	-	-	
Net Receivables	943,813	760,643	759,033	
Inventory	509,969	463,609	421,463	up 10% annually
Other Current Assets	317,624	317,624	317,624	keep it the same
Total Current Assets				
Long-Term Investments	-	-	-	
Property, Plant, and Equipment	596,749	576,749	556,749	up $20M annually
Goodwill	845,324	845,324	845,324	keep it the same
Intangible Assets	70,593	70,593	70,593	keep it the same
Accumulated Amortization	-	-	-	
Other Assets	149,912	149,912	149,912	keep it the same
Deferred Long-Term Asset Charges	503,168	503,168	503,168	keep it the same
Total Assets	7,169,558	6,660,286	6,194,501	
Liabilities				
Current Liabilities				
Accounts Payable	1,518,234	1,518,234	1,518,234	keep it the same
Short/Current Long-Term Debt	64,286	64,286	64,286	keep it the same
Other Current Liabilities	-	-	-	
Total Current Liabilities	1,582,520	1,582,520	1,582,520	
Long-Term Debt	785,714	735,714	685,714	up $50M annually
Other Liabilities	304,676	304,676	304,676	keep it the same
Deferred Long-Term Liability Charges	-	-	-	
Minority Interest	-	-	-	
Negative Goodwill	-	-	-	
Total Liabilities	2,672,910	2,622,910	2,572,910	
Stockholders' Equity				
Misc. Stocks, Options, Warrants	-	-	-	
Redeemable Preferred Stock	-	-	-	
Preferred Stock	-	-	-	
Common Stock	441,369	441,369	441,369	keep it the same
Retained Earnings	2,961,092	2,478,820	2,040,035	60% of NI = div
Treasury Stock	(1,296,981)	(1,196,981)	(1,096,981)	up $100M annually
Capital Surplus	2,114,307	2,037,307	1,960,307	up $77M annually
Other Stockholders' Equity	(276,861)	(276,861)	(276,861)	keep it the same
Total Stockholders' Equity	4,496,648	4,037,376	3,621,591	addition
Total Liabilities and SE	$7,169,558	6,660,286	6,194,501	addition

Financial Budgets

A *financial budget* is a document that details how funds will be obtained and spent for a specified period of time. Annual budgets are most common, although the period of time for a budget can range from one day to more than 10 years. Fundamentally, financial budgeting is a method for specifying what must be done to complete strategy implementation successfully. Financial budgeting should not be thought of as a tool for limiting expenditures but rather as a method for obtaining the most productive and profitable use of an organization's resources. Financial budgets can be viewed as the planned allocation of a firm's resources based on forecasts of the future.

There are almost as many different types of financial budgets as there are types of organizations. Some common types of budgets include cash budgets, operating budgets, sales budgets, profit budgets, factory budgets, capital budgets, expense budgets, divisional budgets, variable budgets, flexible budgets, and fixed budgets. When an organization is experiencing financial difficulties, budgets are especially important in guiding strategy implementation.

Perhaps the most common type of financial budget is the *cash budget*. The Financial Accounting Standards Board (FASB) has mandated that every publicly held company in the United States must issue an annual cash-flow statement in addition to the usual financial reports. The statement includes all receipts and disbursements of cash in operations, investments, and financing. It supplements the Statement on Changes in Financial Position formerly included in the annual reports of all publicly held companies. A cash budget for the year 2009 for the Toddler Toy Company is provided in Table 8-11. Note that Toddler is not expecting to have surplus cash until November 2009.

Financial budgets have some limitations. First, budgetary programs can become so detailed that they are cumbersome and overly expensive. Overbudgeting or underbudgeting can cause problems. Second, financial budgets can become a substitute for objectives. A budget is a tool and not an end in itself. Third, budgets can hide inefficiencies if based solely on precedent rather than on periodic evaluation of circumstances and standards. Finally, budgets are sometimes used as instruments of tyranny that result in frustration, resentment, absenteeism, and high turnover. To minimize the effect of this last concern, managers should increase the participation of subordinates in preparing budgets.

Evaluating the Worth of a Business

Evaluating the worth of a business is central to strategy implementation because integrative, intensive, and diversification strategies are often implemented by acquiring other firms. Other strategies, such as retrenchment and divestiture, may result in the sale of a division of an organization or of the firm itself. Thousands of transactions occur each year in which businesses are bought or sold in the United States. In all these cases, it is necessary to establish the financial worth or cash value of a business to successfully implement strategies.

All the various methods for determining a business's worth can be grouped into three main approaches: what a firm owns, what a firm earns, or what a firm will bring in the

TABLE 8-11 Six-Month Cash Budget for the Toddler Toy Company in 2009

Cash Budget (In Thousands)	July	Aug.	Sept.	Oct.	Nov.	Dec.	Jan.
Receipts							
Collections	$12,000	$21,000	$31,000	$35,000	$22,000	$18,000	$11,000
Payments							
Purchases	14,000	21,000	28,000	14,000	14,000	7,000	
Wages and Salaries	1,500	2,000	2,500	1,500	1,500	1,000	
Rent	500	500	500	500	500	500	
Other Expenses	200	300	400	200	—	100	
Taxes	—	8,000	—	—	—	—	
Payment on Machine	—	—	10,000	—	—	—	
Total Payments	$16,200	$31,800	$41,400	$16,200	$16,000	$8,600	
Net Cash Gain (Loss) During Month	−4,200	−10,800	−10,400	18,800	6,000	9,400	
Cash at Start of Month if No Borrowing Is Done	6,000	1,800	−9,000	−19,400	−600	5,400	
Cumulative Cash (Cash at start plus gains or minus losses)	1,800	−9,000	−19,400	−600	5,400	14,800	
Less Desired Level of Cash	−5,000	−5,000	−5,000	−5,000	−5,000	−5,000	
Total Loans Outstanding to Maintain $5,000 Cash Balance	$3,200	$14,000	$24,400	$5,600	—	—	
Surplus Cash	—	—	—	—	400	9,800	

market. But it is important to realize that valuation is not an exact science. The valuation of a firm's worth is based on financial facts, but common sense and intuitive judgment must enter into the process. It is difficult to assign a monetary value to some factors—such as a loyal customer base, a history of growth, legal suits pending, dedicated employees, a favorable lease, a bad credit rating, or good patents—that may not be reflected in a firm's financial statements. Also, different valuation methods will yield different totals for a firm's worth, and no prescribed approach is best for a certain situation. Evaluating the worth of a business truly requires both qualitative and quantitative skills.

The first approach in evaluating the worth of a business is determining its net worth or stockholders' equity. Net worth represents the sum of common stock, additional paid-in capital, and retained earnings. After calculating net worth, add or subtract an appropriate amount for goodwill, overvalued or undervalued assets, and intangibles. Whereas intangibles include copyrights, patents, and trademarks, goodwill arises only if a firm acquires another firm and pays more than the book value for that firm. For example, in late 2007 when M&F Worldwide acquired the much larger check-printing and software firm John H. Harland Company for $1.7 billion, that equated to $52.75 per share, even though John Harland's stock price was only $44.47. So M&F paid a 19 percent premium over the book value (number of shares outstanding times stock price) for John Harland's stock. M&F now carries this on its balance sheet as goodwill. Paying over book value happens quite often. Cisco Systems in late 2007 paid a 23 percent premium in their acquisition of WebEx Communications.

Phillips Electronics NV recently bought U.S.-based Color Kinetics for $794 million to expand its lighting business. This equated to $34 a share, or a 14 percent premium over Color Kinetics' closing share price that day of $29.79. This total provides a reasonable estimate of a firm's monetary value. If a firm has goodwill, it will be listed on the balance sheet, perhaps as "intangibles." It should be noted that Financial Accounting Standard Board (FASB) Rule 142 requires companies to admit once a year if the premiums they paid for acquisitions, called goodwill, were a waste of money. Goodwill is not a good thing to have on a balance sheet. Note in Table 8-12 that Mattel's goodwill of $845 million as a percent of its total assets ($4,955 million) is 17.1 percent, which is extremely high compared to Nordstrom's goodwill of $51 million as a percentage of its total assets ($4,821 million), 1.1 percent. Pfizer's goodwill to total assets percentage also is high at 18.7 percent. As noted in the "Global Perspective" box, accounting standards worldwide are converging, which is good.

The second approach to measuring the value of a firm grows out of the belief that the worth of any business should be based largely on the future benefits its owners may derive through net profits. A conservative rule of thumb is to establish a business's worth as five times the firm's current annual profit. A five-year average profit level could also be used. When using the approach, remember that firms normally suppress earnings in their financial statements to minimize taxes.

The third approach, letting the market determine a business's worth, involves three methods. First, base the firm's worth on the selling price of a similar company. A potential problem, however, is that sometimes comparable figures are not easy to locate, even though substantial information on firms that buy or sell to other firms is available in major libraries. The second approach is called the *price-earnings ratio method.* To use this method, divide the market price of the firm's common stock by the annual earnings per share and multiply this number by the firm's average net income for the past five years. The third method can be called the *outstanding shares method.* To use this method, simply multiply the number of shares outstanding by the market price per share and add a premium. The premium is simply a per-share dollar amount that a person or firm is willing to pay to control (acquire) the other company.

Business evaluations are becoming routine in many situations. Businesses have many strategy-implementation reasons for determining their worth in addition to preparing to be sold or to buy other companies. Employee plans, taxes, retirement packages, mergers, acquisitions, expansion plans, banking relationships, death of a principal, divorce, partnership agreements, and IRS audits are other reasons for a periodic valuation. It is just good business to have a reasonable understanding of what your firm is worth. This knowledge protects the interests of all parties involved.

TABLE 8-12 **Company Worth Analysis for Mattel, Nordstrom, and Pfizer (year-end 2006, in $millions, except stock price and EPS)**

Input Data	Mattel	Nordstrom	Pfizer
Shareholders' Equity	$2,432	$2,168	$71,358
Net Income (NI)	592	677	19,337
Stock Price	25	55	25
EPS	1.48	2.55	2.58
# of Shares Outstanding	393	257	7,090
Goodwill	845	51	20,876
Total Assets	4,955	4,821	114,837
Company Worth Analyses			
1. Shareholders' Equity plus Goodwill	$3,277	$2,219	$92,244
2. Net Income × 5	2,960	3,385	96,685
3. (Stock Price/EPS) × NI	10,000	14,601	187,374
4. # of Shares Out × Stock Price	9,825	14,135	177,250
5. Enterprise Value according to http://finance.yahoo.com	10,840	14,480	168,990
6. Five Method Average	7,380	9,764	144,508
$Goodwill/$Total Assets	17.1%	1.1%	18.7%

GLOBAL PERSPECTIVE
Globally Standardizing Accounting Standards

The Financial Accounting Standards Board (FASB) in the U.S. and its counterpart, the International Accounting Standards Board (IASB), are each modifying its "rules" in an effort to globally converge accounting standards. It is unusual for the FASB to change simply to meet the IASB, but there is more and more movement from both sides toward convergence. And the FASB is changing too. Standard setters in both the United States and other countries mutually desire that the financial statements of a company—say in France—one day will be comparable to those in the U.S. Accounting standards convergence would greatly simplify cross-border investment, interaction, and trade.

The FASB and the IASB began meeting twice yearly in 2002. The European Union of countries has agreed to adopt the IASB's standards by 2005. About 91 countries worldwide will require their companies to comply with IASB standards by 2005. However, there still exist many differences between FASB and IASB standards. For example, the FASB does not allow for upward reevaluation of property, plant, and equipment, whereas the IASB permits periodic reevaluation up or down of assets. Thus, property, plant, and equipment on the statements of U.S. firms is often worth a lot more than reflected on the books. For another example, the IASB wants to remove net income from the income statement, but the

FASB has not reached a decision on this issue. There are also differences between the FASB and IASB in accounting for acquisitions as well as differences about when revenue should be booked.

The United States and the European Union signed a new agreement in May 2007 that paves the way for a single trans-Atlantic accounting standard by 2009. The agreement allows many public U.S. companies to drop American generally accepted accounting principles (GAAP) in favor of more flexible international financial reporting standards (IFRS). The Securities and Exchange Commission (SEC) voted unanimously on June 20, 2007 to allow companies based outside the United States to file financial results using IFRS, without reconciling the figures to GAAP. Later in 2007, the SEC votes on whether to allow U.S. companies to choose whether to file financial statements either under GAAP or IFRS. Part of the motivation for approving such actions is that U.S. stock exchanges are losing market share to London and Hong Kong. The SEC wants more stock listings in the United States. Some analysts believe GAAP will soon be eliminated entirely for everyone.

South Korean companies must adopt international financial reporting standards starting in 2011. This requirement is aimed at building investor confidence through increased transparency. The new regulations are spurring growth in Korea. The perception of weak accounting and disclosure standards in South Korea has been a problem for years for that economy. All publicly held European Union companies must file results using IFRS.

The statutory authority to set accounting standards for public companies in the United States rests with the SEC, although GAAP is overseen by the Financial Accounting Standards Board (FASB), a 24-year-old private-sector group based in Norwalk, Connecticut.

One day decades in the future, there may be one currency worldwide. Certainly, convergence between accounting systems among countries worldwide would be a step in that direction. Establishment of the euro was a big step, too. Convergence of accounting systems simply makes doing business worldwide much easier.

Source: Adapted from Cassell Bryan-Low, "Accounting's Global Rule Book," *Wall Street Journal* (November 28, 2003): C1; John McKinnon, "U.S., EU to Streamline Accounting," *Wall Street Journal* (May 1, 2007): A8; and Kara Scannell and David Reilly, "Foreign Afffair: Is End Near for 'U.S. Only' Accounting?" *Wall Street Journal* (June 21, 2007): C1.

China, Yunnan, Xishuangbanna, Jinghong, Dai women selling vegetables at busy street market. *Source:* Nigel Hicks (c) Dorling Kindersley

Table 8-12 provides the cash value analyses for three companies—Mattel, Nordstrom, and Pfizer—for year-end 2006. Notice that there is significant variation among the four methods used to determine cash value. For example, the worth of the toy company Mattel ranged from $2.29 billion to $10.84 billion. Obviously, if you were selling your company, you would seek the larger values, while if purchasing a company you would seek the lower values. In practice, substantial negotiation takes place in reaching a final compromise (or averaged) amount. Also recognize that if a firm's net income is negative, theoretically the approaches involving that figure would result in a negative number, implying that the firm would pay you to acquire them. Of course, you obtain all of the firm's debt and liabilities in an acquisition, so theoretically this would be possible.

At year-end 2006, Mattel, Nordstrom, and Pfizer had $845 million, $51 million, and $20.876 billion in goodwill respectively on their balance sheets. Most creditors and investors feel that goodwill indeed should be added to the stockholders' equity in calculating worth of a business, but some feel it should be subtracted, and still others feel it should not be included at all. Perhaps whether you are buying or selling the business may determine whether you negotiate to add or subtract goodwill in the analysis. Goodwill is sometimes listed as intangibles on the balance sheet, but technically intangibles refers to patents, trademarks, and copyrights, rather than the value a firm paid over book value for an acquisition, which is goodwill. If a firm paid less than book value for an acquisition, that could be called negative goodwill—which is a line item on Mattel's balance sheets.

Deciding Whether to Go Public

Going public means selling off a percentage of your company to others in order to raise capital; consequently, it dilutes the owners' control of the firm. Going public is not recommended for companies with less than $10 million in sales because the initial costs can be too high for the firm to generate sufficient cash flow to make going public worthwhile. One dollar in four is the average total cost paid to lawyers, accountants, and underwriters when an initial stock issuance is under $1 million; 1 dollar in 20 will go to cover these costs for issuances over $20 million.

In addition to initial costs involved with a stock offering, there are costs and obligations associated with reporting and management in a publicly held firm. For firms with more than $10 million in sales, going public can provide major advantages: It can allow the firm to raise capital to develop new products, build plants, expand, grow, and market products and services more effectively.

Research and Development (R&D) Issues

Research and development (R&D) personnel can play an integral part in strategy implementation. These individuals are generally charged with developing new products and improving old products in a way that will allow effective strategy implementation. R&D employees and managers perform tasks that include transferring complex technology, adjusting processes to local raw materials, adapting processes to local markets, and altering products to particular tastes and specifications. Strategies such as product development, market penetration, and related diversification require that new products be successfully developed and that old products be significantly improved. But the level of management support for R&D is often constrained by resource availability.

Technological improvements that affect consumer and industrial products and services shorten product life cycles. Companies in virtually every industry are relying on the development of new products and services to fuel profitability and growth.[5] Surveys suggest that the most successful organizations use an R&D strategy that ties external opportunities to internal strengths and is linked with objectives. Well-formulated R&D policies match market opportunities with internal capabilities. R&D policies can enhance strategy implementation efforts to:

1. Emphasize product or process improvements.
2. Stress basic or applied research.
3. Be leaders or followers in R&D.
4. Develop robotics or manual-type processes.
5. Spend a high, average, or low amount of money on R&D.
6. Perform R&D within the firm or to contract R&D to outside firms.
7. Use university researchers or private-sector researchers.

There must be effective interactions between R&D departments and other functional departments in implementing different types of generic business strategies. Conflicts between marketing, finance/accounting, R&D, and information systems departments can be minimized with clear policies and objectives. Table 8-13 gives some examples of R&D activities that could be required for successful implementation of various strategies. Many U.S. utility, energy, and automotive companies are employing their research and development departments to determine how the firm can effectively reduce its gas emissions.

TABLE 8–13 Research and Development Involvement in Selected Strategy-Implementation Situations

Type of Organization	Strategy Being Implemented	R&D Activity
Pharmaceutical company	Product development	Test the effects of a new drug on different subgroups.
Boat manufacturer	Related diversification	Test the performance of various keel designs under various conditions.
Plastic container manufacturer	Market penetration	Develop a biodegradable container.
Electronics company	Market development	Develop a telecommunications system in a foreign country.

Many firms wrestle with the decision to acquire R&D expertise from external firms or to develop R&D expertise internally. The following guidelines can be used to help make this decision:

1. If the rate of technical progress is slow, the rate of market growth is moderate, and there are significant barriers to possible new entrants, then in-house R&D is the preferred solution. The reason is that R&D, if successful, will result in a temporary product or process monopoly that the company can exploit.

2. If technology is changing rapidly and the market is growing slowly, then a major effort in R&D may be very risky, because it may lead to the development of an ultimately obsolete technology or one for which there is no market.

3. If technology is changing slowly but the market is growing quickly, there generally is not enough time for in-house development. The prescribed approach is to obtain R&D expertise on an exclusive or nonexclusive basis from an outside firm.

4. If both technical progress and market growth are fast, R&D expertise should be obtained through acquisition of a well-established firm in the industry.[6]

There are at least three major R&D approaches for implementing strategies. The first strategy is to be the first firm to market new technological products. This is a glamorous and exciting strategy but also a dangerous one. Firms such as 3M and General Electric have been successful with this approach, but many other pioneering firms have fallen, with rival firms seizing the initiative.

A second R&D approach is to be an innovative imitator of successful products, thus minimizing the risks and costs of start-up. This approach entails allowing a pioneer firm to develop the first version of the new product and to demonstrate that a market exists. Then, laggard firms develop a similar product. This strategy requires excellent R&D personnel and an excellent marketing department.

A third R&D strategy is to be a low-cost producer by mass-producing products similar to but less expensive than products recently introduced. As a new product is accepted by customers, price becomes increasingly important in the buying decision. Also, mass marketing replaces personal selling as the dominant selling strategy. This R&D strategy, requires substantial investment in plant and equipment but fewer expenditures in R&D than the two approaches described previously.

R&D activities among U.S. firms need to be more closely aligned to business objectives. There needs to be expanded communication between R&D managers and strategists. Corporations are experimenting with various methods to achieve this improved communication climate, including different roles and reporting arrangements for managers and new methods to reduce the time it takes research ideas to become reality.

Perhaps the most current trend in R&D management has been lifting the veil of secrecy whereby firms, even major competitors, are joining forces to develop new products. Collaboration is on the rise due to new competitive pressures, rising research costs, increasing regulatory issues, and accelerated product development schedules. Companies not only are working more closely with each other on R&D, but they are also turning to consortia at universities for their R&D needs. More than 600 research consortia are now in operation in the United States. Lifting of R&D secrecy among many firms through collaboration has allowed the marketing of new technologies and products even before they are available for sale. For example, some firms are collaborating on the efficient design of solar panels to power homes and businesses.

Management Information Systems (MIS) Issues

Firms that gather, assimilate, and evaluate external and internal information most effectively are gaining competitive advantages over other firms. Recognizing the importance of having an effective *management information system (MIS)* will not be an option in the future; it will be a requirement. Information is the basis for understanding in a firm. In many industries, information is becoming the most important factor in differentiating successful from unsuccessful firms. The process of strategic management is facilitated immensely in firms that have an effective information system. Many companies are establishing a new approach to information systems, one that blends the technical knowledge of the computer experts with the vision of senior management.

Information collection, retrieval, and storage can be used to create competitive advantages in ways such as cross-selling to customers, monitoring suppliers, keeping managers and employees informed, coordinating activities among divisions, and managing funds. Like inventory and human resources, information is now recognized as a valuable organizational asset that can be controlled and managed. Firms that implement strategies using the best information will reap competitive advantages in the twenty-first century.

A good information system can allow a firm to reduce costs. For example, online orders from salespersons to production facilities can shorten materials ordering time and reduce inventory costs. Direct communications between suppliers, manufacturers, marketers, and customers can link together elements of the value chain as though they were one organization. Improved quality and service often result from an improved information system.

Firms must increasingly be concerned about computer hackers and take specific measures to secure and safeguard corporate communications, files, orders, and business conducted over the Internet. Thousands of companies today are plagued by computer hackers who include disgruntled employees, competitors, bored teens, sociopaths, thieves, spies, and hired agents. Computer vulnerability is a giant, expensive headache.

Dun & Bradstreet is an example of a company that has an excellent information system. Every D&B customer and client in the world has a separate nine-digit number. The database of information associated with each number has become so widely used that it is like a business Social Security number. D&B reaps great competitive advantages from its information system.

In many firms, information technology is doing away with the workplace and allowing employees to work at home or anywhere, anytime. The mobile concept of work allows employees to work the traditional 9-to-5 workday across any of the 24 time zones around the globe. Affordable desktop videoconferencing software developed by AT&T, Lotus, or Vivo Software allows employees to "beam in" whenever needed. Any manager or employee who travels a lot away from the office is a good candidate for working at home rather than in an office provided by the firm. Salespersons or consultants are good examples, but any person whose job largely involves talking to others or handling information could easily operate at home with the proper computer system and software.

Many people see the officeless office trend as leading to a resurgence of family togetherness in U.S. society. Even the design of homes may change from having large open areas to having more private small areas conducive to getting work done.[7]

Conclusion

Successful strategy implementation depends on cooperation among all functional and divisional managers in an organization. Marketing departments are commonly charged with implementing strategies that require significant increases in sales revenues in new areas and with new or improved products. Finance and accounting managers must devise effective strategy-implementation approaches at low cost and minimum risk to that firm. R&D managers have to transfer complex technologies or develop new technologies to successfully implement strategies. Information systems managers are being called upon more and more to provide leadership and training for all individuals in the firm. The nature and role of marketing, finance/accounting, R&D, and management information systems activities, coupled with the management activities described in Chapter 7, largely determine organizational success.

We invite you to visit the David page on the Prentice Hall Companion Web site at www.prenhall.com/david for this chapter's review quiz.

Key Terms and Concepts

Cash Budget (p. 284)
EPS/EBIT Analysis (p. 273)
Financial Budget (p. 283)
Management Information System (MIS) (p. 290)
Market Segmentation (p. 267)
Marketing Mix Variables (p. 267)
Outstanding Shares Method (p. 285)
Price-Earnings Ratio Method (p. 285)
Product Positioning (p. 267)
Projected Financial Statement Analysis (p. 278)
Research and Development (R&D) (p. 288)
Vacant Niche (p. 270)

Issues For Review and Discussion

1. Suppose your company has just acquired a firm that produces battery-operated lawn mowers, and strategists want to implement a market-penetration strategy. How would you segment the market for this product? Justify your answer.
2. Explain how you would estimate the total worth of a business.
3. Diagram and label clearly a product-positioning map that includes six fast-food restaurant chains.
4. Explain why EPS/EBIT analysis is a central strategy-implementation technique.
5. How would the R&D role in strategy implementation differ in small versus large organizations?
6. Discuss the limitations of EPS/EBIT analysis.
7. Explain how marketing, finance/accounting, R&D, and management information systems managers' involvement in strategy formulation can enhance strategy implementation.
8. Consider the following statement: "Retained earnings on the balance sheet are not monies available to finance strategy implementation." Is it true or false? Explain.
9. Explain why projected financial statement analysis is considered both a strategy-formulation and a strategy-implementation tool.
10. Describe some marketing, finance/accounting, R&D, and management information systems activities that a small restaurant chain might undertake to expand into a neighboring state.
11. Discuss the management information system at your college or university.
12. What effect is e-commerce having on firms' efforts to segment markets?
13. How has the Sarbanes-Oxley Act of 2002 changed CEOs' and CFOs' handling of financial statements?
14. To what extent have you been exposed to natural environment issues in your business courses? Which course has provided the most coverage? What percentage of your business courses provided no coverage? Comment.
15. Complete the following EPS/EBIT analysis for a company whose stock price is $20, interest rate on funds is 5 percent, tax rate is 20 percent, number of shares outstanding is 500 million, and EBIT range is $100 million to $300 million. The firm needs to raise $200 million in capital. Use the table accompanying to complete the work.
16. Under what conditions would retained earnings on the balance sheet decrease from one year to the next?
17. In your own words, list all the steps in developing projected financial statements.
18. Based on the financial statements provided for Walt Disney (pp 32–33), how much dividends in dollars did Walt Disney pay in 2006? In 2007?
19. Based on the financial statements provided in this chapter for the Litten Company, calculate the value of this company if you know that its stock price is $20 and it has 1 million shares outstanding. Calculate four different ways and average.
20. Why should you be careful not to use historical percentages blindly in developing projected financial statements?

21. In developing projected financial statements, what should you do if the $ amount you must put in the cash account (to make the statement balance) is far more (or less) than desired?

22. Why is it both important and necessary to segment markets and target groups of customers, rather than market to all possible consumers?

23. In full detail, explain the following EPS/EBIT chart.

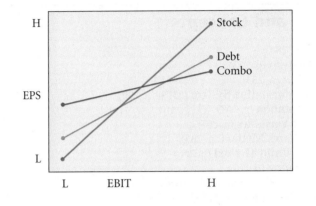

	100% Common Stock	100% Debt Financing	20%Debt–80%Stock
EBIT			
Interest			
EBT			
Taxes			
EAT			
# Shares			
EPS			

Notes

1. Leslie Miller and Elizabeth Weise, "E-Privacy—FTC Studies 'Profiling' by Web Sites," *USA Today* (November 8, 1999): 1A, 2A.

2. Ralph Biggadike, "The Contributions of Marketing to Strategic Management," *Academy of Management Review* 6, no. 4 (October 1981): 627.

3. Phyllis Plitch, "Companies in Many Sectors Give Earnings a Pro Forma Makeover, Survey Finds," *Wall Street Journal* (January 22, 2002): A4.

4. Michael Rapoport, "Pro Forma Is a Hard Habit to Break," *Wall Street Journal* (September 18, 2003): B3A.

5. Amy Merrick, "U.S. Research Spending to Rise Only 3.2 Percent," *Wall Street Journal* (December 28, 2001): A2.

6. Pier Abetti, "Technology: A Key Strategic Resource," *Management Review* 78, no. 2 (February 1989): 38.

7. Adapted from Edward Baig, "Welcome to the Officeless Office," *BusinessWeek* (June 26, 1995).

Current Readings

Dean, Alison and Martin Kretschmer. "Can Ideas Be Capital? Factors of Production in the Postindustrial Economy: A Review and Critique." *The Academy of Management Review* 32, no. 2 (April 2007): 573).

Fine, Leslie M. "Selling and sales management." *Business Horizon* 50, no. 3 (May-June 2007): 185.

Fine, Leslie M. "Spotlight on Marketing." *Business Horizons* 49, no. 3 (May–June 2006): 179.

Herremans, Irene, John K. Ryans, Jr., and Linda C. Ueltschy. "Marketing: Who's Really Minding the Store Globally?" *Business Horizons* 49, no. 2 (March–April 2006): 139.

Katsikeas, C. S., S. Samiee, and M. Theodosiou. "Strategy Fit and Performance Consequences of International Marketing." *Strategic Management Journal* 27, no. 9 (September 2006): 867.

Mani, S., K.D. Anita, and A. Rindfleisch. "Entry Mode and Equity Level: A Multilevel Examination of Foreign Direct Investment Ownership Structure." *Strategic Management Journal* 28, no. 8 (August 2007): 857–867.

• EXPERIENTIAL EXERCISES   DISNEY

Experiential Exercise 8A

Developing a Product-Positioning Map for Walt Disney

Purpose

Organizations continually monitor how their products and services are positioned relative to competitors. This information is especially useful for marketing managers but is also used by other managers and strategists.

Instructions

Step 1 On a separate sheet of paper, develop a product-positioning map for Walt Disney. Include Time Warner, and News Corporation in your diagram.

Step 2 At the chalkboard, diagram your product-positioning map.

Step 3 Compare your product-positioning map with those diagrammed by other students. Discuss any major differences.

A Mickey Mouse Disneyland promotional badge. *Source:* (c) Judith Miller / Dorling Kindersley / Cad Van Swankster at The Girl Can't Help It

Experiential Exercise 8B

Performing an EPS/EBIT Analysis for Walt Disney

Purpose

An EPS/EBIT analysis is one of the most widely used techniques for determining the extent that debt and/or stock should be used to finance strategies to be implemented. This exercise can give you practice performing EPS/EBIT analysis.

Instructions (1-1-08 Data)

Let's say Walt Disney needs to raise $1 billion to revamp its California Adventure theme park. Determine whether Walt Disney should have used all debt, all stock, or a 50-50 combination of debt and stock to finance this market-development strategy. Assume a 38 percent tax rate, 5 percent interest rate, Walt Disney stock price of $30 per share, and an annual dividend of $0.30 per share of common stock. The EBIT range for 2008 is between $7.725 billion and $10 billion. A total of 2 billion shares of common stock are outstanding. Develop an EPS/EBIT chart to reflect your analysis.

Experiential Exercise 8C

Preparing Projected Financial Statements for Walt Disney

Purpose

This exercise is designed to give you experience preparing projected financial statements. Pro forma analysis is a central strategy-implementation technique because it allows managers to anticipate and evaluate the expected results of various strategy-implementation approaches.

Instructions

Step 1   Work with a classmate. Develop a 2008 projected income statement and balance sheet for Walt Disney. Assume that Walt Disney plans to raise $900 million in 2008 to begin serving new countries and plans to obtain 50 percent financing from a bank and 50 percent financing from a stock issuance. Make other assumptions as needed, and state them clearly in written form.

Step 2   Compute Walt Disney current ratio, debt-to-equity ratio, and return-on-investment ratio for 2006 and 2007. How do your 2008 projected ratios compare to the 2006 and 2007 ratios? Why is it important to make this comparison? Use http://finance.yahoo.com to obtain 2007 financial statements.

Step 3   Bring your projected statements to class, and discuss any problems or questions you encountered.

Step 4   Compare your projected statements to the statements of other students. What major differences exist between your analysis and the work of other students?

Experiential Exercise 8D

Determining the Cash Value of Walt Disney

Purpose

It is simply good business practice to periodically determine the financial worth or cash value of your company. This exercise gives you practice determining the total worth of a company using several methods. Use year-end 2007 data as given in the Cohesion Case on pp. 32–33.

Instructions

Step 1   Calculate the financial worth of Walt Disney based on four methods: (1) the net worth or stockholders' equity, (2) the future value of Walt Disney earnings, (3) the price-earnings ratio, and (4) the outstanding shares method.

Step 2   In a dollar amount, how much is Walt Disney worth?

Step 3   Compare your analyses and conclusions with those of other students.

Experiential Exercise 8E

Developing a Product-Positioning Map for My University

Purpose

The purpose of this exercise is to give you practice developing product-positioning maps. Nonprofit organizations, such as universities, are increasingly using product-positioning maps to determine effective ways to implement strategies.

Instructions

Step 1   Join with two other people in class to form a group of three.

Step 2   Jointly prepare a product-positioning map that includes your institution and four other colleges or universities in your state.

Step 3   At the chalkboard, diagram your product-positioning map.

Step 4   Discuss differences among the maps diagrammed on the board.

Experiential Exercise 8F

Do Banks Require Projected Financial Statements?

Purpose

The purpose of this exercise is to explore the practical importance and use of projected financial statements in the banking business.

Instructions

Contact two local bankers by phone and seek answers to the questions that follow. Record the answers you receive, and report your findings to the class.

1. Does your bank require projected financial statements as part of a business loan application?
2. How does your bank use projected financial statements when they are part of a business loan application?
3. What special advice do you give potential business borrowers in preparing projected financial statements?

Part 4 • Strategy Evaluation

9 Strategy Review, Evaluation, and Control

"notable quotes"

Complicated controls do not work. They confuse. They misdirect attention from what is to be controlled to the mechanics and methodology of the control.

SEYMOUR TILLES

Although Plan A may be selected as the most realistic ... the other major alternatives should not be forgotten. They may well serve as contingency plans.

DALE MCCONKEY

Organizations are most vulnerable when they are at the peak of their success.

R. T. LENZ

Strategy evaluation must make it as easy as possible for managers to revise their plans and reach quick agreement on the changes.

DALE MCCONKEY

While strategy is a word that is usually associated with the future, its link to the past is no less central. Life is lived forward but understood backward. Managers may live strategy in the future, but they understand it through the past.

HENRY MINTZBERG

Unless strategy evaluation is performed seriously and systematically, and unless strategists are willing to act on the results, energy will be used up defending yesterday. No one will have the time, resources, or will to work on exploiting today, let alone to work on making tomorrow.

PETER DRUCKER

Executives, consultants, and B-school professors all agree that strategic planning is now the single most important management issue and will remain so for the next five years. Strategy has become a part of the main agenda at lots of organizations today. Strategic planning is back with a vengeance.

JOHN BYRNE

Planners should not plan, but serve as facilitators, catalysts, inquirers, educators, and synthesizers to guide the planning process effectively.

A. HAX AND N. MAJLUF

Time to Receive Diplomas. *Source:* Bryan David

experiential exercises

Experiential Exercise 9A
Preparing a Strategy-Evaluation Report for Walt Disney

Experiential Exercise 9B
Evaluating My University's Strategies

Experiential Exercise 9C
Who Prepares an Environmental Audit?

chapter objectives

After studying this chapter, you should be able to do the following:

1. Describe a practical framework for evaluating strategies.

2. Explain why strategy evaluation is complex, sensitive, and yet essential for organizational success.

3. Discuss the importance of contingency planning in strategy evaluation.

4. Discuss the role of auditing in strategy evaluation.

5. Explain how computers can aid in evaluating strategies.

6. Discuss the Balanced Scorecard.

7. Discuss three twenty-first-century challenges in strategic management.

The best-formulated and best-implemented strategies become obsolete as a firm's external and internal environments change. It is essential, therefore, that strategists systematically review, evaluate, and control the execution of strategies. This chapter presents a framework that can guide managers' efforts to evaluate strategic-management activities, to make sure they are working, and to make timely changes. Management information systems being used to evaluate strategies are discussed. Guidelines are presented for formulating, implementing, and evaluating strategies.

The Nature of Strategy Evaluation

VISIT THE NET

Gives excellent additional information about evaluating strategies, including some analytical tools. (www.mindtools.com/plevplan.html)

The strategic-management process results in decisions that can have significant, long-lasting consequences. Erroneous strategic decisions can inflict severe penalties and can be exceedingly difficult, if not impossible, to reverse. Most strategists agree, therefore, that strategy evaluation is vital to an organization's well-being; timely evaluations can alert management to problems or potential problems before a situation becomes critical. Strategy evaluation includes three basic activities: (1) examining the underlying bases of a firm's strategy, (2) comparing expected results with actual results, and (3) taking corrective actions to ensure that performance conforms to plans. The strategy-evaluation stage of the strategic-management process is illustrated in Figure 9-1.

Adequate and timely feedback is the cornerstone of effective strategy evaluation. Strategy evaluation can be no better than the information on which it is based. Too much pressure from top managers may result in lower managers contriving numbers they think will be satisfactory.

Strategy evaluation can be a complex and sensitive undertaking. Too much emphasis on evaluating strategies may be expensive and counterproductive. No one likes to be evaluated too closely! The more managers attempt to evaluate the behavior of others, the less control they have. Yet too little or no evaluation can create even worse problems. Strategy evaluation is essential to ensure that stated objectives are being achieved.

FIGURE 9-1

A Comprehensive Strategic-Management Model

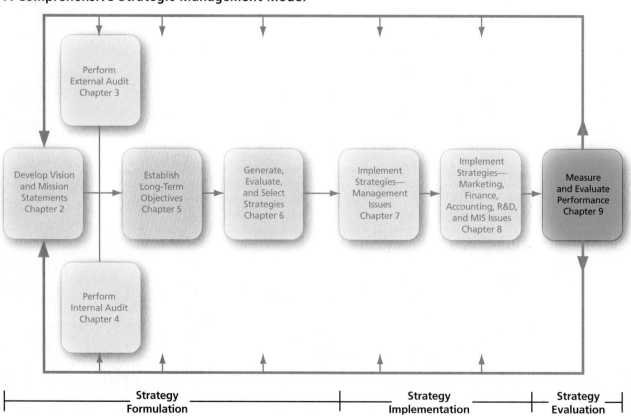

Source: Fred R. David, "How Companies Define Their Mission," *Long Range Planning* 22, no. 3 (June 1988): 40.

In many organizations, strategy evaluation is simply an appraisal of how well an organization has performed. Have the firm's assets increased? Has there been an increase in profitability? Have sales increased? Have productivity levels increased? Have profit margin, return on investment, and earnings-per-share ratios increased? Some firms argue that their strategy must have been correct if the answers to these types of questions are affirmative. Well, the strategy or strategies may have been correct, but this type of reasoning can be misleading because strategy evaluation must have both a long-run and short-run focus. Strategies often do not affect short-term operating results until it is too late to make needed changes.

It is impossible to demonstrate conclusively that a particular strategy is optimal or even to guarantee that it will work. One can, however, evaluate it for critical flaws. Richard Rumelt offered four criteria that could be used to evaluate a strategy: consistency, consonance, feasibility, and advantage. Described in Table 9-1, *consonance* and *advantage* are mostly based on a firm's external assessment, whereas *consistency* and *feasibility* are largely based on an internal assessment.

TABLE 9-1   Rumelt's Criteria for Evaluating Strategies

consistency

A strategy should not present inconsistent goals and policies. Organizational conflict and interdepartmental bickering are often symptoms of managerial disorder, but these problems may also be a sign of strategic inconsistency. Three guidelines help determine if organizational problems are due to inconsistencies in strategy:

- If managerial problems continue despite changes in personnel and if they tend to be issue-based rather than people-based, then strategies may be inconsistent.
- If success for one organizational department means, or is interpreted to mean, failure for another department, then strategies may be inconsistent.
- If policy problems and issues continue to be brought to the top for resolution, then strategies may be inconsistent.

consonance

Consonance refers to the need for strategists to examine *sets of trends*, as well as individual trends, in evaluating strategies. A strategy must represent an adaptive response to the external environment and to the critical changes occurring within it. One difficulty in matching a firm's key internal and external factors in the formulation of strategy is that most trends are the result of interactions among other trends. For example, the day-care explosion came about as a combined result of many trends that included a rise in the average level of education, increased inflation, and an increase in women in the workforce. Although single economic or demographic trends might appear steady for many years, there are waves of change going on at the interaction level.

feasibility

A strategy must neither overtax available resources nor create unsolvable subproblems. The final broad test of strategy is its feasibility; that is, can the strategy be attempted within the physical, human, and financial resources of the enterprise? The financial resources of a business are the easiest to quantify and are normally the first limitation against which strategy is evaluated. It is sometimes forgotten, however, that innovative approaches to financing are often possible. Devices, such as captive subsidiaries, sale-leaseback arrangements, and tying plant mortgages to long-term contracts, have all been used effectively to help win key positions in suddenly expanding industries. A less quantifiable, but actually more rigid, limitation on strategic choice is that imposed by individual and organizational capabilities. In evaluating a strategy, it is important to examine whether an organization has demonstrated in the past that it possesses the abilities, competencies, skills, and talents needed to carry out a given strategy.

advantage

A strategy must provide for the creation and/or maintenance of a competitive advantage in a selected area of activity. Competitive advantages normally are the result of superiority in one of three areas: (1) resources, (2) skills, or (3) position. The idea that the positioning of one's resources can enhance their combined effectiveness is familiar to military theorists, chess players, and diplomats. Position can also play a crucial role in an organization's strategy. Once gained, a good position is defensible—meaning that it is so costly to capture that rivals are deterred from full-scale attacks. Positional advantage tends to be self-sustaining as long as the key internal and environmental factors that underlie it remain stable. This is why entrenched firms can be almost impossible to unseat, even if their raw skill levels are only average. Although not all positional advantages are associated with size, it is true that larger organizations tend to operate in markets and use procedures that turn their size into advantage, while smaller firms seek product/market positions that exploit other types of advantage. The principal characteristic of good position is that it permits the firm to obtain advantage from policies that would not similarly benefit rivals without the same position. Therefore, in evaluating strategy, organizations should examine the nature of positional advantages associated with a given strategy.

Source: Adapted from Richard Rumelt, "The Evaluation of Business Strategy," in W. F. Glueck (ed.), *Business Policy and Strategic Management* (New York: McGraw-Hill, 1980): 359–367.

VISIT THE NET

Describes the how and why of strategy evaluation. (www. csuchico.edu/mgmt/strategy/ module1/sld046.htm)

Strategy evaluation is important because organizations face dynamic environments in which key external and internal factors often change quickly and dramatically. Success today is no guarantee of success tomorrow! An organization should never be lulled into complacency with success. Countless firms have thrived one year only to struggle for survival the following year. Organizational trouble can come swiftly, as further evidenced by the examples described in Table 9-2.

Strategy evaluation is becoming increasingly difficult with the passage of time, for many reasons. Domestic and world economies were more stable in years past, product life cycles were longer, product development cycles were longer, technological advancement was slower, change occurred less frequently, there were fewer competitors, foreign companies were weak, and there were more regulated industries. Other reasons why strategy evaluation is more difficult today include the following trends:

1. A dramatic increase in the environment's complexity
2. The increasing difficulty of predicting the future with accuracy
3. The increasing number of variables
4. The rapid rate of obsolescence of even the best plans
5. The increase in the number of both domestic and world events affecting organizations
6. The decreasing time span for which planning can be done with any degree of certainty[1]

A fundamental problem facing managers today is how to effectively control employees in light of modern organizational demands for greater flexibility, innovation, creativity, and initiative from employees.[2] How can managers today ensure that empowered employees acting in an entrepreneurial manner do not put the well-being of the business at risk? Recall that Kidder, Peabody & Company lost $350 million when one of its traders allegedly booked fictitious profits; Sears, Roebuck and Company took a $60 million charge against earnings after admitting that its automobile service businesses were performing unnecessary repairs. The costs to companies such as these in terms of damaged reputations, fines, missed opportunities, and diversion of management's attention are enormous.

TABLE 9-2   Examples of Organizational Demise

A. Some Large Companies That Experienced a Large Drop in Revenues in 2006 vs. 2005		B. Some Large Companies That Experienced a Large Drop in Profits in 2006 vs. 2005	
Avis Budget Group	−71%	Avis Budget Group	−249%
American Express	−10%	Coca-Cola Enterprises	−322%
Brinks	−44%	Mosaic	−173%
Dynegy	−69%	Dynegy	−423%
First Data	−33%	Sungard Data Systems	−201%
Louisiana-Pacific	−18%	Centene	−178%
Saks	−40%	WCI Communities	−95%
Spectrum Brands	−434%	Spectrum Brands	−1,027%
Visteon	−33%	Clorox	−15%
OGE Energy	−33%	SAIC	−95%
Laidlaw International	−15%	Boston Scientific	−670%
Duke Energy	−16%	New York Times	−309%
Aquila	−14%	R.H. Donnelley	−452%

When empowered employees are held accountable for and pressured to achieve specific goals and are given wide latitude in their actions to achieve them, there can be dysfunctional behavior. For example, Nordstrom, the upscale fashion retailer known for outstanding customer service, was subjected to lawsuits and fines when employees underreported hours worked in order to increase their sales per hour—the company's primary performance criterion. Nordstrom's customer service and earnings were enhanced until the misconduct was reported, at which time severe penalties were levied against the firm.

The Process of Evaluating Strategies

Strategy evaluation is necessary for all sizes and kinds of organizations. Strategy evaluation should initiate managerial questioning of expectations and assumptions, should trigger a review of objectives and values, and should stimulate creativity in generating alternatives and formulating criteria of evaluation.[3] Regardless of the size of the organization, a certain amount of *management by wandering around* at all levels is essential to effective strategy evaluation. Strategy-evaluation activities should be performed on a continuing basis, rather than at the end of specified periods of time or just after problems occur. Waiting until the end of the year, for example, could result in a firm closing the barn door after the horses have already escaped.

Evaluating strategies on a continuous rather than on a periodic basis allows benchmarks of progress to be established and more effectively monitored. Some strategies take years to implement; consequently, associated results may not become apparent for years. Successful strategies combine patience with a willingness to promptly take corrective actions when necessary. There always comes a time when corrective actions are needed in an organization! Centuries ago, a writer (perhaps Solomon) made the following observations about change:

> There is a time for everything,
> A time to be born and a time to die,
> A time to plant and a time to uproot,
> A time to kill and a time to heal,
> A time to tear down and a time to build,
> A time to weep and a time to laugh,
> A time to mourn and a time to dance,
> A time to scatter stones and a time to gather them,
> A time to embrace and a time to refrain,
> A time to search and a time to give up,
> A time to keep and a time to throw away,
> A time to tear and a time to mend,
> A time to be silent and a time to speak,
> A time to love and a time to hate,
> A time for war and a time for peace.[4]

Managers and employees of the firm should be continually aware of progress being made toward achieving the firm's objectives. As critical success factors change, organizational members should be involved in determining appropriate corrective actions. If assumptions and expectations deviate significantly from forecasts, then the firm should renew strategy-formulation activities, perhaps sooner than planned. In strategy evaluation, like strategy formulation and strategy implementation, people make the difference. Through involvement in the process of evaluating strategies, managers and employees become committed to keeping the firm moving steadily toward achieving objectives.

A Strategy-Evaluation Framework

Table 9-3 summarizes strategy-evaluation activities in terms of key questions that should be addressed, alternative answers to those questions, and appropriate actions for an organization to take. Notice that corrective actions are almost always needed except when (1) external and internal factors have not significantly changed and (2) the firm is progressing

VISIT THE NET

Elaborates on the "taking corrective actions" phase of strategy evaluation. (www.csuchico.edu/mgmt/strategy/module1/sld047.htm)

TABLE 9-3 A Strategy-Evaluation Assessment Matrix

Have Major Changes Occurred in the Firm Internal Strategic Position?	Have Major Changes Occurred in the Firm External Strategic Position?	Has the Firm Progressed Satisfactorily Toward Achieving Its Stated Objectives?	Result
No	No	No	Take corrective actions
Yes	Yes	Yes	Take corrective actions
Yes	Yes	No	Take corrective actions
Yes	No	Yes	Take corrective actions
Yes	No	No	Take corrective actions
No	Yes	Yes	Take corrective actions
No	Yes	No	Take corrective actions
No	No	Yes	Continue present strategic course

satisfactorily toward achieving stated objectives. Relationships among strategy-evaluation activities are illustrated in Figure 9-2.

Reviewing Bases of Strategy

As shown in Figure 9-2, *reviewing the underlying bases of an organization's strategy* could be approached by developing a revised EFE Matrix and IFE Matrix. A *revised IFE Matrix* should focus on changes in the organization's management, marketing, finance/accounting, production/operations, R&D, and management information systems strengths and weaknesses. A *revised EFE Matrix* should indicate how effective a firm's strategies have been in response to key opportunities and threats. This analysis could also address such questions as the following:

1. How have competitors reacted to our strategies?
2. How have competitors' strategies changed?
3. Have major competitors' strengths and weaknesses changed?
4. Why are competitors making certain strategic changes?
5. Why are some competitors' strategies more successful than others?
6. How satisfied are our competitors with their present market positions and profitability?
7. How far can our major competitors be pushed before retaliating?
8. How could we more effectively cooperate with our competitors?

Numerous external and internal factors can prevent firms from achieving long-term and annual objectives. Externally, actions by competitors, changes in demand, changes in technology, economic changes, demographic shifts, and governmental actions may prevent objectives from being accomplished. Internally, ineffective strategies may have been chosen or implementation activities may have been poor. Objectives may have been too optimistic. Thus, failure to achieve objectives may not be the result of unsatisfactory work by managers and employees. All organizational members need to know this to encourage their support for strategy-evaluation activities. Organizations desperately need to know as soon as possible when their strategies are not effective. Sometimes managers and employees on the front lines discover this well before strategists.

External opportunities and threats and internal strengths and weaknesses that represent the bases of current strategies should continually be monitored for change. It is not really a question of whether these factors will change but rather when they will change and in what ways. Some key questions to address in evaluating strategies follow:

1. Are our internal strengths still strengths?
2. Have we added other internal strengths? If so, what are they?
3. Are our internal weaknesses still weaknesses?

FIGURE 9-2

A Strategy-Evaluation Framework

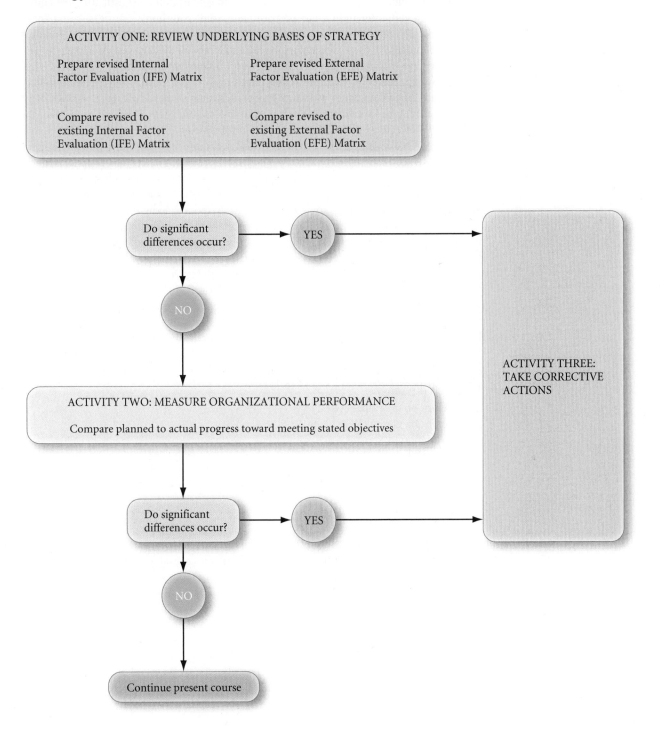

4. Do we now have other internal weaknesses? If so, what are they?
5. Are our external opportunities still opportunities?
6. Are there now other external opportunities? If so, what are they?
7. Are our external threats still threats?
8. Are there now other external threats? If so, what are they?
9. Are we vulnerable to a hostile takeover?

Measuring Organizational Performance

Another important strategy-evaluation activity is *measuring organizational performance*. This activity includes comparing expected results to actual results, investigating deviations from plans, evaluating individual performance, and examining progress being made toward meeting stated objectives. Both long-term and annual objectives are commonly used in this process. Criteria for evaluating strategies should be measurable and easily verifiable. Criteria that predict results may be more important than those that reveal what already has happened. For example, rather than simply being informed that sales in the last quarter were 20 percent under what was expected, strategists need to know that sales in the next quarter may be 20 percent below standard unless some action is taken to counter the trend. Really effective control requires accurate forecasting.

Failure to make satisfactory progress toward accomplishing long-term or annual objectives signals a need for corrective actions. Many factors, such as unreasonable policies, unexpected turns in the economy, unreliable suppliers or distributors, or ineffective strategies, can result in unsatisfactory progress toward meeting objectives. Problems can result from ineffectiveness (not doing the right things) or inefficiency (poorly doing the right things).

Determining which objectives are most important in the evaluation of strategies can be difficult. Strategy evaluation is based on both quantitative and qualitative criteria. Selecting the exact set of criteria for evaluating strategies depends on a particular organization's size, industry, strategies, and management philosophy. An organization pursuing a retrenchment strategy, for example, could have an entirely different set of evaluative criteria from an organization pursuing a market-development strategy. Quantitative criteria commonly used to evaluate strategies are financial ratios, which strategists use to make three critical comparisons: (1) comparing the firm's performance over different time periods, (2) comparing the firm's performance to competitors', and (3) comparing the firm's performance to industry averages. Some key financial ratios that are particularly useful as criteria for strategy evaluation are as follows:

1. Return on investment (ROI)
2. Return on equity (ROE)
3. Profit margin
4. Market share
5. Debt to equity
6. Earnings per share
7. Sales growth
8. Asset growth

But there are some potential problems associated with using quantitative criteria for evaluating strategies. First, most quantitative criteria are geared to annual objectives rather than long-term objectives. Also, different accounting methods can provide different results on many quantitative criteria. Third, intuitive judgments are almost always involved in deriving quantitative criteria. For these and other reasons, qualitative criteria are also important in evaluating strategies. Human factors such as high absenteeism and turnover rates, poor production quality and quantity rates, or low employee satisfaction can be underlying causes of declining performance. Marketing, finance/accounting, R&D, or management information systems factors can also cause financial problems. Seymour Tilles identified six qualitative questions that are useful in evaluating strategies:

1. Is the strategy internally consistent?
2. Is the strategy consistent with the environment?
3. Is the strategy appropriate in view of available resources?
4. Does the strategy involve an acceptable degree of risk?
5. Does the strategy have an appropriate time framework?
6. Is the strategy workable?[5]

Some additional key questions that reveal the need for qualitative or intuitive judgments in strategy evaluation are as follows:

1. How good is the firm's balance of investments between high-risk and low-risk projects?

2. How good is the firm's balance of investments between long-term and short-term projects?
3. How good is the firm's balance of investments between slow-growing markets and fast-growing markets?
4. How good is the firm's balance of investments among different divisions?
5. To what extent are the firm's alternative strategies socially responsible?
6. What are the relationships among the firm's key internal and external strategic factors?
7. How are major competitors likely to respond to particular strategies?

Taking Corrective Actions

The final strategy-evaluation activity, *taking corrective actions*, requires making changes to competitively reposition a firm for the future. Examples of changes that may be needed are altering an organization's structure, replacing one or more key individuals, selling a division, or revising a business mission. Other changes could include establishing or revising objectives, devising new policies, issuing stock to raise capital, adding additional salespersons, differently allocating resources, or developing new performance incentives. Taking corrective actions does not necessarily mean that existing strategies will be abandoned or even that new strategies must be formulated.

> The probabilities and possibilities for incorrect or inappropriate actions increase geometrically with an arithmetic increase in personnel. Any person directing an overall undertaking must check on the actions of the participants as well as the results that they have achieved. If either the actions or results do not comply with preconceived or planned achievements, then corrective actions are needed.[6]

No organization can survive as an island; no organization can escape change. Taking corrective actions is necessary to keep an organization on track toward achieving stated objectives. In his thought-provoking books *Future Shock* and *The Third Wave,* Alvin Toffler argued that business environments are becoming so dynamic and complex that they threaten people and organizations with *future shock*, which occurs when the nature, types, and speed of changes overpower an individual's or organization's ability and capacity to adapt. Strategy evaluation enhances an organization's ability to adapt successfully to changing circumstances. Brown and Agnew referred to this notion as *corporate agility*.[7]

Taking corrective actions raises employees' and managers' anxieties. Research suggests that participation in strategy-evaluation activities is one of the best ways to overcome individuals' resistance to change. According to Erez and Kanfer, individuals accept change best when they have a cognitive understanding of the changes, a sense of control over the situation, and an awareness that necessary actions are going to be taken to implement the changes.[8]

Strategy evaluation can lead to strategy-formulation changes, strategy-implementation changes, both formulation and implementation changes, or no changes at all. Strategists cannot escape having to revise strategies and implementation approaches sooner or later. Hussey and Langham offered the following insight on taking corrective actions:

> Resistance to change is often emotionally based and not easily overcome by rational argument. Resistance may be based on such feelings as loss of status, implied criticism of present competence, fear of failure in the new situation, annoyance at not being consulted, lack of understanding of the need for change, or insecurity in changing from well-known and fixed methods. It is necessary, therefore, to overcome such resistance by creating situations of participation and full explanation when changes are envisaged.[9]

Corrective actions should place an organization in a better position to capitalize upon internal strengths; to take advantage of key external opportunities; to avoid, reduce, or mitigate external threats; and to improve internal weaknesses. Corrective actions should have a proper time horizon and an appropriate amount of risk. They should be internally consistent and socially responsible. Perhaps most important, corrective actions strengthen an organization's competitive position in its basic industry. Continuous strategy evaluation keeps strategists close to the pulse of an organization and provides information needed for an effective strategic-management system. Carter Bayles described the benefits of strategy evaluation as follows:

> Evaluation activities may renew confidence in the current business strategy or point to the need for actions to correct some weaknesses, such as erosion of product superiority or technological edge. In many cases, the benefits of strategy evaluation are much more far-reaching, for the outcome of the process may be a fundamentally new strategy that will lead, even in a business that is already turning a respectable profit, to substantially increased earnings. It is this possibility that justifies strategy evaluation, for the payoff can be very large.[10]

The Balanced Scorecard

Introduced earlier in the Chapter 5 discussion of objectives, the Balanced Scorecard is an important strategy-evaluation tool. It is a process that allows firms to evaluate strategies from four perspectives: financial performance, customer knowledge, internal business processes, and learning and growth. The *Balanced Scorecard* analysis requires that firms seek answers to the following questions and utilize that information, in conjunction with financial measures, to adequately and more effectively evaluate strategies being implemented:

1. How well is the firm continually improving and creating value along measures such as innovation, technological leadership, product quality, operational process efficiencies, and so on?
2. How well is the firm sustaining and even improving upon its core competencies and competitive advantages?
3. How satisfied are the firm's customers?

A sample Balanced Scorecard is provided in Table 9-4. Notice that the firm examines six key issues in evaluating its strategies: (1) Customers, (2) Managers/Employees, (3) Operations/Processes, (4) Community/Social Responsibility, (5) Business Ethics/Natural Environment, and (6) Financial. The basic form of a Balanced Scorecard may differ for different organizations. The Balanced Scorecard approach to strategy evaluation aims to balance long-term with short-term concerns, to balance financial with nonfinancial concerns, and to balance internal with external concerns. It can be an excellent management tool, and it is used successfully today by Chemical Bank, Exxon/Mobil Corporation, CIGNA Property and Casualty Insurance, and numerous other firms. For example, Unilever has a financial objective to grow revenues by 5 percent to 6 percent annually. The company also has a strategic objective to reduce its 1,200 food, household, and personal care products to 400 core brands within three years. The Balanced Scorecard would be constructed differently, that is, adapted, to particular firms in various industries with the underlying theme or thrust being the same, which is to evaluate the firm's strategies based upon both key quantitative and qualitative measures.

Published Sources of Strategy-Evaluation Information

A number of publications are helpful in evaluating a firm's strategies. For example, *Fortune* annually identifies and evaluates the Fortune 1,000 (the largest manufacturers) and the Fortune 50 (the largest retailers, transportation companies, utilities, banks, insurance companies, and diversified financial corporations in the United States). *Fortune* ranks the best and worst performers on various factors, such as return on investment, sales volume, and profitability. In its March issue each year, *Fortune* publishes its strategy-evaluation research in an article entitled "America's Most Admired Companies." Eight key attributes serve as evaluative criteria: people management; innovativeness; quality of products or services; financial soundness; social responsibility; use of corporate assets; long-term investment; and quality of

TABLE 9-4   **An Example Balanced Scorecard**

Area of Objectives	Measure or Target	Time Expectation	Primary Responsibility
Customers			
1.			
2.			
3.			
4.			
Managers/Employees			
1.			
2.			
3.			
4.			
Operations/Processes			
1.			
2.			
3.			
4.			
Community/Social Responsibility			
1.			
2.			
3.			
4.			
Business Ethics/Natural Environment			
1.			
2.			
3.			
4.			
Financial			
1.			
2.			
3.			
4.			

management. In October of each year, *Fortune* publishes additional strategy-evaluation research in an article entitled "The World's Most Admired Companies." *Fortune's* 2007 evaluation in Table 9-5 reveals the firms most admired (best managed) in their industry. The most admired company in the world in 2007 was General Electric, followed by Toyota Motor, Procter & Gamble, Johnson & Johnson and Apple.[11]

Another excellent evaluation of corporations in America, "The Annual Report on American Industry," is published annually in the January issue of *Forbes*. It provides a detailed and comprehensive evaluation of hundreds of U.S. companies in many different industries. *BusinessWeek*, *Industry Week*, and *Dun's Business Month* also periodically publish detailed evaluations of U.S. businesses and industries. Although published sources of strategy-evaluation information focus primarily on large, publicly held businesses, the comparative ratios and related information are widely used to evaluate small businesses and privately owned firms as well.

Characteristics of an Effective Evaluation System

Strategy evaluation must meet several basic requirements to be effective. First, strategy-evaluation activities must be economical; too much information can be just as bad as too

TABLE 9-5   **The Most Admired Companies in Various Industries (2007)**

Industry	The Most Admired Company
Financial data services	Dun & Bradstreet
Insurance: Life and health	Northwestern Mutual
Insurance: Property and casualty	Berkshire Hathaway
Megabanks, credit card companies	American Express
Mortgage services	LandAmerica Financial Group
Securities	Lehman Brothers Holdings
Apparel	Nike #1, Polo Ralph Lauren #2
Beverages	Anheuser-Busch #1, Coca-Cola #3
Consumer food products	Nestle #1, PepsiCo #2
Food production	Bunge #1, Pilgrim's Pride #2
Household and personal products	P & G #1, Estee Lauder #2
Food services	Starbucks #1, McDonald's #2
General merchandisers	Nordstrom
Specialty retailers	Costco Wholesale
Furniture	Herman Miller
Homebuilders	Centex #1, Toll Brothers #4

Source: Adapted from: Eugenia Levenson, "America's Most Admired Companies," *Fortune* (March 19, 2007): 90–100.

little information; and too many controls can do more harm than good. Strategy-evaluation activities also should be meaningful; they should specifically relate to a firm's objectives. They should provide managers with useful information about tasks over which they have control and influence. Strategy-evaluation activities should provide timely information; on occasion and in some areas, managers may daily need information. For example, when a firm has diversified by acquiring another firm, evaluative information may be needed frequently. However, in an R&D department, daily or even weekly evaluative information could be dysfunctional. Approximate information that is timely is generally more desirable as a basis for strategy evaluation than accurate information that does not depict the present. Frequent measurement and rapid reporting may frustrate control rather than give better control. The time dimension of control must coincide with the time span of the event being measured.

Strategy evaluation should be designed to provide a true picture of what is happening. For example, in a severe economic downturn, productivity and profitability ratios may drop alarmingly, although employees and managers are actually working harder. Strategy evaluations should fairly portray this type of situation. Information derived from the strategy-evaluation process should facilitate action and should be directed to those individuals in the organization who need to take action based on it. Managers commonly ignore evaluative reports that are provided only for informational purposes; not all managers need to receive all reports. Controls need to be action-oriented rather than information-oriented.

The strategy-evaluation process should not dominate decisions; it should foster mutual understanding, trust, and common sense. No department should fail to cooperate with another in evaluating strategies. Strategy evaluations should be simple, not too cumbersome, and not too restrictive. Complex strategy-evaluation systems often confuse people and accomplish little. The test of an effective evaluation system is its usefulness, not its complexity.

Large organizations require a more elaborate and detailed strategy-evaluation system because it is more difficult to coordinate efforts among different divisions and functional areas. Managers in small companies often communicate daily with each other and their employees and do not need extensive evaluative reporting systems. Familiarity with local environments usually makes gathering and evaluating information much easier for small organizations than for large businesses. But the key to an effective strategy-evaluation system may be the ability to convince participants that failure to accomplish certain objectives within a prescribed time is not necessarily a reflection of their performance.

There is no one ideal strategy-evaluation system. The unique characteristics of an organization, including its size, management style, purpose, problems, and strengths, can determine a strategy-evaluation and control system's final design. Robert Waterman offered the following observation about successful organizations' strategy-evaluation and control systems:

> Successful companies treat facts as friends and controls as liberating. Morgan Guaranty and Wells Fargo not only survive but thrive in the troubled waters of bank deregulation, because their strategy evaluation and control systems are sound, their risk is contained, and they know themselves and the competitive situation so well. Successful companies have a voracious hunger for facts. They see information where others see only data. They love comparisons, rankings, anything that removes decision making from the realm of mere opinion. Successful companies maintain tight, accurate financial controls. Their people don't regard controls as an imposition of autocracy but as the benign checks and balances that allow them to be creative and free.[12]

Contingency Planning

A basic premise of good strategic management is that firms plan ways to deal with unfavorable and favorable events before they occur. Too many organizations prepare contingency plans just for unfavorable events; this is a mistake, because both minimizing threats and capitalizing on opportunities can improve a firm's competitive position.

Regardless of how carefully strategies are formulated, implemented, and evaluated, unforeseen events, such as strikes, boycotts, natural disasters, arrival of foreign competitors, and government actions, can make a strategy obsolete. To minimize the impact of potential threats, organizations should develop contingency plans as part of their strategy-evaluation process. *Contingency plans* can be defined as alternative plans that can be put into effect if certain key events do not occur as expected. Only high-priority areas require the insurance of contingency plans. Strategists cannot and should not try to cover all bases by planning for all possible contingencies. But in any case, contingency plans should be as simple as possible.

Some contingency plans commonly established by firms include the following:

1. If a major competitor withdraws from particular markets as intelligence reports indicate, what actions should our firm take?
2. If our sales objectives are not reached, what actions should our firm take to avoid profit losses?
3. If demand for our new product exceeds plans, what actions should our firm take to meet the higher demand?
4. If certain disasters occur—such as loss of computer capabilities; a hostile takeover attempt; loss of patent protection; or destruction of manufacturing facilities because of earthquakes, tornados, or hurricanes—what actions should our firm take?
5. If a new technological advancement makes our new product obsolete sooner than expected, what actions should our firm take?

Too many organizations discard alternative strategies not selected for implementation although the work devoted to analyzing these options would render valuable information. Alternative strategies not selected for implementation can serve as contingency plans in case the strategy or strategies selected do not work. U.S. companies and governments are increasingly considering nuclear-generated electricity as the most efficient means of power generation. Many contingency plans certainly call for nuclear power rather than for coal- and gas-derived electricity. As indicated in the "Global Perspective," the United States is well below many countries in the world in the percentage of power derived from nuclear power plants. See the "Global Perspective" for states in the country that lead in nuclear power generation.

GLOBAL PERSPECTIVE
Eastern Europe, Western Europe, and the United States (in That Order) Embrace Atomic Energy

The United States and Western Europe continue to waver on the use of atomic energy, while Eastern European countries build new-generation nuclear power stations to meet rising demand. Note in the following list that the United States is well behind almost all European countries on the use of nuclear fuel for electricity generation.

Country	Percent of Electricity Derived from Nuclear Power
France	78.1%
Lithuania	72.1
Slovakia	55.2
Belgium	55.1
Sweden	51.8
Bulgaria	41.6
Switzerland	40.0
Slovenia	38.8
Hungary	33.8
Germany	32.1
Czech Republic	31.2
Finland	26.6
Spain	22.9
United States	19.9
United Kingdom	13.4

Although coal and natural gas power plants may be safer (and that is debatable), the nuclear option surely is cleaner and more powerful. East European countries are thus building new nuclear plants to meet growing demand, while the United States and Western Europe have this option only in their contingency plans. New nuclear plants today are being built in France, the Czech Republic, Slovakia, Romania, Finland, and Bulgaria, while Germany, England, and the United States discuss closing some of their plants. Germany, in fact, is committed to being a nuclear-free state by 2021, which means closing 19 nuclear plants that today account for 30 percent of that country's power-generating capacity.

TXU Corporation, NRG Energy, Exelon Corporation, and Amarillo Power are firms in Texas that plan to build nuclear power plants in that state in the next decade. Two reasons for the spur in nuclear power in Texas are: (1) Utilities in Texas no longer have monopolistic territories, and (2) environmental groups in Texas are reversing their negative view of nuclear power, having concluded that global warming is so severe and the time for action is so short that nuclear power is a far better option than coal-fired plants. Texas trails only Illinois, Pennsylvania, South Carolina, New York, and North Carolina in quantity of nuclear power kWh generated. California is seventh in the United States.

Finland is building the first nuclear generating plant in Western Europe since 1991. The plant will open in 2010. Switzerland just lifted its moratorium on new nuclear plants. Belarus starts construction of a nuclear plant in 2008 that will begin generating power in 2014. In addition to nuclear energy, countries are also scrambling to install solar photovoltaic power to avoid CO_2 emissions and obtain carbon credits from the government. A recent *USA*

France, River Seine, view of nuclear plants.
Source: Christopher and Sally Gable (c) Dorling Kindersley

Today article reports that 1,744 megawatts of solar photo-voltaic power were installed worldwide in 2006. The following countries reveal where those solar stations were built in terms of percentage of the 1,744 megawatts:

Germany	55 percent
Rest of Europe	11 percent
Japan	17 percent
United States and Other	9 percent

Source: Adapted from Nina Sovich, "Europe's New Nuclear Standoff: Eastern States Embrace Atomic Energy, as Western Neighbors Waver," *Wall Street Journal* (June 29, 2005): A13; Rebecca Smith, "TXU Sheds Coal Plan, Charts Nuclear Path," *Wall Street Journal* (April 10, 2007): A2; Jeffrey Ball, "Cows, Climate Change and Carbon Credits," *USA Today* (June 14, 2007): B1, B2; and Jeffrey Stinson, "Europe Warms to Nuclear Energy," *USA Today* (June 4, 2007): A1.

When strategy-evaluation activities reveal the need for a major change quickly, an appropriate contingency plan can be executed in a timely way. Contingency plans can promote a strategist's ability to respond quickly to key changes in the internal and external bases of an organization's current strategy. For example, if underlying assumptions about the economy turn out to be wrong and contingency plans are ready, then managers can make appropriate changes promptly.

In some cases, external or internal conditions present unexpected opportunities. When such opportunities occur, contingency plans could allow an organization to quickly capitalize on them. Linneman and Chandran reported that contingency planning gave users, such as DuPont, Dow Chemical, Consolidated Foods, and Emerson Electric, three major benefits: (1) It permitted quick response to change, (2) it prevented panic in crisis situations, and (3) it made managers more adaptable by encouraging them to appreciate just how variable the future can be. They suggested that effective contingency planning involves a seven-step process:

1. Identify both beneficial and unfavorable events that could possibly derail the strategy or strategies.
2. Specify trigger points. Calculate about when contingent events are likely to occur.
3. Assess the impact of each contingent event. Estimate the potential benefit or harm of each contingent event.
4. Develop contingency plans. Be sure that contingency plans are compatible with current strategy and are economically feasible.
5. Assess the counterimpact of each contingency plan. That is, estimate how much each contingency plan will capitalize on or cancel out its associated contingent event. Doing this will quantify the potential value of each contingency plan.
6. Determine early warning signals for key contingent events. Monitor the early warning signals.
7. For contingent events with reliable early warning signals, develop advance action plans to take advantage of the available lead time.[13]

Auditing

A frequently used tool in strategy evaluation is the audit. *Auditing* is defined by the American Accounting Association (AAA) as "a systematic process of objectively obtaining and evaluating evidence regarding assertions about economic actions and events to ascertain the degree of correspondence between these assertions and established criteria, and communicating the results to interested users."[14] Since the Enron, Worldcom, and Johnson & Johnson scandals, auditing has taken on greater emphasis and care in companies. Independent auditors basically are certified public accountants (CPAs) who provide their services to organizations for a fee; they examine the financial statements of an organization to determine whether they have been prepared according to generally accepted accounting principles (GAAP) and whether they fairly represent the activities of the firm. Independent auditors use a set of standards called *generally accepted auditing standards* (GAAS). Public accounting firms often have a consulting arm that provides strategy-evaluation services.

Two government agencies—the General Accounting Office (GAO) and the Internal Revenue Service (IRS)—employ government auditors responsible for making sure that organizations comply with federal laws, statutes, and policies. GAO and IRS auditors can audit any public or private organization. The third group of auditors consists of employees within an organization who are responsible for safeguarding company assets, for assessing the efficiency of company operations, and for ensuring that generally accepted business procedures are practiced.

The Environmental Audit

For an increasing number of firms, overseeing environmental affairs is no longer a technical function performed by specialists; rather, it has become an important strategic-management concern. Product design, manufacturing, transportation, customer use, packaging, product disposal, and corporate rewards and sanctions should reflect environmental considerations. Firms that effectively manage environmental affairs are benefiting from constructive relations with employees, consumers, suppliers, and distributors. As indicated in the "Natural Environment Perspective," China is home to 16 of the world's 20 most polluted cities.

Shimell emphasized the need for organizations to conduct environmental audits of their operations and to develop a Corporate Environmental Policy (CEP).[15] Shimell contended that an environmental audit should be as rigorous as a financial audit and should include training workshops in which staff can help design and implement the policy. The CEP should be budgeted, and requisite funds should be allocated to ensure that it is not a public relations facade. A Statement of Environmental Policy should be published periodically to inform shareholders and the public of environmental actions taken by the firm.

Instituting an environmental audit can include moving environmental affairs from the staff side of the organization to the line side. Some firms are also introducing environmental criteria and objectives in their performance appraisal instruments and systems. Conoco, for example, ties compensation of all its top managers to environmental action plans. Occidental Chemical includes environmental responsibilities in all its job descriptions for positions.

Twenty-First-Century Challenges in Strategic Management

Three particular challenges or decisions that face all strategists today are (1) deciding whether the process should be more an art or a science, (2) deciding whether strategies should be visible or hidden from stakeholders, and (3) deciding whether the process should be more top-down or bottom-up in their firm.[16]

The Art or Science Issue

This textbook is consistent with most of the strategy literature in advocating that strategic management be viewed more as a science than an art. This perspective contends that firms need to systematically assess their external and internal environments, conduct research, carefully evaluate the pros and cons of various alternatives, perform analyses, and then decide upon a particular course of action. In contrast, Mintzberg's notion of "crafting" strategies embodies the artistic model, which suggests that strategic decision making be based primarily on holistic thinking, intuition, creativity, and imagination.[17] Mintzberg and his followers reject strategies that result from objective analysis, preferring instead subjective imagination. "Strategy scientists" reject strategies that emerge from emotion, hunch, creativity, and politics. Proponents of the artistic view often consider strategic planning exercises to be time poorly spent. The Mintzberg philosophy insists on informality,

NATURAL ENVIRONMENT PERSPECTIVE
China Vastly Polluted

China has compressed a normal century of economic development into one generation and ravaged its air, soil, and water in the process. China is today home to 16 of the world's 20 most polluted cities, and it battles soil erosion, spreading deserts, polluted water, and smog everywhere. About 40 percent of Chinese cities lack sewage treatment facilities. All of China's major rivers are dangerously polluted, and two-thirds of the country's rivers and lakes are severely polluted. Data indicate that 340 million of the 1.3 billion Chinese (26 percent) lack access to clean drinking water, and 10 percent of China's farmland is polluted.

Research shows that deposits of mercury accumulating in the western United States originated from coal-burning power plants in China. These plants produce 70 to 90 percent of China's energy, but the surging Chinese economy is demanding more and more energy. The deputy director for China's State Environmental Protection Administration (EPA) recently told state media that environmental issues have "become a key bottleneck" for the economy. China's own Modernization Report issued in January 2007 acknowledged that the country has made no progress in protecting the environment over the past three years. Although China signed the Kyoto Protocol, it has been exempted from the treaty's greenhouse-gas limits.

The good news is that China's central government recognizes pollution to be a strategic problem for the country and is taking steps to improve the situation, but it may be too little, too late as global warming and climate issues ravage the country. China's State Environmental Protection Administration recently published a list of 82 large projects, valued at a total of $14.4 billion, that it said had failed to comply with environmental regulations, mostly in the steel, chemical, and metallurgy industries. Chinese officials estimate that one-fifth of the power plants in China are illegal, generating enough power to light up all of Britain.

In 2006, China had 161 serious environmental accidents, the most ever, according to Pan Yue, deputy director of China's EPA. Mr. Pan also says "the year 2006 was the most grim year ever for China's environmental situation." Rising sea levels now threaten the deltas of the Yellow, Yangtze, and Pearl rivers—home to the bulk of China's manufacturing and export business. China will thus soon become concerned about global warming.

China overtook the United States by 7.5 percent as the world's top producer of carbon dioxide emissions in 2006. China's emissions per capita are of course less than those of the United States, but in volume and quantity it now leads all countries of the world in air pollutants.

Source: Adapted from Calurn MacLeod, "China Envisions Environmentally Friendly 'Eco-City,'" *USA Today* (February 16, 2007): 9A; Shai Oster, "China Cracks Down on Power Companies in Tough Antipollution Campaign," *Wall Street Journal* (January 12, 2007): A9; Shai Oster, "China Tilts Green," *Wall Street Journal* (February 13, 2007): A4; and "China Passes U.S. on CO_2 output," *Wall Street Journal* (June 22, 2007): A4.

School for the Arts-Children's Palace, Shanghai. *Source:* Mrs. Feldheim

whereas strategy scientists (and this text) insist on more formality. Mintzberg refers to strategic planning as an "emergent" process whereas strategy scientists use the term "deliberate" process.[18]

The answer to the art versus science question is one that strategists must decide for themselves, and certainly the two approaches are not mutually exclusive. In deciding which approach is more effective, however, consider that the business world today has become increasingly complex and more intensely competitive. There is less room for error in strategic planning. Recall that Chapter 1 discussed the importance of intuition and experience and subjectivity in strategic planning, and even the weights and ratings discussed in Chapters 3, 4, and 6 certainly require good judgment. But the idea of deciding upon strategies for any firm without thorough research and analysis, at least in the mind of this writer, is unwise. Certainly, in smaller firms there can be more informality in the process compared to larger firms, but even for smaller firms, a wealth of competitive information is available on the Internet and elsewhere and should be collected, assimilated, and evaluated before deciding on a course of action upon which survival of the firm may hinge. The livelihood of countless employees and shareholders may hinge on the effectiveness of strategies selected. Too much is at stake to be less than thorough in formulating strategies. It is not wise for a strategist to rely too heavily on gut feeling and opinion instead of research data, competitive intelligence, and analysis in formulating strategies.

The Visible or Hidden Issue

There are certainly good reasons to keep the strategy process and strategies themselves visible and open rather than hidden and secret. There are also good reasons to keep strategies hidden from all but top-level executives. Strategists must decide for themselves what is best for their firms. This text comes down largely on the side of being visible and open, but certainly this may not be best for all strategists and all firms. As pointed out in Chapter 1, Sun Tzu argued that all war is based on deception and that the best maneuvers are those not easily predicted by rivals. Business is analogous to war.

Some reasons to be completely open with the strategy process and resultant decisions are these:

1. Managers, employees, and other stakeholders can readily contribute to the process. They often have excellent ideas. Secrecy would forgo many excellent ideas.
2. Investors, creditors, and other stakeholders have greater basis for supporting a firm when they know what the firm is doing and where the firm is going.
3. Visibility promotes democracy, whereas secrecy promotes autocracy. Domestic firms and most foreign firms prefer democracy over autocracy as a management style.
4. Participation and openness enhance understanding, commitment, and communication within the firm.

Reasons why some firms prefer to conduct strategic planning in secret and keep strategies hidden from all but the highest-level executives are as follows:

1. Free dissemination of a firm's strategies may easily translate into competitive intelligence for rival firms who could exploit the firm given that information.
2. Secrecy limits criticism, second guessing, and hindsight.
3. Participants in a visible strategy process become more attractive to rival firms who may lure them away.
4. Secrecy limits rival firms from imitating or duplicating the firm's strategies and undermining the firm.

The obvious benefits of the visible versus hidden extremes suggest that a working balance must be sought between the apparent contradictions. Parnell says that in a perfect world all key individuals both inside and outside the firm should be involved in strategic planning, but in practice particularly sensitive and confidential information should always remain strictly confidential to top managers.[19] This balancing azct is difficult but essential for survival of the firm.

The Top-Down or Bottom-Up Approach

Proponents of the top-down approach contend that top executives are the only persons in the firm with the collective experience, acumen, and fiduciary responsibility to make key strategy decisions. In contrast, bottom-up advocates argue that lower- and middle-level managers and employees who will be implementing the strategies need to be actively involved in the process of formulating the strategies to ensure their support and commitment. Recent strategy research and this textbook emphasize the bottom-up approach, but earlier work by Schendel and Hofer stressed the need for firms to rely on perceptions of their top managers in strategic planning.[20] Strategists must reach a working balance of the two approaches in a manner deemed best for their firms at a particular time, while cognizant of the fact that current research supports the bottom-up approach, at least among U.S. firms. Increased education and diversity of the workforce at all levels are reasons why middle- and lower-level managers—and even nonmanagers—should be invited to participate in the firm's strategic planning process, at least to the extent that they are willing and able to contribute.

Conclusion

This chapter presents a strategy-evaluation framework that can facilitate accomplishment of annual and long-term objectives. Effective strategy evaluation allows an organization to capitalize on internal strengths as they develop, to exploit external opportunities as they emerge, to recognize and defend against threats, and to mitigate internal weaknesses before they become detrimental.

Strategists in successful organizations take the time to formulate, implement, and then evaluate strategies deliberately and systematically. Good strategists move their organization forward with purpose and direction, continually evaluating and improving the firm's external and internal strategic positions. Strategy evaluation allows an organization to shape its own future rather than allowing it to be constantly shaped by remote forces that have little or no vested interest in the well-being of the enterprise.

Although not a guarantee for success, strategic management allows organizations to make effective long-term decisions, to execute those decisions efficiently, and to take corrective actions as needed to ensure success. Computer networks and the Internet help to coordinate strategic-management activities and to ensure that decisions are based on good information. The Checkmate Strategic Planning Software is especially good in this regard (www.checkmateplan.com). A key to effective strategy evaluation and to successful strategic management is an integration of intuition and analysis:

> A potentially fatal problem is the tendency for analytical and intuitive issues to polarize. This polarization leads to strategy evaluation that is dominated by either analysis or intuition, or to strategy evaluation that is discontinuous, with a lack of coordination among analytical and intuitive issues.[21]

Strategists in successful organizations realize that strategic management is first and foremost a people process. It is an excellent vehicle for fostering organizational communication. People are what make the difference in organizations.

> The real key to effective strategic management is to accept the premise that the planning process is more important than the written plan, that the manager is continuously planning and does not stop planning when the written plan is finished. The written plan is only a snapshot as of the moment it is approved. If the manager is not planning on a continuous basis—planning, measuring, and revising—the written plan can become obsolete the day it is finished. This obsolescence becomes more of a certainty as the increasingly rapid rate of change makes the business environment more uncertain.[22]

We invite you to visit the David page on the Prentice Hall Companion Web site at www.prenhall.com/david for this chapter's review quiz.

Key Terms and Concepts

Advantage (p. 299)
Auditing (p. 312)
Balanced Scorecard (p. 306)
Consistency (p. 299)
Consonance (p. 299)
Contingency Plans (p. 309)
Corporate Agility (p. 305)
Feasibility (p. 299)
Future Shock (p. 305)
Management by Wandering Around (p. 301)
Measuring Organizational Performance (p. 303)
Reviewing the Underlying Bases of an Organization's Strategy (p. 302)
Revised EFE Matrix (p. 302)
Revised IFE Matrix (p. 302)
Taking Corrective Actions (p. 305)

Issues for Review and Discussion

1. Why has strategy evaluation become so important in business today?
2. BellSouth Services is considering putting divisional EFE and IFE matrices online for continual updating. How would this affect strategy evaluation?
3. What types of quantitative and qualitative criteria do you think Meg Whitman, CEO of eBay, uses to evaluate the company's strategy?
4. As owner of a local, independent supermarket, explain how you would evaluate the firm's strategy.
5. Under what conditions are corrective actions not required in the strategy-evaluation process?
6. Identify types of organizations that may need to more frequently evaluate strategy than others. Justify your choices.
7. As executive director of the state forestry commission, in what way and how frequently would you evaluate the organization's strategies?
8. Identify some key financial ratios that would be important in evaluating a bank's strategy.
9. As owner of a chain of hardware stores, describe how you would approach contingency planning.
10. Strategy evaluation allows an organization to take a proactive stance toward shaping its own future. Discuss the meaning of this statement.
11. Explain and discuss the Balanced Scorecard.
12. Why is the Balanced Scorecard an important topic both in devising objectives and in evaluating strategies?
13. Develop a Balanced Scorecard for a local fast-food restaurant.
14. Do you believe strategic management should be more visible or hidden as a process in a firm? Explain.
15. Do you feel strategic management should be more a top-down or bottom-up process in a firm? Explain.
16. Do you believe strategic management is more an art or a science? Explain.

Notes

1. Dale McConkey, "Planning in a Changing Environment," *Business Horizons* (September–October 1988): 64.
2. Robert Simons, "Control in an Age of Empowerment," *Harvard Business Review* (March–April 1995): 80.
3. Dale Zand, "Reviewing the Policy Process," *California Management Review* 21, no. 1 (Fall 1978): 37.

4. Eccles. 3: 1–8.
5. Seymour Tilles, "How to Evaluate Corporate Strategy," *Harvard Business Review* 41 (July–August 1963): 111–121.
6. Claude George, Jr., *The History of Management Thought* (Upper Saddle River, New Jersey: Prentice Hall, 1968): 165–166.
7. John Brown and Neil Agnew, "Corporate Agility," *Business Horizons* 25, no. 2 (March–April 1982): 29.
8. M. Erez and F. Kanfer, "The Role of Goal Acceptance in Goal Setting and Task Performance," *Academy of Management Review* 8, no. 3 (July 1983): 457.
9. D. Hussey and M. Langham, *Corporate Planning: The Human Factor* (Oxford, England: Pergamon Press, 1979): 138.
10. Carter Bayles, "Strategic Control: The President's Paradox," *Business Horizons* 20, no. 4 (August 1977): 18.
11. Eugenia Levenson, "America's Most Admired Companies," *Fortune* (March 19, 2007): 92.
12. Robert Waterman, Jr., "How the Best Get Better," *BusinessWeek* (September 14, 1987): 105.
13. Robert Linneman and Rajan Chandran, "Contingency Planning: A Key to Swift Managerial Action in the Uncertain Tomorrow," *Managerial Planning* 29, no. 4 (January–February 1981): 23–27.
14. American Accounting Association, *Report of Committee on Basic Auditing Concepts* (1971): 15–74.
15. Pamela Shimell, "Corporate Environmental Policy in Practice," *Long Range Planning* 24, no. 3 (June 1991): 10.
16. John Parnell, "Five Critical Challenges in Strategy Making," *SAM Advanced Management Journal* 68, no. 2 (Spring 2003): 15–22.
17. Henry Mintzberg, "Crafting Strategy," *Harvard Business Review* (July–August, 1987): 66–75.
18. Henry Mintzberg and J. Waters, "Of Strategies, Deliberate and Emergent," *Strategic Management Journal* 6, no. 2: 257–272.
19. Parnell, 15–22.
20. D. E. Schendel and C. W. Hofer (Eds.), *Strategic Management* (Boston: Little, Brown, 1979).
21. Michael McGinnis, "The Key to Strategic Planning: Integrating Analysis and Intuition," *Sloan Management Review* 26, no. 1 (Fall 1984): 49.
22. McConkey, 72.

Current Readings

Barsade, Sigal G. and Donald E. Gibson. "Why Does Affect Matter in Organizations." *The Academy of Management Perspective* 21, no. 1 (February 2007): 36.

Berry, Leonard L. "The best companies are generous companies." *Business Horizon* 50, no. 4 (July-August 2007): 263.

Burlingham, Bo. "Small Giants: Companies That Choose to Be Great Instead of Big." *Business Horizons* 50, no. 3 (May-June 2007): 185.

Nag, R., D.C. Hambrick, and M.J. Chen. "What is Strategic Management, Really? Inductive Derivation of a Consensus Definition of the Field." *Strategic Management Journal* 935, no. 28 (September 2007): 935.

Seo, Myeong-Gu. "Being Emotional during Decision Making—Good or Bad? An Empirical Investigation." *The Academy of Management Journal* 50, no. 4 (August 2007): 923.

Stadler, Christian. "The Four Principles of Enduring Success." *Harvard Business Review* (July-August 2007) 62.

• **EXPERIENTIAL EXERCISES** **D**ISNEY

Experiential Exercise 9A

Preparing a Strategy-Evaluation Report for Walt Disney

Purpose

This exercise can give you experience locating strategy-evaluation information. Use of the Internet coupled with published sources of information can significantly enhance the strategy-evaluation process. Performance information on competitors, for example, can help put into perspective a firm's own performance.

Instructions

Step 1 Visit http://marketwatch.multexinvestor.com, http://moneycentral.msn.com, http://finance.yahoo.com, www.clearstation.com to locate strategy-evaluation information on competitors. Read 5 to 10 articles written in the last six months that discuss the family entertainment industry.

Step 2 Summarize your research findings by preparing a strategy-evaluation report for your instructor. Include in your report a summary of Walt Disney's strategies and performance in 2007 and a summary of your conclusions regarding the effectiveness of Walt Disney's strategies.

Step 3 Based on your analysis, do you feel that Walt Disney is pursuing effective strategies? What recommendations would you offer to Walt Disney's chief executive officer?

Mickey Mouse balloons.
Source: Lourens Smak/Almay Images

Experiential Exercise 9B

Evaluating My University's Strategies

Purpose

An important part of evaluating strategies is determining the nature and extent of changes in an organization's external opportunities/threats and internal strengths/weaknesses. Changes in these underlying critical success factors can indicate a need to change or modify the firm's strategies.

Instructions

As a class, discuss positive and negative changes in your university's external and internal factors during your college career. Begin by listing on the board new or emerging opportunities and threats. Then identify strengths and weaknesses that have changed significantly during your college career. In light of the external and internal changes that were identified, discuss whether your university's strategies need modifying. Are there any new strategies that you would recommend? Make a list to recommend to your department chair, dean, president, or chancellor.

Experiential Exercise 9C

Who Prepares an Environmental Audit?

Purpose

The purpose of this activity is to determine the nature and prevalence of environmental audits among companies in your state.

Instructions

Contact by phone at least five different plant managers or owners of large businesses in your area. Seek answers to the following questions. Present your findings in a written report to your instructor.

1. Does your company conduct an environmental audit? If yes, please describe the nature and scope of the audit.
2. Are environmental criteria included in the performance evaluation of managers? If yes, please specify the criteria.
3. Are environmental affairs more a technical function or a management function in your company?
4. Does your firm offer any environmental workshops for employees? If yes, please describe them.

Part 5 • Strategic Management Case Analysis

How to Prepare and Present a Case Analysis

chapter objectives

After studying this chapter, you should be able to do the following:

1. Describe the case method for learning strategic-management concepts.

2. Identify the steps in preparing a comprehensive written case analysis.

3. Describe how to give an effective oral case analysis presentation.

4. Discuss special tips for doing case analysis.

steps in presenting an oral case analysis

Oral Presentation—Step 1
Introduction (2 minutes)

Oral Presentation—Step 2
Mission/Vision (4 minutes)

Oral Presentation—Step 3
Internal Assessment (8 minutes)

Oral Presentation—Step 4
External Assessment (8 minutes)

Oral Presentation—Step 5
Strategy Formulation (14 minutes)

Oral Presentation—Step 6
Strategy Implementation (8 minutes)

Oral Presentation—Step 7
Strategy Evaluation (2 minutes)

Oral Presentation—Step 8
Conclusion (4 minutes)

The purpose of this section is to help you analyze strategic-management cases. Guidelines for preparing written and oral case analyses are given, and suggestions for preparing cases for class discussion are presented. Steps to follow in preparing case analyses are provided. Guidelines for making an oral presentation are described.

What Is a Strategic-Management Case?

A *strategic-management* (or *business policy) case* describes an organization's external and internal conditions and raises issues concerning the firm's mission, strategies, objectives, and policies. Most of the information in a business policy case is established fact, but some information may be opinions, judgments, and beliefs. Strategic-management cases are more comprehensive than those you may have studied in other courses. They generally include a description of related management, marketing, finance/accounting, production/operations, R&D, computer information systems, and natural environment issues. A strategic-management case puts the reader on the scene of the action by describing a firm's situation at some point in time. Strategic-management cases are written to give you practice applying strategic-management concepts. The case method for studying strategic management is often called *learning by doing*.

Guidelines for Preparing Case Analyses

The Need for Practicality

There is no such thing as a complete case, and no case ever gives you all the information you need to conduct analyses and make recommendations. Likewise, in the business world, strategists never have all the information they need to make decisions: information may be unavailable or too costly to obtain, or it may take too much time to obtain. So in preparing strategic-management cases, do what strategists do every day—make reasonable assumptions about unknowns, clearly state assumptions, perform appropriate analyses, and make decisions. *Be practical*. For example, in performing a projected financial analysis, make reasonable assumptions, appropriately state them, and proceed to show what impact your recommendations are expected to have on the organization's financial position. Avoid saying "I don't have enough information." You can always supplement the information provided in a case with Internet and library research.

The Need for Justification

The most important part of analyzing cases is not what strategies you recommend but rather how you support your decisions and how you propose that they be implemented. There is no single best solution or one right answer to a case, so give ample justification for your recommendations. This is important. In the business world, strategists usually do not know if their decisions are right until resources have been allocated and consumed. Then it is often too late to reverse a decision. This cold fact accents the need for careful integration of intuition and analysis in preparing business policy case analyses.

The Need for Realism

Avoid recommending a course of action beyond an organization's means. *Be realistic*. No organization can possibly pursue all the strategies that could potentially benefit the firm. Estimate how much capital will be required to implement what you recommended. Determine whether debt, stock, or a combination of debt and stock could be used to obtain the capital. Make sure your recommendations are feasible. Do not prepare a case analysis that omits all arguments and information not supportive of your recommendations. Rather, present the major advantages and disadvantages of several feasible alternatives. Try not to exaggerate, stereotype, prejudge, or overdramatize. Strive to demonstrate that your interpretation of the evidence is reasonable and objective.

The Need for Specificity

Do not make broad generalizations such as "The company should pursue a market penetration strategy." Be specific by telling *what, why, when, how, where*, and *who*. Failure to use specifics is the single major shortcoming of most oral and written case analyses. For example, in an internal audit say, "The firm's current ratio fell from 2.2 in 2007 to 1.3 in 2008, and this is considered to be a major weakness," instead of "The firm's financial condition is bad." Rather than concluding from a Strategic Position and Action Evaluation (SPACE) Matrix that a firm should be defensive, be more specific, saying "The firm should consider closing three plants, laying off 280 employees, and divesting itself of its chemical division, for a net savings of $20.2 million in 2008." Use ratios, percentages, numbers, and dollar estimates. Businesspeople dislike generalities and vagueness.

The Need for Originality

Do not necessarily recommend the course of action that the firm plans to take or actually undertook, even if those actions resulted in improved revenues and earnings. The aim of case analysis is for you to consider all the facts and information relevant to the organization at the time, to generate feasible alternative strategies, to choose among those alternatives, and to defend your recommendations. Put yourself back in time to the point when strategic decisions were being made by the firm's strategists. Based on the information available then, what would you have done? Support your position with charts, graphs, ratios, analyses, and the like—not a revelation from the library. You can become a good strategist by thinking through situations, making management assessments, and proposing plans yourself. *Be original.* Compare and contrast what you recommend versus what the company plans to do or did.

The Need to Contribute

Strategy formulation, implementation, and evaluation decisions are commonly made by a group of individuals rather than by a single person. Therefore, your professor may divide the class into three- or four-person teams and ask you to prepare written or oral case analyses. Members of a strategic-management team, in class or in the business world, differ on their aversion to risk, their concern for short-run versus long-run benefits, their attitudes toward social responsibility, and their views concerning globalization. There are no perfect people, so there are no perfect strategies. Be open-minded to others' views. *Be a good listener and a good contributor.*

Preparing a Case for Class Discussion

Your professor may ask you to prepare a case for class discussion. Preparing a case for class discussion means that you need to read the case before class, make notes regarding the organization's external opportunities/threats and internal strengths/weaknesses, perform appropriate analyses, and come to class prepared to offer and defend some specific recommendations.

The Case Method versus Lecture Approach

The case method of teaching is radically different from the traditional lecture approach, in which little or no preparation is needed by students before class. The *case method* involves a classroom situation in which students do most of the talking; your professor facilitates discussion by asking questions and encouraging student interaction regarding ideas, analyses, and recommendations. Be prepared for a discussion along the lines of "What would you do, why would you do it, when would you do it, and how would you do it?" Prepare answers to the following types of questions:

- What are the firm's most important external opportunities and threats?
- What are the organization's major strengths and weaknesses?
- How would you describe the organization's financial condition?
- What are the firm's existing strategies and objectives?
- Who are the firm's competitors, and what are their strategies?

- What objectives and strategies do you recommend for this organization? Explain your reasoning. How does what you recommend compare to what the company plans?
- How could the organization best implement what you recommend? What implementation problems do you envision? How could the firm avoid or solve those problems?

The Cross-Examination

Do not hesitate to take a stand on the issues and to support your position with objective analyses and outside research. Strive to apply strategic-management concepts and tools in preparing your case for class discussion. Seek defensible arguments and positions. Support opinions and judgments with facts, reasons, and evidence. Crunch the numbers before class! Be willing to describe your recommendations to the class without fear of disapproval. Respect the ideas of others, but be willing to go against the majority opinion when you can justify a better position.

Business policy case analysis gives you the opportunity to learn more about yourself, your colleagues, strategic management, and the decision-making process in organizations. The rewards of this experience will depend on the effort you put forth, so do a good job. Discussing business policy cases in class is exciting and challenging. Expect views counter to those you present. Different students will place emphasis on different aspects of an organization's situation and submit different recommendations for scrutiny and rebuttal. Cross-examination discussions commonly arise, just as they occur in a real business organization. Avoid being a silent observer.

Preparing a Written Case Analysis

In addition to asking you to prepare a case for class discussion, your professor may ask you to prepare a written case analysis. Preparing a written case analysis is similar to preparing a case for class discussion, except written reports are generally more structured and more detailed. There is no ironclad procedure for preparing a written case analysis because cases differ in focus; the type, size, and complexity of the organizations being analyzed also vary.

When writing a strategic-management report or case analysis, avoid using jargon, vague or redundant words, acronyms, abbreviations, sexist language, and ethnic or racial slurs. And watch your spelling! Use short sentences and paragraphs and simple words and phrases. Use quite a few subheadings. Arrange issues and ideas from the most important to the least important. Arrange recommendations from the least controversial to the most controversial. Use the active voice rather than the passive voice for all verbs; for example, say "Our team recommends that the company diversify" rather than "It is recommended by our team to diversify." Use many examples to add specificity and clarity. Tables, figures, pie charts, bar charts, timelines, and other kinds of exhibits help communicate important points and ideas. Sometimes a picture *is* worth a thousand words.

The Executive Summary

Your professor may ask you to focus the written case analysis on a particular aspect of the strategic-management process, such as (1) to identify and evaluate the organization's existing mission, objectives, and strategies; or (2) to propose and defend specific recommendations for the company; or (3) to develop an industry analysis by describing the competitors, products, selling techniques, and market conditions in a given industry. These types of written reports are sometimes called *executive summaries*. An executive summary usually ranges from three to five pages of text in length, plus exhibits.

The Comprehensive Written Analysis

Your professor may ask you to prepare a *comprehensive written analysis*. This assignment requires you to apply the entire strategic-management process to the particular organization. When preparing a comprehensive written analysis, picture yourself as a consultant who has been asked by a company to conduct a study of its external and internal environment and to make specific recommendations for its future. Prepare exhibits to support your recommendations. Highlight exhibits with some discussion in the paper. Comprehensive written analyses are usually about 10 pages in length, plus exhibits.

Steps in Preparing a Comprehensive Written Analysis

In preparing a **written** case analysis, you could follow the steps outlined here, which correlate to the stages in the strategic-management process and the chapters in this text. (Note—The steps in presenting an **oral** case analysis are given on p. 328, are more detailed, and could be used here).

Step 1   Identify the firm's existing vision, mission, objectives, and strategies.

Step 2   Develop vision and mission statements for the organization.

Step 3   Identify the organization's external opportunities and threats.

Step 4   Construct a Competitive Profile Matrix (CPM).

Step 5   Construct an External Factor Evaluation (EFE) Matrix.

Step 6   Identify the organization's internal strengths and weaknesses.

Step 7   Construct an Internal Factor Evaluation (IFE) Matrix.

Step 8   Prepare a Strengths-Weaknesses-Opportunities-Threats (SWOT) Matrix, Strategic Position and Action Evaluation (SPACE) Matrix, Boston Consulting Group (BCG) Matrix, Internal-External (IE) Matrix, Grand Strategy Matrix, and Quantitative Strategic Planning Matrix (QSPM) as appropriate. Give advantages and disadvantages of alternative strategies.

Step 9   Recommend specific strategies and long-term objectives. Show how much your recommendations will cost. Clearly itemize these costs for each projected year. Compare your recommendations to actual strategies planned by the company.

Step 10   Specify how your recommendations can be implemented and what results you can expect. Prepare forecasted ratios and projected financial statements. Present a timetable or agenda for action.

Step 11   Recommend specific annual objectives and policies.

Step 12   Recommend procedures for strategy review and evaluation.

Making an Oral Presentation

Your professor may ask you to prepare a strategic-management case analysis, individually or as a group, and present your analysis to the class. Oral presentations are usually graded on two parts: content and delivery. *Content* refers to the quality, quantity, correctness, and appropriateness of analyses presented, including such dimensions as logical flow through the presentation, coverage of major issues, use of specifics, avoidance of generalities, absence of mistakes, and feasibility of recommendations. *Delivery* includes such dimensions as audience attentiveness, clarity of visual aids, appropriate dress, persuasiveness of arguments, tone of voice, eye contact, and posture. Great ideas are of no value unless others can be convinced of their merit through clear communication. The guidelines presented here can help you make an effective oral presentation.

Organizing the Presentation

Begin your presentation by introducing yourself and giving a clear outline of topics to be covered. If a team is presenting, specify the sequence of speakers and the areas each person will address. At the beginning of an oral presentation, try to capture your audience's interest and attention. You could do this by displaying some products made by the company, telling an interesting short story about the company, or sharing an experience you had that is related to the company, its products, or its services. You could develop or obtain a video to show at the beginning of class; you could visit a local distributor of the firm's products and tape a personal interview with the business owner or manager. A light or humorous introduction can be effective at the beginning of a presentation.

Be sure the setting of your presentation is well organized, with seats for attendees, flip charts, a transparency projector, and whatever else you plan to use. Arrive at the classroom at least 15 minutes early to organize the setting, and be sure your materials are ready to go. Make sure everyone can see your visual aids well.

Controlling Your Voice

An effective rate of speaking ranges from 100 to 125 words per minute. Practice your presentation aloud to determine if you are going too fast. Individuals commonly speak too fast when nervous. Breathe deeply before and during the presentation to help yourself slow down. Have a cup of water available; pausing to take a drink will wet your throat, give you time to collect your thoughts, control your nervousness, slow you down, and signal to the audience a change in topic.

Avoid a monotone by placing emphasis on different words or sentences. Speak loudly and clearly, but don't shout. Silence can be used effectively to break a monotone voice. Stop at the end of each sentence, rather than running sentences together with *and* or *uh*.

Managing Body Language

Be sure not to fold your arms, lean on the podium, put your hands in your pockets, or put your hands behind you. Keep a straight posture, with one foot slightly in front of the other. Do not turn your back to the audience; doing so is not only rude, but it also prevents your voice from projecting well. Avoid using too many hand gestures. On occasion, leave the podium or table and walk toward your audience, but do not walk around too much. Never block the audience's view of your visual aids.

Maintain good eye contact throughout the presentation. This is the best way to persuade your audience. There is nothing more reassuring to a speaker than to see members of the audience nod in agreement or smile. Try to look everyone in the eye at least once during your presentation, but focus more on individuals who look interested than on those who seem bored. To stay in touch with your audience, use humor and smiles as appropriate throughout your presentation. A presentation should never be dull!

Speaking from Notes

Be sure not to read to your audience because reading puts people to sleep. Perhaps worse than reading is merely reciting what you have memorized. Do not try to memorize anything. Rather, practice unobtrusively using notes. Make sure your notes are written clearly so you will not flounder when trying to read your own writing. Include only main ideas on your note cards. Keep note cards on a podium or table if possible so that you won't drop them or get them out of order; walking with note cards tends to be distracting.

Constructing Visual Aids

Make sure your visual aids are legible to individuals in the back of the room. Use color to highlight special items. Avoid putting complete sentences on visual aids; rather, use short phrases and then orally elaborate on issues as you make your presentation. Generally, there should be no more than four to six lines of text on each visual aid. Use clear headings and subheadings. Be careful about spelling and grammar; use a consistent style of lettering. Use masking tape or an easel for posters—do not hold posters in your hand. Transparencies and handouts are excellent aids; however, be careful not to use too many handouts or your audience may concentrate on them instead of you during the presentation.

Answering Questions

It is best to field questions at the end of your presentation, rather than during the presentation itself. Encourage questions, and take your time to respond to each one. Answering questions can be persuasive because it involves you with the audience. If a team is giving the presentation, the audience should direct questions to a specific person. During the question-and-answer period, be polite, confident, and courteous. Avoid verbose responses. Do not get defensive with your answers, even if a hostile or confrontational question is asked. Staying calm during potentially disruptive situations, such as a cross-examination, reflects self-confidence, maturity, poise, and command of the particular company and its industry. Stand up throughout the question-and-answer period.

Tips for Success in Case Analysis

Strategic-management students who have used this text over 10 editions offer you the following tips for success in doing case analysis. The tips are grouped into two basic sections: (1) Content Tips and (2) Process Tips. Content tips relate especially to the content of your case analysis, whereas the Process tips relate mostly to the process that you and your group mates undergo in preparing and delivering your case analysis/presentation.

Content Tips

1. Use the www.strategyclub.com Web site resources. The software described there is especially useful.
2. In preparing your external assessment, use the S&P Industry Survey material in your college library.
3. Go to the http://finance.yahoo.com or http://moneycentral.msn/investor/home.asp and enter your company's stock symbol.
4. View your case analysis and presentation as a product that must have some competitive factor to favorably differentiate it from the case analyses of other students.
5. Develop a mind-set of *why*, continually questioning your own and others' assumptions and assertions.
6. Because business policy is a capstone course, seek the help of professors in other specialty areas when necessary.
7. Read your case frequently as work progresses so you don't overlook details.
8. At the end of each group session, assign each member of the group a task to be completed for the next meeting.
9. Become friends with the library and the Internet.
10. Be creative and innovative throughout the case analysis process.
11. A goal of case analysis is to improve your ability to think clearly in ambiguous and confusing situations; do not get frustrated that there is no single best answer.
12. Do not confuse symptoms with causes; do not develop conclusions and solutions prematurely; recognize that information may be misleading, conflicting, or wrong.
13. Work hard to develop the ability to formulate reasonable, consistent, and creative plans; put yourself in the strategist's position.
14. Develop confidence in using quantitative tools for analysis. They are not inherently difficult, it is just practice and familiarity you need.
15. Strive for excellence in writing and in the technical preparation of your case. Prepare nice charts, tables, diagrams, and graphs. Use color and unique pictures. No messy exhibits! Use PowerPoint.
16. Do not forget that the objective is to learn; explore areas with which you are not familiar.
17. Pay attention to detail.
18. Think through alternative implications fully and realistically. The consequences of decisions are not always apparent. They often affect many different aspects of a firm's operations.
19. Provide answers to such fundamental questions as *what, when, where, why, who,* and *how*.
20. Do not merely recite ratios or present figures. Rather, develop ideas and conclusions concerning the possible trends. Show the importance of these figures to the corporation.
21. Support reasoning and judgment with factual data whenever possible.
22. Your analysis should be as detailed and specific as possible.
23. A picture speaks a thousand words, and a creative picture gets you an A in many classes.

24. Emphasize the Recommendations and Strategy Implementation sections. A common mistake is to spend too much time on the external or internal analysis parts of your paper. Always remember that the recommendations and implementation sections are the most important part of the paper or presentation.

Process Tips

1. When working as a team, encourage most of the work to be done individually. Use team meetings mostly to assimilate work. This approach is most efficient.
2. If allowed to do so, invite questions throughout your presentation.
3. During the presentation, keep good posture, eye contact, voice tone, and project confidence. Do not get defensive under any conditions or with any questions.
4. Prepare your case analysis in advance of the due date to allow time for reflection and practice. Do not procrastinate.
5. Maintain a positive attitude about the class, working *with* problems rather than against them.
6. Keep in tune with your professor, and understand his or her values and expectations.
7. Other students will have strengths in functional areas that will complement your weaknesses, so develop a cooperative spirit that moderates competitiveness in group work.
8. When preparing a case analysis as a group, divide into separate teams to work on the external analysis and internal analysis.
9. Have a good sense of humor.
10. Capitalize on the strengths of each member of the group; volunteer your services in your areas of strength.
11. Set goals for yourself and your team; budget your time to attain them.
12. Foster attitudes that encourage group participation and interaction. Do not be hasty to judge group members.
13. Be prepared to work. There will be times when you will have to do more than your share. Accept it, and do what you have to do to move the team forward.
14. Think of your case analysis as if it were really happening; do not reduce case analysis to a mechanical process.
15. To uncover flaws in your analysis and to prepare the group for questions during an oral presentation, assign one person in the group to actively play the devil's advocate.
16. Do not schedule excessively long group meetings; two-hour sessions are about right.
17. Push your ideas hard enough to get them listened to, but then let up; listen to others and try to follow their lines of thinking; follow the flow of group discussion, recognizing when you need to get back on track; do not repeat yourself or others unless clarity or progress demands repetition.
18. Develop a case-presentation style that is direct, assertive, and convincing; be concise, precise, fluent, and correct.
19. Have fun when at all possible. Preparing a case is frustrating at times, but enjoy it while you can; it may be several years before you are playing CEO again.
20. In group cases, do not allow personality differences to interfere. When they occur, they must be understood for what they are—and then put aside.
21. Get things written down (drafts) as soon as possible.
22. Read everything that other group members write, and comment on it in writing. This allows group input into all aspects of case preparation.
23. Adaptation and flexibility are keys to success; be creative and innovative.
24. Neatness is a real plus; your case analysis should look professional.
25. Let someone else read and critique your presentation several days before you present it.
26. Make special efforts to get to know your group members. This leads to more openness in the group and allows for more interchange of ideas. Put in the time and effort necessary to develop these relationships.

27. Be constructively critical of your group members' work. Do not dominate group discussions. Be a good listener and contributor.

28. Learn from past mistakes and deficiencies. Improve upon weak aspects of other case presentations.

29. Learn from the positive approaches and accomplishments of classmates.

Sample Case Analysis Outline

There are musicians who play wonderfully without notes and there are chefs who cook wonderfully without recipes, but most of us prefer a more orderly cookbook approach, at least in the first attempt at doing something new. Therefore the following eight steps may serve as a basic outline for you in presenting a strategic plan for your firm's future. This outline is not the only approach used in business and industry for communicating a strategic plan, but this approach is time-tested, it does work, and it does cover all of the basics. You may amend the content, tools, and concepts given to suit your own company, audience, assignment, and circumstances, but it helps to know and understand the rules before you start breaking them.

Depending upon whether your class is 50 minutes or 75 minutes and how much time your professor allows for your case presentation, the following outlines what generally needs to be covered. A recommended time (in minutes) as part of the presentation is given for an overall 50-minute event. Of course, all cases are different, some being about for-profit and some about not-for-profit organizations, for example, so the scope and content of your analysis may vary. Even if you do not have time to cover all areas in your oral presentation, you may be asked to prepare these areas and give them to your professor as a "written case analysis." Be sure in an oral presentation to manage time knowing that your recommendations and associated costs are the most important part. You should go to www.strategyclub.com and utilize that information and software in preparing your case analysis. Good luck.

Oral Presentation—Step 1

Introduction (2 minutes)

a. Introduce yourselves by name and major. Establish the time setting of your case and analysis. Prepare your strategic plan for the three years 2008–2011.

b. Introduce your company and its products/services; capture interest.

c. Show the outline of your presentation and tell who is doing what parts.

Oral Presentation—Step 2

Mission/Vision (4 minutes)

a. Show existing mission and vision statements if available from the firm's Web site, or annual report, or elsewhere.

b. Show your "improved" mission and vision and tell why it is improved.

c. Compare your mission and vision to a leading competitor's statements.

d. Comment on your vision and mission in terms of how they support the strategies you envision for your firm.

Oral Presentation—Step 3

Internal Assessment (8 minutes)

a. Give your financial ratio analysis. Highlight especially good and bad ratios. Do not give definitions of the ratios and do not highlight all the ratios.

b. Show the firm's organizational chart found or "created based on executive titles." Identify the type of chart as well as good and bad aspects. Unless all white males comprise the chart, peoples' names are generally not important because positions reveal structure as people come and go.

c. Present your improved/recommended organizational chart. Tell why you feel it is improved over the existing chart.

d. Show a market positioning map with firm and competitors. Discuss the map in light of strategies you envision for firm versus competitors' strategies.

e. Identify the marketing strategy of the firm in terms of good and bad points versus competitors and in light of strategies you envision for the firm.

f. Show a map locating the firm's operations. Discuss in light of strategies you envision. Also, perhaps show a Value Chain Analysis chart.

g. Discuss (and perhaps show) the firm's Web site and e-commerce efforts/abilities in terms of good and bad points.

h. Show your "value of the firm" analysis.

i. List up to 20 of the firm's strengths and weaknesses. Go over each one listed without "reading" them verbatim.

j. Show and explain your Internal Factor Evaluation (IFE) Matrix.

Oral Presentation—Step 4

External Assessment (8 minutes)

a. Identify and discuss major competitors. Use pie charts, maps, tables, and/or figures to show the intensity of competition in the industry.

b. Show your Competitive Profile Matrix. Include at least 12 factors and two competitors.

c. Summarize key industry trends citing Standard & Poor's *Industry Survey* or Chamber of Commerce statistics, etc. Highlight key external trends as they impact the firm, in areas such as the economic, social, cultural, demographic, geographic, technological, political, legal, governmental, and natural environment.

d. List up to 20 of the firm's opportunities and threats. Make sure your opportunities are not stated as strategies. Go over each one listed without "reading" them verbatim.

e. Show and explain your External Factor Evaluation (EFE) Matrix.

Oral Presentation—Step 5

Strategy Formulation (14 minutes)

a. Show and explain your SWOT Matrix, highlighting each of your strategies listed.

b. Show and explain your SPACE Matrix, using half of your "space time" on calculations and the other half on implications of those numbers. Strategy implications must be specific rather than generic. In other words, use of a term such as "market penetration" is not satisfactory alone as a strategy implication.

c. Show your Boston Consulting Group (BCG) Matrix. Again focus on both the numbers and the strategy implications. Do multiple BCG Matrices if possible, including domestic versus global, or another geographic breakdown. Develop a product BCG if at all possible. Comment on changes to this matrix as per strategies you envision. Develop this matrix even if you do not know the profits per division and even if you have to estimate the axes information. However, make no wild guesses on axes or revenue/profit information.

d. Show your Internal-External (IE) Matrix. Because this analysis is similar to the BCG, see the preceding comments.

e. Show your Grand Strategy Matrix. Again focus on implications after giving the quadrant selection. Reminder: Use of a term such as "market penetration" is not satisfactory alone as a strategy implication. Be more specific. Elaborate.

f. Show your Quantitative Strategic Planning Matrix (QSPM). Be sure to explain your strategies to start with here. Do not go back over the internal and external factors. Avoid having more than one 4, 3, 2, or 1 in a row. If you rate one strategy, you need to rate the other because, that particular factor is affecting the choice. Work row by row rather than column by column on preparing the QSPM.

g. Present your Recommendations Page. This is the most important page in your presentation. Be specific in terms of both strategies and estimated costs of those strategies. *Total your estimated costs.* You should have six or more strategies. Divide your strategies into two groups: (1) Existing Strategies to Be Continued, and (2) New Strategies to Be Started.

Oral Presentation—Step 6

Strategy Implementation (8 minutes)

a. Show and explain your EPS/EBIT analysis to reveal whether stock, debt, or a combination is best to finance your recommendations. Graph the analysis. Decide which approach to use if there are any given limitations of the analysis.

b. Show your projected income statement. Relate changes in the items to your recommendations rather than blindly going with historical percentage changes.

c. Show your projected balance sheet. Relate changes in your items to your recommendations. Be sure to show the retained earnings calculation and the results of your EPS/EBIT decision.

d. Show your projected financial ratios and highlight several key ratios to show the benefits of your strategic plan.

Oral Presentation—Step 7

Strategy Evaluation (2 minutes)

a. Prepare a Balanced Scorecard to show your expected financial and nonfinancial objectives recommended for the firm.

Oral Presentation—Step 8

Conclusion (4 minutes)

a. Compare and contrast your strategic plan versus the company's own plans for the future.

b. Thank audience members for their attention. Seek and answer questions.

INDEX